MW00466444

Believers Church
Bible Commentary

Elmer A. Martens and Willard M. Swartley, Editors

EDITORIAL COUNCIL

David Baker
Brethren Church

Estella B. Horning
Church of the Brethren

Robert B. Ives
Brethren in Christ Church

Lydia Harder
General Conference Mennonite Church

Gordon H. Matties
Mennonite Brethren Church

Paul M. Zehr
Mennonite Church

OLD TESTAMENT EDITOR

Elmer A. Martens
Mennonite Brethren Biblical Seminary
Fresno, California

Allen R. Guenther (for *Jeremiah*)
Mennonite Brethren Biblical Seminary
Fresno, California

NEW TESTAMENT EDITORS

Willard M. Swartley
Associated Mennonite Biblical Seminary
Elkhart, Indiana

Howard H. Charles (for *Matthew*)
Associated Mennonite Biblical Seminary
Elkhart, Indiana

**Believers Church
Bible Commentary**

2 Corinthians

V. George Shillington

HERALD PRESS
Scottdale, Pennsylvania
Waterloo, Ontario

Library of Congress Cataloging-in-Publication Data
Shillington, V. G. (V. George)
    2 Corinthians / V. George Shillington.
        p. cm. — (Believers church Bible commentary)
    Includes bibliographical references and index.
    ISBN 0-8361-9073-4 (alk. paper)
        1. Bible. N.T. Corinthians, 2nd—Commentaries. I. Title.
    II. Series.
    BS2675.3.S47 1997
    227'.307—dc21   97-37900

Canadian Cataloguing-in-Publication Data
Shillington, V. G. (Valentine George), 1937-
    2 Corinthians

(Believers church Bible commentary)
Includes bibliographical references and index.
ISBN 0-8361-9073-4

1. Bible. N.T. Corinthians, 2nd—Commentaries. I. Title. II. Title: Second
Corinthians. III. Title: Two Corinthians. IV. Series.
BS2675.3.S54 1997   227'.307   C97-932021-6

The paper used in this publication is recycled and meets the minimum requirements of American National Standard for Information Sciences—Permanence of Paper for Printed Library Materials, ANSI Z39.48-1984.

Credits for Bible quotations appear on page 6.

BELIEVERS CHURCH BIBLE COMMENTARY: 2 CORINTHIANS
Copyright © 1998 by Herald Press, Scottdale, Pa. 15683
    Released simultaneously in Canada
    by Herald Press, Waterloo, Ont. N2L 6H7. All rights reserved
Library of Congress Catalog Number: 97-37900
Canadiana Entry Number: C97-932021-6
International Standard Book Number: 0-8361-9073-4
Printed in the United States of America
Cover and charts by Merrill R. Miller

07 06 05 04 03 02 01 00 99 98 10 9 8 7 6 5 4 3 2 1

To my sons,
Ralph and Brad

BELIEVERS CHURCH BIBLE COMMENTARY

Old Testament

Genesis, by Eugene F. Roop
Jeremiah, by Elmer A. Martens
Ezekiel, by Millard C. Lind
Daniel, by Paul M. Lederach
Hosea, Amos, by Allen R. Guenther

New Testament

Matthew, by Richard B. Gardner
Acts, by Chalmer E. Faw
2 Corinthians, by V. George Shillington
Colossians, Philemon, by Ernest D. Martin
1 and 2 Thessalonians, by Jacob W. Elias

Credits for Bible Quotations
Scripture versions are used by permission, all rights reserved, and unless otherwise indicated are from the NRSV: *New Revised Standard Version Bible*, copyright 1989, by the Division of Christian Education of the National Council of the Churches of Christ in the USA. Other versions are used briefly in making comparisons: NAB, *New American Bible;* KJV, *King James Version;* NASB, *New American Standard Bible*; NEB, *New English Bible;* NIV, *New International Version;* Phillips, *The New Testament in Modern English;* RSV, *Revised Standard Version;* VGS, by the author.

Contents

Abbreviations and Cross-References

(Barrett, 1973:56ff.)   Sample reference to Bibliography: as needed,
        author's name, date, volume and page numbers
e.g.   for example
lit.   literally
LXX   Greek Old Testament, Septuagint
ABD/ME/MM/TDNT   See Bibliography
notes   Explanatory Notes for each section
NRSV   Sample acronym for Bible version: see copyright page
NT/OT   New Testament/Old Testament
[Opponents, p. 000]   Sample reference to essay at back of book
TBC   Text in Biblical Context, after notes in each section
TLC   Text in the Life of the Church, after TBC in each section

Series Foreword

The Believers Church Bible Commentary Series makes available a new tool for basic Bible study. It is published for all who seek more fully to understand the original message of Scripture and its meaning for today—Sunday school teachers, members of Bible study groups, students, pastors, and other seekers. The series is based on the conviction that God is still speaking to all who will listen, and that the Holy Spirit makes the Word a living and authoritative guide for all who want to know and do God's will.

The desire to help as wide a range of readers as possible has determined the approach of the writers. Since no blocks of biblical text are provided, readers may continue to use the translation with which they are most familiar. The writers of the series use the *New Revised Standard Version*, the *Revised Standard Version*, the *New International Version*, and the *New American Standard Bible* on a comparative basis. They indicate which text they follow most closely, as well as where they make their own translations. The writers have not worked alone, but in consultation with select counselors, the series' editors, and the Editorial Council.

Every volume illuminates the Scriptures; provides necessary theological, sociological, and ethical meanings; and in general, makes "the rough places plain." Critical issues are not avoided, but neither are they moved into the foreground as debates among scholars. Each section offers explanatory notes, followed by focused articles, "The Text in Biblical Context" and "The Text in the Life of the Church."

The writers have done the basic work for each commentary, but not operating alone, since "no . . . Scripture is a matter of one's own interpretation" (2 Pet. 1:20; cf. 1 Cor. 14:29). They have consulted with select counselors during the writing process, worked with the editors for the series, and received feedback from another biblical scholar. In addition, the Editorial Council, representing six believers church denominations, reads the manuscripts carefully, gives church-ly responses, and makes suggestions for changes. The writer considers all this counsel and processes it into the manuscript, which the Editorial Council finally approves for publication. Thus these commentaries combine the individual writers' own good work and the church's voice. As such, they represent a hermeneutical community's efforts in interpreting the biblical text, as led by the Spirit.

The term *believers church* has often been used in the history of the church. Since the sixteenth century, it has frequently been applied to the Anabaptists and later the Mennonites, as well as to the Church of the Brethren and similar groups. As a descriptive term, it includes more than Mennonites and Brethren. *Believers church* now represents specific theological understandings, such as believers baptism, commitment to the Rule of Christ in Matthew 18:15-20 as crucial for church membership, belief in the power of love in all relationships, and willingness to follow Christ in the way of the cross. The writers chosen for the series stand in this tradition.

Believers church people have always been known for their emphasis on obedience to the simple meaning of Scripture. Because of this, they do not have a long history of deep historical-critical biblical scholarship. This series attempts to be faithful to the Scriptures while also taking archaeology and current biblical studies seriously. Doing this means that at many points the writers will not differ greatly from interpretations which can be found in many other good commentaries. Yet these writers share basic convictions about Christ, the church and its mission, God and history, human nature, the Christian life, and other doctrines. These presuppositions do shape a writer's interpretation of Scripture. Thus this series, like all other commentaries, stands within a specific historical church tradition.

Many in this stream of the church have expressed a need for help in Bible study. This is justification enough to produce the Believers Church Bible Commentary. Nevertheless, the Holy Spirit is not bound to any tradition. May this series be an instrument in breaking down walls between Christians in North America and around the world, bringing new joy in obedience through a fuller understanding of the Word.

—The Editorial Council

Author's Preface

Numerous efforts have been made to grasp the mind of Paul, to know his motives and his world mission. The efforts have borne much fruit, but the end of the search is not yet. Paul's thought and life is as elusive as it is illuminating. This quality of the Pauline literature draws interpreters to the text like bees to nectar. And I am no exception.

After completing a doctoral dissertation in the early 1980s on Paul's thought, under the rigorous supervision of Professor E. P. Sanders, I felt as though my adventure with Paul had only begun. What a delight in 1992 to be invited to write a commentary on 2 Corinthians for the Believers Church Bible Commentary series! I accepted without a moment's hesitation and soon began to make plans to carry out serious research, specifically related to this puzzling document in the Pauline corpus.

Concord College graciously granted me a full-year sabbatical study leave for the calendar year of 1994. I gladly record my sincere gratitude to Concord College administration for financial and moral support during my research and writing.

Most of 1994 was spent in New College, University of Edinburgh, Scotland. New College accepted me into their faculty as a visiting scholar, which gave me all the privileges necessary for my work on 2 Corinthians. The substantial library resources in New College related to my research provided most of what I needed to complete the project. Library personnel at New College demonstrated the best in library assistance and deserve well-earned recognition.

To the New Testament editor of the series, Professor Willard M. Swartley, I offer heartfelt thanks for his careful reading of the manuscript and for his insightful comments along the way. Likewise, I owe much to the editorial council of the series for their suggestions on how to make the manuscript sufficiently readable to a wide audience.

Herald Press has earned my vote of confidence for their prompt publication of the manuscript and for the concerted promotion of this volume in the series.

Part of the procedure for writing in this series requires several consultants to read each major section once completed. These readers spent many hours perusing the manuscript in progress. To them I acknowledge an immense debt of gratitude. Professor Gordon Zerbe filled the role of peer consultant. He is an acknowledged Pauline scholar. Cheryl Pauls was the reader for gender and cultural awareness. Cheryl was herself working on her Doctor of Musical Arts at the time of reading my manuscript. Elfrieda and David Duerksen were the lay readers. Their perspective and constant encouragement added an important dimension to the finished product. To all of these I say, Thank you from the bottom of my heart!

In no small way I recognize my wife, Grace, for her patience and encouragement at every phase of the work. Grace was obliged to explore the beautiful city of Edinburgh on her own, for the most part, while I spent my days and several nights of the week in the library of New College. Her support behind this work is greatly appreciated.

—V. George Shillington
  Winnipeg
  July 1996

Introduction to 2 Corinthians

The Thought World of 2 Corinthians

Of all the letters of Paul in the New Testament (NT), none reveals the emotional side of his Christian character more boldly than 2 Corinthians. The letter was written out of personal conflict with the church at Corinth. This language of 2 Corinthians exhibits deep feelings of hurt and grief in the heart of this foremost Christian missionary of the first century.

At the same time, Paul's painful experiences are offset by the grace of Jesus Christ that filled his being. His vision of the Messiah (Christ) past, present, and yet to come guides his thought throughout the multifaceted script of this letter. Whether he is arguing against the charges of opponents, exhorting the congregation to piety, or interpreting the Scriptures for the new cultural situation, a single dynamic center pervades his thought from beginning to end: the grace of our Lord Jesus Christ (1:2; 13:13).

Paul's new vision of God's Messiah corresponds aptly with his recent experience of the call of God into Gentile world mission. The Corinthian congregation(s) of Christians are part of the result of that mission. Paul's correspondence with them in 2 Corinthians provides a window through which to view the kaleidoscope of *Christ-at-work-in-the-world* as transforming agent of the Redeemer-God. The view includes the following:

13

- The Messiah of God, crucified and raised, present in the Spirit, has become the lens through which to interpret the Scriptures (3:7-18).
- The glory of this Christ surpasses even that of Moses, the great mediator of the law of the Lord to Israel (3:7-11).
- The Spirit of the resurrected Christ renews the human spirit (4:13-18).
- The same Spirit guarantees the final glory of believers (5:5; 1:22).
- The new creation through the resurrected Messiah of God ensures the transformation of the mortal body into a body eternal (5:1-17).
- Christ acts as equalizer between different groups, as evidenced in the collection of money from Gentile Christians in Corinth for Jewish Christians in Jerusalem (8:1—9:15).
- Paul's experience of Christ answers the question of suffering in mission, and of the place of human "weakness" in the plan of God to save the world (10:1—12:13).

Reading the Rhetoric of 2 Corinthians

Unlike the dogmatic array of ideas given above, Paul clothes the sweep of his Christian thought in argument. Argument is not a clear-cut setting forth of truth. Argument aims at persuading readers to adopt a point of view by using the literary instrument of rhetoric. Ancient and modern orators employ the rules of rhetoric to convince their audiences to think differently. In this century Martin Luther King Jr., for example, mastered the use of social rhetoric to persuade the American people of the need for equal rights for all ethnic groups, particularly African-Americans in the United States. In his time Paul likewise employed the rules of rhetoric currently in use among the educated people of the Mediterranean world.

There were schools of rhetoric from the time of Aristotle of Athens into the Latin period (as shown, for example, in the works of Cicero and Quintilian). Paul was himself an educated man living in Greek culture. He certainly knew the rules of rhetoric, if not from studying in a school, then from observing rhetoric at work in the speeches and writings of his day. Whatever his formal education in the art of rhetorical address, Paul's argumentation in 2 Corinthians is marked by forms of writing intended to affect the Corinthian audience. He wanted to redirect their thinking from its present course.

Among the many elements of ancient rhetoric, a few stand out in

2 Corinthians, especially in the second main part, chapters 10–13. Paul uses irony, sarcasm, and parody to defuse his opponents' criticisms of him among the Corinthians, and to win back the confidence of his friends at Corinth. For example, in the section often called "the fool's speech" (11:1—12:13), Paul plays the part of the fool to make his rival apostles at Corinth look like the real fools, and himself the genuine apostle of Christ. In response to the charge from the Corinthians that his refusal of financial support is an insult to them and a mark of weakness in Paul himself, he responds sarcastically, *Forgive me this wrong!* (12:13). The form of address is biting throughout the last four chapters (10–13) and may thus be called a **rhetoric of denunciation.**

While the tone of language in chapters 8 and 9 is less sharp, it is no less forceful. The Corinthians have neglected their commitment to complete the collection for Jerusalem. In chapters 8 and 9, Paul seeks to persuade them to keep their word and to collect the money. He uses the example of the generous gift from the Macedonians who are poorer than the Corinthians; he cites the incarnation of Christ in economic terms: *He was rich, yet for your sakes he became poor* (8:9). By this and other rhetorical means, Paul writes *affectively.* He fills the language of his argument in such a way as to make his readers feel that they need to change their thinking and acting to become more equitable. The language of chapters 8 and 9 may thus be called a **rhetoric of equalization.**

The persuasive speech in the first seven chapters of 2 Corinthians is more conciliatory. The language of reconciliation occurs variously at several points. Paul takes some responsibility for causing pain to the Corinthians, and thus his rhetoric takes a different turn. The tone and texture of the arguments are more tender and more empathetic than that of the last four chapters. The readers are persuaded to join Paul rather than to judge him, to accept him rather than to accuse him. The arguments of these early chapters thus manifest a **rhetoric of reconciliation.**

This variety of rhetoric in 2 Corinthians, together with the differences in subject matter from one part to the next, has prompted many questions pertaining to the interpretation of the various texts. The more pertinent of these questions are focused in the Essays at the end of the commentary. For purposes of this introduction, a few other considerations may facilitate the reading of the commentary.

On Reading Other People's Mail

Paul wrote real letters to particular people about specific situations. The letters are not carefully structured treatises for a general reading public. Nor are Paul's letters in the first instance intended for the church at large. They follow the convention of letter writing used in the Greco-Roman world for *occasional* communication. Local circumstances common to both writer and readers gave rise to the letter and shaped the language of its text. The text of a letter alludes to the situation without giving detailed description; it addresses the situation within the common temporal experience of sender and receiver. Second Corinthians is certainly a letter in this sense. Paul adopted the conventional letter of his time according to his own Christian convictions, and in terms of his own purposes in mission.

Recognition of this character of the letter helps explain some of the peculiarities of 2 Corinthians. The content and rhetoric of this letter is situation-specific and reader-specific, as are the content and rhetoric of the other Pauline letters in their own way. In this respect Paul's letters differ from other types of literature in the NT, including the general epistles such as Hebrews or 1 Peter. Hence, when Christian readers other than the original Corinthians read 2 Corinthians, they are, in some measure, reading someone else's mail.

The in-house character of Paul's arguments in 2 Corinthians helps explain why scholarly opinion differs so widely on the puzzling issues in this letter. Modern readers are outsiders to the primary reading circle at Corinth, and to Paul's opponents there. Present-day experience in the local church is not the same as life in the first-century local church. Paul, on the other hand, was not an outsider to his Corinthian converts nor to those depicted as his adversaries. He and they had knowledge in common that readers today do not have. He could simply allude to personalities, experiences, and ideas, and expect the readers to follow his thought. For example, Paul could allude to his *thorn in the flesh* and his first readers would probably know what he meant. Later readers have to imagine creatively (12:7).

Creative imagination is required in all reading of great literature. How much more is required for a letter like 2 Corinthians, written two thousand years ago to a particular group of people in an urban center in Achaia about a particular set of circumstances! Paul assumes, consciously or unconsciously, a common ground between himself and his primary readers. He shares a knowledge of the same social conventions, as well as the particular situation related to Corinth. Paul's writing to the Corinthians is much like a family member writing a letter to the family circle. Family readers live within a cluster of familial clues unknown to a stranger. The stranger has to find as many clues as possible to make good sense of the family letter. So it is with those who read 2 Corinthians today.

Yet this analogy can be taken only so far. Unlike ordinary letters to family members, Paul's letters were eventually collected from their local settings after his death. Later they were canonized by councils to form part of the NT Scriptures of the church for all ages. Thus Christian people living two thousand years after Paul's composition read and interpret his letters in light of current issues in life. As Scripture, Paul's letters, such as 2 Corinthians, are authoritative for believers living out their faith in the present time and situation. The original situation of the writing and reading becomes secondary at best. This contemporary reader-response approach to a text like 2 Corinthians is understandable and valid. But when taken to an extreme, it disconnects with the situation in the life of the primary community of writer and readers. Such a radical reader-response approach truncates the meaning of the text and dilutes the heritage of faith. The journey of faith is "out of faith into faith" (Rom. 1:17, VGS), out of theirs into ours.

Modern readers of 2 Corinthians tend to feel some distance between themselves and the arguments in 2 Corinthians. Perhaps the best counsel is to engage the puzzles in the text sensitively and prayerfully, and expect a renewing of mind and spirit in the engagement.

Overview of Paul's Relations with the Corinthians

From the Corinthian correspondence and from Acts, it is possible to recapture (in part at least) the sequence of events in Paul's missionary experience with the Corinthians. The sketch below provides a framework for understanding the various arguments in 2 Corinthians and the Explanatory Notes that accompany them.

- Paul entered the city of Corinth, made converts to Jesus Christ, both male and female, and formed a community that met in homes.
- Then Paul left the city and the believing community to preach elsewhere, particularly in Macedonia, to the north.
- Paul learned that the converts at Corinth were unsure how to relate to their old friends and their old ways of life.

- Therefore, Paul wrote a letter instructing the Corinthians not to commune with sexually immoral persons (the letter alluded to in 1 Cor. 5:9). That letter did not survive.
- The community wrote to Paul with more questions about the relationship between their new life in Christ and their old life in the religion and culture of Corinth (1 Cor. 7:1). With the letter from Corinth came also an oral report from Chloe's people about divisions in the ranks (1 Cor. 1:11) and about immorality in the community of faith (1 Cor. 5:1).
- In response to the Corinthians' letter and the report, Paul wrote instructions. That letter is preserved in 1 Corinthians of the NT.
- Paul made a second personal visit to Corinth after writing 1 Corinthians. On that visit he was insulted by a member of the congregation. The congregation did not discipline the member for his reproach of Paul. Paul left humiliated and sorrowful (2 Cor. 2).
- Paul wrote a "letter of tears," instructing the congregation to discipline the member and to demonstrate their allegiance to the gospel of God and to the agency of Paul in proclaiming the gospel (2 Cor. 2:1-4; 7:8). The "letter of tears" did not survive.
- Titus, Paul's colleague in the gospel, visited the congregation, presumably bearing the "letter of tears." He returned to Paul with a good report of the congregation's repentance and obedience. Titus also reported on the Corinthians' reception of traveling missionaries carrying letters of recommendation (2 Cor. 2:12-13; 7:6-7; 3:1-3).
- In response to the good word of Titus, Paul wrote a letter of reconciliation, including in the letter also some concern for the intrusion of apostles who boast about letters of recommendation. Paul's letter of reconciliation to the Corinthians is preserved in 2 Corinthians 1-9.
- The congregation lagged in collecting promised support for the Jerusalem saints. So Paul dispatched Titus and two unnamed *brothers* with the conciliatory letter (2 Cor. 1-9) to encourage the completion of the gift for Jerusalem (2 Cor. 8-9).
- Word reached Paul, probably when Titus returned from Corinth, that the intruding apostles were making charges against the genuineness of Paul's apostleship. They were leading the Corinthians to suspect the purity of Paul's motives in rejecting their material support (2 Cor. 10:10; 12:14-18).
- Upset and offended by this news, Paul wrote a severe letter of defense and censure. He sealed it with a promise of a third visit to

discipline the congregation for their folly. That defensive letter is preserved in 2 Corinthians 10-13.

- Paul most likely made the promised third visit, corrected the situation in the congregation, wrote the letter to the Romans at Corinth, and left from there for Jerusalem with the collection.

Probably the letters of Paul to Corinth cited above were all written within an eighteen-month period in A.D. 54-55. The letters incorporated in 2 Corinthians were likely written within a few months of each other in A.D. 55. The arrangement of the letters or parts thereof into the single scroll of 2 Corinthians in the NT is called the canonical form. The shape of the present 2 Corinthians is the same form it was in when the church adopted it for public reading in services of worship and teaching. Interpretation must therefore take account of the function of the canonical form of 2 Corinthians, as much as it does the incorporated letters or fragments of letters. *[Canonical Shape of 2 Corinthians, p. 260.]*

Theology Born in the Crucible of Opposition

Some of the grandest theology of the Christian faith appears in 2 Corinthians: loving forgiveness (2:5-11), transformation of human existence (3:7—5:10), reconciliation and new creation (5:11—6:13), Christian stewardship (8:1—9:15), divine strength in human weakness (11:1—12:13). Yet these great Christian themes are not set out abstractly after quiet reflection, as in systematic theology, but are conceived and written in the missionary crucible of opposition and affliction.

In the first principal part of 2 Corinthians (chaps. 1-9), Paul is aware of interlopers at Corinth who carry letters of recommendation and ask for the same from the Corinthians. The Corinthians criticize Paul for conducting his mission without such letters. Rather than contest the criticism of the interlopers and the rising suspicion of the Corinthians on a purely pragmatic front, Paul weaves his response around a vibrant core of theological thought.

A theology of **suffering with Christ** opens the letter of reconciliation (chaps. 1-9) and permeates the arguments thereafter. Paul ties his suffering tightly to the mission in chapter one, and he connects that mission with the redemptive death of Jesus Christ. When he speaks of being *crushed*, of receiving *the sentence of death*, he identifies with Christ in his suffering, so that with Christ he will be rescued by God. The ultimate rescue of resurrection is yet to come for Paul, but the ongoing experiences of rescue in the missionary situation are sure signs that Paul is aligned with Christ and with God, who raises the dead. By engaging in Christian mission, which brings its own hardships, Paul has God's *Yes* and *Amen* stamped on his life. He can look forward confidently to the day when *the earthly tent* of his physical, suffering body *will be destroyed*, to be replaced by *a house not made with hands, eternal in the heavens* (5:1-10).

In the meantime, though, Paul's true self is *being transformed into the same image* of Christ *from one degree of glory to another* (3:17-18). This **theology of transformation** is not isolated to the situation of opposition current at Corinth. In his later letter to the Romans (probably written from Corinth), Paul appeals to his readers to "be transformed by the renewing of your minds" (Rom. 12:2). Transformation, accomplished by the Spirit of the Lord, is more than a single conversion. The conversion of the Gentiles is their response to the good news of God, and this is itself a transformation. A person who turns to Jesus Christ from a sinful way of life (particularly idolatry, 1 Thess. 1:9) is changed, and the change continues by the grace of God *from one degree of glory to another* (3:18).

Still, in the Letter of Reconciliation (2 Cor. 1–9), Paul touches on a **theology of life after life**, not simply life after death. Paul is more keenly sensitive to the relation between this present life in the flesh and the life that succeeds this life. He speaks of putting off the present existence and putting on the other *eternal weight of glory beyond all measure* (4:17; 5:4). The present form of life is passing. The life that follows this life is permanent. That life is home, true home (5:6-8). In short, Paul puts little stock in the present nature of things. Mortality holds no appeal for him, except as the seedbed of the better life to come (5:1-10; 1 Cor. 15:42-58).

But Paul's vision is not merely personal and individual. It is cosmic. He stitches **a theology of new creation** to his plea for reconciliation with his converts at Corinth. The resurrection of Christ changed Paul's way of viewing the world. He no longer viewed Messiah as a physical, political leader; that would be to think by human standards. Instead, Paul now accepts Messiah crucified, whom God raised out of the old creation of sin and death (5:14-16). The new order of life that came with the resurrected body of Christ was, for Paul, the "first fruits" of a whole new order of the universe (1 Cor. 15:20-21). Paul could see the enormous ramifications of a resurrected Messiah. The old creation of God, ravaged as it was by sin and corruption, had received the touch of the finger of God. The resurrection of the Messiah signaled for Paul the start of the new creation out of the old. The old had already begun to pass away at the moment of resurrection, and the new had begun to appear. People of faith in this resurrected Messiah could lay claim to the new creation here and now. Their faith united them vitally to the Messiah of God. Thus Paul writes: *So if anyone is in Christ [Messiah], there is a new creation: everything old has passed away; see, everything has become new! All this is from God* . . . (2 Cor. 5:17-18).

Linked with Paul's vision of new creation is **an Adam-Christ theology.** Even though the figure of Adam is not named explicitly in 2 Corinthians (as in 1 Cor. 15 and Rom. 5), the theological implications of Genesis 3 (the disobedience of the first parents) echoes through the arguments of 2 Corinthians 4 and 5. Paul views fallen Adam as the progenitor of the whole human family, the representative protohuman. Adam's sin put a stranglehold on every human being, Jewish and Gentile. As Paul writes later, "We have already charged that all, both Jews and Greeks, are under the power of sin" (Rom. 3:9). The only possible way out of the stranglehold is by God's powerful gift of grace in Jesus Christ crucified and raised, the new Adam. The resurrected Christ thus becomes the representative prototype of the new humanity now under way and soon to become fully revealed. Meanwhile God is reconciling the world to himself through the good news of Christ (2 Cor. 5:18-19).

The urgency for Paul to have the Corinthians complete the collection for Jerusalem pushes him to substantiate his two-part plea with **a theology of stewardship** (chaps. 8 and 9). Stewardship applies to all resources of this life, but in 2 Corinthians 8 and 9 Paul focuses specifically on the human resource of money. Stewards of money ask the question, How shall we manage the financial resources entrusted to us? Paul's Christian response recognizes God as the giver of all things, including money, the means of exchange for goods and services. A Christian may say, "I have come by my money honestly." Yet the money is still an entrusted resource from God. How is it used when it ends up in the charge of a Christian individual? That is the question. If money is a good resource from God, then it can be used to help others in need.

The Jerusalem saints were in physiological need that money could resolve, while the Corinthians were not so much in need. Money can bring equity between peoples, in Paul's case between the Jerusalem Jewish group and the Gentile converts to Christ (Messiah). The

Jerusalem saints were the historic and ethnic channel through which the Messiah of the world came. The Gentile Christians at Corinth have a responsibility to recognize the source of their salvation. The offering of money can help fulfill their responsibility.

The Corinthians are not asked to give money to Jerusalem unreasonably or irresponsibly, but only as the Lord has prospered them. The old tithe is not mentioned, probably because its usefulness in the Gentile world situation was dysfunctional. Proportional giving out of the gifted resources, on the other hand, does not leave the low-resource giver destitute. Neither does it allow the affluent rich Christian an enormous surplus of money to expend selfishly. Paul's Christian theology of stewardship calls for voluntary, proportional distribution of monetary resources to create equity between peoples in response to *God for his indescribable gift* of his Son, Jesus Christ our Savior (2 Cor. 9:15).

While all of these aspects of Christian theology of 2 Corinthians 1–9 were born in the crucible of criticism, if not incipient opposition, the theology of the second part, chapters 10-13, emerged unequivocally out of a situation of strident opposition. What emerges in the rhetoric of these four chapters is a theological paradox, **a theology of strength in weakness.** If we are to understand the picture of the paradox painted by Paul, we need some inkling of the kind of opposition that has called it forth. The inkling comes from within the argument of these last four chapters of 2 Corinthians. Those who speak against Paul at Corinth say he is too weak to qualify as a true apostle of Christ: *They say, "His letters are weighty and strong, but his bodily presence is weak, and his [public] speech contemptible"* (10:10; 11:6). To bolster their case (whoever they are), they cite Paul's refusal of money from the Corinthians. If Paul were a strong and loving apostle to the Corinthians, he would have accepted their financial support, to which he is entitled (11:7-11; 12:13). Instead, he is crafty in taking up a collection of money purportedly for Jerusalem, but really for himself. Such a man is not a true apostle, they claim (12:16-18).

What constitutes a true apostle of Christ? That is Paul's key question behind his stinging argument in chapters 10–13. In answer, Paul aligns himself with the Christ crucified in weakness, whom God vindicates by raising him from the dead. Paul's human weakness is his sure sign of his true identity as an apostle of the same Jesus Christ. His apostleship is not triumphalist, as Christ's work of redemption was not. The triumph belongs to God alone. The strength is from God alone. Divine strength is made perfect in human weakness. That was the word of revelation to Paul when he accepted Jesus Christ as his Savior: *My grace is sufficient for you, for power is made perfect in weakness.* Henceforth Paul has contented himself with his human weakness, for which his opponents criticize him so severely: *For whenever I am weak, then I am strong* (12:9-10). [*Opponents*, p. 272.]

In Dialogue with 2 Corinthians

Guided by these theological markers, we now enter into specific dialogue with Paul in reading his text of 2 Corinthians.

Inside each of the two principal parts of 2 Corinthians, the Letter of Reconciliation (chaps. 1-9) and the Letter of Defense (chaps. 10-13), several smaller units of text exist, each with its own rhetorical tone and texture. With every new unit comes a variation on the theme of missionary ministry that runs throughout each major part. Hence the headings in the following analysis.

Letter of Reconciliation, 1:1—9:15

Right Relationship in Ministry
> Variation 1: Solidarity in Affliction and Joy (1:1—2:13)
> Variation 2: The New Ministry in the Light of Christ (2:14—7:4)
> Variation 3: Equity Through a Financial "Gift of Blessing" (8:1—9:15)

Letter of Defense, 10:1—13:13

Response to Betrayal in Ministry
> Variation 4: Weak Minister, Strong God (10:1—13:13)

So Good!

Letter of Reconciliation

Right Relationship in Ministry

2 Corinthians 1:1—9:15

OVERVIEW

The apostle Paul makes the claim in this Letter of Reconciliation that Christian ministry is a matter of a person's right relationship on two indivisible fronts: (1) a right relationship to Jesus Christ, and (2) a right relationship of Christians to each other in an ordered community of life and faith.

The focus is on Paul's own ministry, particularly in relation to the Corinthians, although not exclusively so. His discourse persistently aims at expounding more broadly a theology of ministry in the age of Jesus Christ that has recently dawned upon the world. One can infer from his exposé that Paul has an inkling of an opposing view that has crossed the threshold of the Corinthian community at the time of writing this letter. Proponents of that view see ministry as competitive and self-commending. Paul does not. They seek letters of recommendation from one community to another to authorize their mission and their right to subsistence from the community they serve. To authorize his mission and to sustain him in it, Paul relies entirely on his relationship to God. The others may appeal to Moses as their guiding light in ministry. Paul thinks of Moses merely as a type of present Christian ministry, with Paul and his like-minded comrades as fulfillment of the type (2:16—3:18).

Paul's primary reason for sending this Letter of Reconciliation (2 Cor. 1-9) is to persuade the Corinthians of a view of ministry consistent with the death of Jesus Christ, the Son of God. Paul is principally concerned that his converts know exactly who is reconciling the world. God does this through Jesus Christ. Paul as apostle does not. Instead, Paul's *gift of ministry* from God in Christ acts as the agency of the grace that human beings need to bring them home again to God. In short, Paul views his ministry in the context of right relationships (5:11—6:10; 1:8—2:4).

The rightness of the relationship stems from the character of God.

26

God rescues the sinner, raises the dead, and reconciles the world. God's unique agent in this massive enterprise of bringing the world home again is none other than the divine Son, the wisdom of God personified in Jesus Christ (1 Cor. 1:24). Those who receive the Spirit of this Christ by faith relate to God in the new way of Christ, relate to each other in community in the same way, and likewise relate to the world with the compassionate love of Christ. In these terms of right relationship, argued this way and that throughout 2 Corinthians 1-9, Paul sees God reconciling the world to himself (4:7—5:5; 5:14-15).

Included in this ministry of right relationship is the appeal to the Corinthians to give of their means to *the saints* in Jerusalem. The motive for this, or for any other ministry in the name of Jesus Christ, is the *indescribable gift* of God in the One who *became poor, so that by his poverty you might become rich* (9:15; 8:9).

This leading motif of ministry in the Letter of Reconciliation of 2 Corinthians moves through changes of mood and rhetorical form, yet remains essentially constant through the various textures of the language. Thus, the different sections of the text appear as *variations on the theme of Christian ministry.*

Variation 1: Solidarity in Affliction and Joy

OVERVIEW

After the opening salutation, Paul at once thanks the *Father of mercies and the God of all consolation* for the ministry of consolation given to him. Afflicted on every side to the point of death itself, Paul accepts his suffering in ministry as participation in the suffering and death of Jesus Christ for others (cf. Phil. 3:10). Paul's affliction serves a similar saving purpose for the Corinthians (and others). But Paul banks on the knowledge that God consoles the afflicted and raises the dead, as witnessed in Jesus resurrected (2 Cor. 1:3-11).

Imagine how the listeners in the Corinthian congregation must have felt as they heard this letter read in their house-church setting. Unlike a congregation today, two thousand years removed from the time of writing, the Corinthians could not treat the implications of Paul's sentences with passive objectivity. Paul was in their neighborhood and might visit them at any time. They could lose face in his presence. Through him they had come to faith. How should they feel about their relationship to their afflicted apostle? The answer that follows in the notes suggests itself from the way the text reads.

The apostle has put his life on the line for them in the service of God's salvation of the world. His conscience is clear on this point (1:12). Toward him they should feel sympathy, loyalty, confidence. Paul seems to know they have felt otherwise about him, and thus he writes persuasively. They think he vacillates because he has not visited Corinth as he planned. Not so, says Paul. What you call vacillation between "Yes" and "No" is nothing less than my commitment to

28

the *Amen* of **God's** plan (1:15-22).

Instead of visiting the Corinthians as planned, Paul has decided rather to send a letter *written out of much distress* and *with many tears*. The letter (now lost, except for the reference here and in 2 Cor. 7) censured the congregation for allowing one of its members to cause offense, presumably to Paul. After leaving Corinth offended, Paul writes the "letter of tears" as a substitute for his personal presence. His motive in writing the letter of tears is to save the members undue pain, as God is his witness (1:23). And the Corinthians have responded positively to Paul's appeal in the letter. They have disciplined the offender. Then by the time Paul writes this present Letter of Reconciliation (1-9), he asks the congregation to forgive the offender in the name of Christ, as Paul himself has forgiven him (2:1-11).

This variation on the theme of Paul's ministry ends with a brief note from the memory of his journey to Macedonia to meet Titus, who had news about the Corinthians' state of mind toward Paul (2:12-13; 7:5-16). Mention of Macedonia, where Paul had ministered effectively, sets his mind to thinking on another variation on the theme of his ministry in the name of Christ.

OUTLINE

The Salutation, 1:1-2

Thanksgiving: The Afflicted Consoled, 1:3-7

The Sentence of Death and the Witness of Conscience, 1:8-14

God's Unequivocal "Yes," 1:15-22

Heart Truth: As God Is My Witness, 1:23—2:4

An Offender Forgiven, 2:5-11

Looking for Titus in Macedonia, 2:12-13

The Salutation

2 Corinthians 1:1-2

PREVIEW

Characteristic of the letter-form in Mediterranean society, 2 Corinthians opens with the standard three-part salutation: sender, receiver, and greeting. While these three are standard, they are not uniform in the letters of the time. Nor are they uniform in Paul's letters. For example, in some letters Paul does not designate himself "apostle" in the salutation (Phil. 1-2; 1 and 2 Thess.; Philem.). In opening 2 Corinthians, however, Paul does so designate himself because his status as apostle has come under fire at Corinth. This letter confirms his apostolic ministry according to *the will of God* (1:1).

In short, the salutation corresponds largely to the substance of the body of the letter, and thus it deserves due consideration. Paul has crafted the terms of each salutation in line with his experience of Jesus Christ on the one hand, and included particular terms in line with the character of his argument on the other.

OUTLINE

Senders Designated, 1:1a

Receivers Designated, 1:1b

A Pauline Greeting, 1:2

EXPLANATORY NOTES

Senders Designated 1:1a

Paul consistently uses the single given name of *Paul* to identify himself (cf. Acts 9; 13:9). The title, *apostle of Christ Jesus*, however, is critical in this salutation. In the society of Paul's time, an apostle was one commissioned to carry a message from a superior, a trusted ambassador. According to Luke-Acts, the term *apostolos* ("a person commissioned by a superior") took on special meaning as referring to the twelve disciples who knew Jesus in the flesh, who were witnesses at the first Easter, and whom Jesus commissioned with the liberating word of the gospel (Luke 6:13; Acts 1:2, 25). These were "apostles" of the first order. They occupied a primary position in the earliest church. Paul could not claim to be one of them, despite his claim to have seen the resurrected Lord (1 Cor. 9:1). The primacy of Paul's apostleship has been called into question at Corinth, for reasons not completely known. The two Corinthian letters in the NT bear testimony to the problem Paul is facing.

His answer in 1 Corinthians is that the resurrected Christ appeared to him as "one untimely born" (1 Cor. 15:8-9); that he is "the least of the apostles," but an apostle just the same; in Galatians, that God revealed his Son to him and placed a call upon his life to bring the gospel to the Gentiles (Gal. 1:15-17). Paul accepts the responsibility under God (not under human authority) of bringing the news of God's salvation in Christ crucified and raised to the Gentile world, and woe is he if he does not preach the gospel (1 Cor. 9:16)! His apostolic call and ministry thus are *by the will of God*. In this letter he rests his case for ministry in Corinth—and in the world—on this belief and understanding. Interestingly, the term "apostle" does not come up again in the Letter of Reconciliation, and only once in the Letter of Defense at 2 Corinthians 12:12. But the character of his apostolic ministry is argued variously throughout both The Letter of Reconciliation and the Letter of Defense.

Timothy, known to the Corinthians (1 Cor. 16:10f.), is cited as co-sender of the letter, and designated *brother*, a family metaphor, instituted probably before Paul, for a kindred spirit relationship in the community of faith in Christ. From the designation *brother* (rather than *apostle*), the inference is that Paul does not regard Timothy to have the same apostolic status as himself.

Receivers Designated 1:1b

The receivers of the letter lived in the environs of Corinth, the influential Greek capitol of Achaia, situated on the busy harbor of Cenchreae. The believers addressed in the salutation probably met in the houses of certain members of the group located in various parts of the city and the surrounding area. The houses had to be large enough to accommodate a significant number of people, perhaps as many as thirty in each house. The owners were doubtless the well-to-do members. Paul refers collectively to *all the saints* of the region as *the church of God*, singular. They are all saints, set apart from their old way of life by the grace of God.

This designation of the readers ties in with Paul's concern in this letter for communion in the Spirit. The various groups have but one identity and one allegiance: they are a people called out of the old order of society to belong to God through Christ. Implicit in Paul's designation is a call for the Corinthians' singular loyalty to the God who rescued them from the peril of the world through the apostolic ministry of Paul. Paul will show that these two, God's grace and Paul's ministry, are correlatives. They go together.

A Pauline Greeting 1:2

Grace was a common word in the Greek-speaking culture in which Paul lived. The term meant good-will, favor, gracious act. A benefit or gift from a deity was also seen as a grace in that society. Paul employed the term in his salutations for the good gift of God revealed in the person and action of Christ. This is the grace he wishes for his readers.

Peace in Paul's formula may have its roots in the Jewish greeting *shalom.* Both terms, *grace* and *peace,* speak of divine well-being made available *from God our Father and the Lord Jesus Christ.*

Paul's use of *Father* here for God, doubtless drawn from his Scriptures, and more so from his Jewish liturgy, is his distinctive way of naming God as the source of Christian life.

THE TEXT IN BIBLICAL CONTEXT

The content of the salutation of 2 Corinthians is essentially the same as that of 1 Corinthians, except for the personal name Sosthenes in 1 Corinthians and Timothy in 2 Corinthians. One suspects the reason for the close similarity between the two salutations: the issues are the same in both letters. Paul's status as an apostle of Christ Jesus remains in question at the time of writing the Letter of Reconciliation, and the moral and spiritual condition of the Corinthians also persists. The principal factor for Paul in dealing with both issues is *the will of God* that makes all of the Corinthians saints and makes Paul an apostle. Together Paul and they live under the grace and peace of the same God who delivered Israel from bondage in Egypt and exile in Babylon, and Jesus from the grip of death.

The two-part wish in the greeting, coined by Paul, appears in every one of his letters at the opening and often at the close (cf. E. Martin: 31-32). Later leaders of the church used the form more elaborately in their encyclical epistles to the churches.

THE TEXT IN THE LIFE OF THE CHURCH

It is somewhat surprising that believers, especially those of Anabaptist persuasion, have not made more of Paul's consistent peace-wish in his opening and closing greeting to his churches. Dirk Philips does cite 2 Corinthians 1:2 in his own greeting in the "Three Admonitions, No. 1." He grounds his admonitions on Christian love and grace, but he does not draw out the significance of Paul's deliberate formulation of **grace and peace** in his correspondence with his new communities.

Recently, however, in a book sponsored by the Institute of Mennonite Studies, Ulrich Mauser highlights well the significance of peace in Paul's greetings:

> The address of Paul's letters . . . has the power of a blessing in which the apostle communicates a message whose origin is from God. . . . The letter, whatever it may contain, is ultimately brought about by a divine act of re-creation in which the enmity between God and human beings is overcome, and it imparts a blessing in which the restoration to a life of filial trust and obedience is initiated and nourished. (108)

Modern Christians living in a culture built on competition and in some respects enmity, need to remind themselves repeatedly why Paul incorporated the term *peace* (well-being, harmony, life) into his greeting. Could it be that Paul's experience of the suffering-death of Jesus Christ brought the meaning of peace to life for him in a new way? Apostleship and sainthood, or any other titles of position and role in the church, mean little apart from *grace and peace* from God through the Lord Jesus Christ.

Thanksgiving:
The Afflicted Consoled

2 Corinthians 1:3-7

PREVIEW

The thanksgiving section, which generally follows the salutation in first-century letters, launches the theme of 2 Corinthians 1–9. The thanksgiving extends to verse 7. Verse 8 then bridges the thought of the thanksgiving to Paul's testimony to his ministry among the Corinthians. Some commentators believe the thanksgiving includes verses

8-11, since *prayers* and *thanksgiving* are mentioned in 11 (Barrett, 1973:56ff.; Furnish, 1984:108ff.; Hughes: 9-24). Verse 11, however, is not Paul's thanksgiving for benefits but his hope that many others will have occasion to give thanks in the future. The language of 1:8-11 opens the explicitly persuasive element of the letter (so Talbert: 134; R. Martin: 12ff.; Fallon: 13-15; Watson: 1-6).

In the strict sense, verses 3-7 express a blessing thus: *Blessed be the God and Father of our Lord Jesus Christ . . .* (1:3). It consists of a marvelous paean of praise to the God who consoles the afflicted. Woven into this liturgical language of praise is the paradoxical principle that the affliction of one yields the salvation and consolation of others: primarily Christ for others, resulting in Paul for others (the Corinthians in this case). In the end, both Paul and the Corinthians are consoled by *the sufferings of Christ* (1:5). The thanksgiving creates the effect of winning the confidence of the readers in preparation for the ensuing argument in verses 8-11, that Paul's personal affliction in mission is reason for prayer and praise, not criticism.

OUTLINE

Source: God, 1:3-4

Agent: Christ, 1:5
Agency: Paul's Ministry, 1:6

Christian Paradox, 1:7

EXPLANATORY NOTES

Paul lays out his liturgical eulogy to God in verses 3-7 in a sequence of three movements, each having two complementary parts. The three movements of thought come together in one dominant paradox that pervades the ensuing discussion of chapters 1-9 (Letter of Reconciliation). The structure may be outlined as follows.

a.   God is the source and giver of all consolation (1:3).
a'. Paul and company (*we*) benefit purposefully (1:4).

b.   God's Agent, Christ, suffered abundantly (1:5a).
b'. Paul and company (*we*) are consoled abundantly (1:5b).

c.   Paul's agency (ministry) of consolation is borne in affliction (1:6a).

    c'. The Corinthians (*you*) are consoled as they join in Paul's ministry
       (1:6b-c).
    d. Hope unshaken: Corinthian partners in the paradox of consolation
       through affliction (1:7).

Source: God 1:3-4

In this canticle of praise, Paul boldly acknowledges God as the author
of salvation and consolation. *Blessed be the God*, he says. This literally means "Speak well of God," since God is the Father-provider of
consolation to afflicted humanity. Benefits to human beings in this
life spring exclusively from God's mercies and compassion, not from
human goodness nor from affliction as such. Jesus Christ stands in
close association with God, as Son to Father, the *agent designate* of
the mercies planned for the world, accomplished through suffering.
God has designated Jesus as the one ultimately to re-create humanity and the world.

    The consolation for which Paul praises God is given purposefully:
*so that we may be able to console those who are in affliction with the
consolation with which we ourselves are consoled by God* (1:4b).
The beneficiaries are enabled to act as God acts, redemptively.

    Paul plays out the word-group *console/consolation* as in a poetic
refrain (ten times in 1:3-7). Essentially, the verb means "to call alongside, help, support, encourage, and/or comfort." In the present context of affliction in ministry, *to console* (NRSV) is probably the best
translation, with God as the subject and principal source of the consolation. The prominence of *consolation* in this thanksgiving passage
sets the tone for the later arguments about Christian ministry. The
first pattern is straightforward: (a) God consoles the afflicted;
(a') those consoled do likewise.

Agent: Christ 1:5

In verse 5 the *agent designate* of the consolation of God becomes
Christ, the singular *agent operative* in the saving program of God.
For Paul, the effective agency of Jesus Christ is more than sufficient
for the end-time rescue of alienated human beings from a world of
enmity. The means of rescue is *the sufferings of Christ,* the Messiah.
Herein lies Paul's solution to the question of his own suffering in ministry (and by inference of all human suffering and death), a solution
the Corinthians have difficulty accepting (cf. 1 Cor. 1:18ff.). For Paul
there can be no compromise on the saving significance of the suffer-

ings of Christ. They are *abundant for us* (2 Cor. 1:5).

In his variations on the theme of ministry, Paul will have occasion to return to the Greek word behind *abound, abundant, excel,* as in 8:7, where he aims at collecting money for Jerusalem (cf. 3:9; 4:15).

The suffering Christ at this stage becomes the middle term between Paul's ministry and the consoling God. Through the Agent-Christ, Paul is granted an *agency* or ministry through which God's consolation flows to the Corinthians (and others like them). Paul depicts himself thus in a dependent relationship to the suffering Christ: *so also our consolation is abundant through Christ.* The sufferings of God's Agent abound (b); consolation to and from Paul abounds (b').

Agency: Paul's Ministry 1:6

Paul's use of the plural pronoun *we* in this thanksgiving section, and elsewhere throughout the Letter of Reconciliation, can be puzzling. In 1:4-5 *we* seems to include all believers, Corinthians too, who receive the consolation of God. But in 1:6 it definitely does not. *We* are afflicted/consoled so that *you* will be consoled/saved. Paul's *we* in 1:6 implies persons like himself involved in ministry in the name of Christ, including Timothy the *brother* (1:1). Sometimes he uses *we* to speak about himself alone; other times *we* refers to himself and the Corinthians. The context in each case has to determine the sense. In 1:6 *we* (Paul and associates) console *you* (the Corinthians).

The relational sequence between the thought of 1:5 and that of 1:6 is striking. The sufferings of Christ (5) are borne out in the affliction of Paul in ministry (6). It is not a typological relationship in the standard sense, where a *type* in Israel's sojourn finds fulfillment in the new age of Christ and the Spirit. Instead, this is *type* in the sense of identity. What Jesus Christ was, Paul is (Elias: 45-46, on *typos*). The saving effect of the Christ of the new creation (cf. 5:17) energizes Paul in his ministry of the new covenant (3:6). His affliction on behalf of the Corinthians is marked by the same new covenant affliction of Christ who gave his life as "a ransom for many" (Mark 10:45).

In the corollary line of this third movement of the thanksgiving, the Corinthians become the beneficiaries of both Paul's affliction and his consolation. Hence the scheme: Paul's agency carries the consolation of God in affliction (c), resulting in the Corinthians' being consoled as they participate in Paul's ministry (c'). (Crafton: 137-169, on Paul's agency.)

Christian Paradox   1:7

Paul's hope is unshaken *on behalf of* the Corinthians. His confidence is not in them as Corinthians, but in the grace of God that rescued them from sin through faith in the suffering Christ. On that premise Paul *knows* that they are partners in his sufferings in the ministry of Christ. They are consoled. The paradox stands thus: redemptive consolation comes through suffering, not apart from it. This apparent contradiction will become a recurring refrain in the variations of speech that follow.

THE TEXT IN BIBLICAL CONTEXT

Blessed be God echoes the prayer liturgy of the Jewish synagogue service that Paul knew well. The Eighteen Benedictions of daily prayer resound this blessing, the roots of which go deep into the OT understanding of the Lord who delivers and consoles the people (Exod. 18:10; Ps. 28:6; 41:13; Ruth 4:14; Finkelstein: 494-502). The phrase has limited use in the NT (Eph. 1:3; 1 Pet. 1:3).

Similarly, *the Father of mercies* builds on references to the Lord's mercy scattered throughout OT texts (Exod. 34:6; Ps. 25:6). The idea became liturgical in the synagogue of second-temple Judaism and also in the Jewish sect of the Dead Sea Scrolls (found in caves near Qumran; 1QH 10.14; cf. Wisd. 9:1; 3 Macc. 5:7). Paul, however, shapes the blessing according to his Christian understanding of the messianic sufferings in which he participates in the ministry of Christ.

In Paul's uncontested letters, the term *the sufferings of Christ* appears elsewhere only in Philippians 3:10 (cf. 1 Pet. 1:11; 4:13; Col. 1:24). Paul does not limit the *sufferings* to Jesus in time past. Probably he associates them (as in Judaism) with the coming of Messiah in the end-time, sufferings in which he and his missionary comrades are engaged since the coming of Christ (Barrett, 1973:61f.).

Echoes of the Servant passages of Isaiah 40–55 resound in this "blessing" in 2 Corinthians, as in many other messianic statements in the NT. The prophet sings, "Comfort, O comfort my people, says your God" (Isa. 40:1), then later announces that the comfort comes through the sufferings of the Servant of the Lord: "He was oppressed, and he was afflicted" (53:7). Paul grasped the significance of this thought in his encounter with the crucified-resurrected Christ, and thereafter in his perilous missionary experience (2 Cor. 1:8-10; 11:21-29).

THE TEXT IN THE LIFE OF THE CHURCH

The affliction-consolation theme, so prominent in this eulogy to God, takes on real flesh-and-blood significance at various points in Christian history. At times believers have found themselves in political and cultural situations where they have suffered abuse, ridicule, and even death because of their distinctive confession of faith in Jesus Christ.

As Radical Reformers of the sixteenth century, the Anabaptists are one example of suffering for their convictions concerning Jesus Christ. Perceived as deviants from the true church, these Christians "were persecuted severely" (Oyer in *ME*, 5:696). In the midst of their affliction, their writings bear testimony to their dependence on the grace of God in the Spirit of Jesus Christ. Dirk Philips, for example, writing to a woman imprisoned at Antwerp, consoled her, using Paul's phrase in 2 Corinthians 1:3, *the God of all mercy.* To this God alone Dirk Philips appeals "out of the depths of [his] heart" on behalf of the sister suffering in prison for her Christian faith (Philips: 619; cf. 196, 236). Similarly, Michael Sattler in his sermon "On the Satisfaction of Christ" uses this text of 2 Corinthians to understand the place of suffering in the redemptive plan of God for the world. Affliction for the sake of others reaps God's consoling grace. He asks, "Where would the dear prophets and apostles be left, yea, also Christ Himself, . . . if the members of Christ would not need to suffer just like the head?" (Sattler: 112).

In their situation of religious and political affliction, these believers among many others found comfort in *the God of all consolation* (1:3). They identified with Jesus and with Paul in their redemptive ministry.

Times have changed in the Western hemisphere. Religious freedom is now written into the constitutions of many nations where religious persecution was rife. Does this mean that affliction for the cause of Jesus Christ has vanished? Perhaps the pain takes on different forms in different times and cultural settings. Each generation of believers in Jesus, whose acts of love challenge the conventions of the day, will feel a certain pain of alienation. Whatever their trial in the name of Jesus Christ, true believers are assured of consolation from the God *who consoles us in all our affliction* (1:4).

The Sentence of Death and the Witness of Conscience

2 Corinthians 1:8-14

PREVIEW

In these six verses Paul begins to address the incipient accusations of the Corinthians against him. They have accused him of (1) insincerity by breaking his word about a return visit, and (2) lack of clarity in what he writes. His relationship with them hangs in the balance. Paul seeks to regain their confidence in him and in his apostolic ministry.

In the Greek society in which Paul lived, the rule for opening judicial rhetoric consisted of two parts: a quick narration of events, to establish the defendant's character (*ethos*); and a short proposal of the case, to gain the sympathy of the audience (*pathos*). Paul's opening of his "defense" appears to follow this rule, as shown in the outline.

OUTLINE

Perilous Asian Ministry Narrated, 1:8-11

Case for the Defense Proposed, 1:12-14

EXPLANATORY NOTES

To say that "Paul follows the guidance of Aristotle" (Talbert: 134) is to overstate the evidence. At the same time, Paul was doubtless conscious of the rules of rhetoric among speakers of the world in which he lived and preached. Recognition of Paul's acquaintance with such rules throws light on this text, over which commentators have puzzled repeatedly.

Perilous Asian Ministry Narrated 1:8-11

The formula, *We do not want you to be unaware, brothers and sisters,* is Paul's way of signaling a new thought (cf. 8:1; Rom. 1:13; 11:25; 1 Cor. 10:1; 12:1; 1 Thess. 4:13; Phil. 1:12). In this context, following the introductory eulogy to God, the phrase anticipates the next thought. As it happens, the next thought is so compressed as to create more suspense than solution. Interpreters have puzzled long

39

and hard on Paul's meaning in this text. The problem they see is that Paul says too little about his distress in Asia, so they feel compelled to reconstruct the adverse event(s) that might have caused him to despair of life itself (2 Cor. 1:8). The speculations on Paul's oblique references run the gamut, such as the *thorn in the flesh*, imprisonment in Ephesus, the riots mentioned in Acts 19, a physical illness, attacks of the Corinthians on his character. As Aristotle taught, the narration at best should say "just as much as will make the thing clear or as much as will make the audience suppose that something has happened or that harm has been done . . ." (3.16.4; cf. Quintilian 3.9.6-7).

The speculative reconstruction does not shed light on the effect Paul wants to create. He chooses to present only those aspects that will create empathy with his situation and his perspective on the issues in the case against him. The way he shapes the narrative of his ministry forms a caricature of himself (*ethos*) that will win the sympathy (*pathos*) of his audience in preparation for the argument to follow. The terse narration of the situation without detail is sufficient to set the defense on course: the place was Asia; the condition was affliction; he felt personal injury (*unbearably crushed*, and *despaired of life itself*); Paul felt the sentence of death in himself; God who raises the dead rescued him.

Whatever his specific affliction in Asia, Paul presumably ties it in with the mission there. Its severity led him to think he would die (2 Cor. 1:8b). Death as such would not frighten him (Phil. 1:19-26), but the thought of dying before accomplishing his mission—or before his transformation at the coming of Christ—would be unthinkable to him (cf. 1 Cor. 9:16; 15:51-58; Rom. 11:25-26). His premature death would mean that his ministry is disapproved and his call revoked. The *sentence of death* (2 Cor. 1:9), which he has felt within himself, may thus be taken metaphorically, not as an official sentence from an external authority. Paul depicts the feeling dramatically in his use of the perfect tense rather than the usual simple past: literally, *we **have had** the sentence of death within ourselves* (Dana and Mantey: 204f.).

The term *sentence* hints at the judicial form of this letter. Will the charges that the Corinthians are bringing against him end in a sentence of some sort? Later he will call in "witnesses" to prove that the Corinthians should drop the charges. Meanwhile, they should know that *God who raises the dead* (a phrase from the synagogue) has rescued him and renewed his hope. That being so, the helpful prayer of the Corinthians on Paul's behalf will lead to thanksgiving from the *many* (the Corinthians?) for the gracious gift granted to Paul through the *many*. This way of understanding the puzzling structure of verse 11 makes sense, but "there is no completely satisfactory way to unscramble the syntax of this verse" (Furnish, 1984:115).

Paul's introduction to his defense in these verses (1:8-11) aims to win the confidence of the Corinthians, while at the same time alluding implicitly to the redemptive principle of "the one for the many" current in early Christianity (cf. Mark 10:45; Rom. 5:15-21).

Case for the Defense Proposed 1:12-14

Paul appeals to the Corinthians in these verses to understand his ministry and his letters. His ground for such an appeal, called *our boast*, is twofold: (1) the witness of his own conscience in light of God's grace (1:12), and (2) the knowledge that the Corinthians are on their way to final salvation on account of him (1:14b).

"Boasting" appears more often in 2 Corinthians (twenty-eight times) than in any other letter of Paul. The negative aspect of boasting in Paul's letters has the boasters proud of their own achievements, especially concerning salvation (Rom. 3:27f.). When Paul boasts, as he does here, he attributes the achievement in his ministry to *the grace of God,* not to *earthly wisdom* (2 Cor. 1:12).

His boast, first of all, is the witness of a clear conscience. By *conscience (syneidēsis)* Paul means the moral core of his being that measures consistency between his thought and word, between his word and behavior, in the context of the Christian community and before God (Malina: 202-218). His conscience tells him that his behavior in the world has integrity and *godly sincerity,* and that is happening by the grace of God, *and all the more toward you* Corinthians (1:12b).

"Read my writing and understand my thought!" he proposes for the defense, with a play on the Greek words *anaginōskete (read)* and *epiginōskete (understand;* 1:13; cf. Acts 8:30). "That is how I write, not to mislead you. Otherwise, how could I *boast* of you, or you of me, in the day of the Lord." *The day of the Lord Jesus* depicts the final reckoning at the coming of Christ for both apostle and congregation. Then they will receive reward or suffer loss according to their work (2 Cor. 1:14; cf. 1 Cor. 3:10-15).

By 1:14 the introduction is in place. Paul is ready to demonstrate his innocence in hope of renewed relationship with the Corinthians.

THE TEXT IN BIBLICAL CONTEXT

One can only imagine how Paul must have felt when the sentence of death was ultimately passed on him in Rome. The witness of 2 Timothy pictures him facing death bravely, having fought a good fight, having finished the race, having kept the faith (4:6-8).

In 2 Corinthians 1:8-10 Paul does not tie his experience in Asia directly to the death of Jesus. Yet from other texts it may be assumed that he implies as much here as well (Phil. 3:10-11). Paul considers suffering for Christ part of believing; both are a privilege (1 Thess. 1:6-7; Phil. 1:29-30). Suffering and death lead to resurrection, which for Paul is the greatest promise in this life (1 Cor. 15). In Asia, *God who raises the dead* has rescued Paul from the sentence of death within himself. That experience prefigures the ultimate resurrection-life (Rom. 8:9-25; cf. 4:19-25).

Paul's picture of God as the one who raises the dead draws on "a universally oriental Jewish predicate" (Bultmann, 1985:28). The thought was part of daily prayers in Jewish synagogues throughout the Mediterranean world: "Praised be you, Yahweh [Lord], who makes the dead alive."

THE TEXT IN THE LIFE OF THE CHURCH

The Reformers of the sixteenth century believed strongly in the resurrection of Jesus from the dead, which prefigured the final resurrection of baptized believers in Jesus. They also acknowledged with Paul the foretaste of end-time resurrection, already in this life, beginning with regeneration and baptism. Menno Simons, for example, believed that "in baptism [the regenerate] bury their sins in the Lord's death and rise with him to a new life" (Menno: 93).

However, more than that, reflective of Paul's experience narrated in 1:9-10, the same believers saw themselves "walking in the resurrection," according to article 1 in the Schleitheim Confession of 1527: "Baptism shall be given to all those who have been taught repentance and . . . desire to walk in the resurrection of Jesus Christ" (Sattler: 36). For Paul, as for the Reformers in their situation, the work of God in Christ communicated a "newness of life" in the Spirit, which meant following Jesus in obedience (Rom. 6:4).

When Paul wrote of his experience in Asia of being rescued by *God who raises the dead* from a sentence of death, he was living according to the principle of "walking in the resurrection." Paul's thought in this text (2 Cor. 1:8-11) offers **encouragement and hope** in the present time to people who *despair of life itself*, whose Christian conscience is clear by the grace of God in the presence of the community.

God's Unequivocal "Yes"

2 Corinthians 1:15-22

PREVIEW

In keeping with the form of judicial rhetoric, Paul in the first phase of his defense (1:15-22) cites the circumstances of the charge of fickleness and duplicity, then answers with the argument of a defendant on trial. His defense, however, is not according to *human standards* (1:17), but according to the trustworthy character of God, whom he serves (1:18).

Traditionally, commentators have focused on reconstructing the events to which Paul alludes in 1:16-17, as if understanding the text depended on one or another hypothesis (of which there are several). The first readers knew much more about their own mail than later readers. Yet it is not the Corinthians' knowledge of events that yields the effect Paul wishes to create, but their *hearing of his language* in the way he was inspired to project it. Our hearing likewise should be guided primarily by the forms of language in the text, not by a critical reconstruction of data beyond the text.

[handwritten margin note: UNDERSTAND THE TEXT. DON'T WORRY PRIMARILY ABOUT CONTEXT BEHIND IT.]

This first phase of defense deals with the charge of fickleness, in which a promise is broken. Since Paul has failed to visit the Corinthians as promised, how can they trust his word in weightier matters of the gospel? The short answer is this: If they can trust God's word, they can trust the word of God's servant, Paul!

The three-part structure of Paul's theological argument in verses 18-22 is not trinitarian in the strict sense of later confessions of the church. Yet his reply speaks of a communal completeness and relational harmony within the Godhead, diagrammed thus:

a. As God is reliable (1:18a),
a'. our word is reliable (1:18b).

b. As the promises of God in the Son are "Yes" (1:20),
b'. our preaching of the Son is "Yes" (1:19).

    c.   As the Spirit of God confirms your hearts (1:22),
    c'.   our hearts are also confirmed by the same Spirit (1:22).

OUTLINE

The Question of an Unreliable Apostle, 1:15-17

A Theological Reply, 1:18-22

EXPLANATORY NOTES

The Question of an Unreliable Apostle   1:15-17

Since I was sure of this (1:15) links back to the mutual boast between Paul and the Corinthians in 1:13-14. By his use of the first person singular (*I*) in this part of his defense, Paul takes full responsibility for the case against him. Yet he also draws on the witness of his two missionary colleagues, Silvanus and Timothy (1:19). What exactly is the issue?

Judging from the two rhetorical questions in 1:17, the Corinthians appear to have accused Paul of fickleness and of speaking out of both sides of his mouth. First question: *Was I vacillating when I wanted to do this? Vacillating* is a noun with the article in the Greek text, which implies "the vacillation" with which he is accused. The word signals a fickleness and irresponsibility. Fickleness in what? Verses 15-16 suggest an answer, difficult as the sentences are to unravel.

Paul *at first* (Barrett, 1973:74) planned to visit the Corinthians twice: once *on the way to Macedonia*, to give them the benefit of his presence a second time; and again on his way back from Macedonia to Jerusalem with the offering from the Gentile churches. On this return visit (his third), Paul wants them to provide supplies for his journey, perhaps even traveling companions from among their members (1:16b; Acts 20:2-4). According to 2:1-4, Paul did not follow through with the third visit as planned, but wrote a letter instead *with many tears* following a painful second visit (cf. 13:1). The first question thus addresses his wish before the events: Was I being fickle when I *wanted* to come a second time? Paul expects the answer to be "No," but the Corinthians have said "Yes."

Second question: *Do I make my plans according to ordinary human standards* (lit.: *according to flesh*), *ready to say "Yes, yes" and "No, no" at the same time?* Well, it appears that way to the Corinthians! The form of the *Yes, yes* and the *No, no* with the article, implies that the Corinthians have said as much. This is the charge of duplicity common among flatterers of the time. Paul says one thing to please his audience but intends another. Greek and Roman writers of the time condemned such flattery; they said it "undermines true friendship" (Talbert: 136).

It is up to Paul now to set the record straight, so that the Corinthians will answer his expected "No" to both questions: no, he is not a flatterer; no, he is not double-minded.

A Theological Reply 1:18-22

To facilitate their answer, Paul summons the most reliable witness of all, God—his God and theirs. *As surely as God is faithful* (1:18) brings an air of solemnity to the case for the defense. Furnish (following Windisch, Lietzmann, and Bultmann) argues that the structure of the phrase "should be interpreted . . . as an oath formula" (1984:135). Why not rather view the phrase simply as a form that goes with a judicial way of arguing the case? The appeal to the reliable character of God draws the Corinthians onto his side immediately. This is the God they worship at Corinth. And Paul has brought this God to them in the first place by the word he preached. How then can they say their God is reliable but the word of his minister, Paul, has been "Yes and No"? This is the effect of the appeal to God in 1:18.

Similarly, the appeal to *the Son of God, Jesus Christ* in 1:19 unites Paul's word with the unequivocal *Yes* of the Son who mediates the saving grace of the reliable God. The full title, *the Son of God*, is rare in Paul's letters and makes a close connection with the God of 1:18 (Hengel, 1976:7-15, on Paul's use of the title "Son of God"). Paul's argument here does not turn on the veracity of the words of the earthly Jesus, but on the reality of the Son of God in Jesus the Messiah. "What is at stake is not a Yes or No which Christ utters, but the Yes which he is. He is an unequivocal Yes which God has spoken in him" (Bultmann, 1985:40).

Silvanus and Timothy act as co-proclaimers with Paul of the Yes of God in Jesus Christ, and Timothy also as co-sender of the letter. The two leaders, well-known to the Corinthians, function as complementary witnesses to the reliability of Paul's word.

God's promises (1:20a), granted to Israel past, find their Yes in the Christ of Paul's preaching. Of particular interest to Paul elsewhere in his letters is the promise to Abraham that through him the Gentiles would receive the blessing of God (Rom. 4:13-24; Gal. 3:15-18).

Paul presents Christ as the promised seed of Abraham (Gal. 3:16), and himself as minister of Christ to the Gentiles, including the Corinthians.

The *Amen* (1:20b), taken from the synagogue where it was "spoken as the congregational assent to benedictions" (Furnish, 1984:136), was adapted to the Gentile church service. Here the Amen forms another link in the chain of the defense argument. It means a firm **Yes** of agreement with God. Since Paul has taught the congregation to use this Aramaic *Amen* of affirmation to God, they should think of God when they utter their *"Amen," to the glory of God* in their church meetings (Van Unnik, 1973:221f., says the wordplay on *Amen* and *Yes* is the key to understanding 1:15-22).

Finally, in 1:21-22 Paul makes an elliptical appeal to the Corinthians' baptism in the name of Christ. *It is God who* **establishes** *us with you in Christ and has* **anointed** *us, by* **putting his seal** *on us and giving us his Spirit in our hearts as a* **first installment.** The cumulative effect of the four key terms in bold italics tells several things. The first implies God's ownership of Paul together with the Corinthians (Barrett, 1973:78-79). Second, the anointing (at baptism) confirms divine title to the recipients, as in the anointing of prophets and judges of the OT (R. Martin, 1986:28). Third, the metaphor from the practice of sealing important documents to avoid forging (Hughes: 41) endorses the first two ideas. The fourth, connected to the Spirit in our hearts, guarantees God's ownership into the future, when the full transaction of salvation will be enacted (cf. Rom. 8:23; Plummer: 41).

The force of these four terms in the setting of Paul's defense may be stated thus: God has **confirmed** his genuine ownership of our corporate lives by his **anointing** (as in baptism) in relation to his Anointed. God has **sealed** his ownership by giving us his Spirit in our hearts as the **guarantee** of final salvation. Therefore, you Corinthians are bound to affirm me as one confirmed, anointed, sealed, and guaranteed along with yourselves.

THE TEXT IN BIBLICAL CONTEXT

Paul's theological reply, predicated on the faithfulness of God, draws heavily on the OT view of the covenant-making God. In Deuteronomy 7:9 the Lord is pictured as "the faithful God who maintains covenant loyalty" with the people of his choosing. Numerous other texts of the OT carry the same refrain (e.g., Ps. 89:1-9; Isa. 49:7; Dan. 9:4).

The theme appears variously in the NT beyond Paul. For example, 1 John 1:9 affirms the faithful character of God to forgive sins. Hebrews 10:23 says God can be trusted to keep his word. The fulfillment motif, so prominent in Matthew, reflects the same idea: God is faithful in bringing his word to fruition.

The *Amen* of 2 Corinthians 1:20, related as it is to the faithfulness of God, finds expression also in the ministry of Jesus in the Gospels. The double "Amen" (verily, verily) found frequently in John in connection with the character and word of Jesus vouches for their veracity (as in Matt. 5:18; 8:10; 16:28; Mark 3:28; 10:15; Luke 4:24; John 3:3-5; 5:19, 25; 6:53; 8:58).

God's promises (2 Cor. 1:20) are not simply psychological recipes for the happy life of an individual believer. They belong rather within the great divine plan to reconcile the world to God (5:19). The principal promise of God for Paul was made to Abraham, that "all the nations (or Gentiles) of the earth shall be blessed in him" (Gen. 18:18; cf. 12:3; Gal. 3; Rom. 4).

If baptism is in 2 Corinthians 1:21-22, as seems likely, then the thought connects well with the more explicit reference in Romans 6:1-4. Baptism in the Romans text unites the believer to Christ crucified and raised, and initiates the person into the community-life of Christ. Baptism became the visible act of inclusion into the Christian community. That event includes male and female, Jew and Gentile, slave and free (Gal. 3:28; in Judaism, circumcision as an initiation rite included males only).

THE TEXT IN THE LIFE OF THE CHURCH

In his discourse on baptism, Pilgram Marpeck taught that the Holy Spirit comes to all believers as "a guarantee of the assurance of . . . grace," and he cites 2 Corinthians 1:22 in support. Marpeck understood the "sign" of grace on a believer to be "through faith or through the Holy Spirit" (190), which was then symbolized in the act of baptism. Marpeck did place heavy emphasis on baptism as the seal of inclusion in Christ: "Baptism is a burying of the old being and a resurrection of the new. *Likewise,* it is a portal of entrance into the holy communion or church of Christ. . . . Without it, no one is able to have an assurance of a good conscience. . . . Baptism is similar to a betrothal or a marital union between the believer and Christ" (186).

Several signs of church liturgy surface in 2 Corinthians 1:15-22, including the Amen and the anointing. Believers church people have tended to play down the significance of formal worship. "Hymn singing, prayer, and preaching are the primary elements of nearly all Mennonite worship services" (Slough in *ME*, 5:945). Liturgical acts of worship properly ordered can give the church service depth of meaning. "The Amen," a deeply significant affirmation in Paul's congregations, has become for us a way of ending prayers. The "Amen" in the congregations that Paul founded was probably a congregational response to pastoral declarations about God. The Amen was meaningful then.

The challenge for congregations today, particularly for their leaders, is to create ways of making every corporate expression of praise to the faithful God memorable, meaningful, and current. The various attempts in some churches to create alternate forms of Christian worship point in the right direction. Unfortunately, styles of worship (kinds of music, etc.) have become a source of contention in some cases, and frequently they have become grounds for factious division within congregations. Division of this sort defeats the purpose of making worship relevant. The people of God need to acknowledge also that they are the church of God and body of Christ that does not admit division (1 Cor. 3; Rom. 14:1—15:13).

Heart Truth:
As God Is My Witness
2 Corinthians 1:23—2:4

PREVIEW

With his broad defense now in place, Paul can proceed to answer the specific charges against him and seek reconciliation between himself and his converts at Corinth. He acknowledges two facts for which he is held responsible and advances a motive for each of them. The first fact is that he did not visit Corinth as he had planned initially. The reason was to spare them pain. The second fact is that he wrote a painful letter, because he loved them and wanted to rekindle joy between himself and them.

OUTLINE

A Visit Purposefully Declined, 1:23—2:2

A Letter Painfully Written, 2:3-4

EXPLANATORY NOTES

The two facts and their corresponding motives fall under the umbrella of "protest formula," a language structure that resembles an oath, for establishing the truth of a statement: *I call on God as witness against me* (1:23). Paul employs this strong oathlike formula to affirm forcefully the genuineness of his relationship with the Corinthians. The formula implies that Paul is prepared to have God put a curse on his life if his statement is false. (Similar formulas appear elsewhere in Paul's letters: 2 Cor. 11:31; 12:19; Gal. 1:20; Rom. 9:1. Cf. Josephus, *Wars* 2.8.6; and references in Furnish, 1984:138.)

The fact-motive structure of this text is as follows:

> **Motive**—*to spare you.* (1:23)
> **Fact**—*I did not come again to Corinth.* (1:23)
> **Elaboration**—*I do not mean.* (1:24—2:2)
> **Fact**—*I wrote to you as I did.* (2:3a)
> **Motive**—*so that I might not suffer pain.* (2:3a)
> **Elaboration**—*for I am confident about all of you.* (2:3b-4)

A Visit Purposefully Declined 1:23—2:2

The text begs two related questions: (1) Which visit did Paul decline, the second or the third? (2) From what exactly did he spare the Corinthians by declining to visit them? The first has minimal bearing on the interpretation of the text and calls for only brief comment.

Paul established the church on his first visit and apparently stood on good terms with his converts. It is hard to imagine Paul referring to his first visit to Corinth as a *painful visit* (2:1). It is equally strained to suggest that 1 Corinthians is the letter written *out of much distress . . . and with many tears* after a second painful visit (so Hughes: 54-58; cf. also Batey: 144.). The wording of 1:23—2:2 more naturally assumes a visit after writing 1 Corinthians, when someone insulted Paul, as inferred from 2 Corinthians 7:12. The identity of the wrongdoer, well-known to the first readers, is not known to us, apart from speculation. Some suppose he was an intruder at Corinth (Barrett, 1973:86f.; R. Martin, 1986:33). If so, how could Paul instruct the community first to discipline him and then later to forgive him (2:5-11; 7:5-13)? Paul declined a third visit, responding instead with a letter written *out of . . . anguish of heart and with many tears*. The third visit is still to come, as indicated in the Letter of Defense (2 Cor. 12:14; 13:1; cf. 1:16).

The second question addresses the issue with which Paul is principally concerned: Why did he not pay them a visit? *I made up my mind not to make you another painful visit* (2:1), he says, *to spare you (1:23)*. From what, exactly? Presumably some form of chastisement. Paul apparently suffered abuse from someone in the congregation during the second visit (2:5-9; 7:12), and the congregation did not stand with their apostle and father in the faith. If Paul had returned to Corinth, he would have been obliged to call the church to account for their failure to support him. He has spared them the shame of his presence, one suspects, and thus also his discipline in the face of their indifference to the wrongdoing.

Paul elaborates in 1:24 on his stated motive. Far from a parenthesis (Furnish, 1984:151), this remark is a sensitive, pastoral inflection on the implication of his "sparing" them. His action toward the Corinthians was not as a tyrant domineering their life of faith, but as a concerned co-worker for their joy. Paul's solidarity with the Corinthians is signaled in his emotionally charged question of 2:2: *If I cause you pain, who is there to make me glad but the one whom I have pained?*

A Letter Painfully Written 2:3-4

The verb *I wrote* (2:3-4) is a simple past tense here, not a letter-writing past referring to the present letter. This means that Paul is here pointing to an earlier letter written *out of much distress and anguish of heart and with many tears* (2:4). Does such a letter exist in the NT?

Interpreters have given several answers. The traditional one is that 1 Corinthians is the letter of anguish. But 1 Corinthians really does not fit Paul's description here, nor does the incestuous man of 1 Corinthians 5 fit the description of the one who injured Paul (against the protests of Hughes: 54-64; cf. Plummer: 53-55). Many commentators identify 2 Corinthians 10-13 with the tearful letter, declaring that the severe tone and texture of those four chapters qualifies. This view thus puts chapters 10-13 chronologically *before* chapters 1-9. The other view, adopted in this commentary, is that the tearful letter of 2:3-4 did not survive, and that chapters 10-13 were written subsequent to chapters 1-9. *[Integrity of 2 Cor., p. 266.]*

More to the point of these two verses (2:3-4) is the reason for Paul's letter of tears. *I wrote as I did*, he says, *so that . . . I might not suffer pain from those who should have made me rejoice* (2:3). His point is sharp. The Christian community of faith and love does not inflict pain on its members, and certainly not on its own apostle. The

THE FAMILY OF GOD TO BRING JOY TO EACH OTHER, NOT PAIN BUT COMFORT.

mutual aim of the community of Christ is joy, not injury or pain. For
this reason also Paul strives to persuade the Corinthians that his aim
in writing as he did was to restore joy between himself and them, not
to inflict pain.

A compassionate note, prevalent throughout this section of the
letter, comes through clearly in 2:4. It pained Paul to write the letter
of tears, a corrective letter by all accounts, but it had to be done, because of *the abundant love* he had for them (2:4)

WE DISCIPLINE OUT OF LOVE.

THE TEXT IN BIBLICAL CONTEXT

Several elements in 1:23—2:4 call for comment as to their context in
the Bible. **The oath-formula** of 1:23 is not the same as the swearing
prohibited in Matthew 5:33-37. In Matthew's context, the swearing
(or oath-taking) is related to carrying out vows "made to the Lord." In
Paul's setting in 2 Corinthians, the formula is part of the persuasive
manner of speech that establishes the truth of his word among the
believers at Corinth. He adopts this formula for apologetic effect at
several points in his letters (11:31; 12:19; Gal. 1:20; Rom. 9:1).

There are many instances of such so-called oath rhetoric among
Greek-speaking Jews. Josephus, for example, citing Abraham's betrothal of Isaac to Rebecca (Gen. 24), uses a Greek formula similar to
Paul's: "They called upon God as the witness of what was to be done"
(*Antiq.* 1.16.1; cf. Deissmann: 413ff.). According to Josephus, the Es-
senes, a sect of Palestinian Jews, avoided taking an oath of any kind,
considering it "worse than perjury. . . . He who cannot be believed
without [swearing by] God is already condemned" (*Wars* 2.8.6). The
prohibition against oath-taking in Matthew 5:33-37 is close to this
Essene interpretation.

The solidarity that Paul feels toward the Corinthians is rooted in
the OT notion of the corporate personality of Israel, and less so in the
Stoic idea of harmony. Paul's body politic expressed imaginatively in
1 Corinthians 12 and in Romans 12 could well be the frame for his
empathetic language of pain and joy in the text of 2 Corinthians
1:23—2:4. A similar thought is reflected in the theme of mutual in-
dwelling so prominent in John 15 and 1 John 4.

The I-we interplay in these verses is instructive. Paul's personal
pronoun *I* (*egō*) in this text is not a generic or inclusive *I* of humanity
(in the sense of Rom. 7:7-15: I and every human being with me). Nor
is it the *I* of common Christian confession (as in Gal. 2:18-21: I and all
believers with me). Instead, it is a distinctly personal *I* of accountabili-

ty. In saying *I call on God. ... I did not come. ... I wrote as I did*—he is
"carrying his own load" (Gal. 6:5).

At 2 Corinthians 1:24, however, the plural personal pronoun *we*
draws Paul's colleagues into the circle of Christian ministry: ministers
do not lord it over the faith community. The same thought on compassionate Christian ministry appears explicitly also in 1 Peter 5:1-5.
Leading elders are exhorted to "tend the flock of God," not for "sor-
did gain," but as "examples to the flock." Paul's *we* in this text, like the
injunction in 1 Peter, is a communal way of thinking. It is a *we* of mutual trust, of common concern, even while the minister is physically
separated from the congregation. Minister and congregation work together, Paul tells the Corinthians from his heart, "whether they work
together or apart" (Frost, "The Tuft of Flowers": 22-23).

THE TEXT IN THE LIFE OF THE CHURCH

Many Christian groups do not believe in taking an oath under any circumstance. They read the words of Jesus in Matthew 5:33-37 quite
literally as the touchstone of this confessional stand. For example, the
Russian Mennonite Brethren confessional tradition reflects this position. The article reads: "We believe and confess, that to the fathers
under the old covenant it was permitted to take oath by the name of
God. But the Lord Jesus, . . . Founder of the new covenant, has in the
following words [of Matt. 5] forbidden believers to swear with an
oath" (Loewen: 172).

The same groups of Christians seem not to be particularly dis-
turbed when Paul calls God to witness. Paul invokes the name of God
in the context of the faith community, not in a nonfaith setting, as in
lawcourts of society (1 Cor. 6). The community at Corinth knows the
God whom Paul invokes. He has preached that God to them. Paul
has lived under the call of God, and then in turn he has called on God
as witness to the truth of his word. Paul's oath-formula thus is part of
his theological language operating in the context of faith.

Paul makes much of his solidarity with the believers at Corinth,
and theirs with him. A community of believers in Jesus Christ does
well to keep in sharp focus the *abundant love* that filled Paul's relationship with the Corinthians. Discipline, like any other form of Christian ministry, operates in the context of self-giving love. Modern
Christian believers run the risk of losing the Christian art of "speaking
the truth in love" (Eph. 4:15). Paul's example of corrective action in
the context of love for the purpose of joy in 2 Corinthians 1:23—2:4
is not a personal option. It is a theological necessity for the church.

[CORRECTIVE ACTION IN LOVE.]

An Offender Forgiven

2 Corinthians 2:5-11

PREVIEW

This section alludes to the cause of Paul's pain on his interim visit, and why he wrote the tearful letter in response. Someone in Corinth defamed Paul in some way, causing him personal grief. At the time of the incident, the community as a whole withdrew themselves and let the insult fall on their apostle, who had brought "the truth of the gospel" to them initially (Gal. 2:14). By implication, therefore, the insult was as much on them as it was on their apostle, Paul.

Once Titus returned from Corinth with a good report (2 Cor. 7:5-12), Paul celebrates with the Corinthians, because his letter of tears achieved its desired end. The community has taken the offender to task and placed him under discipline. Paul's pastoral counsel to them, by the time of writing this passage, is to lift the disciplinary measures. It is time to forgive and console the offender, and to reaffirm their love for him as Paul does.

OUTLINE

Compassionate Counsel, 2:5-8

A Test of Obedience, 2:9-11

EXPLANATORY NOTES

The chiastic (crisscross) structure of these seven verses (2:5-11) focuses on three principal actors: the offender, the offended (Paul), and the community caught between the two. Paul's persuasive language, however, operates more in line with the notion of "the one and the many," with the effect of reducing the principal actors to two in each line of the two scenarios. The structure may be diagrammed as shown on the next page.

Compassionate Counsel 2:5-8

At verse 5 Paul alludes to the situation that led to the letter of tears. Some person caused Paul pain. *He has caused it not [only] to me, but to some extent—not to exaggerate it—to all of you* (Bruce: 185). Paul argues here from the principle of "the one and the many." The pain that was his was, by extension, pain to the whole community, since Paul was their apostolic father.

Paul does not disclose the identity of the offender in these verses. Of course, the Corinthians and Paul both know who he is. He can hardly be an intruder at Corinth (so Barrett, 1973:93; R. Martin, 1986:38). How can the community exert discipline on an outsider? How can Paul counsel them to lift the measures and restore the man again in love? Probably the man is an outspoken member of the church at Corinth whose outburst has became a rude offense to the apostle. The incestuous man of 1 Corinthians 5 scarcely fits the description in 2 Corinthians 2:5-8. Paul's disciplinary sentence pronounced in 1 Corinthians 5:5, "hand this man over to Satan for the destruction of the flesh," simply does not square with the language in 2 Corinthians 2 and 7. The issue in 2 Corinthians calls for limited discipline rather than the more-ultimate language of 1 Corinthians 5:5.

Paul counsels the community: *This punishment by the majority is enough for such a person.* Barrett renders *punishment* as *reproof,* guided perhaps by his view that the offender is an outsider. Yet there is good ground for taking the word to have some punitive connotation (such as barring the individual from the love feast—severe punishment in that social context). The English term *the majority* implies that there was a minority who sided with the offender. *The majority* could just as easily read "the many" and mean the full membership of the congregation, as it does in the community scroll of the Dead Sea sect of Judaism (1QS 6.8-13, where the Hebrew term *ha rabbim,* "the many," refers to the whole membership [*TDNT,* 6:538]; cf. Rom. 5:19; Dan. 9:27; 11:33).

Paul then asks the congregation to *forgive and console [the offender], so that he may not be overwhelmed by excessive sorrow.* The word for forgiveness here means giving the offender the gift of their love. Active restoration is in view. Console the offender in his sorrow, Paul says in effect, and confirm your love for him as you would a member of your own family.

Paul's attitude and language of reconciliation in this text become effective for his own case. If Paul treats his offender with such compassion and grace, how much more should the Corinthians look upon their apostle with love and acceptance!

Scenario 1: Offense-Forgiveness (2:5-8)

The Offense:

A. Paul is offended (one)   >   B. Community is offended (many) (5-6)

The Forgiveness:

B'. From the community (many)   >   A'. To Paul's offender (one) (7-8)

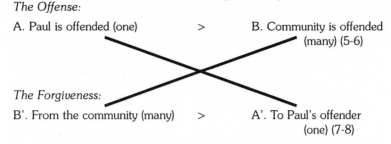

Scenario 2: Test-Forgiveness (2:9-10)

The Test:

A. Paul letter (one)   >   B. The community obeys (many) (9)

The Forgiveness:

B'. From the community (many)   >   A'. From Paul (one) (10)

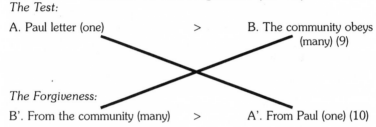

A Test Of Obedience 2:9-11

The letter of tears has put the Corinthians' character to the test, whether they were *obedient in everything* (2:9). Paul is happy to let them know that they have passed the test of obedience. Does Paul mean obedience to him as an official apostle of the church? Probably not in those terms. His concern, rather, is that the Corinthians follow the "obedience of faith" in relation to Christ (Rom. 1:5). The demand of the gospel requires that they acknowledge wrongdoing and deal with it, as they have now done. But the gift of the gospel calls both apostle and community to forgive the offender *in the presence of Christ* (2 Cor. 2:10).

Far from lording it over the community, Paul aligns himself with their Christian heartbeat, almost to the point of putting himself under their authority. *Anyone whom you forgive, I also forgive. What I have forgiven, if I have forgiven anything, has been for your sake in the presence of Christ* (2:10). The translation, *if I have forgiven anything*, can be misleading. The implication of the parenthesis is that the Corinthians are the offended party, Paul being only one of the many. An alternate translation might read: *What I have forgiven (if [in this instance] it has been my place to forgive anything) has been on your account before Christ.*

The bottom line of Paul's thought here is that the community of Christ stands ever ready to forgive. If it does not stand thus, it runs the risk of being *outwitted by Satan* (2:11). The *presence of Christ* and the designs of *Satan* are juxtaposed in verses 10 and 11. The Hebraic title *Satan* represents the archenemy of God and Christ, and it captures everything ungodly (1 Chron. 21:1; Job 1-2; Zech. 3:1-2 *[Satan, p. 278]*. *We do this* forgiving so as not to be caught in satanic ways of thinking (2:11).

THE TEXT IN BIBLICAL CONTEXT

There is some warrant for placing 2 Corinthians 2:5-11 alongside other disciplinary texts of the NT. The letter of tears, to which this text points, presumably called for corrective action toward the wrongdoer in the community of faith. In that respect, the call for community action in the Letter of Tears may have resembled the instruction of 1 Corinthians 5. But that is as far as the similarity goes. The two cases are not the same.

1 Corinthians 5 represents an instance of extreme discipline toward a serious sex offender. Paul advises the church at Corinth to expel the offender ceremonially from the community into the realm of Satan for the destruction of the flesh (5:5). That text echoes the atonement liturgy of Leviticus 16-18 and of second-temple Judaism. In the scapegoat ceremony of the Day of Atonement, the goat takes the sins of Israel into the wilderness of Azazel (a demon figure, Lev. 16:6-10). This typifies what Paul pronounces for the offender of 1 Corinthians 5:5. On the other hand, judging from the language of 2 Corinthians 2, Paul's advice in the Letter of Tears could not have carried the same sentence.

Handing over to Satan in 1 Corinthians 5:5 should not be considered the norm for discipline in the NT. That text is about ultimate censure: a loss of *one* "fleshly" member to save the spiritual life of *the many* in the community in the day of the Lord (cf. Acts 5; Josh. 7). Second Corinthians 2:5-11, on the other hand, is about corrective discipline of a member. Corrective discipline within the church and expulsion from the church are two different practices in the NT and should not be confused. The corrective measures in Matthew 18:15-20 do not address the same extreme sin and sentence of 1 Corinthians 5:5. Matthew's formula for discipline is more in keeping with the inferred in-church censure prescribed in the Letter of Tears. (Background to discipline and excommunication in the NT may be found in the Community Rule scroll of the Dead Sea community [1QS6; see Delcor: 79-80]).

In the end, 2 Corinthians 2:5-11 focuses on the center of the gospel of Jesus Christ that forgives an erring member. Forgiveness is live-giving, restorative, communal. Jesus' parables reflect this compassionate gift of restoration (Luke 15:1-32; Matt. 18:23-35). In his death Jesus asked forgiveness for his enemies (Luke 23:34). He was the unique representative of the Lord of Israel, who pardons iniquity and delights in showing mercy (Mic. 7:18). Paul's counsel on forgiveness in 2 Corinthians 2, moreover, springs from his experience of the Son of God "who loved [him] and gave himself for [him]" (Gal. 2:20).

THE TEXT IN THE LIFE OF THE CHURCH

The practice of church discipline (otherwise called "the ban," *Meidung*) among the Radical Reformers of the sixteenth century is well-known. Following the Schleitheim Confession of 1527, the ban, in various forms, became part of confessions of faith in believers church tradition. The stated purpose of the ban was to restore the sinning member, and also to keep the church pure and faithful. But as Ervin Schlabach has indicated, "In spite of the repeated emphasis of the early Swiss leaders to practice the ban only in sincere Christian love, the potential punitive implications of the ban became increasingly problematic after Schleitheim" (*ME*, 5:239).

Church discipline is part of the ongoing pastoral and educational task of the church, not to be done from a legalistic checklist. In each situation, the gospel should determine how the member in question is best led into discipleship and harmony with the church and its leaders. The governing center is Christ, who humbled himself and gave himself for the sake of the other. Discipline apart from this profound consciousness of Christ is not worthy of the believers church.

Believers in Christ live and act, as Paul says in 2 Corinthians 2:10, *for your sake in the presence of Christ*. The Christ of the gospel welcomes the sinner, forgives the wrongdoer, and includes the alienated in the community of faith. While *exclusion* from community life may be necessary on rare occasions, the church's confession should emphasize the *inclusiveness* of the gospel of Christ (Rom. 14:1-4; 13:1-12).

Looking for Titus in Macedonia

2 Corinthians 2:12-13

Paul's note about his search for Titus, first at Troas and then in Macedonia, adds a finishing touch to the effectiveness of his defense against the Corinthians' charge of fickleness and duplicity. Titus has gone to Corinth, probably with the Letter of Tears (2:1-4; 7:5-13). Paul's *mind could not rest* until he heard how the community at Corinth received Titus and the letter, so he went on to Macedonia. His restlessness accents his concern for the Corinthians and serves to exonerate him from the charge.

As at other points in his defense, so here Paul has only to mention his longing for Titus. The Corinthians will catch the significance immediately. But Paul does not abandon the idea about finding Titus in Macedonia. He will narrate the event again to round off the next large variation on the theme of ministry (7:5-16).

The content and form of these two verses (2:12-13) make a rather awkward literary transition to Paul's jubilant thanksgiving in 2:14. The reader experiences an abrupt change of thought and mood from verse 13 to verse 14. The abruptness of the change has led some interpreters to the opinion that 2:14 is the beginning of another letter. However, sudden changes of topic are not uncommon, even within 2:14—6:13. A word or idea can spark another argument with little transition. Moreover, Murphy-O'Connor's point about the break between 2:13 and 2:14 has merit: mention of Macedonia triggers praise to God for the triumphant ministry in that region. That then leads into a discussion of the new ministry of the Spirit in the light of Christ (1985:99-103).

2 Corinthians 2:14—7:4

Variation 2: New Ministry in the Light of Christ

OVERVIEW

This large section of 2 Corinthians (2:14—7:16) pulls back the curtain on Paul's life in mission as no other in the Pauline letters. The ebb and flow of the argument "presents one of the most moving portrayals of ministry to be found anywhere in Scripture" (Baird: 78).

Paul opens the section abruptly at 2:14, without a clear connection with the search for Titus in verses 12-13. Yet he develops the thought of ministry from the previous arguments about his own ministry in solidarity with the Corinthians. The defensive tone persists in this second variation on the theme of ministry, but in a modulated way. Paul shapes the argument of this second main section more in terms of rival missionaries to Corinth, who have challenged the adequacy of his ministry there. ,

The argument about the new ministry in the light of Christ is more objective and reflective than the personal agenda that occupied the first section (1:3—2:13). The thought of this second main part is larger in scope, and at points more complicated. But the language, while mildly defensive, is not nearly as sharp and sarcastic as the tone and texture of the Letter of Defense (chapters 10–13). The form of language of those four chapters suggests that the situation at Corinth has taken a sharp turn for the worse after the writing and delivery of the Letter of Reconciliation; this situation calls for sterner speech ("Overview" in Introduction) [Integrity, p. 266].

However one puts the subject matter into English words, there can be little doubt about the controlling theme: *the new ministry in the light of Christ.* Some form of the word *ministry (diakonia)* appears twenty times in this passage alone, out of a total of thirty-six uses in all of Paul's letters. Concerned that the Corinthians will accept the opponents' criticism of his mission, Paul advances an impressive case for his place within the new ministry inaugurated by Christ crucified and raised. He highlights the *newness* of the ministry by his use of two key terms: *new covenant* (3:6) and *new creation* (5:17). Around these two categories of "newness" he develops three ways of looking at the ministry in which he is involved. First, this ministry is a new operation of the Spirit of God (2:14—3:18). Second, it renews the human spirit (4:1—5:10). Third, it reconciles the world to God (5:11—7:4).

Clothed as they are in personal, literary garb, these ideas about the new ministry in the light of Christ are not static dogma. They arise from within Paul's heart, and they speak to the situation at hand. So he writes about qualification, commendation, and recommendation (2:16; 3:1, 6; 4:2; 5:12; 6:4). Apparently his rivals commended themselves to the Corinthians and also produced written credentials, as Paul did not or could not, since he was always breaking new missionary ground. Lacking such credentials, Paul's ministry at Corinth could become suspect, if the rivals' notion of ministry is adopted. In view of this unsavory prospect Paul aims at forestalling an impending loss of the Corinthians' confidence in him.

Throughout his discussion of the theme of the new ministry in 2:14—7:16, Paul weaves in *three major appeals.* He points first to the gospel of God in Christ, which he preaches; second, to God's unequivocal call upon his life at the turn of the ages; and third, to the effect of his own mission among the Corinthians. As Paul presents his role in the new ministry of Christ, his language moves from one idea to the next without fair warning, from one image to the next in quick flashes of insight. He draws images from Scripture, as in the veil and glory of Moses; and from common Mediterranean life, as in the processional aroma, clay jars, and the temporary tent.

2 Corinthians 2:14—7:16 beckons Christian readers of every age to engage with Paul in the ministry of the new covenant and new creation.

OUTLINE

The New Operation of God's Spirit
2 Corinthians 2:14—3:18

OVERVIEW

After a jubilant note of thanksgiving to God for leading him and his companions in a triumphal march of ministry, Paul raises the question of adequacy or sufficiency in ministry. His conclusion is that no human being is sufficient for the task, not Paul and not his opponents at Corinth. God alone empowers his ministers through the Spirit.

The intruders at Corinth claim to have letters of recommendation that give them entrance into the community, a convention of the time. Paul, on the other hand, has no such letters, nor does he need them. The Corinthians themselves are his letter. Paul is their primary apostle, with the news of Jesus Christ. Let the outsiders read the Corinthian believers' lives. They are what they are by the grace of God through the ministry of Paul.

Mention of the letters of recommendation prompts Paul to compare the difference between *letter* and *spirit*. *The letter kills;* the spirit gives life. Paul has in mind the letter of the law of Moses chiseled on stone tablets. Paul's opponents from the synagogue may be advocating the significance of the scrolls of the Law, read in the synagogue service. Paul rejects the old-covenant code of the law, considering it not to be life-giving. In the new covenant, *the Spirit gives life* (3:6).

Then follows one of the most difficult passages in all of Paul's letters (3:7-18). He compares the glory of the ministry of Moses with the glory of the new ministry in the name of Christ. Paul concludes that the glory of ministry with Christ surpasses the glory of Moses so as to render Moses' ministry inoperative. The method or pattern of thought Paul uses here is typological. In the old covenant, the glory associated with Moses was a sign of salvation. In the new covenant of the Spirit, Moses' glory finds its fulfillment in the glory of Christ. In a sense Paul interprets backward from his experience of the new age of Christ to the old age of Israel. Seen in the light of Christ, the ministry of the old age has come to have no glory at all because of the glory that surpasses it (3:10).

Paul's thought then moves to the veil that Moses wore to cover his face when he appeared before the Israelites. In the new ministry, in which Paul and his co-workers are engaged, Christ has lifted the veil. On the other hand, Paul's contemporaries in the synagogue (from which the opponents probably come) read Moses apart from Christ and have a "veil" over their minds. They cannot see the glory of Christ in the glory of Moses, since they have not accepted the cruci-fied Jesus as Messiah (Christ). *But when one turns to the Lord*—which means, for Paul, believing in Jesus as Messiah—as Mo-ses did, they find the veil removed and see the true glory of God in the face of Jesus Christ, and are thus *transformed into the same im-age from one degree of glory to another* (3:18).

OUTLINE

Qualification for the New Ministry, 2:14—3:6

The Old Glory Veiled, the New Unveiled, 3:7-18

Qualification for the New Ministry
2 Corinthians 2:14—3:6

PREVIEW

Implicit in Paul's defense to the Corinthians in 2:14—3:6 is a ques-tion from opponents: Is Paul qualified for the kind of apostolic minis-try in which he is engaged? The question comes from outsiders to Corinth, probably from a Jewish synagogue setting of Christian mis-sion *[Opponents of Paul, p. 272]*. These critics of Paul carry official letters of recommendation from some church authority and thus gain entrance into the community as bona fide missionary preachers. In turn they request letters from the Corinthians for their next stop.

Their commendation of themselves and their ministry, implied in Paul's questions in 3:1, casts a shadow over Paul and his ministry. Hence the defensive tone in this text.

Paul's competence in ministry, he argues, springs not from a sense of self-importance but from a deep sense of mission under the control of God in the name of Christ and in the power of the Spirit. Earlier he wrote in this vein to the Corinthians: "Obligation is laid upon me, and woe to me if I do not proclaim the gospel" (1 Cor. 9:16). The same conviction pervades this passage in 2 Corinthians. Given the primacy of the call of God on his life in mission, Paul is not about to seek letters of recommendation from some secondary source. Least of all would he ask for letters from the Corinthian believers, who owe their spiritual life in Christ to his ministry. God has called and qualified him for the new ministry (2 Cor. 3:1-3).

Paul's thought then turns from letters of recommendation to the "letter" of the old covenant as compared to life in the Spirit (3:3-6). The text contains multiple metaphors, not always easily deciphered. Echoes of various Scripture texts punctuate the kaleidoscopic movement from one image to the next. In short, Paul argues for a ministry authorized by God, and energized by the Spirit of the new covenant in Christ [New Covenant, p. 271].

OUTLINE

God Qualifies True Ministers, 2:14-17
    2:14-16a   Imagine a Victory Parade
    2:16b   Posing the Question
    2:17   True Ministers Versus Gospel Hucksters

Ink and Spirit, Letter and Life, 3:1-3

New-Covenant Competence, 3:4-6

EXPLANATORY NOTES

God Qualifies True Ministers 2:14-17

2:14-16a Imagine a Victory Parade

Paul opens his case for the new ministry by thanking God profusely in a form that could be put to music. At the head of the order of ministry is God; under God stand the ministers; through the agency of the ministers, the *aroma* or *fragrance* of Christ spreads to human-

kind; the consequence is life to some and death to others. The chias-
mus (crisscross structure) in the "consequence" accentuates the life-
and-death paradox.

Thanks be to God,
  who . . . always leads us in triumphal procession. (2 Cor. 2:14a)
Through us
  spreads in every place the fragrance. . . . (14b)
  For we are the aroma of Christ to God (15a)

a. among those who   b. and among those who
   are being saved (15b)   are perishing; (15c)

b'. to the one a fragrance   a'. to the other a fragrance
   from death to death, (16a)   from life to life. (16b)

Used only here and at Colossians 2:15, one Greek verb, *thriambeuō*, stands out in the thanksgiving: *God . . . leads us in triumphal
procession* (2 Cor. 2:14). Writers used the word for the procession of
a victorious Roman general after battle with foreigners. In his chariot
the general would ride into Rome through the Porta Triumphalis
(gate of victory), followed by his troops, to the cheers of citizens. The
display ended with the army general making an offering to Jupiter
(Versnel).

Many commentators believe Paul uses the image of the Roman
triumphus to illustrate the triumph of God, and to put ministers in
their place. Ministers are on display in the procession, but they are
God's captives in the parade. Paul wrote elsewhere in this vein, calling himself a prisoner (Philem. 1:1) and a bond slave (Rom. 1:1). If
Paul does have the metaphor of the Roman triumphal procession in
mind, as seems likely, then he uses it here as a paradox, along the
lines of *power . . . in weakness* (2 Cor. 12:9-10). He is a captive in the
victory celebration of Christ, but he participates gladly in the public
display of the triumph of God (Williamson: 325-30; Beker: 355-
367).

Yet Paul does not actually spell out the metaphor of the Roman
triumph, if in fact he does have it in mind. He may simply intend the
basic meaning of the word, "to put on display" (Furnish, 1984:174,
187). Either way, the point is clear. Paul is not the leader of the procession. God is the leader, and Paul is his joyful captive-minister.
"Usually, of course, such captives are a sorry sight and form a wretch-

ed procession of despondent and spiritless people. But here Paul presents the picture of a paradox, . . . for this captive is rejoicing!" (Bosch: 28-29).

Complementing the sight of the triumphal procession is the aroma that accompanied the entourage. The sense of smell is underscored in Paul's metaphor (2:14b). As the retinue marches after their general through the city streets, some in the parade wave the scent of pleasant-smelling incense in the air to counteract the odor from open sewers and the like. Paul's missionary role in God's plan for the world is like the diffusion of such *fragrance*, which he identifies with knowing God (2:14b). *Knowledge* was a favorite catchword in Corinthian spirituality (e.g., 1 Cor. 8:1-3). Now it serves Paul's case for his ministry over against the claims of his rivals. The good news of the knowledge of God in Christ diffuses through the world like the fragrance of sweet-smelling incense.

Fragrance may carry a hint of sacrifice, especially if the Roman procession that culminated in a sacrifice to Jupiter is implied. In Paul's argument, however, the fragrance of sacrifice would come from his own background in Jewish worship, rich in sacrificial symbolism, and in his present experience of Christ "our paschal lamb" (1 Cor. 5:7). There is no set system of sacrificial imagery in Paul's letters, just echoes of his own heritage in Jewish worship transposed into the new experience of Christ in world mission. As a new person in Christ, he considers all of life a sacrificial service to God (Rom. 12:1-2). So he thinks of his ministry in mission as a *fragrance . . . to God*, effective *in every place* (2 Cor. 2:14). In real terms, Paul is presenting an image of himself, not as a triumphant minister, but as a captive servant in God's self-disclosure in Christ crucified and raised. *We* (Paul and his colleagues) *are the aroma of Christ to God* (2:15).

If there is a hint of sacrifice in the word *fragrance* in 2:14, then in 2:15 *the aroma* almost certainly signifies an offering of praise to God. In Paul's thought, the sacrificial offering is two-phase: the sacrifice of Christ crucified (cf. Rom. 3:25), and the sacrifice of Paul's life in missionary service as one crucified with Christ (cf. Gal. 2:19f.). Paul saw his ministry in mission, and the hardship that accompanied it, as a spiritual sacrifice, *carrying in* his *body the death of Jesus* (2 Cor. 4:10). In short, his life in mission testifies to the paradox of God's saving grace in the death of Jesus. As the bringer of this good news, Paul has become an *aroma of Christ.*

Paul's preaching of this Christ yields two opposite effects in his audience. Some accept "the message about the cross" (1 Cor. 1:18-

25) and *are being saved* (2 Cor. 2:15). The present passive form of the participle *are being saved* is characteristic of Paul's view of salvation in his letters. Salvation is present and thus progressive throughout this life; it is performed by the grace of God. Final salvation comes at the end of the age, at the completion of the present mission-ministry (Rom. 11:25), when God will raise the dead and transform the living remnant (1 Cor. 15:42-57). But not all who experience the *aroma* of the gospel *are being saved*. Some are *perishing* (2 Cor. 2:15).

The aroma of Christ is to some a deadly odor, *from death to death*. Herein lies the paradox. The same word that brings life to one group brings death to another. "Paul was not unfamiliar with the notion of a message that could be both healing and poisonous in its effects." Jewish sources speak similarly of the Law (Torah): "As the bee reserves her honey for her owner and her sting for others, so the words of the Torah are an elixir of life (*sam hayyim*) for Israel and a deadly poison (*sam ha-maweth*) to the nations of the world" (Barrett, 1973:101). *From death to death* can also imply that those who reject the resurrection of the crucified Jesus remain in death.

More likely than not, Paul is thinking of those who see only offense in the death of Jesus. To them, the ugly death of Jesus brings death. On the other hand, those who accept the offense of the crucified Messiah receive newness of life (Rom. 6:4). Paul has already wrestled with this problem in 1 Corinthians. The preaching of the cross is an offense to both Jewish and Gentile minds, but to the ones called, it is the power of God (1 Cor. 1:23f.). In the present text of 2 Corinthians, the same thought may well be present in the metaphor of the aroma. To unbelievers, the aroma is an odor of an offensive death by crucifixion, nothing more. To believers, the crucifixion is a fragrance of life that gives life to them. The ground is thus laid to pose the question that will guide the argument to its end at 7:4.

2:16b Posing the Question

Who is sufficient for these things? That is, the *things* he has just now set out in metaphor and cryptic phrases in 2:14-16a. Who is qualified for a paradoxical ministry like this? The question is posed from Paul's perspective. The answer he intends his readers to give is this: No one. In one's self, no one is qualified. Not Paul, and certainly not his opponents. One must assume from the form of address that the opponents were calling for Paul's credentials for ministry. Who has authorized him to preach the gospel of God's Messiah? Who among the Gentiles is to say whether his preaching is authentic?

Paul's rhetorical question stands as his answer. The ministry is too much for any human being. While answering thus, Paul stands in the tradition of Moses, whose self-assessment as minister of the Lord was similar: "I am not *qualified*" (*hikanos,* LXX, Exod. 4:10), the same word Paul uses here for *sufficient.* The enabling for such a ministry comes strictly from the Lord, not from any human source.

Yet the force of the argument is that Paul is abundantly qualified for the ministry in Corinth or anywhere else in the world, because God has called him and qualified him (see 2 Cor. 3:4-6; cf. Gal. 1:15-17). What greater qualification can anyone have? This manner of speech is more than an effective way of writing for Paul. He deeply believes in God's enabling grace for ministry. He will testify in the Letter of Defense to an enabling oracle of God to him: *My grace is sufficient for you, for power is made perfect in weakness* (2 Cor. 12:9).

2:17   True Ministers Versus Gospel Hucksters

At this point Paul attacks the *many* who are in ministry for money (*many, polloi;* some manuscripts read *the rest/others, loipoi*). *Peddlers of God's word,* he calls them. They adulterate the gospel, as some wine makers water down their wine and sell it for profit (Barrett, 1973:103). In his effort to shape his language for the best effect in his defense, Paul is not averse to imposing motives on opponents that they would hardly accept for themselves.

Nevertheless, Paul seems to know that these rivals do take money for their ministry at Corinth. They probably criticize Paul as inadequate and unqualified because he does not take money from the Corinthians for his ministry. Paul has proclaimed the gospel at Corinth "free of charge" (1 Cor. 9:18). If indeed the rival missionaries are accusing him of incompetence because he does not accept money from the Corinthians, he is turning that charge against them here: *We are not . . . like so many.* They huckster the gospel, and that renders them false ministers. *But in Christ we speak as persons of sincerity, as persons sent from God and standing in his presence* (2 Cor. 2:17).

Paul rests his case on his sense of mission as one *sent from God,* vindicated and approved by that highest of courts. His plea before the Corinthians on the charge of being unqualified as apostle of Christ is unequivocally "Not guilty." At 3:1 Paul begins to prove his case.

Ink and Spirit, Letter and Life   3:1-3

Two questions laden with irony launch Paul's argument for his God-given qualification for ministry. *Are we beginning to commend ourselves again? Surely we do not need, as some do, letters of recommendation to you or from you, do we?* (3:1). The implication is unmistakable. Paul was the first to present the gospel of Christ to them. He has led the Corinthians into a community of faith. Their very existence as a new community of Jesus Christ proves his competence. What need has he to begin again to commend himself to them? *Commending* here has to do with persons coming together, literally standing together. Paul's question implies that he senses a distance developing between himself and his Corinthian converts, a condition his theology of community in Christ will not tolerate. But the problem has not started with the Corinthians themselves, as the second question intimates.

The telltale phrase, *as some do*, points to rival missionaries. Apparently they have presented letters of recommendation to the Corinthians from an established congregation. Such letters were customary at the time *[Letters of Recommendation, p. 270]*.

The idea of these letters triggers a string of metaphors in Paul's mind, not always neatly tied together in the text. First, he cites the Christian lives of the Corinthians as his letter. Their standing in Christ is Paul's primary proof for the genuineness of his ministry. At verse 2, the NRSV reads, *You yourselves are our letter, written on **our** hearts.* Some manuscripts of 2 Corinthians read *your hearts,* adopted by the RSV (also by Barrett and Martin). The meaning then would be: Your own hearts of faith in Christ constitute our letter of recommendation. Yet the wording of the NRSV is preferable on two counts: (1) this more-difficult reading is well attested, and (2) it fits the context. In effect, *written on **our** hearts* (3:2) means that Paul carries the Corinthians with him wherever he goes. They are his letter of recommendation, *known and read by all.*

The difficulty with this image is that *all* cannot know and read what is written in Paul's heart (3:2), unless, of course, he speaks what is in his heart. And this is probably what he intends (cf. Rom. 10:9). No doubt Paul talks about his Corinthian community wherever he preaches, praising their enthusiastic acceptance of the message of the gospel.

The idea is further qualified in verse 3. The Corinthians are *a letter of Christ, prepared by us* (NRSV). The RSV has *delivered by us,* and the Jerusalem Bible *drawn up by us.* In this context, the verb signifies intermediate agency. Paul administers the word of Christ to them. That kind of *letter*, he argues, is greater than any letter of recommendation written with ink. That kind is written *with the Spirit of the living God* (3:3).

With the mention of the writing medium of the Spirit (cf. liquid ink), Paul's mind flies immediately to the stone tablets of the law, written by the finger of God and delivered by the intermediate minister, Moses, to the people of Israel (Exod. 31:12-18). Paul then promptly begins to draw a comparison between himself and Moses. Yet he does not draw a straight line from Moses to himself. He echoes two intervening prophets, Jeremiah and Ezekiel.

These two figures signal the character of a new age. Jeremiah anticipates the divine laws written on the hearts of the people (Jer. 31:33), while Ezekiel envisions God changing stony hearts to hearts of flesh (Ezek. 11:19; 36:26). Paul's mixture of these metaphoric images, in such compressed form, is hard for a modern critical mind to accept. Paul strikes his Scripture with his theological hammer wherever he will from his new perspective in Christ, then watches the sparks fly up before his mind's eye. He writes what he sees into the situation of the moment. We have to watch with him as he strikes and writes (Hays: 122-153; 168-178) *[Use of Scripture, p. 284]*.

New-Covenant Competence 3:4-6

According to this text (2:14—3:6), Paul's critics infer that he is too self-assured. He ministers without proper approval. He answers that his confidence is *through Christ toward God* (3:4). That thought leads him back to his earlier question of 2:16b, not completely answered to this point: Who is *qualified* or *competent*? The same word is used again in 3:5-6 as adjective, noun, and verb. The point is moot for Paul, not because the criticism is a personal affront to him, but because his competence and his call go hand in hand. If he is not competent for the ministry, then he is not called to the ministry. But he knows he is called, therefore he is competent.

However, his competence is not simply innate; it is a gift from God (3:5). God *made* Paul competent by a divine authority that outranks human convention. The Corinthians are thereby left with little choice. Either they accept Paul on these terms or they reject him. To reject him is to reject God and enter the path that leads to death (2:16a).

Verse 6 then identifies Paul more precisely as a minister of the *new covenant*. The accent falls on *new*, not on *covenant*. The thought of a *new* covenant existed already in Israel since the time of Jeremiah (31:31f.; LXX, 38:31). It rose to prominence in the Jewish sect of the Dead Sea Scrolls and entered early Christian liturgy in the words of the institution of the Lord's Supper (1 Cor. 11:23-26; cf. Luke 22:20). The *letter* (versus spirit) in 2 Corinthians 3:6 signifies the covenant enacted in the written law in Judaism. Whatever worthy functions the law of Moses had, and Paul admits elsewhere that it had a purpose (Gal. 3:19-27; Rom. 7:7-12), as *letter* the law *kills* (3:6b). That covenant Paul sees reconstituted in Christ, communicated through the Spirit, and in that sense it is *new [New Covenant, p. 271]*.

THE TEXT IN BIBLICAL CONTEXT

Paul's thoughts woven into his literary form of address in 2 Corinthians 2:14—3:6 are at home within the biblical world. Four ideas in particular may be highlighted.

Prophetic Defense. Paul's defense of his ministry among the Corinthians is thoroughly consistent with the prophetic call in ancient Israel and in early Christianity. Moses defended his right to lead the wilderness people of God (e.g., Num. 16:12-50). Elijah provocatively proved his ministry in Israel at Mount Carmel (1 Kings 18:30-46). Jesus stood his ground before Caiaphas and Pilate (Matt. 26:57-75; 27:1-26; cf. John 18:33—19:16). Stephen offered a critical apology for his preaching and suffered stoning for doing so (Acts 7:1-60). The prophetic call, of which Paul is deeply conscious (Gal. 1:11-17), binds the prophet to the mission.

Ability for ministry. Georgi believes Paul's opponents at Corinth claimed the status of "divine men" in the tradition of Moses. Jewish teachers, such as Philo of Alexandria, characterized Moses as a "divine man." Georgi's application of the term "divine men" to Paul's opponents goes beyond the direct evidence of the text of 2 Corinthians. Yet there are hints that Paul's rival missionaries considered Jesus Christ to be the new Moses, and themselves endowed with the same spirit of Christ/Moses. The clearest hint occurs in Paul's question at 2:16b: *Who is sufficient for these things?*" The question echoes Moses' reply to God's call as given in the Greek translation of the OT (LXX): "I am not sufficient" (Exod. 4:10). The interconnection between Exodus 4:10 and 2 Corinthians 2:14 occurs in the key word *sufficient* both in the texts and in the context of a commissioned ministry. The point is this: whether the ministry is that of Moses or Paul, the enabling comes from God, not from within the character of the minister.

Letters of Recommendation. Paul argues against letters of recommendation with respect to his own pioneer mission at Corinth, as elsewhere (2 Cor. 3:1-6). The Corinthians themselves are his letter. By comparison, Acts 18:27 says that Apollos carried a letter to Corinth from the believers at Ephesus. The interplay in Acts 18-19 between Paul, Apollos, Corinth, and Ephesus begs the question of Apollos's rival ministry at Corinth. According to Acts, Apollos proved himself at Ephesus to be "an eloquent man, well-versed in the scriptures, . . . [who] spoke with burning enthusiasm." Yet Priscilla and Aquila, *Paul's* co-workers, "took [Apollos] aside and explained the Way of God to him more accurately" (18:24-26).

After Apollos went to Corinth from Ephesus, Paul arrived at Ephesus and found believers in need of his correction. The question: Did the Corinthians (or a group of them) see in Apollos a gifted minister beyond the stature of Paul, with a letter from Ephesus to prove it? The allusion to letters of recommendation in 2 Corinthians 2:14—3:6 does not point directly to Apollos. Yet one may link the allusion in this text with the references in Acts to a letter from Ephesus and with the mention in 1 Corinthians 3 of rivalry at Corinth between Paul and Apollos. Then Apollos and his companions present themselves as likely candidates to be Paul's rival missionaries, as implied in 2 Corinthians.

Covenant. Paul regarded highly the covenant-promise that God enacted with Israel through Abraham: "All the Gentiles shall be blessed in you" (Gal. 3:8; Rom. 4:16f.; cf. Gen. 18:18; cf. Gen. 12:3). Paul believed the promise to Abraham to be fulfilled in his own mission among the Gentiles. He regarded the written Mosaic covenant to be reconstituted in Christ and the Spirit. In that sense the effective function of the Mosaic covenant was rendered inoperative. Paul is merely exploiting Jeremiah's "new covenant" and Ezekiel's "new spirit" and "covenant of peace" in his own new call to the Gentile world mission (Jer. 31:31; Ezek. 36:26; 37:26).

The term and theme of *new covenant* entered the church's thinking early. Paul quotes a eucharistic formula in 1 Corinthians 11:25 in which "new covenant" defines the meaning of the bloody death of Jesus. His was a life-giving death, carried forward in the community of Christ by the eating of bread and the drinking of wine. The community thus "proclaims the Lord's death" (1 Cor. 11:26; 12:12-13; cf. Luke 22:20). The theme reached its fullest Christian expression in the later text of Hebrews. There the new covenant is heavenly, the old one is earthly. God has made the first earthly covenant (as in Judaism) "obsolete," soon to disappear in the presence of the new (Heb. 8:13).

THE TEXT IN THE LIFE OF THE CHURCH

Signs of triumphalism are evident in some parts of evangelical Christianity today. God is said to grant success and prosperity in this life to persons of faith. Proponents of this teaching have mistakenly used 2 Corinthians 2:14-15 in support of their view. Paul's idea, rather, is that God leads his followers in God's triumph. Paul is simply honored to be a captive in God's parade (Williamson: 317-332). Paul carried the death of the Lord Jesus in his body; he felt the sentence of death within him; he knew the sting of the thirty-nine lashes, and the pain of a thorn in his flesh. Paul's life in mission was hardly one of physical and material victory. He lived and worked with the Christian paradox in which *power is made perfect in weakness* (12:9).

The replacement of that paradox with the modern cult of success and consumerism menaces the church's life of faith and mission in the name of the crucified Messiah of God. A missiologist of the University of South Africa, David Bosch, said in 1978: "The missionary enterprise has become indissolubly fused with the ethic of capitalism. In everything we undertake we think in categories of success, of yield and dividends, and we have transposed that to our missionary enterprise as well" (31). God's captive servants operate in the Spirit of God, not in the spirit of capitalism. The two are not synonymous, judging from Paul's testimony in 2 Corinthians 2:14-15.

Membership in a believers church can happen in one of three ways: by baptism on the basis of faith, by reaffirmation of faith without rebaptism, or by **a letter of recommendation** from another congregation. The third means of entrance relates to our text. Are letters of recommendation ruled out altogether by Paul's defensive argument in 2 Corinthians 3:1-2? Not really. Paul's apostolic ministry was primary and needed no such letters to Corinth or to any other community. Letters of recommendation for the transfer of membership serve a worthy purpose and should not be written or received lightly. Paul himself wrote such a letter for Onesimus to the church that met in Philemon's house.

Characteristic of the believers church tradition, a "covenant" spells out the shape of life in community, after the model of the biblical covenant with Israel. In most cases, the **church covenant** states in writing what the members believe and practice as a community of faith. New members, in turn, receive a copy of the church covenant to indicate what is expected of them in their life and witness.

In its proper place, the church covenant can be a helpful guide for new members. At the same time, a written covenant, however well intended, carries an element of risk to the church's life in Christ, as any physical element of the church does. An Anabaptist leader, Balthasar Hubmaier, quoting 2 Corinthians 3:6, said the same of the Lord's Supper. "If the spiritual eating and drinking does not first take place, then the outward breaking of bread, eating and drinking, is a killing letter" (397). So too a written covenant. Once it becomes the measure of a member's right to life in the community, a church covenant is as much *the letter* that *kills* as the old covenant of Judaism in Paul's time. The new covenant enacted in Christ communicates life through the Spirit. This thought for Paul was not merely a statement of doctrine. It was reality for him, as it should be for the church today. *The Spirit gives life*—always (3:6).

The Old Glory Veiled, The New Unveiled
2 Corinthians 3:7-18

PREVIEW

In this next stage of Paul's move toward reconciliation with his converts, he compares his ministry with that of Moses, using the Scripture text of Exodus 34:29-35. The comparative argument in 2 Corinthians 3:7-18 is one of the most complex and subtle to be found anywhere in Paul's letters. "This utterance is perhaps the most surprising. The greatest man in the history of Israel is put beneath the traveling tent-maker" (Munck: 61). Yet the comparison is not a simple matter of weighing the strengths of the two figures, Moses and Paul. It is a question of where each of the two ministers figures in the plan of God for the salvation of the world. Reminiscent of Jewish apocalyptic thought, Paul's thought operates on the premise of two ages. The second age emerges out of the first, rendering the first inoperative. For Paul, the emergence of the new age has begun with the resurrection of the crucified Messiah.

Paul's call at the turn of the ages (1 Cor. 10:11) undergirds his interpretation of Exodus 34:29-35 about Moses' "glory" (*doxa*, LXX).

Exodus 34 says the skin of Moses' face shone after speaking with the Lord. As he came down the mountain with the two tablets of the covenant in his hands, the Israelites saw his shining face and were afraid. After Moses spoke to them, he put a veil on his face. When he went in before the Lord, he removed the veil until he had emerged and relayed to the Israelites what the Lord had commanded. Paul reads the text of Exodus 34 as a minister of the new covenant, standing at the threshold of the new aeon. Within this schema the old-covenant ministry of Moses becomes for Paul a type of his own new-covenant ministry. The *glory* of Moses' ministry points forward to the greater *glory* of Paul's ministry in the name of Christ. The glory of Moses is veiled; the glory of Paul and companions is unveiled.

Paul's typology here is not at all a slavish matching of particulars between the text of Exodus 34 and his own Christian experience. The typology is shaped largely by the situation at Corinth. The effect of the comparison is to discredit those who adhere to the synagogue where Moses is read apart from Christ. Moses' glory is old, veiled, and temporary; Paul's is new, unveiled, and permanent (2 Cor. 3:10-11). The new glory has surpassed the old, as the church of Christ has surpassed the synagogue of Moses. Paul is thus led to say that those who read the law *to this very day* (3:14-15) have a veil over their minds. If they turn to the Lord (accept Christ), they will find the veil removed, the glory of the Lord revealed, and they themselves transformed *from one degree of glory to another* (3:18) [*Jewish-Christian Relations, p. 270*].

REMARKABLE CONTRAST BETWEEN THE OLD AND NEW.

OUTLINE

New-Ministry Glory Sets the Old Aside, 3:7-11

3:7-9   The Glory of the Two Ministries Compared
3:10-11   The Second Renders the First Inoperative

Veiled and Unveiled Faces and Minds, 3:12-18

3:12-13   Bold New Ministers
3:14-15   Veiled Minds While Reading Moses
3:16-18   Radical Unveiling of the Spirit

GOOD SECTION EXPLAINING PAUL'S THOUGHTS IN COMPARING THE OLD AND THE NEW 75

EXPLANATORY NOTES

New-Ministry Glory Sets the Old Aside 3:7-11

3:7-9 The Glory of the Two Ministries Compared

The argument compares the two ministries (*diakonia*; RSV: *dispensation*) of Moses and Paul. It does not contrast works of the law with faith in Christ. That discussion occurs in Galatians and Romans. (The term "law" [*nomos*] does not appear in 2 Cor.). Having said that, this comparison between Paul's ministry and that of Moses carries an implicit commentary on the Jewish law in light of the new order of Christ and the Spirit.

The operative word, taken from the Greek version (LXX) of Exodus 34:29-35, is *glory* (*doxa*), alternately translated *splendor* or *radiance*. Paul acknowledges a glory that attended Moses' ministry in Israel. But he views Moses' glory through the lens of the new covenant inaugurated by Christ and implemented by the Spirit in his own mission. The effectiveness of the comparison is inescapable: those inclined to elevate Moses' ministry in the present time (e.g., through adherence to the synagogue) will feel slighted. They have opted for a lesser type and thereby forfeit the greater antitype (the fulfillment to which the type pointed). They cannot have both, since the new incorporates all the good of the old, thus rendering the old form inoperative. The categories of the two glories are clear in 3:7-9:

Glory 1: The Ministry of Moses	Glory 2: The Ministry of Paul
of death (7)	of the life-giving Spirit (6, 8)
of condemnation (9)	of justification (9)

This stark contrast leads one to wonder whether Paul believes what the contrast implies: that religion (Judaism) based on the law of Moses is inferior and should be abandoned in favor of the superior religion based on faith in Christ. Taken in this way, Paul's argument becomes the seed of Christian anti-Semitism. Although such anti-Semitism was at times expressed in the writings of the early Fathers (Barnabas, Justin), it mostly developed in the wake of Constantine's decree in the fourth century to make Christianity an official religion in the empire. The Christian church thereafter saw itself as the God-ordained replacement of Judaism by virtue of its privileged place in the world. What is important to note, however, is that Paul argues here as a *Jewish* person alongside Jewish counterparts. Against them, he believes that the crucified and resurrected Jewish Messiah

(Jesus) fulfills the hopes of the people of God and saves the world from the tyranny of sin and death. To convince his readers, he argues in this stark manner *[Jewish-Christian Relations, p. 270]*.

The shape Paul's argument takes in this passage is instructive. Moses' ministry is portrayed as one of death, as shown in the image of the two lifeless stone tablets engraved with the Ten Commandments. Paul is not here claiming that the whole Mosaic law is lifeless (against Furnish, 1984:226f.), but that "stone tablets," used to depict the age and agency of Moses, were in themselves not life-giving. Compared to the life-giving ministry of the Spirit in Paul's present missionary experience, the ministry of stone tablets in the former time of Moses is one of death. Paul demonstrates this point from the engraved laws that condemn the transgressor. *Condemnation* (3:9) involves the penalty for breaking the covenant, which often could mean the death of the transgressor (e.g., Exod. 31:15). Condemnation in this sense is then set against its counterpart, *justification* (RSV: *righteousness*), that leads to life. God justifies the sinner; the tablets condemn the transgressor (cf. Rom. 4:5; 8:33).

The word group "justification/justify/righteous" is rare in 2 Corinthians. The passive verb form "justified," abundant in Galatians and Romans, is understandably absent from 2 Corinthians. The situation in Corinth is different from that of Galatians or Romans; it calls for different terminology and argument. But the noun at least is here in 2 Corinthians 3:9, signaling the life-giving ministry of the Spirit in which Paul is engaged.

Two other terms in this section of the argument are juxtaposed: *set aside* (3:7), referring to the glory of Moses' ministry, and *much more* (3:9), referring to the glory of Paul's ministry. The word translated *set aside* in the NRSV signifies a process of something "being rendered inoperative," as in the old age in which Moses exercised his ministry (cf. 1 Cor. 7:31; 13:10).

On Paul's side of the comparison, the *much more* of fulfillment (2 Cor. 3:8-9) applies. This form of argument is akin to a "well-established rabbinic exegetical procedure" known as *qal wahomer*, building "from the lesser to the greater" (Furnish, 1984:203). Beyond this observation, Paul's argument turns on the premise that he ministers at the turn of the ages on the side of newness and life; but Moses ministered within the old order of condemnation and death. The point of the *much more* is this: If there was a glory attending the ministry of Moses in the old order of condemnation and death, imagine the glory attending the ministers of the new covenant of justification and life!

To suggest, as many commentators do, that Paul here describes the "inferiority" of Moses' ministry against the "superiority" of his own is misleading (e.g., Bultmann, 1985:78-84; Furnish, 1984:226-233; Watson: 34; Plummer: 92). In this text, inferiority and superiority are inappropriate terms within Paul's horizon and argument. The issue is not that of two competing ministries in one economy, but one ministry for each of two economies. The second ministry, having arrived in Christ and the Spirit, and having incorporated the good of the old in itself, effectively renders the first inoperative by its presence. The next section confirms the point.

3:10-11 The Second Renders the First Inoperative

The issue is now out in the open: *Indeed what once had glory has lost its glory because of the greater glory; for if what was set aside came through glory, much more has the permanent come in glory!* (3:10). Having admitted that *glory* surrounded Moses' ministry, Paul presses his point that the arrival of the *greater* and *permanent* glory of Christ effectively renders the glory of Moses' ministry inoperative. That is, the ministry of Messiah has taken over from the ministry of Moses in Paul's Jewish Christian experience. His argument runs along a typological track, characteristic of his thinking as a minister of Christ in the new age of the Spirit (Rom. 5:12-21; 1 Cor. 10:1-13). He is not comparing two established religions, Judaism and Christianity *[Jewish-Christian Relations, p. 270]*.

The Greek text of 3:10a reads like a self-contradiction: *that which had glory did not have glory* (Martin, 1986:64; Furnish, 1984:229). But in 3:10b, Paul immediately rules out the contradiction. Moses' face really did shine; his ministry really did have a certain glory. Nevertheless, by the sheer force of his comparison in 3:7-9, Paul is led to say that Moses' glory has come to have no glory because of the glory that surpasses it.

Verse 11 sums up the thought of verses 7-10 and brings the typological relationship between the two glories to a head: *For if what was set aside came through glory, much more has the permanent come in glory!* The glory of Moses' ministry, characteristically a fading glory, has faded away with the coming of the *much more* permanent glory of Christ.

Veiled and Unveiled Faces and Minds 3:12-18

3:12-13 Bold New Ministers

Another part of Exodus 34 comes into focus: Moses is said to have veiled his face to keep the Israelites from being afraid (34:29-35). Connection is made with the conclusion in 2 Corinthians 3:10-11: *Since, then, we have such a hope* (3:12). Hope belongs to the abiding glory of the new ministry of the Spirit, but it speaks of an out come yet to be realized in the future. The present reality of the Spirit is permanent (3:11) but not ultimate. The resurrection and transformation of the body is ultimate for Paul (1 Cor. 15:50-57; cf. Phil. 3:12-14). Given this *hope*, guaranteed by the present reality of the permanent Spirit of Christ (2 Cor. 1:22; 5:5), Paul and his colleagues in mission *act with great boldness* (3:12).

Within the strained language of verses 12-13, a single point comes through: Paul and his co-workers are *bold* in their ministry as compared to Moses, who veiled his face, as one perhaps ashamed (Van Unnik, 1963:153-169). According to Paul's understanding of that veiled face, Moses lacked the confidence in his ministry that Paul and comrades enjoy in theirs. If the interlopers at Corinth claim to have proper ties to the synagogue where Moses is read, they can hardly miss the cutting edge of Paul's argument. Paul's poor relationship with the synagogue—because of his law-free Gentile mission—is cast here in a highly positive theological light.

The *boldness* is a way of behaving toward God on the one hand, and toward people of Paul's mission on the other. This confidence is not a presumptuousness based on certain personality traits or acquired skills. It springs from the hope produced by the surpassing glory of the new covenant cited in the previous verses.

The reasoning in the text of 3:13 is difficult to untangle. The NRSV reads: *We act with great boldness, not like Moses, who put a veil over his face to keep the people of Israel from gazing at the end of the glory that was being set aside.* Paul is still interpreting the text of Exodus 34:29-35, but on his own terms. Exodus 34 does not give the motive for Moses putting the veil on his face. The text only hints that he did so because the Israelites were afraid when they saw his shining face. Nor does Exodus 34 say anything about the end of the radiance on Moses' face. A Jewish tradition says the radiance remained until his death (van Unnik, 1963:198).

Two questions: (1) What does Paul mean by the term *end* (*telos*)? (2) Why did Moses not want the people to see the end of the radiance on his face? In answer to the first, *end* could imply goal and purpose, or termination, or perhaps a combination of these meanings (cf. Rom. 10:4). If Paul construes the goal and purpose (*telos*) of the glory of Moses to be Christ, why does he say that Moses veiled his face to keep the people of Israel from gazing at the end of the glory, since the end is Christ (2 Cor. 3:13)? In the context of 3:7-13, with its repeated indication that something about Moses was being rendered inoperative, *end* must connote a temporal end. If *end* in this text implies goal or purpose (Hays: 137), Paul's argument suggests that the purpose of Moses' fading glory has been attained in Christ; it has thus come to its temporal end in the transient form it had in the old age of Moses. Paul attempts to prove that Moses knew the temporal limitation of his own ministry and was therefore not bold when he veiled the luster of his face from the Israelites.

The second question, about Moses' motive for veiling his face, has several possible answers, none of which Paul states in the text. The people would lose hope. They would disparage Moses without his glory. They would not obey the commandments of the Lord and thus profane the glory (Hickling, 1975a:390f.). Any one of these would serve Paul's purpose to persuade his readers of the sufficiency of the new order of glory in Christ Jesus. Unlike the bold new ministers of Christ, Moses lacked boldness because the glory attending his ministry was coming to an end. Thus Moses veiled his face in timidity (or shame: van Unnik, 1963:153-169).

Paul is effective in projecting this overall picture of Moses' glory as veiled, and Moses himself as lacking confidence. Rival missionaries to Corinth, supposing the glory of Moses in the synagogue and the glory of Christ in the church to be coordinates, will taste a bit of Paul's derision here. Why would anyone still want to adhere to the ministry of Moses as perpetuated in the synagogue? By its nature, the coming of Christ *renders everything pertaining to Moses inoperative* (an attempt to render a troublesome neuter Greek participle of 3:13). Simply put, Paul reads Exodus 34 about Moses from the perspective of the whole system of synagogue worship. There *Moses is read . . . to this very day* (2 Cor. 3:15) apart from the new glory of Christ. The succeeding verses take the symbol of the veil further.

3:14-15 Veiled Minds While Reading Moses

Large-scale Jewish rejection of the gospel haunted Paul throughout his mission. In a later letter to the Romans (9–11), Paul addresses the issue more fully and with less polemic than here. Still, in Romans

also he labels Jewish resistance to the gospel as "a hardening." Despite *our* unveiled confidence in the glory of the new covenant in
Christ, the people reading Moses still do not see.

On that note Paul transfers the figurative veil from Moses' face to
the Jewish Scriptures, called the *old covenant*, a term used only here
in the NT. The veil of Exodus 34 now answers why synagogue worshipers cannot see the end of the transient glory of Moses and the beginning of the permanent glory of Christ. *To this day* in which Paul
lives, *the same veil* that concealed the face of Moses *remains un-
lifted*, concealing the temporality of the Mosaic covenant now *old*.

One suspects that Paul's opponents, if their synagogue mentors
are anything like Philo of Alexandria, tout their spirit of wisdom for
unveiling the secret truth of Scripture (Fallon: 32). Against such a
view, Paul says, *Only in Christ is [the veil] set aside.* Herein lies the
pattern of Paul's own interpretation of Exodus 34. He lives "in Christ"
and reads the text with Christian eyes.

Paul moves the veil in his argument once more at 2 Corinthians
3:15, so that it *lies over* synagogue worshipers' *minds* when they read
Moses. *Moses* is a way of referring to the five scrolls of the Law
(Gen.-Deut.), which Moses was said to have written. *Mind* here stands
for the Greek *kardia*, usually translated "heart." *Kardia* connotes the
center of a person's being. A veil, says Paul, lies over the center of
their being *when Moses is read.* Hence, the readers have a blurred vision of Moses. If they were "in Christ," as Paul and his converts are,
they would find the veil removed and the covenant of Moses rendered inoperative.   *Thank you Jesus for removing the veil!*

3:16-18 Radical Unveiling of the Spirit

In rhythmic style Paul wraps up his discussion of Moses' *glory* and
veil and makes transition back to the personal agenda of his own
apostolic ministry (4:1ff.).

Verse 16 echoes Exodus 34:34a: "Whenever Moses went in before the Lord to speak with him, he would take the veil off." Paul then
transposes the narrative into a principle of conversion operating in
his mission among the Gentiles: *When one turns to the Lord, the veil
is removed* (3:16). Of the Gentiles at Thessalonica, Paul said, "You
turned to God from idols, to serve a living and true God" (1 Thess.
1:9). Their turning, like that of Moses, unveiled the glory of the Lord
in the person of Jesus Christ.

Who is *the Lord* (*kurios*) in these verses? In Paul's Greek Bible

(LXX), *kurios* translates *Yahweh*, the name of the covenant God of Israel (Exod. 3:15, NRSV note). *Kurios* was commonly used to indicate dignity, majesty, and sovereignty. It soon became a title for the resurrected Jesus Christ of the church, *the Lord Jesus Christ*. The Lord of Moses' ministry in the tent of meeting is the same Lord of Paul's ministry among the Gentiles. It does not occur to Paul to apply the title *Lord* to one form of God in Exodus 34 and to another in his letter to the Corinthians. Precise delineation of divinity, as we find in later trinitarian confessions, does not concern Paul, as the next verse intimates (cf. Dunn, 1970:309-320).

The Lord is the Spirit (2 Cor. 3:17). That is, the Lord to whom Moses turned (16), whose glory shone on his face, is the Spirit of Christ, who gives life to all who turn to Christ now. To assume that Paul is thinking of the distinct person of the Holy Spirit in both contexts, not of Christ, strains the form of Paul's language in this text. Similarly, Paul elsewhere interchanges titles (Rom. 8:9-11) and has "Christ" present in the wilderness (1 Cor. 10:4). Here Paul has the active power of God's Spirit in view.

Paul's return to his earlier thought of the life-giving Spirit at verse 17 prompts the idea of freedom. *Where the Spirit of the Lord is, there is freedom.* Paul may intend freedom from the letter of the old covenant (3:6), or freedom from the law of sin and death (Rom. 8:2). More likely than not, freedom here relates to the boldness of the previous verses: boldness in approaching God, and boldness in mission. The Spirit grants such freedom to be bold. A Jewish contemporary of Paul, Philo of Alexandria, also linked the terms "boldness" and "freedom." He claimed that freedom came from the immortal law of *logos*, not from "perishable parchment or stone slab," and generates boldness. Even slaves can be free by this rule (*Every Good Man Is Free*, lines 45-46, 152-153).

Verse 18 gathers up the leading ideas in a grand melodic finale around one central predicate: *all of us . . . are being transformed.* The two parts of the predicate are expanded with rhythmic qualifiers structured thus:

> **And all of us,**
> *with unveiled faces,*
> *seeing the glory of the Lord*
> *as though reflected in a mirror,*

[handwritten margin note: FREEDOM MEANS HERE: FREE TO BE BOLD. I NEED THAT KIND OF FREEDOM.]

> *are being transformed*
> > *into the same image*
> > > *from one degree of glory to another;*
> > > > *for this comes from the Lord, the Spirit.* (3:18)

Transformed translates the Greek work, *metamorphoumetha*, from which comes the English word *metamorphosis*, an inherent change in character. Paul earlier defended his own character and ministry and that of his associates. Now he includes *all* those who have turned to the Lord Jesus Christ through his preaching. All such converts, including the Corinthians who question his ministry, *are being transformed into the same image* by the Spirit of the Lord.

Consider the qualifying phrases. The converts live *with unveiled faces* and thus are free and bold to speak. They see the glory of the Lord *as though reflected in a mirror*, the reflected image being Christ, the image of God (2 Cor. 4:4; 1 Cor. 15:49). The *mirror* can hardly mean the converts themselves, who reflect the glory of the Lord with unveiled faces. They would then be transformed into the same image they reflect—which doesn't make sense. The first option is preferable. The converts turn to Christ, the reflection of God, and are thereby transformed into the same image, the image of Christ, who is the image of God. They become "Christians."

In the next qualifier, they are being transformed *from one degree of glory to another*. Literally the text reads, *from glory into glory*. Is there here an oblique reference to the two glories of verses 7-11? Probably. The Spirit changes believers from the transient glory of the old covenant to the permanent glory of the new (cf. John 1:17-18). From Paul's experience in mission, the transformation is ongoing, spiritual, and moral in the community of faith until the final transformation at the coming of Christ (Rom. 11:25; 12:1-2; 1 Cor. 15:50-57; Rom. 8:18-30). This dynamic change from one glory to the other comes, not from within Christians themselves, but *from the Lord, the Spirit*. They *are being transformed* (passive voice of the verb).

THE TEXT IN BIBLICAL CONTEXT

2 Corinthians 3:7-18 is loaded with issues of biblical theology and ethics. Is Paul's use of Scripture in this argument valid? Is his unique evaluation of the figure of Moses shaped by the critical situation at Corinth? What is Paul's attitude toward his own Jewish people? Does Paul's argument in this text signal a tension between the synagogue

CAN WE EVEN ASK THAT?
THIS IS INSPIRED TEXT.

and the church that will eventually reach breaking point? *[Use of Scripture, p. 284; Jewish-Christian Relations, p. 270]*.

Subtexts in Paul's Text. The notes above make it clear that Paul has Exodus 34 in mind as he argues for the greater glory of the new-covenant ministry. He is not carrying out a line-by-line interpretation of the Exodus text after the manner of a rabbinic midrash. His interpretation reflects backward on the glory of Moses from his present experience of Christ and the Spirit. As far as Paul is concerned, the transforming glory that has come with Christ has replaced the glory of Moses' ministry, rendering the latter inoperative.

Without doubt, Exodus 34 is "the single obvious sub-text" (Hays: 132), but there may be at least one other text interconnected with it. Paul, like other NT writers, invokes the prophecies in Isaiah 40–66 to define his new experience of Christ. The text and context of Isaiah 63 could well be the interface between Paul's thought in 2 Corinthians 3:7-18 and the text of Exodus 34.

Ideas in Isaiah 63 would provide Paul with much of the prophetic tone and radical interpretation of the glory of Moses who veiled his face. Most of the key words in Paul's text appear in Isaiah 63: *glory* (several times) associated with *Moses; hardening* of the *hearts* of the Israelites, "the *spirit* came down from the *Lord* and guided them." More than the word connections, the prophetic insight about the proclamation of a Savior for "the end of the earth" (62:11) is coupled with the hardening of the Israelites' hearts despite the glory of the Lord through Moses (63:10-12). This text of Isaiah is an apt interface between 2 Corinthians 3:7-18 and Exodus 34:29-35.

The Figure of Moses. Did Paul really disparage Moses the minister? Did he put this giant hero of Israel beneath himself (Munck: 61)? On the surface it may seem so. On closer reading, though, Paul is not casting aspersion on the minister as such, but on the era of Moses' ministry. Further, Paul does not say that the transformed Moses gradually lost the glory of the Lord on his person. Rather, the degree and extent of transformation reflected in Moses is outshone by the arrival of the new covenant of Christ and the Spirit. The change of aeons guides Paul's argument: the old and transient covenant has yielded to the new and permanent covenant. If the person of Moses is disparaged in this text of 2 Corinthians 3:7-18, then this is the only text of its kind in all of Jewish or Christian literature. But such is not the case. Paul's argument does not denigrate the figure of Moses, but the transient glory with which Moses happened to be associated.

The Jewish People. What does this text of 2 Corinthians reveal about Paul's attitude toward the Jewish people? The short answer: only as much as the form of speech in this particular text allows. This text gives the impression that Paul views the Jewish people of his day in a negative light: they have a veil over their minds when they read the Scripture; their hearts are hardened. The issue centers on why Paul makes such a judgment. His situation at Corinth, where Jewish Christian missionaries are trying to discredit his ministry, has colored his language and shaped his argument. Given another situation devoid of any immediate Jewish (or Jewish-Christian) critique of his life and work, Paul can speak sympathetically of the Jewish people, as in Romans 9-11. There Paul exhibits a more reflective attitude toward the Jewish people. Of them he declares with deep emotion, "I could wish that I myself were accursed and cut off from Christ for the sake of my own people, my kindred according to the flesh. . . . They are beloved, for the sake of their ancestors; for the gifts and the calling of God are irrevocable" (Rom. 9:3; 11:28-29; Sanders, 1978:175-187; 1983:171-210) [Jewish-Christian Relations, p. 270].

Synagogue and Church. By his own confession, Paul has received the thirty-nine stripes five times from the synagogue authorities (2 Cor. 11:24). From this biographical note alone, it is clear that his relationship with the synagogue is not a congenial one. No doubt he has proclaimed in the synagogue the crucified Messiah whom God raised from the dead. He has taught in the synagogue a new interpretation of the law of Moses, one that welcomes Gentiles into community with full election status, equal to that of the Jewish believers in this Messiah. The tension created by Paul's inclusion of Gentiles by faith apart from the works of the Law has led ultimately to the complete separation of the Pauline communities from the synagogue. That development was probably not in Paul's vision when he launched the Gentile mission. His receiving of the thirty-nine stripes repeatedly (2 Cor. 11:24) is testimony to his persistent attempt to keep ties with the Jewish community.

The tension between church and synagogue reached a critical stage at the time of the Fourth Gospel (ca. A.D. 90). This Gospel indicates that the synagogue had believers in Jesus, but "they did not confess it, for fear that they would be put out of the synagogue; for they loved human glory more than the glory that comes from God" (John 12:42-43). The two "glories" in this text of the Fourth Gospel (as elsewhere in John) correspond to the Jewish synagogue and Christian church respectively (cf. the two "graces" of 1:16-17). Written toward the end of the first century, the two glories of the Fourth

Gospel represent a later stage in the trajectory from Paul's two glories in 2 Corinthians 3:7-18, written in midcentury.

THE TEXT IN THE LIFE OF THE CHURCH

The argument of 2 Corinthians 3:7-18 poses at least two interrelated questions for the church today. How are Christians to interpret the writings of the "old covenant"? What is the nature of spiritual development? And a third is waiting in the wings: What is the state of Jewish-Christian relations after two thousand years of tension and conflict?

Allegorizing the "Old Covenant." The old-covenant Scripture challenged Christian interpreters in the postapostolic period. Marcion and his people of the second century took the most radical position on the OT. Rather than allegorize the text, they simply set the whole of the Jewish Scriptures aside. Like the glory of Moses, the whole of the writings of the old covenant were rendered inoperative with the coming of the Spirit of the resurrected Christ. The orthodox church branded Marcion and his kind as heretics of Gnostic persuasion.

Yet the orthodox church, while it kept the OT, found it difficult to interpret many of its texts. The church in the West, influenced by the interpreters in Alexandria, Egypt, resorted to an allegorical and typological method for understanding the teaching of the OT. Paul's method was cited as the model. His interpretation of the glory and veil of Moses constituted an apt example for the allegorists, even though Paul's approach was far removed from the spiritualizing of later interpreters. Paul interpreted according to his understanding of the change of aeons; the allegorists interpreted by a spiritual meaning they thought they saw beneath the literal meaning of the text.

The allegorical method of Alexandria prevailed in the church until the Reformation, despite the insistence of the Eastern church, centered in Antioch, on the literal reading of Scripture. Martin Luther decried the allegorical method vehemently, but in the end he adopted a form of allegorizing by proposing that Christ is the principle by which all Scripture should be read. The Anabaptists allegorized the text in their own way. Of 2 Corinthians 3:7-8, Dirk Philips writes,

> The law is the letter which kills, but the gospel is the Spirit which makes alive. . . . So we discover that the meaning, content, and actual understanding of the law accords with the gospel. . . . Thus that literal command of the Lord about circumcision of the flesh has come to an end.

> Nevertheless, that command of the spiritual circumcision of the heart
> thus remains. . . . All the figures of the law have . . . come to an end so far
> as the letter is concerned. . . . [The] essential significance of these same
> figures remains and harmonizes with the gospel. (268)

The "literal" and the "figures" of the old covenant yield their
meaning in light of the spiritual gospel of Christ. This approach follows closely the rule of Luther. But the church of the nineteenth and
twentieth centuries frowned upon the allegorical approach, choosing
rather the literal, critical, historical approach to reading the OT. Perhaps the time has come in the life of the church for an appropriate
"synthesis of Antioch and Alexandria," using the literal (Antiochian)
and the spiritual (Alexandrian) approaches to a text (Meyer: 45-49).

Spiritual Development and Christian Discipleship. One of the
great texts about spiritual transformation in the NT is 2 Corinthians
3:17-18. Various traditions of the church understand the idea differently. Some believe that monastic life is the way to achieve spiritual
renewal. Christians in the Anabaptist tradition have generally chosen
the way of discipleship as the means of spiritual formation. Discipleship for them has meant obeying the life and teaching of Jesus in the
strength of the Spirit. Piety and devotion were completely congruent
with acts of love and kindness in the name of Christ, who gave his life
for the salvation of others.

As people in the believers church tradition moved to different
parts of the world, especially to North America, they fell under the influence of other traditions, such as Evangelical and Charismatic
movements. Increasingly, spiritual life was understood as an inner experience quite apart from the life of discipleship (Smucker in *ME*,
5:850-851). The separation of inner experience and ethical deci-
sions is artificial. Spiritual life is a life of discipleship. What Christ was
in his life, so also are Christians in theirs. Jesus Christ was one indivisible reality on earth, not part spiritual and part physical. The incarnation of God in Jesus admits no such false dichotomy. Nor did Paul
consider the change *from one degree of glory to another* to be a private introspective experience. For him transformation was a renewing of the mind that kept on transforming all of life into the image of
Jesus Christ in a spiritual worship of God (Rom. 12:1-2).

Michael Griffiths, writing on *The Example of Jesus*, points repeatedly to Paul's thought in 2 Corinthians 3:18. The attitude, action, and
lifestyle of Jesus is communicated to the believer through the mediation of the Spirit. "How can we possibly even attempt to live as beau-
tifully as the Lord Jesus?" Griffiths asks. "Are we not just kidding our-

selves, that we could ever hope to achieve likeness to his image?" He answers, "No. . . . God is not mocking us. . . . It is the work of the Holy Spirit to reproduce the image of Christ in us. . . . It is his work to transform us into Christ's likeness from one degree of glory to another (2 Cor. 3:18)" (180-181).

Jewish-Christian Dialogue. The interpretation of 2 Corinthians 3 is difficult at several levels. Nowhere is it more strained than in the effort to present a proper Christian attitude toward the Jewish people. The notes above are not meant to imply that Christianity has superseded Judaism. The aim was to represent Paul's polemical argument on its own terms, written by this Jewish believer in Jesus the Messiah, against an opposing Jewish front. Paul's argument should not therefore be confused with the later attitude of the fourth-century church toward the Jewish people [Jewish-Christian Relations, p. 270].

There is much good that may be said of contemporary Western society, but there is still room for improvement in people's attitude toward the "other" next door. One might ask, for example, why Quebec wants to separate from the rest of Canada. What was the intent of the Million Man March in Washington despite the political move toward cultural pluralism? We should be grateful for government legislation that has served to increase the tolerance level between different ethnic groups. One day tolerance may become understanding, and understanding become love. The process is ever so slow. A few hopeful signs have appeared on the horizon.

Anti-Semitism, for example, persisted into the middle of the twentieth century, where it reached its barbaric climax in the holocaust of Nazi Germany. Now it is gradually losing its impetus. Jewish scholars in religion are in dialogue with Christian scholars, and they are writing sympathetically on Christian history, including the NT. Similarly, Christian scholars engage the Jewish story. Teachers in conservative Christian institutions of higher learning now invite Jewish rabbis to speak to their classes about Judaism. Christian students are now encouraged to visit synagogues to observe the reading of Torah. One can only hope that the old polemical fires of ages past are dying out, and that in their place will come the glory of love, and of mutual respect for the religious and cultural convictions of the "resident alien" (Exod. 12:49; Num. 15:15).

Renewal of Human Life

2 Corinthians 4:1—5:10

OVERVIEW

At 2 Corinthians 4:1, Paul's ministry is still in focus and continues so throughout this section (4:1—5:10). Since his ministry ultimately is *by God's mercy,* Paul does not lose heart, however severe the criticism against him. Paul envisions life and world beyond his affliction, beyond the verbal daggers of opponents, beyond the present age of human mortality. Paul sees this newness of life in the gospel of Jesus Christ, *the image of God* (4:4).

Some people at Corinth probably have accused Paul of preaching a *veiled* gospel, one that people cannot grasp because of the element of human weakness in Paul. He agrees that the gospel is veiled to unbelievers. But to those who see the shining light of God, his preaching of the gospel, weak as it appears, contains a treasure of immeasurable proportion. He preaches in a mortal body, like an expendable clay pot. But the substance of his preaching is life eternal, life of the resurrected Jesus promised to those who believe.

Meanwhile, a mysterious renewal of human life continues. It is mysterious because it happens in the absence of human initiative, by the power of the gracious God. The *outer* person of flesh wastes away in time; the *inner* person of spirit experiences life from the future, guaranteed by the Spirit of the resurrected Christ (5:5). Paul's metaphors on this score are telling. Fragile human existence in a physical body is a temporary tent; eternal human existence in a spiritual body is a building of God, not made with hands. The new existence provides new clothes for the same self. In short, the mortal is *swallowed up by life* (5:4).

Genesis 1–3 reverberates throughout the whole section (Pate: 107-157). The image and glory of God in the first human (Adam), lost by disobedience to the divine will, appears again *in the face of Jesus Christ* (2 Cor. 4:6), the second human of the *new creation* (5:17) that Paul proclaims. When the first parents' mortal offspring respond to Paul's gospel in faith, they see the face of Christ and find themselves renewed in spirit, prepared for the age to come.

Paul's vision of Christian existence present and future was not for him a pipe dream. Nor was it packaged doctrine to be memorized. It was reality that controlled his life in mission.

OUTLINE

Nothing to Hide in Light of the Gospel, 4:1-6

Eternal Life in Expendable Jars, 4:7-15

New Life in Two Bodies, 4:16—5:10

Nothing to Hide in Light of the Gospel
2 Corinthians 4:1-6

PREVIEW

In many respects these six verses form a summary of Paul's various arguments that extend from 2:14 to 3:18. The present text reaffirms Paul's confidence as a minister of Christ, denies charges of cunning or deceit, and presents Paul and his fellow leaders as *slaves* to the Corinthians for the sake of Christ. Stated otherwise, the thoughts that open the series of arguments on Paul's worthiness as a minister are recast in these verses to bring closure to the line of argument. Other hints in this summary statement connect with earlier points: the veil over Moses' face, over the old covenant, and over Jewish minds. Now that veil appears in relation to the gospel Paul preaches. *The face of Christ* (4:6) that reflects the glory of God in this section echoes the face of Moses in the earlier section.

However, these verses are more than a summary statement of earlier points. They form a transition to the next major movement in the second variation on the theme of ministry. If the new ministry in the light of Christ operates in terms of the Spirit of God (rather than any human spirit), what does the new ministry hold out to human existence? Paul's answer begins in part already in these verses. Christ, *the image of God* (4:4), the illuminating presence of God (4:6a), enters human hearts (4:6b) so as to renew them (4:16) and prepare them for life in the age to come (5:1-10).

Some of Paul's phrasing in this text is distinctive, as the explanatory notes will illustrate: *image of God, face of Christ, gospel is veiled, and god of this age.* While these forms of speech advance the persuasive character of the Letter of Reconciliation, they belong to a developing Christian self-definition that Paul had a hand in shaping in the first century.

OUTLINE

On Staying in the Ministry, 4:1-2

Why Some Cannot Grasp the Good News, 4:3-4

Enlightened Slave-Ministers, 4:5-6

EXPLANATORY NOTES

On Staying in the Ministry 4:1-2

Therefore could be more literally translated *on account of this.* If Paul has something specific in mind for *this,* it is not clear to his modern interpreters. Is he thinking of the transformation of the Spirit in the verses immediately preceding (3:17-18)? The new covenant with its new ministry of the Spirit (3:6, 8)? The enabling of God for ministry (2:14-16)? Or is Paul thinking forward to *God's mercy* in the next phrase of 4:1? Maybe all of these together, or any one of them.

The point is, on account of any or all of them, he does not *lose heart* (4:1b). He does not shrink back from a ministry graciously granted by God. On the human side, he has *every* reason to withdraw. His afflictions are reason enough. His humiliation in receiving the thirty-nine lashes five times could easily make him lose heart in the ministry. Vilification by opponents is hard to take. But he does not lose heart. Paul knows God's mercy and sees God's plan for the world unfolding in the Gentile mission in which he is engaged. For this reason he does not lose heart.

If Paul has something to hide, something to be ashamed of, that indeed would be a different matter. In that case he could not commend himself at all. But he has *renounced the shameful things that one hides*, by virtue of his unwavering faith in God and Christ; he refuses to *practice cunning or to falsify God's word* (4:2) so as to make himself popular (cf. 2:17). Paul has nothing to hide from the Corinthians or from anyone else.

On the contrary, he lays bare *the truth* and bears the consequences. *The truth* in 4:2 is another word for the gospel of God in Christ crucified and raised, the *gospel* that Paul preaches (4:3). On another occasion he also blends the two terms together: "the truth of the gospel" (Gal. 2:14). On the strength of his conviction that he has been true to the gospel, he is prepared to commend himself and his associates to *the conscience of everyone in the sight of God* (2 Cor. 4:2b).

[handwritten marginal note: WE DO NOT LOSE HEART BECAUSE OF THE QUALITY OF CHRIST]

Strange as it may seem, Paul appeals to every human *conscience*, not merely to those of his own company or to those of Christians generally. He believes that his own moral integrity in relation to his ministry will commend itself to the moral core of *human* conscience resident in the community of Corinth. To be expected, though, Paul will not leave himself at the mercy of the human court alone. His life and ministry come under the scrutiny of the divine mind (cf. 1 Cor. 4:4). What the Corinthians cannot see in Paul, God sees. Thus he commends himself and his comrades.

Why Some Cannot Grasp the Good News 4:3-4

In these verses, Paul returns to the notion of the veil. Now he admits conditionally that his gospel itself is *veiled*. This admission raises a hard question about his own preaching and the preaching of every minister since: Why do so many human beings reject the good news designed specifically for their good? Surely people have enough sense to know what is good for them. Paul could answer as he did in 1 Corinthians 1:18—2:16 that the cross in the good news is the stumbling block to both Jews and Greeks, that the paradox is the veil. But he stops short of making that case, even though the paradox of the cross seems to stand in the background of this and many of the texts of 2 Corinthians. In this text he answers in another way, not easily understood by modern critical thinkers.

If our gospel is veiled, it is veiled to those who are perishing (4:3). And if opponents happen to be among the ones for whom Paul's gospel is veiled, they will have to swallow hard on his judgment call: they too are perishing with the rest of the unbelievers. Paul's categorical statement is only part of the answer as to why some people do not believe the gospel of Christ. The other part is most unusual for Paul.

Unbelievers cannot see the light of the gospel, he says, because *the god of this world has blinded their minds* (4:4a). *This world* is more literally *this age* (*aiōn*) as compared to the age to come. While the future age of glory has to a degree broken in upon the present one, the present age of sin and death is still a reality (cf. 1 Cor. 10:11, the overlap of the ages). Yet Paul does not say simply that the character of the present age of sin and death has blinded the minds of unbelievers. Rather, *the god* of this age is the culprit.

The wording of this statement is found only here in Scripture, and it raises a thorny issue. All his life Paul has held idolatry to be an abomination and has been zealous for the glory of the one true God.

Hence, it is startling to find him using this "great and horrible description of Satan" (Bengel) and applying the term *theos* [god] to "the archenemy of God and of [human]kind" (Plummer: 115) *[Satan, p. 278]*. Some think Paul intended *theos* (god) to mean the Creator-Redeemer God, not Satan. In that case, the saving God blinds the minds of unbelievers. Possible, but not likely. Imagine Paul as a missionary preaching that the God of his gospel blinds the minds of those for whom that gospel is intended!

Paul is well aware of demonic power that pervades the present age (1 Cor. 2:6; 5:5; 8:5; 10:20; cf. John 12:31). He uses the general term for divinity, *theos* (god), to describe the evil persona of spiritual powers seeking to ruin the human family that God wills to save. Nor is Paul dualistic in this text, to the extent that his contemporaries at Qumran were. For them, two spirits live in the universe and "control humankind and determine who is good and who is evil" (Wise: 129; 1QS 3.13-14). For Paul, there is one Creator-Redeemer God working out the plan of the ages. In the meantime, the present age falls under the spell of the evil one, as it has since the sin of the first human parents.

At the head of the old creation, the first humans were created in the image of God (Gen. 1:27). Now, Paul says, Christ is *the image of God* (4:4b) that heads up the new creation (5:17). This climactic phrase *image of God* links the Christ with God uniquely, and with humanity redemptively, as the Lord renews and restores that image in believers (3:18).

Image of God implies not a photographic copy but a true representative character (cf. Heb. 1:3). Philo used similar image-language in defining the relation of the Logos to the Existent God (e.g., *Special Laws* 1.81). The Greek-speaking Jewish church likewise used this language to understand the inherent relation of Jesus Christ to the one true God. Paul drew from that fountain, as in the early hymn to Christ incorporated into Philippians at 2:6: Christ is "the form of God" (cf. Col. 1:15; Jervell: 197).

Image of God also implies Christ's identity with humankind. In 1 Corinthians 15, Paul looks forward to resurrection-transformation, when human beings from the first humankind of earth will take on the image of the second humankind from heaven (15:49). *The light of the gospel of the glory of Christ* (2 Cor. 4:4b) reveals above all this mysterious plan of redemption for human life (1 Cor. 15:51-58).

Enlightened Slave-Ministers 4:5-6

The defensive tone of earlier texts comes through here again. *For we do not proclaim ourselves* sounds as if some at Corinth have said he does so proclaim himself. He has, after all, corrected the Corinthians' behavior as a person with authority. That much is clear from 1 Corinthians 5. If such correction has appeared to the Corinthians as though Paul is lording himself over them, this text clears up that misconception. *We proclaim Jesus Christ as Lord, and ourselves as your slaves for Jesus' sake* (2 Cor. 4:4).

One would expect Paul to say in the second part of his statement, as he does elsewhere, that he is a slave of Christ (e.g., Rom. 1:1; 6:15-23). Not so here. He calls himself and his colleagues slaves of the Corinthians. That is, he has committed himself to serving them in the ministry of the gospel. His correction of their community life in Christ was part of that service. All of his service to them came under the lordship of the risen Christ. Hence his qualifier here: *your slaves for Jesus' sake*. A question anyone might ask and one that Paul himself might ask: Why would Paul enslave himself to the Corinthians? Verse 6 answers why.

For it is the God who said, "Let light shine out of darkness," who has shone in our hearts to give the light of the knowledge of the glory of God in the face of Jesus Christ (2 Cor. 4:6). Divine illumination makes Paul a slave to the Corinthians and others like them. Otherwise it would not occur to him as a free Roman citizen to make himself slave to anyone.

His thought in this statement draws in part on the creation story of Genesis 1:3, where God says, "Let there be light," and also on Isaiah's "light to the nations" (Isa. 49:6; 9:1-2; see TBC below). God caused light to shine in the first creation; he has done so again in the re-creation under the agency of Christ. The shining in the second instance happens in the believing hearts of human beings. A new way of knowing occurs in that light, an "epistemology at the turn of the ages" (Martyn: 269-287). The glory of God that once shone on Moses' face now shines on the face of Christ, and thence to believing hearts. The illumination is not by Paul's own volition.

Many commentators tie Paul's metaphor about the shining light to his conversion experience, which was likewise not of his own choosing. Acts (written many years after 2 Corinthians) speaks of "a light from heaven [that] flashed around him" (9:3) at the time of his transformation. It must be admitted, however, that Paul does not explicitly link his thought about the light of God in 2 Corinthians 4:6 to his own call and conversion. The light he has in mind has shone *in our hearts*, not exclusively in his own. All who believe receive the enlightenment of the glory of God in the face of Jesus Christ. Thus they become slave-ministers of people like the Corinthians, just as Jesus took on the form of a slave and became obedient unto death (Phil. 2:8).

THE TEXT IN BIBLICAL CONTEXT

The section 4:1-6 rounds out the argument that began at 2:14, and sets the stage for further development of the idea of Christian ministry. The metaphor of the light at 4:4-6 is new and has a much wider context within the biblical tradition.

There may be an echo of Genesis 1:3-4, where it is said that God created light and saw that it was good. If Paul had this text in mind, his quotation at 2 Corinthians 4:6—*"Let light shine out of darkness"*—is quite free, a feature not unusual for him. His mind is probably turning on the thought of the new creation in advance of the explicit statement of 5:17: *So if anyone is in Christ, there is a new creation: everything old has passed away; see, everything has become new!*

Given this judgment, it is also fair to say that Paul's quotation almost certainly blends in something of Isaiah's insight at 9:2. Speaking of Gentiles as well as Jews, all those in anguished darkness, Isaiah envisions a new experience for them: "those who lived in a land of deep darkness—on them light has shined." From this text Paul has his words *darkness* and *shine.*

In addition to these two highly probable allusions in 2 Corinthians 4:4-6, the OT has numerous ideas about the light of God. Of these, another possible candidate behind Paul's quotation is Psalm 27:1: "The Lord is my light and my salvation; whom shall I fear?"

Contemporary thinkers in Paul's biblical world reflected deeply on the metaphor of divine light in human understanding. For example, the Jewish community at the Dead Sea referred to themselves as "the sons of light." Their knowledge came from God: "My light has sprung from the source of His knowledge; my eyes have beheld His marvelous deeds, and the light of my heart, the mystery to come" (1QS 11). As in Paul's text, so here in the Dead Sea scroll, "light" is associated with "knowledge," and both are said to reside in the "heart."

Another Jewish thinker, Philo of Alexandria, made much of the image of light in relation to God's revelation of himself. Apart from

God's light shining into human hearts, there cannot be any true vision of God. Philo writes, "The seekers for truth are those who envisage God through God, light through light" (*On Rewards and Punishments* 46).

All of these references to light predate Paul and form part of the background for grasping his thought. Many post-Pauline texts carry similar ideas. Chief among later NT texts that accent the light motif is the Gospel and Epistles of John. In these writings Christ, the Logos of God, judges and gives life by the light. "In him was life, and the life was the light of all people. The light shines in the darkness and the darkness did not overcome it" (John 1:4-5). Light and election are linked in 1 Peter 2:9. People are called of God "out of darkness into his marvelous light." Distinctively, James 1:17 calls God the "Father of lights" (cf. Apoc. Mos. 36:3, "Father of light").

Light imagery had powerful and pervasive religious significance in the biblical world. Paul's text in 2 Corinthians 4:4-6 is the earliest Christian appropriation of the image of light on record (cf. 1 Cor. 4:5; also Eph. 5:8-14; 1 Pet. 2:9; Acts 13:47; 26:18; James 1:17).

THE TEXT IN THE LIFE OF THE CHURCH

One of the troublesome elements of this text for Greek and Latin bishops and leaders of the church after Paul was *the god of this age.* Augustine, for example, interpreted the phrase to mean the one true God has blinded the minds of the unbelievers of this age. To attribute the term *god* to Satan was bordering on error. Many others of the same period offered similar interpretations, assuming that Paul's idea could be found in the OT (e.g., Isa. 6:10; cf. John 12:40).

Whatever difficulty they had with the notion of God being responsible for the destruction of unbelievers was slight compared to the problem of positing two divinities in the universe. The Jewish community of the time had accused the church of propagating multiple gods in its doctrine of the Trinity. Not surprisingly, the church avoided every sign of polytheism in its thinking from the second to the fourth century.

Since the Reformation the church has come to understand Paul's peculiar use of the term *god* for Satan (cf. "ruler of this world," John 12:31). And few are troubled by the idea that Satan blinds the minds of unbelievers so that they cannot grasp the significance of the gospel for their lives. Menno Simons, convinced that his Roman Catholic counterparts were apostate, called them a "blind generation" of evildoers and said, "Their works are done according to the will of the devil" (91). Like Paul's argument against his Jewish counterparts, Menno's polemic against his fellow priests (and people) should be interpreted within the context of Reformation fires.

Yet the same is not true for the positive side of the same argument. "Free" human beings are responsible for their own salvation by their act of faith. Voluntarism is one of the hallmarks of the Radical Reformers' teaching and practice. "It was assumed by all that [human beings] had the capacity to respond to God's call" (Klaassen, 1981:162). Nonetheless, the early Anabaptists usually were careful to credit God with illumination and with the sealing of faith by the Holy Spirit. Many evangelical groups stress the importance of the individual's repentance and personal acceptance of Christ for salvation. Paul's consistent refrain, however, is that God is responsible for the salvation of humankind, and of himself in particular (Phil. 3:12). God causes the light to shine *in our hearts to give the light of the knowledge of the glory of God in the face of Jesus Christ* (2 Cor. 4:6). Human "free will" merely responds to the sovereign will and grace of God that brings newness of life to human beings caught in the plight of sin and death.

[handwritten annotation: Healthy Anabaptist view on salvation. Calvinists would take this a bit further.]

Eternal Life in Expendable Jars
2 Corinthians 4:7-15

PREVIEW

Paul's defense of the character of his ministry continues in 4:7-15, but from a different angle. Beginning in this text, he elaborates on three aspects of the ministry: (1) the relationship between the mortality of the minister and the substance of the ministry; (2) the necessity of adversity in relationship to the crucified-resurrected Christ; (3) the necessary connection of the minister to the congregation of converts (in this case the Corinthians). Paul intertwines these three perspectives in his argument that extends to 5:10.

A striking metaphor shapes the thought (4:7). The text assumes that the first readers will easily understand the significance of a *treasure in clay jars* without explanation. Interpreters (including this one) feel constrained to take apart the pieces and thereby run the risk of losing the metaphoric bite in the language as it stands. The effect of the metaphor is matched well by the ensuing catalog of hardships

(4:8-9). Several such catalogs appear in 2 Corinthians. Their form is not unlike those of Greek philosophers of Paul's day.

Paul closes the section with an exposition of his underlying conviction about the life-giving death of Jesus. This conviction informs the whole development of his thought on the restored image and glory of the first human being through the suffering, death, and resurrection of the second human being, Jesus Christ. Paul's ministry, so he argues, belongs squarely in the restoration program now under way by God's grace (4:10-15).

A diagram of the structure of this text may help focus the meaning and the notes that follow.

Thesis
The fragile life of mortal ministers is necessary
   to show God's extraordinary power. (4:7)

Antithesis
Paul catalogs four hardships and their corollaries. (4:8-9)

Synthesis
Ministers carry the death of Jesus in their bodies (4:10),
so that the life of Jesus
   might become visible in the world of mortality (4:11-12),
because the resurrection life of Jesus
   is in store for all who believe,
   to the glory of God. (4:13-15)

OUTLINE

The Necessity of Fragile Jars for the Treasure of Ministry, 4:7

A Catalog of Hardships in Ministry, 4:8-9

Interpretation 1: Purpose in Adversity, 4:10-12

Interpretation 2: Purpose in Adversity, 4:13-15

EXPLANATORY NOTES
The Necessity of Fragile Jars
for the Treasure of Ministry 4:7

Before exploring the significance of the metaphor in 4:7, some review of the situation at Corinth is needed. The visiting missionaries at

Corinth cast a shadow over Paul's ministry because it appears to lack the kind of power that they display in their speech and action. They are able to commend themselves well to the Corinthians, not only by letters but by their stunning presence and preaching (2:16—3:3; cf. 11:5-6). Alongside them, Paul appears weak, lacking the dynamic of the Spirit that should mark an apostle of Christ. Paul then counters this conception (or misconception!) of ministry in his argument, beginning with the striking metaphor in 4:7.

But we have this treasure in clay jars, so that it may be made clear that this extraordinary power belongs to God and does not come from us (4:7). Pottery, common in Paul's world, was used for storing precious commodities, including money, jewelry, and the like. Religious groups stored their sacred scrolls in clay jars, the Qumran community at the Dead Sea being a prime example. Those Dead Sea scrolls, discovered in the late 1940s, survived for two thousand years in brittle clay pots. Those scrolls take their place among the greatest archaeological treasures in the world.

Paul, however, employs this common practice metaphorically. He compares the physical treasure in clay jars imaginatively with the character of his ministry. This figurative language may be called "rhetorical metaphor" because it stands out explicitly in the text to make a particular point in an argument. But the rhetorical metaphor does not stand alone. It rests on the pervasive "generative metaphor" of the death and resurrection of Jesus Christ. This generative metaphor is how Paul construes the world, including his own ministry within the world (Kraftchick: 169-177).

It remains now to discover as nearly as possible (1) what constitutes *this treasure*, and (2) why it is necessary to contain it in *clay jars*. On the first of these two, several options present themselves. The treasure can be viewed simply as the gospel that Paul preaches (Windisch: 141-142). The hearing of the good news of Jesus Christ brings renewal to the human spirit. Or Paul may mean the treasure of the unveiled glory of his ministry, as compared to that of Moses (Bultmann, 1985:112). Or again, the treasure can refer to the light of the knowledge of the glory of God in 4:6 (Plummer: 126). These all have something in common: they relate to the renewal (or restoration) of human life by the act of God in Jesus, whom Paul preaches.

In other words, "the glory of the Last Adam (the treasure) presently exists within the frailty initiated by the first Adam (the earthen vessel)" (Pate: 87; cf. Rom. 8:18-39). What the Corinthians perceive as weakness, Paul sees as a necessary precursor to the coming glory, guaranteed by the presence of the Spirit (2 Cor. 5:5), just as death is precursor to resurrection. This thought leads directly to the second point of the metaphor, why it is necessary to have the treasure in clay jars.

Clay jars are fragile, expendable, and cheap. As such they constitute an apt metaphor for the physical body, subject as it is to suffering, death, and decay. The metaphor is not new with Paul. The OT makes much of it (Isa. 29:16; 45:9; 64:8; Jer. 18:1-11; 19:1-13; cf. Gen. 2:7). Paul's contemporary in Alexandria, Philo, also spoke of the body as "a vessel for the soul. . . . It comes to maturity, wears out, grows old, dies, is dissolved" (*On Dreams* 1.26). Yet Paul exploits the metaphor in a way peculiar to his own Christian thought and situation in the ministry of Christ. Unlike Philo and the Stoics, Paul does not here consider the physical body a container for the soul. Instead, his mortal body, like that of Jesus, exists as a foil for the power of God in renewing human life.

Paul probably draws upon the motif, found in Jewish literature, of the restoration of glory to humanity (Adam) through righteous suffering. He has then adapted the idea to his Christian worldview, and in particular to his argument in this text of 2 Corinthians (Pate: 196). The stated purpose of such a situation in ministry, however, is to make clear that the *extraordinary power belongs to God and does not come from us* (4:7b). On this point Paul effectively dismantles the opposing view that apostles of Christ display super powers in their bodily presence and preaching. In this present stage, he argues, apostles display the suffering mortality of Jesus so that the resurrection life of God might come through.

A Catalog of Hardships in Ministry 4:8-9

To illustrate his thesis of verse 7, Paul lays out a catalog of four hardships in antithetical form. The same device of listing hardships was prevalent among Greek philosophers of Paul's time. The sage would list personal trials to prove his worth as a true philosopher. Wisdom so shaped the sage's character that the hardships of life bore testimony to the veracity of his person and teaching and commended both to the audience (Fitzgerald, 1988:47-116).

However, "Paul's own use of these traditions and the catalogs associated with them is highly creative" (Fitzgerald, 1988:207). In the first place, Paul has come under the direct influence of the OT tradition of the Suffering Servant, already well established in the church, and the suffering righteous person, as in Job. In the foreground, however, Paul transforms the catalog of hardships out of "his fixation on the cross of Christ." Whatever his trials in mission, they connect in Paul's mind with the trial(s) of Jesus who "humbled himself and became obedient to the point of death—even death on a cross" (Phil. 2:8). In this sense, the catalog of hardships is more than an effective convention. It "takes us to the center of Paul's understanding of God and his own self-understanding" (207).

The antithetical corollary to each of the hardships on the list points to the power of God in sustaining his suffering servants. The accent falls on the antithesis thus:

> Afflicted in every way, *but not crushed;*
> perplexed, *but not driven to despair;*
> persecuted, *but not forsaken;*
> struck down, *but not destroyed.*

The rest of the section (4:10-15) offers two interpretations of Paul's hardships in Christian mission.

Interpretation 1: Purpose in Adversity 4:10-12

Here is where Paul's "generative metaphor" or central conviction rises to the surface of his argument. What is the meaning of his suffering? Why does he continue in a mission that brings such affliction? His answer is that he is *always carrying in the body the death of Jesus* (4:10). *The body* here means his identifiable person: his senses (*flesh*, 4:11b), emotions, mind, spirit, appearance, and whatever gives Paul identity in the time-space world in which he lives. His body, like that of Jesus, bears the suffering associated with the mission.

His word for death (*nekrōsis*) in 4:10 is rare in the letters. It depicts more the process of *dying* than the actual event of *death* (*thanatos*, 4:11) that ends physical existence (Bultmann, 1985:117). Of course, every mortal is in process of dying, but Paul operates from a different premise in this text. The death he experiences comes with the mission, and in that respect his afflicted *body* has on it the stamp of the dying of Jesus. Without that stamp, so Paul implies here, his mission is a lost cause, his preaching vain.

Paul believes his preaching has to conform to his life, and his life to his preaching. If the saving death of Jesus is central to his preaching (1 Cor. 1:18ff.), then the experience of such a death has to be visible in the person of the preacher. As he says elsewhere, he has to conform to Jesus' death (Phil. 3:10). Not that death, even death in mission, is an end in itself. Like the death of Jesus, Paul's death lets the resurrection life of God come through. "The destruction of the earthenware vessel (verse 7) reveals more clearly the treasure it contains" (Barrett, 1973:140).

Verse 11 repeats the thought of 4:10 with slight variation. In 4:11 Paul is *given up to death* as in a sentence passed upon him (cf. 1:9). The language is reminiscent of the trial of Jesus before the Roman and Jewish authorities, recorded in the Gospels. Paul experiences "trial" in mission *for Jesus' sake*, but always with the purpose of bringing the resurrection life of Jesus into the open.

The conclusion of 4:12 may seem strange at first glance: *So death is at work in us, but life in you.* The contrast effectively highlights the character and intent of Paul's ministry to the Corinthians. Paul has the same taste of the future life as they have. His point, however, is that his apostolic affliction that leads to death brings life to the Corinthians. Thus he stands with his Lord as a person for others.

Interpretation 2: Purpose in Adversity 4:13-15

In the first interpretation of the trials of a missionary of Jesus Christ, Paul forges a theological link between his personal experience and his proclamation. Similarly, in the second interpretation he ties believing to speaking. The speaking he has in mind is his preaching of the gospel of the glory of Christ, the image of God (4:4-5). In his heart he is convinced of the truth of what he speaks (cf. Rom. 10:9). Believing and speaking cannot be separated.

So important is the connection between believing and preaching that in support Paul cites a psalm from his Greek Bible (Ps. 116:10; LXX: 115:1). Paul's mind probably ran to Psalm 116, not only for the two key words *believed* and *spoke* but more so on account of its context of affliction and death (see below).

Why *believed* and *spoke*? Why suffer and die in mission? Paul's answer: *Because we know that the one who raised the Lord Jesus will raise us also with Jesus, and will bring us with you into his presence* (2 Cor. 4:14). Final salvation for Paul lies ahead, constituted and guaranteed by the resurrection of Jesus in the recent past. To be raised *with Jesus* means to be raised as he was raised. Paul's ultimate goal in this life and ministry is to attain resurrection-transformation. That is why he suffers now in connection with Christ (Phil. 3:11).

The two groups *us* and *you* on the way to resurrection life in

2 Corinthians 4:14 are Paul and associates (*us*) and the Corinthians (*you*). Whatever the contingent problems at Corinth, Paul *knows* that the Corinthians will participate with him in the renewal of human life. They have received his gospel, which makes them part of the plan of God for the renewal of humankind.

At 4:15, Paul finishes interpreting his affliction in mission with yet another connection: the *grace* of God and human gratitude. This balance is missing in the Corinthians' attitude. While Paul had been an agent of God's grace to the Corinthians, their current response to him is one of adversarial critique, not gratitude. The proper response to grace at any level is gratitude, and the more of it the better. As grace extends *to more and more people,* gratitude should abound more and more, and that to the glory of God. If God is glorified in the gratitude of believers, then Paul's living and dying shall not be in vain.

THE TEXT IN BIBLICAL CONTEXT

As indicated in the notes above, the implied biblical background for this section is the Genesis account of the creation and fall of the first human parents (Gen. 1–3). They mirrored the glory of God in that they bore the divine image. The tragedy of Adam and Eve was in their disobedience to the divine will, which led to the loss of the divine glory, making them subject to "the power of sin" and death (Rom. 3:9). The clay jars of 2 Corinthians 4:7, breakable and expendable, depict the mortal state of the human family. The good news announces the restoration of the lost image and glory of the first human pair through Jesus Christ, the image of God.

Jewish literature prior to Paul and contemporary with him contemplates the restoration of original glory in humanity. Informed by the Servant Songs of the second part of Isaiah (esp. Isa. 53), Jewish writers saw the restoration happening, not mystically or painlessly, but through affliction on the part of the righteous remnant. Paul can hardly have escaped the theme of righteous suffering for future glory, circulating widely in the Jewish communities. It was standing ready for Paul to adapt to his new understanding of the cruel death of Jesus that resulted in resurrection, and also for the application of the theme to his own role of *carrying the death of Jesus* in mission in hope of resurrection life. "When the Adamic glory/suffering motif is applied to . . . [2 Cor. 4:7—5:21], the conundrum of interpretation posed by those verses is more readily solvable" (Pate: 65).

For the first time in 2 Corinthians, Paul quotes his Greek Scripture directly and verbatim at 4:13. He uses only one short statement from Psalm 116, *I believed, and so I spoke*, principally for the two key words, *believed* and *spoke*. What is striking, however, is that the context of these two words in Psalm 116 concerns bodily affliction and the Lord's deliverance, much like that of 2 Corinthians 4:7-15. Here are sample lines from the Psalm. "The pangs of death seized me. . . . I found affliction and sorrow. . . . I was brought low, and he saved me. . . . He has delivered my soul from death. . . . ***I believed, wherefore I have spoken***: but I was greatly afflicted. . . . Precious in the sight of the Lord is the death of his saints" (LXX: 114:3, 6, 8; 115:1, 6; = NRSV: 116:3, 6, 8, 10, 15).

Paul consistently taught that believing and suffering go together, and that together they pave the way to future glory. For example, of the Philippians he says, "[God] has graciously granted you the privilege not only of believing in Christ, but of suffering for him as well" (1:29). Believing and suffering constitute evidence of salvation already at work in them (1:28).

Colossians 1:24 goes so far as to unite "rejoicing" and "suffering" to advance "Christ's afflictions for the sake of his body, that is, the church." First Peter develops the theme of rejoicing in the sufferings of Christ so as to participate in the final "glory" of Christ: "Do not be surprised at the fiery ordeal that is taking place among you. . . . Rejoice insofar as you are sharing Christ's sufferings, so that you may . . . shout for joy when his glory is revealed" (4:12-13; cf. Matt. 5:11-12).

THE TEXT IN THE LIFE OF THE CHURCH

While I was writing on this text of 2 Corinthians, the "Mirror of the Martyrs" exhibit arrived at Concord College in Winnipeg. One cannot but be moved by the commitment of those depicted on the panels of the exhibit, who went to cruel death for their Christian convictions.

The Radical Reformers of the sixteenth century sought to recapture the pattern of faith in the early Christians. Their new vision and practice brought the fury of the established church and state down on their heads, so that many of them suffered the pain of death by burning or drowning. They were radicals, daring to say that only believers should be baptized, that infant baptism availed nothing for salvation. These radicals went so far as to rebaptize people of the church on the basis of their own personal faith in Christ. Hence the designation *Anabaptists* from their opponents.

The model of Paul's affliction, articulated in 2 Corinthians 4:7-15, filled the minds of the many martyrs throughout the history of the church. Trial comes from being radical on one hand, and on the other hand from being thoroughly convinced of beliefs against the accepted traditions. Nowhere is this condition any more evident than in the witness of the Radical Reformers of the sixteenth century. They understood themselves to be the extended body of Christ, as shown in Conrad Grebel's postscript letter to Thomas Müntzer: "Christ must suffer still more in his members" (in L. Harder: 293; cf. Col. 1:24).

Michael Sattler, burned at the stake on the old road to Tübingen in 1527, taught his congregation that suffering was integral to Christian experience and witness in this present life. Participation in the Lord's Supper, he said, declares the believers' participation in the real suffering of Christ in the world.

> Just as if Christ had not established the Lord's Supper primarily because they must suffer, just like their head Christ, and through death enter into glory, yea, that their death would not be their own but the Lord's and that they should also be resurrected just like the head. And where would the dear prophets and apostles be left, yea, also Christ himself, who prophesied for so many years of the great suffering of the friends of God in this time, if the members of Christ would not need to suffer just like the head? (Sattler: 112)

As in Paul's text, so here, suffering is not an end in itself. It is the clay jar that contains the treasured glory of the resurrection. This thinking can easily slip off center in the modern pursuit of happiness and personal fulfillment. Religion in most Euro-American settings is protected under civil law, unlike the worlds of Paul and the sixteenth-century Anabaptists. Many modern Christian believers belong to the religious establishment in the affluent one-third world and feel "secure" in their faith. They live comfortably; they are well respected by their neighbors; they attend church services without threat on their lives.

Yet even in a setting of political protection, believers can bear effective witness (Greek: *martyreō*) to the great grace of God in a pluralistic society. Witness is borne in various ways, depending on the situation. Each generation of Christians carries the responsibility for bearing in their bodies the mark of the death of Jesus, configured according to the situation in which they live (2 Cor. 4:10).

Take, for example, the witness of parents in relation to their children. Many parents experience hardship as they spend themselves for the well-being of their children. The result is not always commensurate with the effort, but the witness is borne none the less. The same is true in the workplace. Christian employees, employers, and professionals exhibit the reality of Christ in the equity of their relationships. The gospel of Christ crucified sets the terms of reference for behavior in any sphere of human society. The treasure of resurrection life shines through the redemptive cracks in the clay jars of mortality.   Amen

New Life in Two Bodies
2 Corinthians 4:16—5:10

PREVIEW

As much as this text offers hope and encouragement to believers, it presents vexing questions to the interpreter. What aggravates the interpretation as much as anything is the tendency to read Paul's thought in this passage in isolation from the larger apology for his ministry that opened at 2:14. Paul has already dealt with the frailty of his present human existence as a missionary of Christ. Now he lets the accent fall on the future state of glory that awaits him and others like him.

Paul's vision of future life for believers is quite visible within the form of argument, like the rays of the rising sun through a pine forest. Paul is not here speculating calmly on the meaning of life and death, nor on the character of life after death, although one can glimpse some standing convictions coming through. His aim, rather, is to deflect criticism of his "weak" apostolate, and to win back the confidence of his Corinthian converts. *We do not lose heart* (4:16), he says, recalling his phrase from 4:1. *We are always confident* (5:6), he affirms again, notwithstanding any appearances to the contrary.

Paul's bodily presence, alongside the interlopers at Corinth, lacks the luster associated with apostolic stature at Corinth. He grants their human perception but challenges their vision that comes from faith in Christ. Paul sees his mortal body as an earthen vessel, temporarily designated to carry the treasure of God (4:7). The treasure is what counts in the end; it carries eternal weight (4:17). His *outer nature* is wasting away while his *inner nature* is being renewed every day (4:16). This process continues until the final day, when God will give him a new body for the new human life that he possesses within his dying body of flesh. This glorious outcome, as Paul sees it, is guaranteed by the gift of the Spirit of God (5:5).

The mixture of metaphors in 5:1-5 serves one principal purpose for Paul: the metaphors explain to his readers the reason for his present suffering and death in a mortal body. In such suffering God is *preparing us for an eternal weight of glory beyond all measure* (4:17).

The structure of the text exhibits a balanced effect, as one might expect, given Paul's two-stage scheme of thought: (1) present Christian experience, and (2) the projected future life.

Present Experience	*Future Envisioned*
4:16 outer nature (*anthrōpos*)	inner nature (*anthrōpos*)
wasting away	renewed every day
4:17 slight affliction	immeasurable weight of glory
4:18 what can be seen,	what cannot be seen,
temporary	eternal
5:1 earthly tent	building from God
5:3-4 clothed,	further clothed,
mortal [existence]	eternal life

OUTLINE

Renewed Every Day While Wasting Away, 4:16-18

Exchanging the Old Body for the New One, 5:1-5

Living in the Present, with an Eye to the Future, 5:6-10

EXPLANATORY NOTES

Renewed Every Day While Wasting Away 4:16-18

Picking up on his phrase of 4:1, *We do not lose heart,* Paul affirms again that he does not shrink back from a ministry shot through with physical adversity (4:16). Paul understands, as his opponents apparently do not, the significance of his suffering in the flesh. And he is bent on making them see his way, even if he has to use their terms to do so.

At this stage of the argument, his approach is to distinguish between two sides of Christian personality. One is still tied to the first humankind of Genesis 1–3, and one is related to the second humankind of the gospel. To make his point, Paul uses two puzzling terms of reference which the NRSV translates *outer nature* and *inner nature*.

They are puzzling because Paul elsewhere refrains from separating human personality into two parts (physical body encasing metaphysical soul) in the manner of many of his Greek-thinking contemporaries (see references in Furnish, 1984:261).

As for the Corinthians, they tend to think the spiritual being can somehow escape from the body in a state of ecstasy, to receive a vision of God. Paul seeks to correct that tendency in 1 Corinthians, but he is still conscious of their urge in that direction. His use of *inner* and *outer* may well be accommodation for the sake of persuasion.

By his use of the term *anthrōpos* (human, person) in the context of the argument, Paul connects his thought tangentially with the first human being of Genesis 1–3 (Pate: 110-114; cf. Moule, 1965:122-123). The first human (*anthrōpos*) pair disobeyed the divine will (Gen. 3) and thus cast the blight of mortality over the human family without exception. From Paul's experience of God's second *anthrōpos*, Jesus Christ, he now views physical existence as belonging to the order of the first *anthrōpos* that *is wasting away*. Physical existence is *outer humanity*, whereas the new Christ experience transforms *inner humanity*. This inner *anthrōpos* constitutes the beginning of resurrection life of the future as secured by God in Christ and guaranteed by the presence of the Spirit (2 Cor. 5:5).

Subject to the same diseases and afflictions as the rest of humanity, the human Paul is wasting away, just as the old creation as a whole is (cf. 5:17). But the new order of life from the future is *being renewed day by day* in Paul's mind and heart, as in the minds and hearts of all believers (4:16). The concept is similar to the progressive transformation from one degree of glory to another at 3:18.

The thought advances in 4:17, giving some purpose to the present affliction of the *outer humanity*. Suffering prepares the believer for the new life of the future. In comparison to the future *eternal weight of glory beyond all measure*, the present affliction is light and momentary. *Weight* (as in the measure of a substance) has positive connotations in this context. The burden (weight) of the present suffering cannot compare to the immeasurable amount (weight) of glory in store for the believing heart. Implicitly, Paul puts no ultimate stock in the present *outer* human existence, as the visiting missionaries to Corinth tend to do. In the end, present existence, mortal that it is, has no lasting value.

Paul is thinking more of future/present rather than of inner/outer. This comes through in 4:18. He fixes his scope on (*skopountōn, pays attention to*) what the physical eye cannot see, since the physical eye sees only the things of time and mortality. Paul has an eye to the *eternal* character of the future, a future already present in his mind (inner *anthrōpos*). "He keeps his gaze fixed on the invisible eternal realities" (Thrall, 1994:355).

Exchanging the Old Body for a New One   5:1-5

For connects the thought of 5:1-5 with the preceding verses (against Bultmann, 1985:130, "5:1-5 is actually a digression"). The phrase *for we know* may introduce "a traditional Christian affirmation" (Talbert: 160), although not necessarily so. *We know* could refer to a saying of Jesus about the destruction and rebuilding of the temple (Collange: 187f.; Mark 14:58). More likely, though, the force of *we know* amounts to an appeal to common Christian experience. *We know*, as all Christians should, that God has planned to restore the lost glory of the first parents of the human family. In the ensuing verses Paul then sketches snippets of the plan as he envisions it.

His roughly sculpted metaphors in this text leave the mystery of human destiny virtually intact. A problem arises when interpreters try to fill in gaps beyond what the text allows. The *unseen* becomes all too visible, and faith too diminished (see 1 Cor. 13:12). In a sentence, Paul's metaphors of tent and building, of unclothing and reclothing, signal his belief in God's plan to exchange the destructible body of the believer in Christ for an indestructible one. First Corinthians 15, written earlier to the same community, dealt with the same subject. It helps to keep that text in mind while reading this paragraph (2 Cor. 5:1-5).

To the first metaphor then. *If the earthly tent we live in is destroyed, we have a building from God, a house not made with hands, eternal in the heavens* (5:1). As in the case of the clay jars at 4:7, so here the tent speaks of the fragile, temporary body of flesh destined for destruction when its earthly purpose is complete. The "if" clause reckons with the possibility that some earthly bodies will not suffer destruction. Some will make it through to the coming of Christ at the end of the age. In his earlier letter to the Corinthians, Paul implied that he himself expected to experience bodily transformation at the reappearance of Christ: "We will not all die, but we will all be changed, in a moment, in the twinkling of an eye, at the last trumpet" (1 Cor. 15:51-52). Now here in 2 Corinthians 5:1, he raises the possibility that the tentlike temporal body will be destroyed, as in death. *Destroyed* can hardly mean anything other than physical death (see

Thrall, 1994:357-370).

Is Paul despondent or fearful at the prospect of such a disman-
tling of his earthly tent-body? Not at all. This is a happy prospect for
him: the exchange of the tent for a *building from God, a house not
made with hands, eternal in the heavens.* The exchange of bodies,
and the manner of exchange, is the point at issue throughout this
paragraph. "2 Corinthians 5 concerns the manner, rather than the
moment, of the change. . . . The new is received only *in exchange for
the old*" (Moule, 1965:116). *Made with hands* conveys the notion of
earthly, temporal, human construction. Anything to do with human
intention and construction is subject to disintegration. The physical
body falls into this category. Not so the body (*building*) *from God.*
Like God's own dwelling, the resurrection body God has planned for
believers in Jesus Christ transcends the present age of mortality. That
house is *made* by God, *not with* human *hands* (cf. Mark 14:58; Acts
17:24; Heb. 9:11). So the prospect is a happy one for Paul.

Why then does he write of *groan*ing *in this tent?* Such groaning
represents a deep longing for the new body from God, not a haunting
fear of the destruction of the tentlike body in death. He longs *to be
clothed with our heavenly dwelling* (5:2). At this point Paul merges
(however indiscreetly) a clothing metaphor with his building image.

The Greek word he uses for *clothed* is a composite form. Most
commentators translate the word *clothe over,* because of the prepo-
sitional prefix *epi,* meaning "over" or "upon." Thus the majority opinion about Paul's compound metaphor is "that this compound form
. . . has the distinct meaning of 'to put on over,' to clothe oneself with
some additional garment" (Furnish, 1984:267; so also R. Martin,
1986:107; Lincoln: 65; Pate: 115f.; Barrett, 1973:152; Talbert: 161;
Plummer: 145; Thrall, 1994:372; cf. Bultmann, 1985:136).

The result of this way of reading Paul's compound word in the
context is misleading, the majority opinion notwithstanding. According to this view, Paul hopes he will not lose his physical body in death,
but will survive until the coming of Christ. Then God will put his new
body **over** the old tentlike one, as a person puts on "another garment
over those he is already wearing" (Barrett, 1973:152). "Clothe over"
is thus supposed to mean that Paul wants "to have his resurrection
body without losing his earthly body" (R. Martin, 1986:107).

The idea borders on the absurd and makes Paul blatantly inconsistent. He has stated unequivocally in the earlier letter to the Corinthians that "flesh and blood cannot inherit the kingdom of God"
(1 Cor. 15:50). How then can he say here that he wishes to wear his

new resurrection body *over* his old tentlike body of flesh and blood? The prefix (*epi*) in this case, as in so many similar instances in the NT, probably carries what is called a perfective force. That is, the prefix signifies being "really clothed," "finally clothed," clothed in a way that will not require any further exchange of clothing. The resurrection body is the ultimate form of identity for the person "baptized into Christ" and "clothed . . . with Christ" (Gal. 3:27). If the preposition *epi* attached to this word implies clothed *over*, then Paul can mean clothed over his "inner person" rather than his "outer person" (the *earthly tent*), that by nature is destructible (2 Cor. 4:16).

Paul parenthetically shudders at the thought of being *found naked* when he has taken off the tentlike body (5:3) (or naked when he has "put on" the new body. Manuscripts vary between "take off" and "put on" in verse 3). Greek thinkers (and some Corinthians also, no doubt) desire the naked self, but Paul's Hebraic mind recoils from the idea of a disembodied soul. He looks forward rather to being *further clothed.*

Many interpreters of Paul see in this text part of his vision of the so-called intermediate state between the death of the physical body of a believer in Christ and the final resurrection body. The interim state, so it is held, is a state of disembodied existence that Paul wants to avoid by living in his mortal body until transformation time at the coming of Christ (R. Martin, 1986:107f.; Hughes: 171). Against this view, however, Paul simply does not present an image of a state of Christian human existence between the death of a believer and the resurrection of the believer. His "thinking on these subjects often stops short at the point where we would like him to continue" (Strachan: 100).

In short, 5:3 implies that Paul does not accept the Greek idea of a naked state for the believer who has put on Christ by faith and baptism (Fallon: 45; cf. Barrett, 1973:153). In any case, a period of waiting in nakedness for the new body is a projection of history onto the eternal. "In the consciousness of the departed believer, there is no interval between dissolution and investiture, however long the interval may be by the calendar of earth-bound human history" (Bruce: 204).

With one last imaginative stroke, Paul expresses the prospect for mortal believers in Christ. Their mortality will be *swallowed up by life* (5:4). This graphic language of transformation from mortal to immortal, from destructible to indestructible (1 Cor. 15:53), belies the earlier terms of transformation in this letter: *transformed . . . from one degree of glory to another* (2 Cor. 3:18); *the inner person is being re-*

newed day by day (4:16). As an expansion of these images, the image of life swallowing up mortality points to the future ultimate change toward which Paul moves in the present experience of the Spirit.

No need to fear. God has *prepared us for this very thing* and has given us *the Spirit as a guarantee* in the present time, a guarantee that the new resurrection body awaits. This term for *guarantee* appeared at 1:22, where the NRSV translated it *first installment.* The same idea fits here as well. The Spirit is the first installment of the kind of life that awaits believers in the resurrected Christ (1 Cor. 15:20; Rom. 8:23).

Living in the Present, with an Eye to the Future   5:6-10

The conclusive *so* at verse 6 (*oun = therefore*) is Paul's way of connecting two thoughts on the same subject. The second is not always a logical conclusion from the first, as here. *[Therefore] we are always confident* (5:6). Confident in the faith-reality that God has prepared another body of eternal weight that will equip the believer to be fully alive in his presence. Confidence figures prominently in 2 Corinthians; only in this letter does Paul use this verb form (5:6, 8; 7:16; 10:1-2). No doubt Paul knows about his critics' claim to boldness. They probably tout their ecstatic experiences and abilities among the Corinthians and thus, unlike Paul, try to validate their apostolic prowess (Fallon: 46-7).

Paul too can boast of visions, as the later development at Corinth compels him to do (12:1-10). But for Paul such visions, however meaningful, are not the final outcome of faith in Christ crucified and raised. Paul believes that as long as he is *at home in the body* of physical existence, he is exiled from the Lord (5:6b). Even though Paul claims to be "in Christ" in his present state, his experience of the Lord is partial compared to "the glory about to be revealed to us" in the resurrection body (Rom. 8:18). Paul here looks forward to being present with the Lord, whose resurrected state transcends mortality.

Verse 7 (of 2 Cor. 5), while it comes across as a parenthesis, is key to Paul's argument against his opponents. *We walk by faith, not by sight* is a way of saying that the full restoration of Adamic glory in the lives of believers is still future. In the meantime, those who live in Christ see with the inner eye of faith what physical eyes cannot see.

Paul has a confident eye to the future: *Yes we do have confidence* (5:8). He has confidence that what has already been accomplished through Christ will reach fulfillment. For Paul, the fulfillment is to be exiled from the mortal body and thus to be *at home with the Lord*. To be at home with the Lord requires a body like that of the Lord, a resurrection body (see again 1 Cor. 15:42-57). His preference is to live in full vision of his Lord in a body like the Lord's. The point is not that "Paul prefers nakedness to present life" (R. Martin, 1986:112; cf. Kruse: 117). Nakedness is not at issue in this paragraph. The comparison, rather, is between the imperfect experience of Christ while *at home* in a tentlike body, and the full glory of being *at home* with Christ in *a building from God*, a resurrection body.

Verse 8 is polemical. Paul seeks to undermine the position of the opponents who make too much of their present ecstasy in a mortal body. Paul's alternative is a new body from God in the future, to house his personal human identity. Paul puts no stock in the present mortal state, except as it works toward the future. And that it does. The last two verses of the paragraph state as much (2 Cor. 5:9-10).

So whether we are at home or away, we make it our aim to please him. Unlike the first humans who tried to please themselves and lost their glory, Paul has found in the second human a Savior who has emptied himself for the sake of the other (Phil. 2:1-8). Having found this newness of life (Rom. 6:4), Paul's goal is to please the Lord by serving others in a ministry of suffering (2 Cor. 4:7-12).

No doubt Paul was urged on by the love of Christ (5:14), but he knows the judgment day is coming. *For all of us must appear before the judgment seat of Christ, so that each may receive recompense for what has been done in the body, whether good or evil* (5:10). Paul's Jewish counterparts have taught their people to prepare now for the day of reckoning in the future, when their destiny in the age to come will be determined. Paul has modified that doctrine. *All of us* in this text refers to all in the community of Christ on their way to final salvation. Their final salvation is not determined at the judgment seat of Christ. Instead, Paul envisions rewards commensurate with work done in the mortal bodies of believers.

Thus far in this letter, what constitutes *good* work in Paul's estimate is suffering service in the name of Christ. Implicitly, *bad* work is marked by self-praise and self-serving, which Paul sees in his opponents at Corinth. Paul and they will **all** appear *before* the final *judgment seat of Christ*, whose ministry was to suffer and die in the service of others. This statement about the coming judgment begs the question: Who will fare better in the presence of this Christ? Those who avoid affliction and seek ecstasy in this life, or those who put their lives on the line for the sake of the gospel of Christ?

THE TEXT IN BIBLICAL CONTEXT

As with the previous passage (4:7-15), here Adam Christology undergirds Paul's argument for the renewal of human life in 4:16—5:10. Key words in Paul's text come from his Greek version of the Genesis story of Adam's descent from glory to mortality (Gen. 1–3): *human person* (Greek: *anthrōpos* = Heb.: *adam*, humankind, Gen. 1:26), life (*zōē* = Eve, living, Gen. 3:20), *mortal, naked, clothed, spirit, groan.* Around these words Paul weaves his argument about God's reversal of the mortal plight of humanity (sin, suffering, death).

In conjunction with the Genesis story of the first parents, Paul's language echoes several terms and ideas from Psalms 8 and 103, and from Isaiah 25. In Psalm 8 God takes note of mortal human beings and crowns them with glory. In Psalm 103 the psalmist's mortal soul (= Paul's *inner being*, 2 Cor. 4:16) blesses the Lord for showing redemptive compassion. Isaiah envisions the Lord swallowing up death forever, and God wiping tears from mortal eyes (25:7-8). Similarly, in the resurrection life Paul foresees God in Christ swallowing up mortality (2 Cor. 5:4b; also 1 Cor. 15:54).

Paul was familiar with biblical allusions to the fallen condition of the old humanity. He was also conversant with diverse speculations in Judaism about God's plan to restore humanity to its original state. His new Christian understanding of the unfolding of God's plan for humankind overlays this biblical-Jewish background (Pate: 115ff., references to Jewish sources).

Second Corinthians 4:16—5:10 assumes the Corinthians' acquaintance with Paul's thought concerning God's reversal of Adam's mortality (*we know,* 5:1; cf. 1 Cor. 15). Nor is Paul's Adam Christology restricted to the Corinthian correspondence. In his later letter to the Romans (5:12-21), Paul again invokes Adam Christology for the purpose of subordinating the Mosaic Law to Christ in the plan of God for the salvation of humanity.

Resurrection life, guaranteed *already* in the believer's mortal body but *not yet* realized in a new body, figures consistently in Paul's undisputed letters (e.g., 1 Cor. 15:1-57; Rom. 8:9-30; 1 Thess. 4:13-18; Phil. 3:10-16). He was, after all, a member of the Jewish party called Pharisees, who believed firmly in the resurrection of the dead at the end of the age (against their Palestinian rivals, the Sadducees; Acts 23:8; Mark 12:18). Paul's new Christian insight knows of one resurrection as having already occurred in the person of Jesus. God will likewise raise persons of faith in Jesus at the reappearance of Christ at the end of the age.

Paul was not alone among NT writers in his view of resurrection. Resurrection language and thought became the hallmark of Christian self-definition (e.g., the early formulation of the faith in 1 Cor. 15:3-5; the teaching of Mark 12:18-27 and par.; John. 11:25; Acts 17:18-34). But whereas Paul in his early letters (including 2 Cor.) reserved resurrection language for the future of believers, in the later writings of the NT, present Christian experience is couched in the language of "resurrection" (e.g., John 11:25; Col. 2:12; 3:1; Eph. 1:3, 2:5-6; cf. Rom. 6:4-5).

Finally, Paul's word about end-time judgment "would have been intelligible to Jews (2 Esdras 7:113-115), to pagans (Lucian, *Dialogues of the Dead* 10.13), and to non-Pauline Christians (Heb. 9:27; Matt. 25:31-46; Mark 8:38; 1 Pet. 4:5; 2 Pet. 3:10-12; James 5:9; Rev. 20:11-15)" (Talbert: 162-163). In Romans 14:10 the judgment seat of Christ becomes the judgment seat of God without any material change of thought from one term to the other. In 2 Corinthians 5:10, *all of us* does not mean "all persons in general" (Bultmann, 1985:143), but those who profess faith in Christ.

The judgment seat does not determine life in the age to come; it determines recompense for work done in the mortal body. Paul made the point explicitly in his earlier letter to Corinth: "The work of each builder will become visible, for the Day [of judgment] will disclose it, . . . and the fire will test what sort of work each has done. . . . If the work is burned up, the builder will suffer loss; the builder will be saved, but only as through fire" (1 Cor. 3:12-15).

These three Christian guideposts—Adam Christology, resurrection life, and final judgment—stand at various junctures on the biblical landscape and serve to encourage believers on their journey.

THE TEXT IN THE LIFE OF THE CHURCH

Eschatology (the doctrine of final events and ultimate human experience) has played a significant role in the life of the church from its inception to the present day. Interest in end-time events tends to increase, understandably, in periods of hardship and social, religious, and political upheaval. The Apocalypse of the NT (Revelation) arose out of a time of Roman persecution of the church. Its cosmic visions and symbols served in their own way to encourage the church to be faithful to its confession.

The sixteenth century in Europe also saw its share of upheaval. Those who dared to disturb the status quo found themselves in trou-

ble with authorities. Many of the more radical believers in that century suffered for their convictions. Their leaders harmonized Paul's eschatology with apocalyptic passages elsewhere in the NT and applied
their results to events and circumstances of their own time. Proponents of apocalyptic eschatology sought meaning in large-scale cosmic language behind the meaningless experiences of their lives.
"Apocalyptic thought was a standard feature of the sixteenth-century
theological furniture" (Klaassen in *ME*, 5:29). Paul's thought in this
text (2 Cor. 4:16—5:10) entered the discussion marginally. Dirk Philips, for example, appealed to 4:18 in support of those who forsook
the world, despised "all perishable and temporal things," and were
persecuted and killed (239). But a great deal more attention was paid
to figuring out the signs of the end. Hans Hut went so far as to set the
time of Christ's return to judge the wicked and reward the righteous
at Pentecost 1528. Most of these radicals named the pope as the antichrist. All were persuaded that the coming of Christ was near (Klaassen, 1981:316-343, on Anabaptist eschatology).

Apocalyptic eschatology still abounds in some branches of the
church. Recently an evangelical from New Zealand spent three eve-
nings in Edinburgh, Scotland, speaking at length from numerous biblical texts on how the world was rapidly moving toward the end. He
projected the signs of the end on an overhead screen in conjunction
with a massive chart of the dispensations of the world. The signs of
doom and judgment included the small print on the United States
dollar, the European Economic Community, and the widespread use
of credit cards (especially gold cards). All of these are the work of the
antichrist. The last sign, currently being manufactured, according to a
newspaper clipping this preacher found in South Africa, is a comput-
er microchip that can be implanted in the forehead or the right hand.
This is the mark of the beast, he said.

His charts and talks and newspaper clippings had a tantalizing effect. However, they bore little sign of the good news of Christ that
brings hope and renewal to suffering humanity. His fatalistic apocalyptic speculation about the "last days" for the world left many to suffer and die, such as the Rwandan refugees, Bosnian orphans.

The system of dispensationalism espoused in this century has become a mark of orthodoxy in some evangelical confessions. Dispensationalism strings together certain apocalyptic texts of the Bible to
construct a chart of the history of the world through the period of the
millennium (Rev. 20) into eternity. Systems of this sort are all post-
biblical *human* constructs and should not be confused with the

thought of biblical writings in their own context. Paul's text in 2 Corinthians 4:16—5:10 deserves to be read on its own terms, recognizing the situation that gave rise to it. To read Paul's text through the lens of a modern apocalyptic system dilutes the life-giving power of the text and makes it an insipid system of human ingenuity.

Paul's thought in 2 Corinthians 4:16—5:10, like that of 1 Corinthians 15, governed his life in mission. His eschatology revolved around the hope of receiving a body fit for resurrection life. Present renewal for him related to future resurrection life by means of the Spirit. This way of conceiving eschatology brings hope and healing to the people of God. Ongoing renewal of persons in the world is related to God's new life of the future. The present *walk by faith* (2 Cor. 5:7) expresses itself in community life, in environmental concern, in family and work relations, in social consciousness and action. And it prepares the believer for death. Believers seek to please the Lord.

In summary, this noteworthy text of Paul instructs the church in every age not to lose heart (4:16); to discover a purpose in affliction (4:17); to grasp the mystery of the invisible world behind the visible (4:18); to understand that houses and clothes of this world are not permanent realities (5:1-5); to experience the *guarantee* of the Spirit as life from the future (5:5); to *please* God in life and thought (5:9); to treat mortality realistically as *exile* from God (5:6-9); to await divine judgment confidently (5:10).

KEY SUMMARY

The Reconciling of the World to God

2 Corinthians 5:11—7:4 (6:14—7:1)

OVERVIEW

Dominating the landscape of this long passage of 2 Corinthians (5:11—7:4) is one of Paul's most beloved and most difficult themes: the reconciling of the world to God. Of the possible situations that could have given rise to Paul's thought and arguments on this theme, the most likely is the deterioration of the relationship between himself and his converts at Corinth. At several points Paul's statements present problems for interpretation; at others his words reveal his unrestricted heart of faith unmatched in his or any other time.

Problems for Interpretation

In 5:14-15, what does Paul intend by his balanced sentence, *One died for all, therefore all died?* Inclusiveness is uppermost in the schema of the one and the many (encountered earlier in the letter). Yet Paul probably does not mean that the death of the One (Christ) secures the eternal salvation of all human beings.

In 5:16, Paul says he once knew Christ according to the flesh. Does he mean that he was acquainted with the historical Jesus? *According to the flesh* probably indicates a way of knowing rather than a description of the earthly figure of Jesus. Paul's new understanding of the resurrection of Christ (the Messiah) has changed his way of knowing.

According to 5:19, does God reconcile the world to himself unconditionally and universally? Or is the reconciliation conditional upon acceptance of Christ? In the latter view, the reconciled world is representative humanity rather than universal.

In 5:21, to what extent did God make Christ *to be sin who knew no sin?* If the sinless nature of Christ is restricted to the earthly life of Jesus, Paul's sentence is scarcely meaningful.

Regarding the passage 6:14—7:1, a principal problem has to do with its place in the middle of Paul's patient, persuasive plea for reconciliation. The sudden warning not to be unequally yoked with unbelievers is strident, and in several respects quite unlike Paul.

Paul's Unrestricted Heart of Faith

In 5:11-12, Paul assumes that a wholesome relationship with the Christian community is normative. When relationship among people of faith breaks down, the situation constitutes a denial of the gospel of God. The gospel mends broken relationships. Hence, Paul seeks to persuade the Corinthians to renew their love for him.

In 5:14, Paul's preaching mission has burst the old ethnic boundaries in his world by the power of the love of Christ. Love has compelled him to serve others, whatever their cultural orientation.

In 5:17, participants in Christ experience a new creation. Old ways of thinking about the world and life pass away in the presence of the new order of life signaled by the resurrection life of Christ.

In 5:20, *Be reconciled to God* is a strange imperative coming from Paul to a community purportedly already committed to Christ. In effect, their estrangement from Paul is estrangement from God.

In 6:11-13, Paul issues one of his most affectionate appeals in this text. His heart is open wide to the Corinthians. He asks his readers to accept his openness and return it in kind.

Serious study of the arguments that clothe these problems and affirmations is bound to reap its own harvest of reconciliation.

OUTLINE

Compelled by the Death of One for All, 5:11-15

God's New Creation Already Under Way, 5:16—6:2

Commendable Marks of God's Reconciling Agents, 6:3-13; 7:2-4

Insert: Exclusive Covenant Community, 6:14—7:1

Compelled by the Death of One for All
2 Corinthians 5:11-15

PREVIEW

This text brings us to the threshold of the center of gravity in the Letter of Reconciliation (2 Cor. 1–9): the death-and-resurrection of Christ for all (5:14-15, the threshold) inaugurates a new creation in

which God reconciles the world to himself (5:16-21, the center).
Resting his case on this far-reaching theology, Paul seeks to persuade
the Corinthians to continue their support of him in his ministry. Paul's
awareness of criticism against him at Corinth shapes the language of
the text, as often throughout 2 Corinthians.

The continuing task for interpreters of Paul in 2 Corinthians is
twofold: to determine his abiding thought as a Christian apostle, and
to distinguish between *Paul's thought* and the *rhetorical shape* his
thought takes in the setting of 2 Corinthians.

This short paragraph in the letter (5:11-15), taken with its following counterpart (5:16-21), "is one of the most pregnant, difficult, and
important in the whole of the Pauline literature" (Barrett, 1973:163).
It puts forward the true motive and power behind Christian mission
and ministry and pinpoints succinctly the moral demand that these
place on the recipient of the life of Christ. The motive is partly *the
fear of the Lord* (5:11) but principally *the love of Christ* (5:14). This
latter becomes the controlling force in Paul's life and thought and issues in selfless living for others (5:15b).

The following diagram focuses the structure of this passage:

Motive and Power in the Paradox of the Gospel (5:11-15)

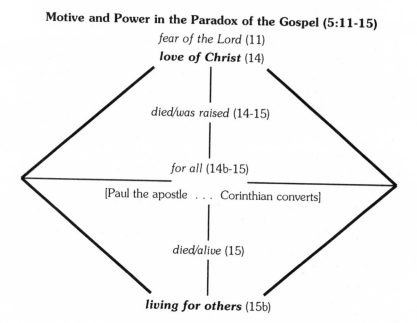

fear of the Lord (11)

love of Christ (14)

died/was raised (14-15)

for all (14b-15)

[Paul the apostle . . . Corinthian converts]

died/alive (15)

living for others (15b)

OUTLINE

Motive and Power for Life and Ministry, 5:11-14a

Quality of Life in Relation to Christ, 5:14b-15

EXPLANATORY NOTES

Motive and Power for Life and Ministry 5:11-14a

The fear of the Lord (5:11) connects with the idea of final judgment in 5:10. By reason of his accountability to the Lord (*therefore*), Paul persuades people. The fear of the Lord comes from Israelite tradition, especially wisdom, which Paul "knows" well (Ps. 2:11; 111:10; Job 28:28; Isa. 2:10; Prov. 1:7; etc.). His *knowing* in this context, however, is more than an intellectual recognition of the fear-of-the-Lord tradition. It is a profound consciousness of the plan of God to save the world. Paul's ministry is part of that divine plan. As he wrote earlier to the Corinthians, "an obligation is laid on me, and woe to me if I do not proclaim the gospel!" (1 Cor. 9:16; cf. Amos 3:8). Out of this sense of responsibility to the call of the Lord, Paul is driven to persuade people.

The NRSV translates the present tense of the Greek verb, *we try to persuade*, but the basic idea of the present tense (continuation-progression) is probably the focus, rather than the start of action (2 Cor. 3:11). Through his preaching of the gospel, Paul kept on persuading people to accept God's grace offered in the death of Christ, and thus to be ready for the judgment. Some scholars suspect that Paul has in mind here the specific persuasion of wavering Corinthians and/or the visiting missionaries who slander him. Yet the target of *others* in Paul's persuasion is as unrestricted as the gospel. *Others* includes Jewish people like Paul and Gentile people like the Corinthians; it includes male and female, slave and free (cf. Gal. 3:28).

What is puzzling, though, is Paul's use of the word *persuade*, since he knows of his critics' readiness to accuse him of using persuasive words to lead the Corinthians astray. Perhaps Paul deliberately turns the term to his own advantage. His persuasion, unlike that of his accusers, comes under the scrutiny and control of the One who died for all. Paul's life in mission, as the earlier arguments have shown (e.g., 2 Cor. 1:3-14), shows his close identity with the suffering and dying Servant of God. Within that identity, Paul persuades people, including his critics.

Still on the theme of judgment (5:10), Paul declares himself open and transparent before God, who knows human hearts. *We ourselves are well known to God*, he says. And he *hopes* (*thinks*, Plummer: 169; *believes*, Hughes: 187) that the same is true for the *consciences* of the Corinthians (on Paul's use of *conscience*, see notes on 1:12). The shift from *we* to *I* in midthought of the verse signals a move to a more personal appeal. Surely the Corinthians know their apostle, Paul, the one whose persuasion brought them to faith in Christ!

Paul, keenly aware of an impending accusation of his self-praise, quickly deflects the charge: *We are not commending ourselves to you again* (5:12a; cf. 3:1). His language at times does sound a bit egoistic, but his explanation turns the focus from himself to the Corinthians. He is providing **them** with an opportune answer (5:12) for those critics who boast about a person's external appearance but not about the heart. The words are reminiscent of 1 Samuel 16:7: "mortals . . . look on the outward appearance, but the Lord looks on the heart." One can only guess what externals Paul has in mind: knowledge of the historical Jesus (cf. 2 Cor. 5:16)? acquaintance with the Jerusalem apostles? an impressive demeanor in public?

The general position taken in this commentary is that Paul has lost his good standing in the synagogues of the Diaspora (cf. Acts 18:5-11). He and his mission churches are regarded as apostate from the tradition of salvation in Israel. Paul's opponents can cite this situation against him. Ultimately, Paul's appeal, as always, is to the redemptive death of Jesus Christ (2 Cor. 5:14-15). In the light of such an act of grace, all facile self-praise dissolves itself into a dew.

Verse 5:13 consists of two equally balanced sentences, the first of which is fraught with ambiguity: (1) *If we are beside ourselves, it is for God.* (2) *If we are in our right mind, it is for you.* The difficulty with the first of these comes with the phrase translated *beside ourselves.* Paul's word is *exestēmen,* from which we derive the English term *ecstasy.* But this observation may not in itself lead us directly to Paul's meaning. Possibly Paul's critics have accused him of madness or unreasonable megalomania, to which this word may refer. Mark 3:21 uses the same word to describe the response of Jesus' relatives to his behavior: "He has gone out of his mind." If Paul is responding to a charge of this sort, his own view of his behavior is quite different. Paul apparently has had many ecstatic experiences (2 Cor. 12:1-4; cf. 1 Cor. 14:18), but they are a personal matter between himself and God. In public at Corinth, he used the normal speech of one in his *right mind* (cf. 1 Cor. 14). This explanation accounts for the various assumed layers in the context of 2 Corinthians 5:13.

Then comes the central motive and power of Paul's Christian life and ministry in 5:14. The several parts of the statement should be taken together before any one of them is singled out for discussion. *For the love of Christ urges us on, because we are convinced that one has died for all; therefore all have died.* Herein lies the source and substance of Paul's affliction in ministry. Paul sees himself related integrally to this Christ who, as he says, "loved me and gave himself for me" (Gal. 2:20). He sees his ministry thus as the agency through which *all* come to faith-death-life (Crafton: 94-99).

Observe the various parts of this striking statement from Paul. Does *the love of Christ* refer to Christ's love for Paul (subjective genitive) or to Paul's love for Christ (objective genitive)? That scholars have raised the question to the level of discussion is itself puzzling. Paul's letters show little interest in the Christian's love for Christ, only as an implicit outflow of the principal love from Christ to the believer. It is unthinkable that Paul would introduce the thought of his love for Christ at such a crucial point in his argument (cf. Hering: 41-42). Instead, his consistent refrain is that Christ has loved him and given himself up for him and for the rest of humanity. Nor should one compromise the point (as does Spicq: 88) and read a two-way love into 5:14. It is the love demonstrated in Christ alone that directs Paul's missionary career (cf. Rom. 5:8).

This love of Christ *urges us on*, as the NRSV has it. Paul's Greek verb denotes control or pressure. He uses the same word in Philippians 1:23, where he is "hard pressed" (NRSV) between two alternatives. The context of 2 Corinthians 5:14, on the other hand, suggests that motivation and control come together in this compound word. Paul finds himself *kept on course and driven onward* by Christ's love.

Quality of Life in Relation to Christ 5:14b-15

Having thus come on side with Christ, Paul has made one principal judgment (NRSV: *we are convinced*) which has led him to a related conclusion. Both judgment and decision come to expression here: *One died for all* (principal judgment); *therefore all died* (related conclusion).

Two words in the principal judgment have given rise to considerable debate: *for* and *all*. On the first one, *for*, two alternate meanings present themselves. (1) Christ died "instead of" (substitution), or (2) Christ died "for the benefit of" (participation-redemption). Several scholars hold the first view, which conforms to the doctrine of expiation or substitutionary sacrifice (R. Martin, 1986:129; cf. 143; Hughes: 193; Bultmann, 1985:152-153; Collange: 254; cf. Furnish, 1984:310, who is uncommitted). Paul can indeed express the idea of Christ's death as expiatory, as in Romans 3:25 and 5:8, yet not as prominently as the idea of transfer, participation, and identification. It was Paul, after all, who coined the term "in Christ," a phrase he uses repeatedly to indicate the new state of being of his converts (e.g., 2 Cor. 5:17).

The second alternative is therefore more in line with the heart of Paul's thinking about the death of Christ. Paul says he is "crucified with Christ" (Gal. 2:19); converts are "baptized into Christ" (Rom. 6:3); the Corinthians participate in Christ and therefore must not participate in the worship of idols (1 Cor. 10:14-22). Given the weight of evidence in Paul's writings for benefit and participation in Christ's death, it is highly unlikely that the idea of expiatory substitution is uppermost in his mind here at 2 Corinthians 5:14.

Furthermore, the context and the related conclusion virtually rule out "instead of" (against R. Martin, 1986:129; Hughes: 193). If Paul means that Christ died "instead of" all, how can he then propose the consequence that *all died*. If he intends substitution, surely he would use a different word and say, "Christ died instead of all, therefore all do not have to die." Paul concludes otherwise. Christ's death draws *all* into his death so that they die with him, and thus they find life (cf. Rom. 6:3-8). This concept is quite different from substitutionary death (Barrett, 1973:168; Hanson: 48; Sanders, 1977:465-466; cf. Seifrid: 255-270).

What of the second ambiguous word *all* in this faith formulation, *One died for all*? If Paul relies on an early Christian formula at 2 Corinthians 5:14, as he probably does, he has modified the tradition in keeping with his argument in this letter. At 1 Corinthians 15:3 Paul explicitly cites a similar form: "Christ died for our sins in accordance with the scriptures." The formula in 2 Corinthians 5:14 is radically abbreviated. "Christ" becomes *One*; "our" becomes *all*; the elements of "sins" and "scriptures" are omitted altogether. *One died for all* signals the inclusiveness of the death of Christ. All human beings, whatever their social, cultural, or ethnic divisions (Gal. 3:28: Jew/Gentile, male/female, slave/free), have only one representative whose death is their death. The one Christ died on behalf of all classes of people, whose lot without exception is death. That being so, all have died with *the One* and thus receive the benefit of his new life (Dunn: 125-131; Hanson: 55-77).

Paul's conclusion falls short of the modern notion of universal salvation of all humanity. His statement carries three implications. First, humanity has only one Re-creator. Second, all human beings (of Adam's progeny, cf. Rom. 5:12-21) are caught in the plight of sin and death. Third, all human beings in Adam who would be redeemed are bound to accept the death of the One by dying to themselves and sin. By thus dying with the *One* in his death, Adam's offspring are transferred into a new Christ-sphere of living. They experience a new quality of life, just as the crucified Jesus received the new resurrection life from God (Rebell: 14, "Leben in einer neuen Qualität"; Pate: 138-140).

If one could ask Paul, "What do you mean by dying with Christ?" he might answer with his concluding ethical statement of 2 Corinthians 5:15. *[Christ] died for all, so that those who live might live no longer for themselves, but for him who died and was raised for them.* The transfer into Christ's death-and-resurrection transforms human life from one of self-serving to one of self-giving.

THE TEXT IN BIBLICAL CONTEXT

The thought of 2 Corinthians 5:11-15 belongs squarely in the context of Paul's modest defense of his apostolic ministry in 1 Corinthians 1-9. His defense sounds like self-praise, so he finds himself, as in earlier arguments, driven to clear himself of this criticism: *We are not commending ourselves* (2 Cor. 5:12; see also 1:12-14; 2:14—3:3).

Paul has but one way of clearing himself of the various charges against him. He appeals to the One who died for all. In so doing, he stands within two trusted traditions. The first is the prophetic tradition, specifically that of Isaiah. The phrase *One died for all* recalls the well-known song about the Suffering Servant of the Lord who was afflicted for the sake of the people (Isa. 53:3-5). In Paul's thought, the One who suffered and died for all is God's righteous Servant, Jesus Christ.

The second tradition, linked to the first, was that of early Christian faith in its thinking about Christ. At an early period, the persecuted believers of Antioch shaped their thought about Christ into formal credal statements, such as the one found in 1 Corinthians 15:3-5. Paul has inherited these formulations and used them in his preaching and teaching (cf. Phil. 2:6-11; Rom. 1:2-4). A remnant of one such statement is preserved in 2 Corinthians 5:14: *One died for all.* This statement of faith became the central tenet of the Christian community at an early stage and continued so for many years to follow.

In later writings of the NT, similar ransom statements appear as sustaining elements for the church's life in the world. The Son-of-Man saying of Mark 10:45 is a prime example: "The Son of Man came not to be served but to serve, and to give his life a ransom for many." The same sentiment appears in 1 Timothy 2:5-6, with an emphasis that God is "one" and God's mediator is "one." "For there is one God; and there is also one mediator between God and human-kind, Christ Jesus, himself human, who gave himself a ransom for all." This sounds like Paul's word in (2 Cor.) 5:14: *One died for all.*

THE TEXT IN THE LIFE OF THE CHURCH

Second Corinthians 5:11-15 conveys both comfort and challenge to the church past and present for those who have ears to hear. Its scope is severalfold.

First, *knowing the fear of the Lord* (5:11) strikes a serious note of responsibility in the hearts of those who bear the grace of the gospel in their lives and ministry. Martin Luther reckoned the fear of the Lord to be necessary in the proclamation of the gospel of Christ. Faith sees a certain divine judgment ahead that urges Christians to rely on God's mercy and grace for themselves, and to persuade others to accept the gospel. "Such fear is necessary," Luther says (1976: 11.70).

Second, that Christ died for all (5:14) eradicates the superficial walls that human groups erect and maintain around themselves, as if "good fences make good neighbors" (Robert Frost, "Mending Wall"). The gracious act of Christ in dying for the human species should always teach us that no one is above another in the sphere of the gospel of Christ, who died for all. The Radical Reformer, Dirk Philips, saw this inclusiveness as a cardinal truth that came to expression at the Lord's Supper. "We have become participants in Christ," he says (251). "Whoever has a true faith in Christ Jesus, and is baptized through the Spirit into one body with all believers, may not be turned away from the Supper of the Lord. Yes, since they are one body and one loaf with all believers, so they must also be partakers of that one loaf" (101).

In the present time, nations and cultures around the world are beginning to take responsibility for the creation of a just society. The recent democratic election in South Africa is one example. How much more should the church of Jesus Christ, who died for all, demonstrate the inherent oneness of its members? Men should not take a secondary position to women nor women to men. Rich should not take a secondary place to the poor nor the poor to the rich. One ethnic group should not set itself above another. None of this in the community of Christ, who died for all equally.

Third, the text leads ultimately to the life experience of participating in the death and resurrection of the One, Christ: *so that those who live [in Christ] might live no longer for themselves, but for him who died and was raised for them* (5:15). Those who accept the death of Christ in wholehearted faith cannot live as before. Change comes over them. They experience a kind of death that leads to a new quality of living. Menno Simons preached the sentiment of this text passionately. "[God] has roused us from the dead and led us into life. . . . For we feel His living fruit and moving power in our hearts, as may be seen in many places by the lovely patience and willing sacrifices of our faithful brethren and companions in Christ Jesus" (633). Menno expounded the newness of life that comes from participation in Christ.

The church with its leaders, having died with Christ, embodies the good news of a new way of living that serves "the other." Yet the old self-serving human spirit continues to exist in the church (perhaps now more than ever), making news headlines that bring shame to the One who died for all: marital infidelity, sexual promiscuity, spouse and child abuse, shady business deals. . . . In Christ resurrected, a new creation has appeared, and with it a new community that bears the name of the One who gave himself away in cruel death for others.

God's New Creation Already Under Way
2 Corinthians 5:16—6:2

PREVIEW

Of all the celebrated statements in Paul's letters, none surpasses that of 2 Corinthians 5:16—6:2 in lyrical grandeur, cosmic scope, theological depth, and emotional appeal. These elements combine to make it one of the more complex of Paul's arguments in this letter.

Once his argument is unraveled, however, Paul's Christian conviction shines through with the brilliance of the North Star on a clear night: God has acted in Christ to re-create the world and restore humankind to a right relationship with the divine mind. Although not found widely in Paul's writings, the key word in this argument is *reconciliation,* the termination of enmity between estranged parties. Intertwined with *reconciliation* are other terms of equal weight: *new creation* (5:17), *righteousness of God* (5:21), and *day of salvation* (6:2). By using the idea and term of *reconciliation* in this manner, Paul implicitly declares the Corinthians at enmity with God if they are at odds with Paul, God's ambassador of reconciliation. In short, Paul is still at pains, as he has been since 2:14, to reestablish a right relationship between himself and his converts at Corinth. To do so, he calls forth some of the richest Christian thought and language.

The thought in the text as a whole moves from the general to the particular, or from the principle to the personal. The thought in 5:16 is transitional. People of faith in Christ (*we*) recognize the profound significance of the death of the One for all (5:14-15). What follows in 5:17—6:2 is a call to incorporate the work of God into the changes of life. Now there is a *new creation* out of the old one. God has reconciled the world to himself through the sinless One, whose emissaries we are. So *be reconciled to God* in this day of salvation now present.

Paul makes a personal appeal to the Corinthians to be reconciled to God. This appeal is set in the sweep of a vision of God's activity in the world. It is a highly charged way of calling the church to task for their lack of concord with Paul himself. At the end of the section, the language becomes urgent, even implicitly judgmental: *We urge you also not to accept the grace of God in vain. . . . Now is the acceptable time; see, now is the day of salvation!* (6:1-2).

An analysis of the narrative structure shows a matching parallelism in thought (a, b, c, with *c', b', a'*) with line *d* as the emphatic declarative center of the text:

a. Through Christ, there is a new creation (5:17).
   b. God has reconciled us to himself through Christ (18a-b).
      c. God has given us the ministry of reconciliation (18c).
         d. God was in Christ, reconciling the world to himself (19a).
      c'. God entrusts the word of reconciliation to us (19c).
   b'. God appeals through us ambassadors, "Be reconciled to God" (20).
a'. That we might become the righteousness of God (21).

Recent interpreters detect traditional material here in Paul's argument, though not as easily identified as elsewhere (e.g., 1 Cor. 11:23; 15:3-5). These early liturgical forms are confessional (2 Cor. 5:18-19) and christological (5:21; see Käsemann, 1971:52-54; Thrall, 1982b:129; Furnish, 1984:334; R. Martin, 1981:71-79; 1986:139-140):

A. Forms About Reconciliation 5:18-19
- God was in Christ, reconciling the world to himself (19a),
- not counting their trespasses to them (19b).
- God has reconciled us to himself through Christ (18b),
- entrusting to us the word of reconciliation (19c).

B. Christological Forms 5:21a
- The one not knowing sin,
- he [God] made him [Christ] to be sin for us.

Paul has these confessional elements of early-church life at hand (probably from the Hellenistic Jewish church at Antioch). To persuade the Corinthian congregation, he proceeds to weave his own terms and comments around them, as guided by the Spirit:

A.   • All things are from God (18a).
      • He [God] has given to us the ministry of reconciliation (18c).
      • On behalf of Christ, we are ambassadors, God having made his appeal through us (20a).
      • We beseech you on behalf of Christ, be reconciled to God (20b).
B.   • So we become the righteousness of God in him [Christ] (21b).

A closer examination of the whole argument (5:16—6:2) reveals how Paul employs reconciliation language and thought to convince the Corinthians to act accordingly.

OUTLINE
New Creation out of the Old, 5:16-17

Reconciliation in Principle, 5:18-19

Reconciliation in Practice, 5:20-21

Transitional Word of Appeal, 6:1-2

EXPLANATORY NOTES
New Creation out of the Old 5:16-17
Therefore links 5:16 to the preceding thought on the death of one for all and the resulting life of all in the One. Simultaneously, the thought of verse 16 points forward to the vision of a world of people reconciled to the God of the new creation. The interpretation of this transitional statement (5:16) turns primarily on Paul's use of the verb "to know" (Martyn: 269-287; cf. Thrall, 1994:420).

Second Corinthians 5:16 has prompted numerous scholarly articles, all of them seeking to unpack Paul's compressed language. It
may help to work from a literal rendering of the Greek text with its
word order (cf. NRSV). *Therefore, we from the now know no one according to flesh. If indeed we knew according to flesh Christ, yet now
no longer we know [him].* This text gives rise to the question of Paul's
personal knowledge of Jesus of history. Does this verse prove that
Paul was personally acquainted with the pre-Easter Jesus? Does the
account of Paul's conversion in Acts require that Paul was personally
acquainted with Jesus in Jerusalem up to and including his crucifixion? (Weiss: 17-53; cf. also Hughes: 198-200). Not really.

In 2 Corinthians 5:16, Paul recognizes that he no longer knows,
according to the flesh, the Christ of God, implying that he now knows
Christ by the insight of the Spirit. Nor is this text suggesting that Paul
has repudiated the idea of the historical Jesus, Messiah according to
the flesh (Bultmann, 1969:235-246). Instead, Paul's **way of knowing** God's Messiah has changed since his encounter with the once-
crucified Jesus now resurrected.

The form of the text itself neither proves nor disproves Paul's acquaintance with the pre-Easter Jesus. By the phrase *according to the
flesh*, Paul is not describing the Christ, but is instead depicting in negative terms his old way of knowing. He no longer understands people, including the person of Christ, along the usual lines of sense perception (*according to flesh*). His insight *now* enables him to see
through the physical, political, and historical circumstances that crucified Jesus of history. Now he can discern the act of God in bringing
the new creation out of the old.

What is the time-reference in *now*? It can hardly mean the present
time of writing this Letter of Reconciliation. But *now* could imply
Paul's present experience of Christ since his conversion. Prior to his
conversion, he persecuted the church because he had heard the
church's message of a crucified Messiah and interpreted the news by
human standards (*according to flesh*). From a human point of view,
Roman crucifixion marked the miserable and bloody end of a human
life. As the end of the Messiah's life, crucifixion was unthinkable to a
devout Jewish mind (cf. Deut. 21:22-23; Hengel, 1977:84-90). Since
his conversion, Paul could say, "From now on we no longer think of
the Messiah from a human point of view."

Yet Paul's horizon in 5:16-17 is wider by far than his personal
faith experience since the time of conversion. He, in the company of
the new people of Christ, lives inside the threshold of the new age of

resurrection life. God raised the crucified Messiah out of the realm of the dead, hence a new creation is born. Paul now "stands at the juncture of the ages" (Martyn: 272), where the first dawning of the new creation has already flashed before his mind's eye. In that light, his knowledge of people generally, and of Christ specifically, is no longer by the standard of the old order. *Now* he understands the cross differently, as the act of God to bring the tyranny of the old order to an end. *Now* since God raised the crucified One from among the dead, *now* since the Spirit of the resurrected One fills the church (5:5; 1:22), *now* since Paul and colleagues are engaged in world mission—since all of these, *now is the day of salvation* (6:2).

The idea of *new creation* in 5:17 has already entered the discussion of verse 16, as well it should since the new way of knowing (5:16) fits together with the new creation (5:17). But Paul's view of the *new creation* is not immediately disclosed in the phrases clustered around this loaded term. *New creation* appears here and in Galatians 6:15; nowhere else in the NT. Paul has adopted the term from apocalyptic Judaism and adapted it to his new insight on the significance of the death and resurrection of Jesus Christ for the world (e.g., 2 Esdras 7:75; 2 Baruch 32:6; Jubilees 4:26; 1QS 4:25; cf. Rev. 21:1; 1 Enoch 45:4-5; 72:1; 91:15-16). The phrase expands his earlier *new-covenant* term (2 Cor. 3:4-6), giving it cosmic scope in the present context. (See Mell for an exhaustive study of Paul's new-creation theology against its background in Hebrew Scripture, and in Jewish and Greek literature; especially 327-388 on 2 Cor. 5:16-17.)

Interpreters in the past (and some in the present) have taken 5:17 as Paul's way of describing personal conversion, or personal new birth. Most English translations (following KJV, *he is a new creature*) until recently support this reading of the text.

Paul's Greek phrasing is terse, leaving the door open for interpreters to constrict the meaning to individual salvation. Yet Paul does not supply a personal pronoun (*he*, KJV), nor does he provide a verb. Furthermore, he is not known to refer to a Christian personality as a *creature*. The Greek word *ktisis* is best understood as "creation" rather than "creature." This understanding does not rule out completely the individual new life of faith in Christ. Even so, "Paul is not describing in this context the personal dimension of a new birth; rather he is announcing as a kerygmatic statement *the advent of the new creation 'in Christ,'* the dramatic recovery of the world" (R. Martin, 1986:146; cf. Barrett, 1973:175).

Anyone can become part of the new order provided they are *in*

Christ. Union with Christ *now* guarantees the believer a place in the new world to come. For Paul, the glorious new world of the future has already broken into the present by God's act of raising the crucified Christ. The resurrected Christ was (and is) God's first installment of the new world emerging out of the old (cf. 1 Cor. 15:20-49).

Paul envisions "a total replacement of the old by the new, not just a rehabilitation of the old" (Furnish, 1984:316). The *old things* do pass away, whether they be the old religious traditions, the old state of sin and death, or the old material universe as a whole. The "newness" in Paul's vision brands him as "a proclaimer of another salvation" in the opinion of his opponents (Georgi, 1986:168). "Total replacement" may, however, connote dislocation of the new from the old. What Paul does imply in the context of 5:17 is that the new creation emerges out of the old, thus rendering the old inoperative in the presence of the new. The process is redemptive, not destructive, for the new creation does not destroy the old, but re-creates it. This does not mean to destroy and begin again with a clean slate.

Accordingly, the paradigm for new creation in Paul's thought is the new life of the crucified Christ, raised *out of* the realm of sin and death by the act of God. Paul consistently identifies the resurrected Christ with the historical figure of Jesus crucified in the old order (e.g., the Adam-Christ framework of 1 Cor. 15:42-49; Rom. 5:12-21; cf. 8:3-11; see also Hughes: 203).

Finally, 2 Corinthians 5:17 exhibits a certain exhilaration in language that looks forward to the new world whose dawn has already begun to break. *Look, all things have become new!* (VGS). How can Paul see the new world so clearly from his place in an old world still caught in the vice of sin and death? He sees through the lens of the crucified Christ, whom God has raised from the dead, whose spirit he possesses. His ministry in relation to Christ, so he will argue in the verses to follow, belongs within the work of God in reconciling the world to himself. In the setting of 2 Corinthians, Paul weaves this exhilarating vision of a new world into a "rhetoric of reconciliation," through which he hopes to win concord between himself and the Corinthians against the threat of opponents. The "rhetoric of reconciliation" in 1 Corinthians is applied to the community's internal factions (Mitchell: 296-304). At this point in 2 Corinthians, the same rhetoric also applies to the community's discord with Paul.

Reconciliation in Principle 5:18-19

Throughout 5:18-21 Paul has, in all likelihood, adapted material from the confessional life of the church before him (Preview). The task at hand is to examine Paul's argument as a whole to discover his understanding and use of the material for the situation at Corinth.

Verses 18-19 set out the theme of reconciliation with God as chief actor throughout. Verse 18 spells out the terms of reference; verse 19 recapitulates the theme of 18 in an antiphonal stanza, with some elaboration:

Verse 18
a. One power source as starting point: *All things are from God* (18a).
  b. The action is reflexive: *[God] reconciled us to himself* (18b).
    c. Implemented by an intermediate agent: *through Christ* (18c).
      d. Accommodated by a gifted agency: *[God] has given to us the ministry of reconciliation* (18d).

Verse 19
a. *God was*
  b. *reconciling the world to himself*
    c. *in Christ (not counting their trespasses against them)*
      d. *and entrusting the word of reconciliation in* (or among) *us.*

The **first principle of reconciliation,** conceived in cosmic terms, is that God is the single mover in the redemptive drama of the universe. *All things are from God* (18a), *yes, God in Christ reconciling the world to himself* (19; VGS). This rules out mere human achievement in the grand scheme of reclaiming the world for God. God reclaims the world for himself.

The **second principle** is that the action **of reconciliation** is reflexive: God reconciles the world *to himself* (18b, 19b). The language refers to a prior separation between parties, a breach in relationship, an estrangement—in this case, between God and his world (*kosmos*). The compound words translated *reconcile* and *reconciliation* are used infrequently in Paul but abundantly in Greek literature. They denote "a change or alteration of relations between individual persons or groups of persons (e.g., nations); it is a change from anger, enmity, or hostility to love, friendship, or intimacy" (Fitzmyer, 1981:164-165).

In Paul's view, the created world, particularly humanity, is estranged from God because of sin that led to transgression of the divine law (5:19c; cf. Rom. 5:12-21). Such a state of trespasses ("under the power of sin," Rom. 3:9) required divine action to restore the human world to a state of love, obedience, and friendship with God. So God acted by *not counting their trespasses against them.* Understood thus, the language of reconciliation is closely akin to the language of justification found elsewhere in Paul (e.g., Gal. 3; Rom. 3–4). *God makes the relationship right* between himself and his transgressing image-bearers in the created world. (The theme is developed further in the later letters of Colossians and Ephesians.)

The **third principle of reconciliation** in 2 Corinthians 5:18-19 is that the action is performed exclusively by God's agent, Christ (18c, 19c). On the strength of this principle, Paul is able to call for unity in the church amid cultural and social diversity. At the same time and in the face of competing religions, he preaches the universal relevance of the good news (e.g., 1 Cor. 7:21-24; cf. Gal. 3:28). For Paul there is but one God who reconciles, one world of humanity to be reconciled, and one intermediate agent between the two whose death and resurrection has put the process into effect.

The **fourth principle of reconciliation** is that God's reconciling program is carried forward to fulfillment through the ministry or agency (Crafton: 59-102) of Paul and his colleagues. *[God] has given us the ministry of reconciliation* (18d). *[God] entrusted the message of reconciliation to us* (19d). *We/us* in these verses probably includes only apostolic types like Paul involved in mission. If *we/us* were to include the Corinthians together with all believers (Furnish, 1984:317), the argument would lose its edge. Paul's subsequent imperative to the Corinthians, *Be reconciled to God,* would lose its force.

The force of the four antiphonal principles is felt in the way the fourth is cemented to the other three. Paul's *message (logos, word) of reconciliation* is a gift to Paul from God. Paul's ministry is valid only as it relates to God's agent, Christ, and as it brings people into a right relationship with God. If the Corinthians take offense at Paul, they thereby take offense at God, for God's world program of reconciliation is inseparable from the world ministry in which Paul and his partners are engaged.

Reconciliation in Practice 5:20-21

Therefore (20a) connects the thought of verses 20-21 to the preceding, as practice connects to principle. Paul's ministry in the urgencies of life in Corinth and elsewhere is the outworking of the grand scheme of God to reconcile the world to himself.

Paul acts in ministry as a representative of Christ in the world. He stands in *for Christ* (5:20a); he entreats *on behalf of Christ* (20b., same phrase both times). In this respect Paul carries in his person and preaching the same self-giving character as Christ, as intimated earlier in this letter (4:10). Thus identified with Christ, Paul sees himself as God's ambassador, acting for God in relation to Christ, analogous to an official of Rome acting for Caesar. Local people in the empire hear the word of peace from Caesar through his representatives. Corinthi ans hear the word of peace from God through Paul and associates: *As ambassadors, God is making his appeal through us* (5:20a; cf. Talbert: 166).

On these grounds Paul can make his strong appeal to the Corinthians *on behalf of Christ* (5:20b): *Be reconciled to God.* He addresses them as though they are strangers to the gospel of God. In a sense they are, even though Paul addresses them as *the church of God* and *saints* (1:1). Estrangement from God's representative means they are estranged also from God. Accordingly, Paul's plea to the Corinthians to be reconciled to God is simultaneously an appeal to be reconciled to Paul.

Paul's imperative, *Be reconciled to God*, appears to conflict with his foregoing statement extolling God's initiative in reconciling the world to himself. Does the imperative contradict the earlier indicative? Does the duty finally fall to the human person to be reconciled to God? Here is a classic example of how Paul forges a theological reality with a command to mortals to make the theology operative. The two elements (God reconciles; you be reconciled) may seem to be contradictory, but they do come together: God was in Christ reconciling the world to himself without the cooperation of Adamic humanity; human transgressors merely submit to God and accept the divine offer. They do not negotiate a deal with God by which God is reconciled to them. On the contrary, transgressors can only accept the reconciling grace of God by which they are reconciled to him.

The passive of the verb *be reconciled* implies that the subjects submit to the reconciling action of God. Taken in the context of 5:18-21, moreover, the imperative of 5:20b removes transgressing humans from the process of reconciliation. Some people find it "very difficult to eliminate the element of personal response from the process of reconciliation itself" (Thrall, 1982:228).

Verse 21 constitutes a slight shift of focus. Paul, having cited the *trespasses* of mortals in 5:19, draws on a line from a christological confession that magnifies the sinless character of Christ. *The one [Christ] not having known sin he [God] made sin on our behalf* (I prefer this word order from the Greek). It could be that "there is no sentence more profound in the whole of Scripture" (Hughes: 211). Certainly the thought is weighty and its meaning debated. On the sinless nature of Christ in this text, there are essentially two views: (1) the statement points to the earthly life of Jesus, who kept God's law perfectly; (2) it refers to the transcendent Christ prior to his earthly existence, his existence "in the form of God" (Phil. 2:6).

The first view is too restrictive in the context of Paul's thought. Apart from his focus on Jesus' death by crucifixion, Paul shows more interest in the pre-earthly Christ and the post-Easter Christ than he does in the behavior of the earthly Jesus in Jewish Palestine.

The second alternative, therefore, with some modification, conforms more adequately to Paul's thought in 2 Corinthians and elsewhere in his letters. In the plan of the ages, the Christ of God knew no sin. Unlike Adam and Eve, Christ did not transgress the divine law (cf. Rom. 5:12-21) in that he was the true *image of God* (2 Cor. 4:4), "the power . . . and wisdom of God" (1 Cor. 1:24), existing eternally in "the form of God" (Phil. 2:6). This is the One who knew no sin whom God made (to be) sin (2 Cor. 5:21a).

The second clause in the Greek text, *[God] made him sin for us*, has likewise generated debate. Again there are principally two views: (1) God made the sinless One an offering for sin. (2) God made the sinless One enter into the human state of sin and death in order to reconcile the world.

The first position draws on the possibility that the text echoes the Servant passage of Isaiah 53:4-6, where sacrificial language dominates. In its favor also is the fact that 2 Corinthians 5:19 cites *trespasses* as the offense that God does not reckon against sinners. God does not reckon the trespasses, says this view, because Jesus bore the brunt of the penalty and satisfied the divine justice.

The second position recognizes Paul's limited use of sacrificial language elsewhere, and points to the abundant use of participatory language in 2 Corinthians and throughout Paul's letters. Paul's point in citing this formulation, therefore, is to signal the participation of the sinless Christ in sinful humanity, epitomized in the cruel death of Jesus. Participating thus in humanity's plight, Christ has opened the door for humanity to participate with Christ in God (cf. Col. 3:3). Hence, this line belongs under the overarching theme of the whole section: *God was in Christ reconciling the world to himself.* This reading of the text is preferable, especially so in light of the concluding purpose clause at the end of verse 21: *that in him we might be-*

come the righteousness of God.

The vision of reconciliation is still in view at the end of 5:21. When God reconciles the world to himself, this involves a transfer of unrighteous people into the righteous character of God. Such an exchange (Hooker: 354) is accomplished *for our sake* (5:21a) but quite apart from human initiative. "Christ became what we are, in order that (in him) we might become what he is" (Hooker: 354).

The *righteousness of God*, a central feature of Paul's gospel (cf. Rom. 1:17), is nevertheless somewhat elusive (Käsemann, 1969: 168-169). Does *the righteousness* belong to God and flow from God through Christ to humanity? Or is *the righteousness* the kind that God approves and accepts from human beings? While the latter view dominates Protestant theology (Käsemann, 1969:169), the former is more probable in the context of Paul's participatory theology so evident in the present text. "We have a sort of exchange which makes no sense apart from the notion of solidarity: [Christ] entered into our sinful situation . . . that we might enter his solidarity of righteousness."

By this interpretation, *the righteousness of God* is "God's own righteousness, his own covenant loyalty . . . which [human beings] conspicuously lack" (Ziesler: 159-160). When believers participate *in Christ* (a key phrase in Paul) they are "justified." *In him* they *become the righteousness of God.* Their status of sin and death is exchanged for one of righteousness and life. The exchange itself is God's doing; God reconciles the world; those reconciled to God participate in the new creation.

Transitional Word of Appeal   6:1-2

Bolstered by the word of the Lord to his Servant in Isaiah 49:8, Paul's appeal of 2 Corinthians 6:1-2 recalls the thought of God's *new* creation already under way (5:16-21) and glances forward to Paul's credentials as God's ambassador in the current ministry of reconciliation (6:3-10). The two verses thus form at once a literary transition and a formal appeal to the Corinthians to keep faith with Paul and associates, who enjoy assurance of God's salvation.

The *urging* of 6:1, supported by the prophetic word from the Servant passage of Isaiah in 6:2a, is clinched promptly by Paul's interpretive comment on the Isaiah text in 6:2b. The plea in 6:1 *not to accept the grace of God in vain* is hinged to the qualifying participle, *as we work together.* The NRSV adds *with him*, God, assuming that the thought is directly related to the reconciling ministry of 2 Corinthians

5:19-20. If there should be such a sure connection, then a more appropriate translation would be, *as we work together for God* (Bruce: 211). Paul conceives of himself as an ambassador under orders from his Sovereign, not as a partner with God—equal or otherwise. The fact is, the Greek text has only a one-word participial qualifier: *as we work together.* At this transitional stage in his appeal, Paul is more likely to be linking his work in ministry with the supportive efforts of the Corinthians, which seem to him to be sagging even as he writes (against Thrall, 1994:451).

The implication is unmistakable. If the Corinthians' reception of God's grace is to remain effective for salvation, they had better keep their ties with God's ambassador intact. To accept one is to accept the other; to abandon one is to abandon the other. The prophetic word lends urgency to the apostle's plea. There is an acceptable time when God will listen; there is a day of salvation when God will help (6:2). From Paul's standpoint at the juncture of the ages, *look*, that time of grace is *now* as never before (cf. 5:16-17). By the end of 6:2, the appeal turns into a veiled warning: Put reconciliation into practice in the present critical moment, or forfeit your place in the final salvation of God.

THE TEXT IN BIBLICAL CONTEXT

The interrelated themes of new creation, reconciliation, and servant-salvation in 2 Corinthians 5:16—6:2 interface with similar ones in the biblical tradition.

Mention of creation echoes immediately the classic story of the original creation found in Genesis 1-2. Sin entered God's created order through the disobedience of the first man and woman to the divine will (Gen. 3). Their offspring fell under a curse. A recurring theme in biblical literature, in prophetic literature especially, is the restoration or recreation of the original state of the first parents in harmony with God. The theme takes on several different hues in Israelite and later Jewish history. Jeremiah pictured a new covenant through which God would restore the broken relationship (31:31-34; 2 Cor. 3:4-6). The Servant Song of Isaiah 43 looks forward to a new order to replace the old (43:18-19; similar language to 2 Cor. 5:17). The later part of Isaiah envisions a new heaven and a new earth (Isa. 65:17; 66:22). These texts from Isaiah (probably from the exilic and postexilic periods) arise out of the experience of Israel's separation from the presence of God in the temple and in the land.

The restoration from exile probably forms the primary background to Paul's theme of new creation and reconciliation in 2 Corinthians 5:17-21. In this view the new creation is simply a development of the earlier theme of new covenant in chapter 3 (see 3:6; Webb: 112-158; Beale: 552-566). Restoration theology does seem to be embedded in the new creation-reconciliation language of 2 Corinthians 5, but only as an allusive layer of meaning. Paul does not actually cite restoration texts from the second main section of Isaiah (chapters 40-55).

Paul's scope, rather, is wider and more cosmic than Israel's return home to Jerusalem. His vision follows more the pattern of new heaven and new earth evident in the last section of Isaiah. It encompasses the restoration of glory lost in Eden, the redemption of the image of God in humanity (Pate: 137-157). That layer of Scripture tradition is closer to the surface of 2 Corinthians 5:18-21 than any other. The Adam Christology, sculpted here in the language of new creation and reconciliation, provides Paul the universal scope his mission demands. He looks for the constitution of a new order out of the world of Jewish and Gentile humanity.

While the term *new creation* itself appears only in Paul (5:17; Gal. 6:15), belief in a new world coming at the end of history is "adequately attested for the Judaism of Paul's day" (Thrall, 1994:422). The Jewish notion is apocalyptic and futuristic, similar to the vision of the NT Apocalypse (Rev. 21:1-4). Paul, by contrast, considers the new order of existence to be present *now* that God has raised the crucified Christ from the dead.

One may conjecture that Paul has drawn on Christian traditions predating his mission for his view of a new creation in which Jewish and Gentile people are reconciled to God and to each other (Mell: 298-299). On the other hand, the text proves only that Paul believed in a new reality and preached the same to the Gentiles, and that he employed the term *new creation* to capture the significance of what he believed. Other NT writings refer to the new reality in Christ in accordance with their own time and setting (Eph. 2:10-16; 2 Pet. 3:13; Rev. 21:1-5).

Of the NT documents that develop the theme of reconciliation, Ephesians ranks highest. In Ephesians the mystery of the new order in Christ is that Jewish humanity and Gentile humanity come together in "one new humanity" (a term used only in Eph. 2:15). Christ broke down the dividing wall of hostility so as "to reconcile both groups to God in one body" (2:16; cf. 4:24). There is no mistaking the

Pauline theme of reconciliation transposed from 2 Corinthians 5:18-21. But the theme is adapted in Ephesians to the needs of the world-wide church on the verge of fracture.

One final word on Paul's use of the Servant passage from Isaiah 49:8. Isaiah's meaning is set in the context of the prenatal appointment of the servant (49:5) to be *a light to the nations* worldwide (49:6). Even though Paul does not divulge this context to the Corinthians, he clearly sees himself in the role of God's servant (ambassador) to the Gentiles. The Corinthians know he sees himself thus, whether or not they know the context of Isaiah 49:8. Paul's plea to the Gentile Corinthians in 2 Corinthians 6:1-2 echoes the Isaianic servant's role as one divinely commissioned to bring God's reconciling grace to those outside Israel.

THE TEXT IN THE LIFE OF THE CHURCH

With the thought of 2 Corinthians 5:16—6:2 in its possession, the church at large could be expected to exhibit the new creation of God and act as agency of God's reconciling grace in the world. But the record proves that possession of a sacred text does not guarantee engagement with its thought, much less the practice of its teaching. Internal strife and public disgrace have from time to time marred the church's ministry and cast a shadow across the reconciling love of God. The case of the Corinthian church is a prime example.

One generation after Paul dispatched this text on *new creation* and *reconciliation*, Clement of Rome found discord rampant in the church in Corinth. Late in the first century, he wrote, "It is disgraceful, brethren, . . . and unworthy of Christian conduct, that of the stable and ancient Church of the Corinthians, . . . it should be reported that it revolts against its presbyters. . . . Owing to your folly you bring revilings on the name of the Lord." Clement then, echoing the thought of 2 Corinthians 5:17-21, aimed at bringing the *reconciliation* and *righteousness* of Christ into that community (1 Clement 47-48). The Corinthians' possession of Paul's sacred letter on reconciliation was no substitute for following its guidance.

Summarizing the various aspects of reconciliation in this text into a manageable creedal statement can likewise delude the church into thinking it has obeyed the message. Summary statements aid in fixing Christian doctrine in the mind. But such statements of belief are worthy only as they translate into situations of living in community and world. The reality of the new creation and of the reconciliation of

God requires instruction—repeated instruction that ends up in loving human relationships (Thrall, 1982b:230-231).

Reformers in their own way taught new creation and reconciliation. They understood *new creation* in Paul to mean the new birth of the inner being of the individual (see notes above), as taught in John 3:3-8. Some gave reconciliation a more juristic meaning than it has in 2 Corinthians 5. Calvin, for example, applied the thought of 2 Corinthians 5:18-19 to the justification of a sinner, thus combining "new creature" with the right standing of the individual before God (reconciliation). True to the situation of his time, he repudiated the doctrine of penance with the support of 2 Corinthians 5:19. He understood reconciliation to include as well the free forgiveness of sins: God does not count trespasses against sinners (Calvin, 2:35-36).

Anabaptist Reformers distinguished themselves from their Protestant counterparts in their application of the new-creation theme. Like the Calvinists they did see new creation in this text as a way of describing regeneration of the individual. They departed from the Calvinists by their defense of believers baptism, against infant baptism. Baptism as such does not result in a "new creature." Faith in Christ is the ground of becoming a "new creature" in Christ (Menno: 123; cf. Dirk: 298-299).

These rebaptizers also confessed the implications of being "new creatures" and of having *the ministry of reconciliation* committed to them as to Paul. Echoing an earlier confession that cited 2 Corinthians 5:17, Olive Branch Confession of Amsterdam (1627) became the basis of reconciliation among "many congregations of the Frisians and High Germans" (*ME*, 1:102-103). These and other Anabaptist groups sought to reflect the peacemaking God "through the putting on of the new [person], which after God is created in righteousness and true holiness; these show forth the image of Christ in their mortal bodies" (*MM:* 30; cf. 394). The emphasis falls on the outworking of God's new creation in the form of peaceable relations. Pilgram Marpeck's allusion to this text is among the most poignant. He wrote of the followers of Christ as representatives of Christ's character and ministers of his liberating grace. He emphasized the liberation from guilt that comes from being reconciled to God through Christ (95; 319). What these believers wrote about reconciliation, they bore out in life and in death.

If any inconsistency existed among these forebears of present-day Mennonites, it was in their sometimes harsh practice of the excommunication of wrongdoers from their fellowship. In this context their thoughts on the reconciliation theme of 2 Corinthians 5 appear muted. God's ambassadors are first and foremost reconcilers, not supreme judges to condemn and sentence. Judgment must at times be passed and discipline meted out, but the goal throughout is reconciliation among members in the community of faith in Christ.

It has remained for later communities of faith in Christ to extend the implications of Paul's teaching on this important topic. "Since peace between God and humanity is established in the cross of Christ, reconciliation in our human world means our calling, our mission, to establish peace. The task is a quite concrete one: the Christian *community* becomes *a place of reconciliation*" (Lochman: 79). In the last quarter of a century, more and more agencies have formed to make concrete the new creation of God in bringing concord between persons and groups. The Community Justice Initiatives based in Kitchener, Ontario, is an umbrella organization in support of several programs in reconciliation. The Victim-Offender Reconciliation Program (VORP), started in 1975, seeks to bring victim and offender together through a third-party mediator in a post-trial stage. Sometime later the Community Mediation Service began working with victims and offenders at the pretrial stage. Currently the reconciliation programs in Canada come under the Network for Community Justice and Conflict Resolution.

The United States has similar programs: The Mennonite Conciliation Service (1975); chapters of Christian Conciliation Service; Victim-Offender Reconciliation (1978). The reconciling work of these and other organizations has gained the respect of the courts and continues to expand (Northey in *ME*, 5:746). All such Christian agencies in society are viable only if they are backed by churches that exhibit within themselves signs of the new creation, whose members live at peace with each other.

Commendable Marks of God's Reconciling Agent
2 Corinthians 6:3-13; 7:2-4

PREVIEW

Paul's apology for the ministry of reconciliation (5:20) in this section takes the form of a deeply personal appeal (6:3-13; 7:2-4). It "is certainly one of the high peaks of all Paul's writings" (Hughes: 238). As appeal, the thought extends the entreaty of 6:1-2 into a self validation forced on Paul by the Corinthians' growing criticism of his person and work. Consistent with his self-understanding in relation to the suffering righteous servant, Christ, Paul's self-praise accents God's power (6:7a) in his human weakness (6:4b-5), God's triumph in Paul's hardships. In that stance Paul issues his affectionate plea to the Corinthians to open their heart to him, as he opens his to them (6:11-13; 7:2-4).

The rhetorical flow of the appeal in these verses (6:3-13; 7:2-4) is interrupted by the compiler's insertion of a stern warning taken from another source (6:14—7:1). Each of these, the compassionate appeal and the stern warning, will receive separate treatment in the notes *[The "Unequal Yoke" Passage, p. 281]*.

Within the appeal, Paul presents one of his best crafted lists comprising hardships, virtues, ups and downs, and paradoxes. The composite list commends Paul to the Corinthians as a true apostle of Jesus Christ and a worthy minister of God's reconciling grace. The affectionate appeal together with the list invites the Corinthians to open wide their hearts to their apostle (6:3, 11-13; 7:2-4).

OUTLINE

A No-Fault Ministry, 6:3-4a

Witness the Evidence, 6:4b-10
    6:4b-5   A List of Hardships
    6:4b, 6-7a A List of Moral Virtues
    6:7b-10   A List of Paradoxical Antitheses

An Appeal for Open Hearts, 6:11-13; 7:2-4

EXPLANATORY NOTES
A No-Fault Ministry 6:3-4a

Grammatically, the language of 6:3-4a relates to that of 6:1. The main verb of 6:1, *We urge you*, finds a complement in the participle of 6:3, *putting no obstacle in anyone's way*. Beyond the grammatical connection, the earlier focus on a God-given ministry of reconciliation (5:18—6:2) is now turned explicitly on the character and behavior of the agent to whom God entrusts such a ministry.

As God's appointed servant, Paul can say of his ministry that it is faultfree. *We are putting no obstacle in anyone's way,* he says. The language is emphatic (double negative in Greek), no offense whatsoever. That is, no offense other than the offense of the cross (1 Cor. 1:23). A faulty ministry blurs the single saving offense of the crucified Christ, through whom God reconciles the world. For this reason Paul is at pains to commend himself as a true agent of God's reconciliation: *so that no fault may be found with our ministry, but as servants of God we have commended ourselves in every way* (2 Cor. 6:3-4). In this respect Paul is not boastful; instead, he is obliged to lay bare his person and behavior before the eyes of the Corinthians so as to move them to accept him as God's true minister.

Witness the Evidence   6:4b-10

This section (6:4b-10) contains a composite list of hardships, virtues, and paradoxes. Before engaging the various parts of the list, a general comment about this listing device in Paul's argument is in order.

Some say the list comes from a preexisting source, perhaps in Stoicism, which Paul has then edited to suit his Christian purposes (e.g., R. Martin, 1986:161). Such a listing was common among Greek thinkers and teachers as a way of setting forth their credibility among their patrons and students. In particular, the sage often cataloged hardships he endured as proof of his good character and of the truth of his philosophy. A list of moral virtues frequently accompanied the list of hardships to vouchsafe the veracity of the sage's teaching (Fitzgerald, 1988:47-116). No doubt Paul was aware of this practice in the Greek world. However, his own rhetorical use of a catalog of hardships and virtues comes not from Stoic serenity but from participation in the spirit and character of Christ crucified.

The list in 6:4b-10, however much it was spontaneous, reflects careful construction. Verses 4b-7a contain a total of eighteen phrases, each beginning with the preposition *en* (*in/by/through*), nine hardships and nine virtues. The nine hardships are headed by the virtue *endurance* (6:4b), followed by the remaining eight virtues (or character traits). Endurance of trials was considered the most important trait of character for the true sage (Fitzgerald, 1988:191). The hardships fall into three triads, each triad emphasizing one kind of trial. The accompanying nine traits of character are patently Pau-

line, found elsewhere in the letters, particularly in another list under
the fruit of the Spirit (Gal. 5:22-23).

After the hardships and virtues comes a catalog of antitheses or
paradoxes under a military metaphor, *the weapons of righteousness
for the right hand and for the left* (6:7b-10). The antitheses illustrate
the paradox of divine strength in human weakness, so prominent in
2 Corinthians.

6:4b-5 A List of Hardships

Some interpreters go to great lengths to reconstruct the historical
moments represented in each of the hardships on the list, as though
the interpretation of the text (6:4-10) depends on proper reporting of
corresponding events. Without doubt, the descriptive phrases bear
out the kind of experiences Paul has had in the ministry of Christ, but
"his words are not to be treated as a matter-of-fact account of his
work" (Barrett, 1973:188). The phrases are selected, arranged, and
linked together to create a persuasive effect in the mind and emotion
of the readers. Taken as a whole, the list of hardships is meant to
prove that Paul has the quality of endurance that marks the true
apostle. The words are his own, not a prepared list that apostles carry
with them as credentials (Collange: 294), and the experiences represented in the phrases were really his. The form of the list is as follows:

Leading virtue (6:4b)	*through much endurance (en hupomenē pollē)*
General external hardships (4b)	*in afflictions (en thlipsesin)* *hardships (en anagkais)* *calamities (en stenochōriais)*
Hardships arising from the mission (5a)	*beatings (en plegais)* *imprisonments (en phulakais)* *riots (en akatastasiais)*
Self-imposed hardships (5b)	*labors (en kopois)* *sleepless nights (en agrupniais)* *hunger (en nēsteiais)*

With such an impressive list of hardships to his credit, Paul's claim
to be minister of reconciliation in the name of the suffering Servant
(Christ) should be settled at Corinth. Interpreters debate whether it
was settled or not. If Paul wrote the Letter of Defense (2 Cor. 10–13)
some time after this section, as proposed in this commentary, then

clearly the Corinthians were not completely convinced by the rhetoric of this list. In the later letter, Paul sent yet another list of hardships,
written in a different tone (11:23-29).

6:4b, 6-7a A List of Moral Virtues

Following the list of hardships that show the virtue of endurance
(6:4b), Paul adds eight other virtues that endorse his ministry as faultfree (6:6-7a). Whether the eight should be called virtues, spiritual
gifts, or traits of moral character makes little difference for the interpretation of their place in the text. These Christian attributes appear
elsewhere in Paul's writings along with other traits not mentioned
here. Just as the list of hardships represented Paul's experience in
ministry, so here, the selected traits of apostolic character are
representative of the kind of minister Paul is. The primary purpose of
the select list is to commend the ministry of Paul effectively to the Corinthians' conscience.

The order of the virtues on the list seems to be random, except
that Paul may have placed the final characteristic deliberately at the
end as an all-encompassing quality: *the power of God* is a major
theme stamped on every facet of this canonical letter (cf. 1 Cor. 1:18-
25).

Purity signifies a person who has nothing to hide, whose behavior
is consonant with thought and feeling (Louw, 1:746). *Knowledge* is
the insightful ability to understand and grasp truth; the Corinthians
(some at least) apparently delight in their possession of this gift
(1 Cor. 8:1-3; 13:2, 8). *Patience* is "a state of emotional calm in the
face of provocation or misfortune and without complaint or irrita-
tion" (Louw, 1:307). *Kindness*, in tandem with *patience*, is "the sympathetic kindliness or sweetness of temper which puts others at their
ease and shrinks from giving pain" (Plummer: 196).

Holiness of spirit, as the NRSV translates, is laden with ambiguity
within this list of moral virtues. With this form of the phrase (without
the article or the divine name), *spirit* often refers to the Holy Spirit of
God (Rom. 5:5; 9:1; 14:17; 15:13; 1 Cor. 6:19; 1 Thess. 1:5-6). A
number of scholars interpret the phrase thus in 2 Corinthians 6:6.
(R. Martin, 1986:176-177; Furnish, 1984:345, 256; Hughes: 228;
Thrall, 1994:460). Yet it is strange to include the Holy Spirit of God
in a list of attributes describing the human instrument of reconciliation. Consistent with the other eight attributes in the list, *pneumati
hagiō* (*holy spirit*) most naturally means the kind of spirit *Paul* pos-

sesses as a minister of God, a spirit "set apart for the gospel of God" (Rom. 1:1; so Barrett, 1973:187; Plummer: 196-197). In this list, however, the phrase *holy spirit* may encompass something of both alternatives. Just as the attributes of purity, knowledge, patience, kindness, love, etc., are the fruit of the Holy Spirit of God (Gal. 5:22), so Paul's spirit is holy and energized for ministry by the Holy Spirit of God (cf. Kruse: 132).

Genuine *love* acts sincerely, not for show (cf. 1 Cor. 13), like the love of God in Jesus Christ crucified for the sake of estranged humankind. The adjective *genuine* may be aimed at opponents whose claims lack a basis in reality. Similarly, the next quality, *truthful speech* (2 Cor. 6:7), is probably so framed to distinguish Paul's preaching from other would-be missionaries whose words are leading the Corinthians astray. The list is then capped by *the power of God*. Paul highlights *the power of God* at various points in 2 Corinthians, paradoxically in the presence of human weakness (4:7; 12:9; 13:4; cf. 1 Cor. 1:18-25). The gospel which Paul preaches is the power of God that brings salvation to everyone who believes (Rom. 1:16). Hence, it belongs at this place of emphasis in the list of credentials.

6:7b-10 A List of Paradoxical Antitheses

With the change of introductory prepositions from *en* to *dia* (*through/by*), the terms of reference also change. In 6:7b-8a, the phrases introduced by *dia* appear to provide transition (Fitzgerald, 1988:195) from a series of positive virtues to a series of antithetical experiences that form the paradox of Paul's ministry (cf. A. Hanson, 1987:55-78). Using a military metaphor, Paul commends himself as one who advances God's good news of peace *with* (*dia*) *the weapons of righteousness for the right hand and for the left* (6:7b).

Paul was not alone in his use of such metaphors to describe the experience of preaching and teaching. His picture of himself as an "armed soldier" is "in keeping with the military imagery that is prominent in the depictions of the sage in his battle with Fortune" (Fitzgerald, 1988:195; cf. Windisch: 207; Furnish, 1984:346; Thrall, 1994:462). Yet Paul's use of the image is distinct in that *the weapons* describe his righteous life in the ministry of reconciliation. The operative *righteousness* in such a ministry is doubtless the same as the reconciling *righteousness of God* in 5:21, not human justice in the sense that Plato taught.

What Paul means by his image of wearing righteousness on the right hand and on the left is not immediately obvious. Since the metaphor is military, he may have in mind the offensive sword in the right hand and the defensive shield in the left (cf. Eph. 6:11-17; 1 Thess. 5:8). His ministry involves him in both at once. In any case, the phrase introduces the duality in the ensuing list of antitheses, reflecting the struggle between good and evil in the present advance of the salvation of God (6:2; cf. Thrall, 1994:462 on the good and evil spirits in humankind described in the Dead Sea Scrolls).

The two remaining *dia*-phrases in 6:8a illustrate the *left* and *right* of Paul's experience in ministry: *in honor and dishonor; in ill repute and good repute.* These general vicissitudes of ministry in the name of Christ are further specified by a series of seven paradoxical antitheses, each introduced by another particle, *hōs* (as). Suggestions about the relationship between the pairs vary: the first of each pair is external while the second is taken as internal; the first is a false estimate by worldly standards, and the second is true by divine standards; the first is human judgment and the second is God's (Thrall, 1994:463-464). The mixture in the list engages all of these to some extent. The overall impression the antitheses leave with the reader is that Paul's ministry heralds truth contained in paradox, in keeping with the paradox of life-through-death in the Christ-event (A. Hanson, 1987:55-78).

Paul has opponents and followers as Jesus had; unbelievers and believers; persecutors and supporters. And Paul recognizes these as belonging to the very nature of the gospel of God that he preaches, *to the one a fragrance from death to death, to the other a fragrance from life to life* (2:16, notes; cf. 1 Cor. 1:18-30). More than that, these antitheses reflect Paul's own dialectical experience of living "between the times," in the overlap of the old age and the new age (1 Cor. 10:11). He has tasted the future glory of God in Christ in his present affliction in ministry. These two together, present affliction [A] and future glory [B], inform Paul's list of antitheses, as the following analysis illustrates (2 Cor. 6:8b-10).

We are treated as impostors [A], *and yet are true* [B]; *as unknown* [A], *and yet are well known* [B]; *as dying* [A] *and see—we are alive* [B]; *as punished* [A], *and yet not killed* [B]; *as sorrowful* [A], *yet always rejoicing* [B]; *as poor* [A], *yet making many rich* (with the gospel; cf. 2 Cor. 8:9) [B]; *as having nothing* (cf. Phil. 3:7-11) [A], *yet possessing everything* [B]. The force of the antitheses pushes the Corinthians to ask themselves whether they come under category *A* or *B*.

Seeing the hardships, virtues, and paradoxical antitheses, some questions come to mind: What feeling will this triple list evoke in the hearts of the Corinthian readers-hearers? Will it yield united support at Corinth for Paul and his ministry? Will it silence those who have questioned his motives, his credentials, and his change of travel plans (2 Cor. 1:15—2:4)? If Paul's subsequent letter (2 Cor. 10-13) is any indication, the answer is negative. Interloping opponents apparently have gained the confidence of (at least a group of) the Corinthians against Paul, despite his effort to prove himself open and true to his beloved converts.

6:11-13; 7:2-4 An Appeal for Open Hearts

Every turn of phrase in this section is wrapped in a blanket of warm affection without equal in the letters. The direct address, *Corinthians* (6:11), itself is "a sign of strong feeling" (Barrett, 1973:191; cf. Gal. 3:1; Phil. 4:15). More than that, though, the audience at Corinth will hear the title with ears more sensitive than those of modern readers. What does it mean to be called a Corinthian? Is it merely an indication of where the readers live? Probably much more than that.

Corinth was "one of the most celebrated cities in the ancient Mediterranean world" (Murphy-O'Connor, 1983:xiii). The milieu of this highly cultured Hellenistic city was impressive, from its architecture to its theater and games, and its spiritual gifts from the gods. All this gave its citizens a corresponding mind-set that marked them out as "Corinthian" (153-172). Paul himself was not a "Corinthian," but in keeping with his missionary practice of becoming "all things to all people" (1 Cor. 9:22), he aimed at applying the truth of the gospel to the Corinthians (cf. Beker: 11-36). Despite that, the Corinthians offer veiled criticism of Paul in their fragile relationship to him: "Your character and behavior scarcely measure up to our Corinthian standard of what a true messenger of God should exhibit."

Paul in the end throws himself wide open to their sense of common decency and fair play without discrediting their Corinthian reputation. Moreover, 2 Corinthians 6:11 could read, *Our mouth is open toward you, Corinthians, [as] our heart stands wide* (as in an open playing field). The two phrases complement each other. Paul conceals nothing of himself from them, neither in his word to them nor in his feeling for them.

The same sentiment is reinforced in 6:12a as ground for the appeal that the Corinthians should open themselves to Paul. *There is no restriction in our affections* (lit.: no constriction in our intestines), *but only in yours.* Then comes the imperative, clothed in a telling metaphor: *In return—I speak as to children—open wide your hearts also* (6:12). *Children* may be a term of endearment; Paul is likely alluding to his status as a spiritual parent to them. As such, he can make this appeal (so R. Martin, 1986:187; Plummer: 204; Hughes: 240). On the other hand, the parenthesis is not explicit on this point since the text does not refer to **my** children. Paul may simply be slipping a parenthetical note into his dictation to the effect that children expect fair play of each other (cf. 11:21). Moffat's translation reads: "A fair exchange now, as children say! Open your hearts wide to me" (also Strachan: 124). Paul seems to say, "Please abandon your suspicion and mistrust of me and return my love for you."

Paul rounds off the appeal in 7:2-4 (likely written right after 6:13). In keeping with the earlier list of hardships, virtues, and antitheses, this closure reiterates in brief the ground of the appeal. Paul vindicates himself and his co-workers in three terse negations: *we have wronged no one, corrupted no one, taken advantage of no one* (7:2). Behind these disclaimers may lie the criticism (1) of Paul's way of collecting money for Jerusalem (1 Cor. 16: Thrall, 1994:482), or (2) of Paul breaking his promise to visit them (2 Cor. 1:15—2:1), or (3) of what seemed to be his sharp discipline of the offender (2:3-11). Since Paul treats all three subjects in the sections immediately following, his three negations in 7:2 probably relate in a general sense to these three criticisms.

Paul is careful not to distance himself from the Corinthians by the defensive tone of 7:2. So he quickly reminds them that his purpose is not to condemn them but to retain them in his heart as always, *to die together and to live together* with them (7:3). There may be an allusion here to the death and life of Christ in which believers all participate (5:14-15). More to the immediate point of the personal appeal, however, Paul has just explained his ministry as a life-in-death experience in which he expects the Corinthians to participate; hence the phrase, *to die together and to live together.*

Paul closes his highly personal appeal by turning attention positively toward the Corinthians in four jubilant phrases arranged in an ascending scale (7:4). He has great confidence in them, boasts greatly about them, is filled with encouragement, and is overflowing with joy. All of these exist *in all our affliction.* Affliction is thematic in 2 Corinthians and fits Paul's thought generally (cf. Phil. 1:29; 3:10-11). In affliction he identifies with Christ crucified, knowing that suffering service in the name of Christ will lead to resurrection glory like that of Christ. This is the theological context for Paul's confidence, boasting, encouragement, and joy with regard to the Corinthians. They are a *new creation* in Christ Jesus as a result of his affliction in ministry (2 Cor. 5:17).

THE TEXT IN BIBLICAL CONTEXT

Second Corinthians 6:3-13 and 7:2-4 consist of two types of material: a catalog of credentials and an affectionate appeal for loving, spiritual support from the Corinthians. The two types relate to each other insofar as the credentials provide the basis of the appeal for support.

In the context of 2 Corinthians, the list of credentials in 6:4b-10 is an extension of the list of hardships in 4:7-12. Elaborately formulated, the list of credentials in chapter 6 may be Paul's way of providing the Corinthians with the *opportunity to boast about* him and his associates to the rival missionaries (5:12). On the surface such listing of credentials seems inconsistent with Paul's repeated concern "never [to] boast of anything except the cross of our Lord Jesus Christ, by which the world has been crucified to me, and I to the world" (Gal. 6:14). If a believer finds occasion to boast, Paul wrote earlier to the Corinthians, "let the one who boasts, boast in the Lord" (1 Cor. 1:31; 2 Cor. 10:17; cf. Jer. 9:23-24). That Paul follows his own directive to others in this list of his credentials is plain. The hardships are those of a suffering servant of Christ; the virtues have their source in God; the antitheses describe Paul's dialectical (up-and-down) experience in the Gentile world mission. Overall the list extols the power of God in Paul's mortal body (cf. 2 Cor. 4:10).

Noticeably absent from Paul's list of credentials in 2 Corinthians 6 are elements of status and achievement set forth in the character witness of Acts 22: Paul's birth of Jewish parents in the important Diaspora city of Tarsus; his education in historic Jerusalem under the prominent Gamaliel; his expertise in the law. For Paul to have put any or all of these on the list in 2 Corinthians 6 would render his "self-commendation" in conflict with his identity as participant in the death-and-life of Jesus Christ.

As for the literary practice of listing credentials, whatever their content, Paul follows a pattern current among Greek philosophers of the time. Paul's list has much in common with the self-commending lists composed by the Greek sage to prove his genuineness by enduring hardships (Fitzgerald, 1988:47-116). In this context, Paul's list provides help for the Corinthians' defense of Paul against his critics. Those opponents have probably come from a hellenized Diaspora synagogue setting where a catalog of this type is respected.

Paul's affectionate appeal in 6:11-13 and 7:2-4 for the Corinthians to reciprocate is without equal in the NT. Reciprocity in principle in Christian community comes to sharpest expression in the later Johannine writings. In the passion discourses of the Gospel of John, for example, Jesus instructs the disciples to love one another: "Just as I have loved you, you also should love one another" (13:34). First John's emphasis on reciprocal love (e.g., 4:7-16) reflects a development of the Pauline idea of participation together in Christ, the touchstone of Paul's personal appeal to the Corinthians to return his love for them.

THE TEXT IN THE LIFE OF THE CHURCH

Preaching on the text of 2 Corinthians 6:11-13, fourth-century archbishop of Constantinople, John Chrysostom, calls Paul's appeal to the Corinthians a rebuke out of love. Excerpts from Chrysostom's sermon will illustrate his point of view:

> Having detailed his own [trials] and afflictions. . . , and having shown that the thing was a great good. . . , and having hereby represented God's abundant care and power. . . , and that he was not only entitled to reverence on this account but also for his trials. . . , he purposeth now also to rebuke them, as not being too well minded towards him. But though purposing he does not immediately come upon this, but having first spoken of the love which he had displayed towards them, he then enters also upon his discussion of these things. . . . Therefore the apostle also having stepped out of the subject of his own trials, and toils, and contests, passes on into speaking of his love, and in this way toucheth them to the quick. What then are the indications of his love? *O ye Corinthians, our mouth is open unto you.* The addition of their name is a mark of great love, and warmth, and affection; for we are accustomed to be repeating continually the bare names of those we love. [Love] opened the mouth of Paul and enlarged his heart. (161-164)

Paul's hardships and virtues endured for the sake of the gospel have encouraged many Christians in similar circumstances. In a letter written from prison in 1569, Tijs Jeuriaenss draws on Paul's testimonial in 2 Corinthians 6. "We must arm ourselves in weakness with the mind of Jesus Christ. . . , with the armor of light, and with the power of God, on the right hand and on the left" (*MM:* 829). In another pris-

on at about the same time, Willeboort Corneliss experienced something of the paradox of Paul's antitheses:

> My dearest and beloved sister in the Lord, in this miserable and sorrowful
> world we are counted a prey to every one. . . . Yea, we are counted as de-
> ceivers, and yet are true; we are become a spectacle; we are troubled on
> every side, yet not distressed; we are perplexed, but not in despair; perse-
> cuted, but not forsaken; cast down, but not destroyed. (*MM:* 669)

Despite their efforts not to give offense in their ministry, those
persecuted in the name of Christ did offend the religious and political
authorities. The question for them, as for all ministers of the gospel in
all ages, is this: Is the offense true to the character of the gospel of
Christ crucified? (1 Cor. 1:18-25)

There also may be a lesson for modern ministers, and for believers generally, in Paul's so-called self-commendation. Present-day
churches, particularly the evangelical, congregational ones, appear to
have developed a psychology of the unworthy self, which purportedly translates into spiritual correctness in speech and confession. As
Christians are able to say they are faltering, wavering, subject to falling into sin, and generally unworthy of Christ, so they are applauded
for their spiritual maturity. It is said, for example, that Christians
should refrain from passing judgment on immoral behavior because
everyone is subject to the same weakness. Yet that betrays a disbelief
in the power of God in the Spirit of Christ.

Paul's *Christian* self-understanding in 2 Corinthians or elsewhere
in his letters (on exegetical grounds, Rom. 7 does not count against
this point) is one of healthy self-assurance in the sphere of Christ crucified. He believes it quite in place to say there is no fault in his ministry (6:3), and quite in order to list his hardships and virtues as commendable credentials. Paul lives and works within *the power of God.*

In a sermon delivered in the midseventies, Frank C. Peters made
the point that Christians have developed the unhealthy habit of de-
grading themselves, speaking frequently of their faults and failings.
Of all people, said Peters, Christians ought to be able to come onto
the world's stage like Mighty Mouse, filled with moral fortitude in the
power of God, and equipped with honed skills for life and ministry.
The problem for Christians is not with professional skills and abilities,
but with the way in which these are held and used in the confession of
Christian character.

Insert: Exclusive Covenant Community
2 Corinthians 6:14—7:1

PREVIEW

Of the several puzzling passages in 2 Corinthians, none carries more enigma for the interpreter than 6:14—7:1. Its "tone is strident and severe" (R. Martin, 1986:211), quite unlike the tone in the verses immediately preceding and following this unit. The text is self-contained, having no obvious grammatical or thematic connection with the surrounding text.

In the classic way of giving advice, the text persuades the readers to maintain community life completely separate from the defilement of the faithless world. Each of the five rhetorical questions in 6:14-16 aims at this goal of covenantal exclusiveness, similar to that of the Jewish covenantors of Qumran, who separated themselves from the compromising situation in Roman-occupied Jerusalem.

The approach taken here is to analyze the cohesion and objective of the unit itself in the notes and then to address the key questions the text raises in TBC. These questions include the issue of whether this passage is an insertion into the middle of Paul's affectionate, personal appeal to the Corinthians to open their hearts to him.

OUTLINE

Formal Elements

Theme and Objective

Inherent Questions

EXPLANATORY NOTES

Formal Elements

This type of text is usually called *paraenetic* or *exhortatory:* it lays down an ethical injunction to persuade the faithful in community to maintain their moral life in keeping with their confession as members of the community. The internal exhorting structure of this unit (6:14—7:1) is fourfold: (1) an introductory prohibition (6:14a); (2) five rhetorical questions to yield an appropriate response (6:14b-

16a); (3) a chain of phrases from Scripture to undergird the command-response (6:16b-18), and (4) a concluding interpretive comment on the Scripture chain as final validation for the ethical demand (7:1). A closer analysis of each of these and of all of them together will illuminate the theme and objective of the passage.

Theme and Objective

The intent of the opening negative imperative is unequivocal: *Do not be mismatched with unbelievers* (6:14a). The metaphor of *mismatched* is vivid, coming from the practice of cultivating land with a double yoke of animals. As an ox should not be yoked to a donkey (Deut. 22:10; cf. Lev. 19:19; see below), neither should the faithful in community be *yoked* to the faithless. *Faithless* is perhaps a better rendering of the Greek word, *apistoi*, than *unbelievers* in an exhortation that enjoins covenant loyalty. Assuming the prohibition is directed to a confessional community, as the plural nouns throughout strongly suggest, the objective of the prohibition is clear: members of the faith community are not to associate with persons outside the community, here designated *faithless*.

Traditionally, church leaders interpreted the "unequal yoke" in this text to mean the marriage between believers and unbelievers. The latter were often subjected to further specification beyond the text. As it stands, the prohibition is not restricted in this way. Partnership of any sort—business, marriage, cultural, religious, political—beyond that of the confessing community is stridently ruled out. The five rhetorical questions, all of them expecting a negative answer, seek to persuade the readers that human society is bipolar: persons are either in the covenant community of God or they are outside the community. Persons in one or the other cannot be party to both at the same time.

For what partnership is there between righteousness and lawlessness? Here as nowhere else in Paul's letters, righteousness is equated with law observance. *Lawlessness* characterizes outsiders who put no stock in the law of God observed in the community. The question of *light* versus *darkness* (2 Cor. 6:14b) further enforces the stark partitioning of human society (similar to the Jewish attitude and imagery in the Qumran scrolls). The juxtaposition of *Christ* and *Beliar* (6:15) is peculiar to this text within the NT. As a metaphysical figure, Beliar appears in Jewish texts, particularly the Dead Sea Scrolls (Fitzmyer, 1971:205-217), as the chief opponent of the lawgiving Creator God.

The fourth question in the text, *What does a believer share with an unbeliever* (6:15b)? may seem anticlimactic after the pointedness of the first three. It is so only as long as *believer* and *unbeliever* are construed as open-ended terms. But when these two opposing adjectives are understood as a *faithful person* and a *faithless person,* a more restricted meaning emerges. The *faithful person* observes the law of God in covenant community with fellow members; the *faithless person* disregards the law of God espoused by the covenant community.

In this understanding, the fourth question is closely related to the final one, *What agreement has the temple of God with idols?* (6:16a). Here *the temple of God* refers to the Jewish temple of Jerusalem, as opposed to Gentile shrines that house idols. The traditional Jewish temple is then extended typologically beyond the question to mean the living community of faith, occupied by *the living God* (6:16b).

The series of short statements (6:16b-18) is taken from cultic texts of the Greek Bible of the synagogue (LXX: Lev. 26:12; Ezek. 37:27; Isa. 52:11; Ezek. 20:34; 2 Sam. 7:14). They undergird the intent of the rhetorical questions and establish the central theme of the unit as a whole. God promises to live within the faithful community and call its members his children as long as they maintain separateness and ethical, religious purity.

The unit concludes with an exhortation in the first person plural, *let us* (2 Cor. 7:1; cf. 6:14, the command to *[you],* pl.), drawn from the chain of ideas in the quoted Scriptures. Fulfillment of God's promises to the community requires cleansing from defilement *of body* (lit.: *flesh*) and *of spirit.* Complete holiness calls for separation from that which defiles. This is the goal *in the fear of the Lord* (7:1).

Inherent Questions

Careful readers have noticed the distinctive character of this text, both in language and in thought, and its abrupt intrusion into the thought of 6:13. They have raised a number of crucial questions of interpretation. All of them may be conveniently subsumed under these two: (1) What is the origin of 6:14—7:1 as it stands in 2 Corinthians? (2) How does one explain its place and purpose within the context of 2 Corinthians 6? Both of these questions are addressed in some detail in an essay *[The "Unequal Yoke" Passage, p. 281].*

THE TEXT IN BIBLICAL CONTEXT

The essay [The "Unequal Yoke" Passage, p. 281] demonstrates that
2 Corinthians 6:14—7:1 was not written at the same time as the rest
of 2 Corinthians 1-9, and it seems not to have been written originally
by Paul. The passage was probably incorporated into the present
form of 2 Corinthians when Paul's letters were collected.

At first glance, the wisdom of incorporating the fragment at that
particular point in 2 Corinthians may seem strange. Yet where better
to balance Paul's unrestricted vision of reconciliation (5:18-21) with
covenant theology than at the very point where he opens wide his
heart to willful Gentile converts? When Paul's writings were collected
and compiled, some Gentile churches had carried Paul's freedom in
the Spirit apart from the law to an extreme. Sensing the need to balance Paul's gospel, the compiler inserted this text of Jewish-Christian
origin at a point where Paul's gospel is most vulnerable. He has
opened his heart wide to a Gentile congregation of questionable
moral character.

The foregoing is a hypothesis in the search to understand the significance and context of this piece of ethical instruction within Paul's
Letter of Reconciliation. One can argue that Paul simply stopped in
the middle of his reconciling address, added this exclusivistic injunction without any connecting word or thought, and then immediately
thereafter returned to conclude his message of reconciliation. It is not
plausible to call this move on Paul's part an excursus. An excursus
happens when an idea within an argument prompts expansion of
that idea, rather than the ongoing development of the argument. By
that definition, this text of 6:14—7:1 is not an excursus but an insertion. Nothing in the argument preceding or following the injunction
connects with the unique words and ideas inside the injunction.
Moreover, this unique text looks more like an insertion during the
compiling and canonizing of Paul's letters. That view does not make
this text less important. It stands in the canon and is therefore authoritative.

THE TEXT IN THE LIFE OF CHURCH

All of the earliest existing manuscripts of 2 Corinthians (late second
century) have the text of 6:14—7:1 in its present place. One may
reasonably infer, therefore, that this text had long been used in public
and private instruction and found easy (and early) access into the

church's authoritative writings of the NT (as compared to the epistle of James, for example).

Radical Christians in the sixteenth-century Reformation identified strongly with the sentiment in this text. They separated themselves from the structures and practices of the Roman Catholic Church, which they considered immoral (such as indulgences, infant baptism, the mass, adoration of images). Menno Simons alluded to this text of 2 Corinthians:

> These words of Paul are plain and intelligible, and it is therefore utterly impossible that those . . . who have become a fit temple of the Lord, . . . should once more be at one with darkness, with Belial, with unrighteousness, with infidels and idolaters. . . . Their doctrines, sacraments, church service, and life are fundamentally false and spurious. . . . How can you again be joined to them and say yes to their abominations? (Menno: 609)

When a Roman Catholic examiner asked Hans de Vette why he had "not continued in the faith of the Roman church," he replied with the help of this text from 2 Corinthians 6: "I . . . separated from her so as not to become a partaker of her plagues, since darkness can have no communion with light, nor Christ with Belial, nor the righteous with the unrighteous, etc. Hence we must come out from among her" (*MM:* 620).

Some groups of Anabaptists, such as communites of Amish and Hutterites, find support for their radical separation from society in this text. Their members marry those in fellowship with their people, and their children are educated in the confines of their covenant community.

Most churches, however, do not interpret this text to mean physical withdrawal from the social and cultural world, but from what they consider immoral practices going on outside the church (cf. 1 Cor. 5:10). Of course, various Christian communions differ in their interpretations of morality. For example, some Christian churches find it morally appropriate for a nation to go to war against another nation for "the cause of peace," while other churches view war efforts as destructive to human life and therefore morally wrong in light of the gospel. Peace churches have therefore sought to separate themselves from a political system that supports military killing of human beings. Hence, they refuse to join the military and in some cases refuse to pay taxes.

Gordon Fee argues that 2 Corinthians 6:14—7:1 above all warns the community against participation in idol worship (1977:140-161).

Even though his reading of the text limits its scope too much, his point is well taken. In Judaism, idolatry was considered the number-one sin against God. Yet idolatry was prevalent and obvious in the surrounding world. Complete separation from idolatry constituted a notable mark of loyalty to the will of the *living God*. That attitude carried over into Christianity.

Idols come in many forms and guises. Humans beings shape reality and meaning into fixed structures and proceed to live within those structures. When the structures, whatever form they take, are treated as ultimate reality, they become idolatrous. The process of making idols is subtle, and it even happens within the church. Denominationalism, for example, can become an idol, as can marriage, property, education, career, clothing. But the most subtle form of idolatry is in the realm of ideas. When ideas, religious or otherwise, are construed as universally fixed reality, they become idols. Believers in the life-giving God of the universe are instructed in this text not to yoke themselves with the structures of the world that function in opposition to the will of God. Structures in themselves are not idols; they become idols by human imagination and will that are separated from the redemptive will of God.

Titus's Positive Report: Retrospect and Prospect

2 Corinthians 7:5-16

PREVIEW

Paul has defended his ministry of reconciliation on theological and moral grounds (2:14—7:4). So now he resumes the matter of his own personal relationship with the community at Corinth (7:5-16), introduced in chapter 2 (2:1-13). The history of that relationship has been at Corinth carries a powerful punch. It is situated at the end of a long argument about the authenticity of Paul's ministry (2:14—7:4) and at the beginning of a fervent appeal to complete the collection for Jerusalem (8:1—9:15). Its refrain of joy, upon hearing the news from Corinth, functions as a threshold to the appeal for the collection in chapter 8. "A conciliatory tone at this point is politic, prior to the plea in chap. 8 for a renewal of effort in respect of the collection" (Thrall, 1994:478).

One might call the form of the text "a narrative of confident joy." Yet it is not a simple story about Titus's report of goodwill at Corinth, his feeling toward the Corinthians, and Paul's response to the report. Charged with theological and emotional significance (not to mention syntactical difficulty), the narrative functions as a confidence builder. One wonders, How can any reasonable Corinthian Christian refuse the appeal of one who says in conclusion, *I rejoice, because I have complete confidence in you* (7:16)?

Paul's **narration** about Titus and about his own elated response to the news comes in two stages. Between the first and second stage, Paul offers an **explanation** of the hurt he (Paul) caused the Corinthians by that "regrettable" letter concerning their attitude toward the wrongdoer. The analysis in the outline below illustrates this structure of the passage.

OUTLINE

Narrative 1: Paul Rejoices in the Positive Report, 7:5-7

Paul's Perspective on the "Regrettable" Letter, 7:8-13a

Narrative 2: Titus's Joy and Paul's Confidence, 7:13b-16

EXPLANATORY NOTES

Narrative 1: Paul Rejoices in the Positive Report   7:5-7

Mention of Macedonia in verse 5 immediately recalls the short note at 2:13. Yet this narrative in chapter 7 has a literary world of its own quite apart from Paul's earlier word about his time in Macedonia. At this point he recalls a state of fatigue in Macedonia with no recourse to rest. *Our bodies* (lit.: *flesh*) *had no rest*, he says. His physical being has limited energy, like all things physical. In Paul's case, his mission has brought with it exhaustion from being *afflicted in every way*. Forms of this word *afflicted* recur in 2 Corinthians with deliberate intensity, as here (cf. 1:4, 6, 8; 4:8; 6:4). Here the term is qualified by two balanced phrases, *disputes without and fears within*. The external disputes are not hard to understand. Paul's preaching has conflicted with authorities on both sides of his mission, Jewish and Gentile (cf. Acts 16–17).

The internal fears are more difficult to comprehend. Can he mean "states of depression, perhaps caused by illness" (Hering: 54)? This suggestion cannot be dismissed out of hand. Paul has just stated that he has had no rest for his physical being; exhaustion can lead to emotional collapse. Nevertheless, taken as belonging to the argument as a whole, the *fears within* are probably those related to the state of relations between himself and the Corinthians. Have they abandoned his apostolic authority in favor of another? For Paul, that was a great inner fear related to his divine calling as an apostle of Jesus Christ.

As always in Paul's narrative statements, the principal actor is God. So here, *God who consoles the downcast, consoled us by the arrival of Titus* (7:6). The context dictates the translation *downcast* rather than "humble," although "humble" is a strong connotation of the Greek word (Louw, 1:748; cf. Matt. 11:29). God consoles the humble and resists the proud (James 4:6). Paul views the arrival of Titus not as a matter of chance in an uncontrolled universe, but in standard prophetic style, as a divinely ordered event.

The arrival of Titus itself encouraged Paul, as the personal presence (*parousia*, coming) of a beloved friend and colleague does. But more than that, Titus's good news about the church at Corinth multiplies Paul's joyous consolation (7:7). Here Paul shifts into the first person singular, as he does periodically in subsequent verses. Thus in effect he says, "Your encouragement was not only to Titus and by extension to me; it was to me personally." On the other hand, it is possible that by his use of the first person singular, Paul wants "to exempt his associates from any involvement" in the cause of the grief at Corinth (Furnish, 1984:397).

Paul then summarizes Titus's report about the Corinthians' devotion to him in three striking words, *longing, mourning,* and *zeal.* The first of these Paul seems to interpret as their desire to renew their relationship with him, or perhaps their desire to have him return to them at Corinth. The *mourning*, related no doubt to the *repentance* of 7:9, he probably understands as their regret at allowing the offense against him in their community. And their *zeal* he may be taking as their positive enthusiasm to participate in the collection for Jerusalem (although *zeal* can have negative connotations, as in jealousy). However rightly Paul has interpreted these words from Titus's report, he *rejoiced still more* when he heard them.

Paul may have misconstrued Titus's report, since chapters 10–13 show the Corinthians' rather halting support of Paul. On the other hand, Paul is not merely recounting facts for their own sake. Instead, he puts them into honed language aimed at securing a favorable response to a request. Numerous parallels to this form of address exist in the Hellenistic world in which Paul lives. "Like other Hellenistic writers, Paul makes use of expressions of confidence in his addressees to undergird the purpose of his letter, by increasing the likelihood of a favorable hearing" (Olson: 295). That this text conforms to such a genre is beyond dispute.

Paul's aim in writing chapters 1 to 9 is at least twofold: (1) to restore the confidence of Corinthians in his person and apostolate (chapters 1-6), and (2) to persuade them to collect the money for Jerusalem (chapters 8-9). As with other texts of this kind, the expression of confidence in 2 Corinthians 7 comes at the critical juncture after Paul's defense of his person and ministry ("self-praise" in the service of God) and before launching his appeal for the collection for Jerusalem. Given this persuasive function, moreover, "such expressions must be used with great caution when trying to reconstruct the relationship between the writer and his readers" (Olson: 295).

Paul's Perspective on the "Regrettable" Letter 7:8-13a

Something in the report from Titus has led Paul to resurrect the matter of a letter that brought pain to the Corinthians. The report apparently has intimated how the Corinthians were hurt by Paul's rebuke of their behavior. In the present context of 2 Corinthians 1-9, Paul's "expression of confidence" aimed at their compliance requires from Paul an explanation of the purpose of the letter that caused them grief. Even in this explanation of a difficult point in the report, Paul attempts to turn the event in question into an occasion for praising the Corinthians. This literary blend is not an easy one for Paul, and it shows in the awkwardness of the text's structure. (Assuming that Paul had someone else write his letters for him, one can imagine how difficult it must have been for a scribe to put Paul's dictation of such a delicate matter into the desired literary form!)

Verse 8 is perhaps the most difficult part of the explanation to unravel, its structure being "grammatically intolerable" (Barrett, 1973:209). The NRSV, like many other versions, has tried to solve the problem by putting part of the statement inside parentheses. This strategy may lead readers to consider the bracketed part to be of little importance. Paul probably expects the thought behind the bracketed English words to be vital to his explanation in the Greek text, which lacks the parentheses. The NRSV of verse 8 reads: *For even if I made you sorry with my letter, I do not regret it (though I did regret it, for I see that I grieved you with that letter, though only briefly).*

Paul's statement has three conditional elements (*ei kai*, 7:8a; *ei kai*, 7:8b; and *ei kai*, 7:8c), each one in tandem with the other. The NRSV translates the first of these *even if*, places the second and third within the parentheses, and translates both of the bracketed conditions *though*. Paul's *regret* of 7:8a is present indicative, expressing present time. The *regret* of 7:8b is imperfect indicative and the *pain* of 7:8c is aorist indicative, both tenses expressing time past. Another problem arises in the verb *I see*. Some important manuscripts have the participle *seeing* instead of the finite verb, which alleviates the awkwardness and allows a smoother translation. But the more difficult reading in several manuscripts is probably Paul's wording, awkward as it is.

Working with these clues from the three conditions and three tenses, and joining the conditions of verse 8 with the affirmations of verse 9, Paul's thought and argument emerge without parentheses. Paul wrote a letter some time back that grieved the Corinthians; in light of Titus's report, he does *not regret* writing as he did. After he had written the letter, though, he *was regretting* (imperfect tense) having done so. In the present situation, however, he *sees* (present tense) that the grief was *short-lived* (lit.: *for an hour*), so he no longer regrets having sent the letter. Instead, he is rejoicing now (7:9). With this understanding of the syntax of 7:8-9c, the following translation is possible: *For even though I grieved you with the letter, I am not regretting it. Even if I was regretting it, even if I see that that letter brought you pain for an hour, I am now rejoicing, not because you were hurt, but because you were hurt unto repentance.*

The letter in question can hardly be other than the one referred to in 2:3-4, since both references identify the painful nature of a letter that chastised the congregation for allowing a wrongdoer to go unchecked. First Corinthians does not fit the description of this painful letter in either of these texts in 2 Corinthians. First Corinthians answers questions the Corinthians asked of Paul and addresses reports Paul received from travelers. It can hardly be described as a letter written *out of much distress and anguish of heart and with many tears* (2:4) that has caused the Corinthians *pain* (2:5; 7:8). Such a letter is not known to exist. It may have been destroyed shortly after its reception in Corinth, understandably so (Barrett, 1973:209).

The shame created by Paul's "regrettable" letter to the Corinthians presents a roadblock to his aim to have the Corinthians comply with his upcoming appeal for money in chapter 8. That obstacle must be cleared away in the minds of the Corinthians before Paul can proceed to the appeal. Verses 9 through 12 constitute that clearing away.

Paul rejoices not because they were hurt, but because the hurt led to *repentance* (7:9a). Repentance *(metanoia)* means literally a change of mind *(TDNT,* 4:1005). In this text it probably means that the Corinthians are sorry for their attitude and behavior that led Paul to discipline them in the letter. Paul rarely uses the word *repentance* (once outside 2 Cor., in Rom. 2:4), and certainly not to describe how Gentiles enter into Christ and his community. Nor is the sparse occurrence of the word merely Paul's attempt to avoid Greek intellectualism with its belief in the power of the human mind to change for the better (Windisch: 211).

Instead, Paul may have deliberately refrained from much use of the term *repentance* because of its importance for covenantal Judaism. In that pattern of religion, Gentiles were expected to "repent" of their sins before they could enter the covenant community of Israel. Paul may want to guard against a view of repentance as human achievement, of which a convert might boast. For Paul, the principle of faith in Christ relies exclusively on divine initiative for the change of heart and behavior (cf. 3:18; 4:7, 16; 5:19; Rom. 3:27).

In 2 Corinthians 7:9-10, the word *repentance* applies to Christians whose *godly grief* resulted in a change of heart. Three times in verses 9-11 Paul calls their experience upon receiving his letter a *godly grief* (lit.: *grief according to God).* That is, the grief and the resultant repentance are God's doing, not Paul's and not merely their own action. Paul knows as much because the positive effect of the letter proves as much. On this ground, Paul can say to the Corinthians, *you were not harmed in any way by us* (7:9b).

The effect of the painful letter, now evident from Titus's report, is that the Corinthians have come to see it Paul's way. They regret that they did not show him favor when someone from the community injured him in some way. Their *godly grief* that changed their minds means they are on the road to salvation again. *Salvation* in 7:10 can signify "wholeness," "well-being," "deliverance from guilt" in present experience. Genuine sorrow for their wrong attitude and behavior, accompanied by obedience to the right, leads to a healthy, integrated life. However, since Paul contrasts *godly grief* that *leads to salvation* with *worldly grief* that *produces death,* he probably means final salvation toward which Christians are moving in faith (Thrall, 1994:492). In short, the Corinthians' *godly grief* that has led to re-

pentance puts them on course again in the direction of final deliverance into the glory of God. The implication is clear. If they had continued to nurse their grief and become embittered against Paul, they
would thereby forfeit final salvation.

After exonerating himself and affirming the Corinthians in their
new stance toward him, Paul then invokes the evidence of their positive responses garnered from the report of Titus: *behold/see* (cf.
5:17; 6:2) these commendable attitudes and actions of yours! (7:11).
Each item on the list of seven stands as an exclamation of Paul's confidence in the Corinthians. The number seven probably has no more
significance than the effect of impressing upon the readers Paul's
confidence in them.

Earnestness probably relates to how they followed through with
Paul's directive in the letter; *eagerness to clear* themselves of any criticism from Paul; *indignation* at the affront; *alarm* at how the incident
threatened their life as a community; *longing* to return to a right relationship with Paul; *zeal* in trying to do so through Titus; *punishment*
of the one who did wrong. The words translated *punishment* and *the
one who did the wrong* "are terms borrowed from criminal law"
(R. Martin, 1986:236). The *punishment* can mean that Paul is
avenged of his opponent at Corinth. However, it seems reasonably
clear from chapters 2 and 7 that Paul is more concerned with the attitude of the community as a whole toward him.

As if this list were not enough to demonstrate Paul's confidence in
the Corinthians, he concludes it with a sweeping affirmation of their
innocence: *at every point you have proved yourselves guiltless in the
matter*, the case of the member injuring another. In what sense is the
congregation innocent in the matter? Paul had to write them a hurtful
letter of censure because they were anything but innocent in the matter. Furthermore, Paul has just admitted that they have worked at
clearing themselves of his charge against them. The most plausible
explanation of the inconsistency in 7:11 is that Paul is willing to de-
clare the Corinthians innocent now that they have taken action in accordance with his directive in the letter.

The *so* of 7:12 introduces a summary of the foregoing explanation by stating the purpose of the letter from the perspective of the
good report of Titus. Looking back from this new position, Paul can
say, *Although I wrote to you, it was not on account of the one who
did the wrong, nor on account of the one who was wronged, but in
order that your zeal for us might be made known to you before God*
(7:12). The identity of the one who did the wrong is impossible to de-

termine. He is not the incestuous man of 1 Corinthians 5. That man did not simply injure someone; he brought shame into the congregation by his immorality. Nor is the wrongdoer the party of 1 Corinthians 6, who took another member to an outside court. In that incident both parties were in the wrong. The narrative in 2 Corinthians about a wrongdoer represents a new incident not cited in 1 Corinthians.

Barrett proposes that an outsider entered Corinth and criticized Paul in the congregation that he had founded, with the congregation allowing it to happen unchallenged. Yet this proposal ties the wrongdoer in with the opponents of chapters 10–13 without sufficient reason (1970:149-157). If Paul recommended that the congregation discipline the person who did the wrong, then he must have been a member of the congregation. An outsider could simply walk away from discipline.

The injured person of 7:12 is not any easier to identify. Taking the evidence of chapter 2 along with that of this passage, Paul himself seems to be *the one who was wronged.* The use of the third person (rather than the first) is Paul's way of distancing himself from the incident so as to demonstrate the larger purpose behind the writing of the "regrettable" letter. In the end, now that the report of Titus is in hand, Paul can state that the purpose behind the letter was *in order that your zeal for us might be made known to you before God* (7:12).

Zeal in this purpose statement is more the idea of eagerness or even devotion (Louw, 1:298), as in verse 11, where the same Greek word (*spoudē, earnestness*) heads the list of seven laudatory nouns. According to this statement of purpose, the Corinthians were not aware of their commitment to Paul in relation to God (7:12c, *in the awareness of God*) until they acted upon the directive in Paul's distressful letter. Now their devotion to Paul is plain (to him, at least), and he is consoled (7:13a). *In this we find comfort* (7:13a) concludes Paul's explanation of the "hurtful" letter he wrote earlier. *This* is ambiguous but probably points to the statement immediately preceding about the Corinthians' awareness of their devotion to Paul as a result of the letter.

Narrative 2: Titus's Joy and Paul's Confidence   7:13b-16

With the explanation of the letter now in place, Paul astutely turns the spotlight on Titus. Titus has become Paul's worthy emissary to Corinth and will soon return there to *complete this generous undertaking* of the collection for Jerusalem (8:6). But before Paul issues the appeal in chapter 8, he seeks to establish a bond between Titus and the Corinthians and himself. Moreover, the narrative of 7:13b-16 has the effect of building the Corinthians' confidence in Titus and Paul on a par with the confidence Paul is expressing toward the Corinthians.

Paul's understanding that Titus's *mind has been set at rest* by the Corinthians (13b) implies that Titus at one time felt ill at ease about the Corinthians. How could that be, since Paul has boasted about them to him (7:14)? One solution to the puzzle in 7:13b-14 is that Titus carried the letter in question and knew its contents, and thus he knew its potential for generating an adverse reaction against Paul and himself. When Paul dispatched Titus with the letter, he may have spurred him on with words of assurance about the Corinthians. In any case, he has returned to Paul filled with contagious joy and *his mind set at rest* by the Corinthians. Paul's word translated *mind* here is *pneuma*, usually translated *spirit*. The *spirit* of Titus refers to that which energizes his whole person. His positive encounter with the Corinthians has quelled the disturbance in his being.

In the following verses, Paul matches the joyous assurance of Titus about the Corinthians with his own. What Titus has found at Corinth, Paul has already boasted about, and that without being put to shame for false boasting. This word *boasting* looms large in 2 Corinthians, probably with good reason. Critics could have accused Paul of overstating his call and apostleship, or of praising himself unduly, or of misrepresenting the gospel. Evidence of these accusations comes out more noticeably in the Letter of Defense (2 Cor. 10-13). Even here in 7:14, the word is carefully qualified: *if indeed* (7:14a) it should be called *boasting* about the Corinthians, Titus has proved my so-called boasting true, *just as everything we said to you was true.*

If Titus had proved Paul's statements false, that would have meant disgrace for Paul and would have rendered him unworthy of the gospel. Hence, the expression of confidence is a two-way street. Paul has confidence in the Corinthians; they appear to have confidence in him and his colleagues, according to Titus.

The focus on Titus sharpens again in 7:15. He holds deep feelings for the Corinthians *as he remembers the obedience of all* of them, and how they *welcomed him with fear and trembling*. In the context of the passage, the *obedience* is specifically their compliance with Paul's directive in the letter on the *punishment* of the wrongdoer. In his sense of apostleship, of which he is profoundly aware, Paul expected his converts to follow his guidance. His word as God's minister of world reconciliation (5:20) is tantamount to being the word of God to them. *Obedience* to the gospel is the only true expression of faith.

To say that *all* obeyed is surprising, except that *all* in this expression of confidence is probably hyperbole. The sense is that Titus was impressed with the groundswell of compliance with Paul's demands, and with their welcome *in fear and trembling*—a phrase used exclusively by Paul in the NT (1 Cor. 2:3; Phil. 2:12; cf. Eph. 6:5; Isa. 19:16). The phrase can signal profound respect on the part of the Corinthians for Paul and his co-worker Titus. Paul earlier referred to his own "fear and trembling" when he arrived in Corinth (1 Cor. 2:3). It was not "a nervous anxiety to do his duty" (Plummer: 228), but a profound consciousness of the call of God on his life. "The phrase occurs in the LXX to indicate the attitude of [one] in face of the numinous" (Thrall, 1994:500).

Paul has used the phrase in this sense at Corinth, and he is now interpreting the Corinthians' reception of Titus in the same way. They have demonstrated deep concern about their relationship to God with respect to Paul. To disobey Paul is to disobey God and jeopardize their status as a community of faith in Christ on the way to salvation. In this context the idea of "alarm" is possible for *fear and trembling*. They are "alarmed" that they could lose their status by their disobedience to Paul's counsel (Bruce: 219).

Paul brings crisp closure to his extended statement of confidence in his audience at Corinth: *I rejoice, because I have complete confidence in you* (7:16). Was his complete confidence misplaced? In light of his strong disapproval of the Corinthians' attitude in the last four chapters of 2 Corinthians, apparently it was.

THE TEXT IN BIBLICAL CONTEXT

One of the leading ideas in 2 Corinthians 7:5-16 is that Paul is *consoled* (7:6) by the arrival of Titus, fortified in spirit to move forward. Various forms of the Greek word *parakaleō* (to console) appear prominently in the opening narrative (7:6-7), at the close of the explanation of the letter (7:13a), and at the introduction of the second narrative (7:13b). On the basis of being consoled and fortified by the good report of Titus, Paul passes along a vote of confidence to the Corinthians.

In the context of the Corinthian correspondence, this consolation means a great deal to Paul. His relationship with that community was frequently in the balance. Factions were rife (1 Cor. 3), immorality permitted (1 Cor. 5), the Lord's Supper perverted (1 Cor. 8-10), the future resurrection denied (1 Cor. 15), and the collection for Jerusalem in the balance (16:1-4). In addition, someone in the community offended him seriously, probably by repudiating his person or preaching or both. That offense led to the painful letter that Paul regretted having to write (2 Cor. 2:1-4; 7:8-13a). Titus may have delivered the letter and while there found the Corinthians (at least a majority of them) ready to obey Paul's demand. They disciplined the person who injured him.

With that sign of allegiance to his message in the report of Titus, Paul is consoled, encouraged, fortified. To lose the Corinthian community would constitute a serious blow to Paul's self-understanding as God's end-time minister of reconciliation. A short time later, Paul's consolation turned into dismay when he learned that the Corinthians doubted that Christ was really speaking through him (13:3).

In the larger biblical context, Paul's note about God consoling him at a point of weakness is anchored firmly in the prophetic tradition, particularly in the Servant tradition of Isaiah. The Servant Song in Isaiah 49:13 (LXX) heralds the same words to the exiled people of Israel in Babylon: "God has shown mercy to his people and has consoled the humble of his people." This part of Isaiah draws on the tradition of the Exodus to encourage the exiles in Babylon to trust in the Lord, who delivers the oppressed (48:10, 17, 20). Paul in his downcast state is likewise fortified by the same God who consoles the downcast. His body *had no rest, . . . afflicted in every way—disputes without and fears within* (2 Cor. 7:5). His relations with the Corinthians were at a low ebb. Yet Paul could identify with the Servant of Isaiah in his circumstance, "I have labored in vain, I have spent my strength for nothing and vanity; yet surely my cause is with the Lord, and my reward with my God" (Isa. 49:4).

Paul's phrase, *God, who consoles,* takes an interesting turn by the time the Gospel of John and the epistle of 1 John are written. In the passion discourses of the Fourth Gospel, the Spirit of truth, whom the resurrected Jesus will send, is called the *paraklētos,* one who consoles, encourages, comforts the bereaved (John 14:16, 26; 15:26; 16:7). Then in 1 John 2:1 the resurrected Christ himself is referred as the *paraklētos,* the "advocate" who pleads the case of the offender as in a court. In both of these texts, the Johannine writer (or writers) transforms Paul's participle (*ho parakalōn, who consoles,* 2 Cor. 7:6) into a substantive title (*paraklētos*) for the divine Spirit of Christ that consoles the helpless.

THE TEXT IN THE LIFE OF THE CHURCH

This text has received less attention in the life of the church than it deserves. Yet its lessons are manifold: it speaks to the church's attitude toward members who insult and injure others; the character and purpose of godly repentance; the agency of a Christian colleague in bringing divine benediction; building confidence in the church; receiving God's consoling strength.

The last of these "lessons" runs through the literary landscape of 2 Corinthians like a stream down a mountain. Divine strength is made perfect in human weakness (12:9; cf. 1:8-11; 4:7-12; 7:4; 8:9). Commenting on Paul's description of God as one *who consoles the downcast* (7:6), John Calvin wrote, "The more we have been afflicted, so much the greater consolation has been prepared for us by God. Hence, in the epithet here applied to God, there is a choice promise contained, . . . that it is peculiarly the part of God to comfort those that are miserable and are abased to the dust" (2:270).

God's consolation comes to the downcast in various ways. Raphel Van Den Velde, imprisoned for his nonconformist confession, wrote to his wife from his cell in response to her letter of encouragement to him. "My heart was greatly comforted and rejoiced, so that for joy I could not refrain from weeping; which was a sure sign of godly sorrow, and the same worketh to salvation" (*MM:* 1027). Sustaining encouragement of this kind comes from God through people of true faith and compassion. Titus was the channel through whom God's consoling grace flowed to Paul.

Not all downcast people are in prisons or in hospitals or in refugee camps. Many are within the church membership, some of them hiding their feeling in fear of recrimination of one sort or another. Still many others in church have good news and good spirit, like that of Titus upon his return from Corinth. When these good souls join hand and heart with the downcast in the church, as Titus did with Paul, God's consolation flows freely to its target. Then the congregation can rejoice together.

Variation 3: Equity Through a Financial "Gift of Blessing"

OVERVIEW

In his third major variation on the theme of Christian ministry in 2 Corinthians 8-9, Paul turns the spotlight away from his own ministry to a ministry belonging to the Corinthians. In particular, he appeals to them to complete the collection of money (without mentioning the term) for the saints in Jerusalem. They have begun the process some time before (*last year*, 8:10) but have apparently lagged behind in completing the project. Now Paul encourages them to complete it, so that he will have an offering from them when he goes to Jerusalem in the near future.

Not wanting to be seen as using his apostolic authority in this delicate matter, Paul rather makes several appeals for the completion of the collection. He insists all the while that the gift must spring from their own voluntary generosity. He appeals first to the *grace of God* (8:1), then to the example of the Macedonians, how they gave joyfully out of their poverty (8:2-6). Paul mentions the gifts already in effect at Corinth in the absence of this gift for Jerusalem (8:7); the Christ of God, who divested himself to enrich the Corinthians (8:9); and the Scripture about the collecting of manna for a *fair balance* among the people of God (8:14-15). In addition to these appeals to stimulate the collection, Paul recommends his partner and co-worker Titus and two unnamed brothers from the churches to collect the gift in trust for Jerusalem (8:16-24).

Chapter 9 revisits the earlier appeal (chap. 8), a practice not uncommon with Paul in making a case (as in 1 Cor. 7; between 1 Cor. 8 and 10; cf. Rom. 6:12-14, 15-19). What appears as repetitive appeal in 2 Corinthians 9 is actually a reworking of the form of appeal advanced in chapter 8. This is not to say that the two chapters represent two distinct letters written at different times to the churches in Achaia and Corinth (Betz, 1985:38-41, 88-90, 129-140). The two appeals more probably arise out of the same occasion, forming a parallel structure. The first appeal is forceful, direct, and somewhat critical. The second is modulated, implicit, and complementary. Paul may have set out to create this parallelism, or he may have decided on it after reading back over the strong and rather critical appeal of chapter 8. In this latter case, he would not discard the first appeal now written, but add to it to soften the blow, so to speak.

Together the two appeals for the collection constitute another variation on the theme of ministry: the Corinthians (and other Gentile Christians) serve God by giving financially to equalize and unify the church. In preparation for this variation on the theme in 2 Corinthians 8 and 9, Paul has told the story of his joy, when he came to Macedonia, at hearing the good report of the Corinthians from Titus (7:5-7). He has praised the Corinthians for their *eagerness* to do right (7:5-16). Picking up the key word *eagerness* (8:7-8) and the reference to Macedonia (8:1), Paul now proceeds with his appeal for the Corinthians to complete the collection for *the saints* (8:4).

OUTLINE

Collection Encouraged, Collectors Commended, 8:1-24

A Second Appeal for the Collection, 9:1-15

Collection Encouraged,
Collectors Commended
2 Corinthians 8:1-24

PREVIEW

The collection of money from the Gentile congregations for the "saints at Jerusalem" (Rom. 15:26) is not an incidental matter in the ministry of Paul. The subject surfaces variously in his four principal letters (Gal. 2:10; 1 Cor. 16:1-4; 2 Cor. 8-9; Rom. 15:25-28), and nowhere more poignantly than in the present passage (2 Cor. 8:1-24). However practical the funds will be in helping *the poor* in Jerusalem, Paul no doubt has mapped the purpose for the collection on a larger canvas. The collection constitutes a symbolic forging of unity between Paul's uncircumcised Gentile congregations and the parent Jewish-Christian enclave in the Holy City. In Paul's view, both groups participate equally in the grace of God in Jesus Christ. Their solidarity in the grace of Christ signals the approaching end of the age for Paul. "His pilgrimage to Jerusalem, bearing gifts from the [Gentiles], reflects the prophetic picture of the last days (Isa. 2:2-5; 60:5-22; Micah 4), as the rabbis believed" (R. Martin, 1986:258).

Moreover, the monetary gift from Corinth will speak loudly on four counts: (1) about the spirit of the Corinthians, (2) about Paul's commitment to the history of salvation epitomized in Jewish Jerusalem, (3) about the full participation of Gentiles in the community of Christ, and (4) about the eschatological gathering of the Gentiles to Zion. Each of these factors is documented and developed in the essay *[The Collection, p. 264]* (see also Nickle: 100-143; Munk: 282-308).

At the center of Paul's appeal to complete the collection stands the grace of God in the gift of eternal life (Rom. 6:23; Käsemann, 1964:64). This word *charis* (used ten times in 2 Cor. 8-9) can be translated *gift, generosity,* or *grace* (8:1). The idea of spiritual giftedness has seized the Corinthians' mind-set, as evidenced in 1 Corinthians 12-14 especially. Paul now presses *charis* into the service of completing the collection before he sets out for Jerusalem. Rich in material goods, rich in spiritual gifts (*charismata*), the Corinthians are called to account for their lack in completing this *gift.*

Using the paradoxical example of the impoverished Macedonians giving joyfully out of their limited means, Paul implicitly shames the

Corinthians into completing their appointed task out of their material abundance. They are to do so voluntarily, but Paul nevertheless employs a variety of handy linguistic forms to persuade them thus. As if that were not enough, he sends representatives ahead of him to assist in achieving the goal.

The three-person embassy includes Paul's representative Titus and two unnamed *brothers* (8:18, 22) representing the churches (presumably of Macedonia). The three are recommended thus by this letter (chapters 1-9, which the delegates probably carry with them to Corinth; cf. 3:1). They have been commissioned to assist in the collection and then to act as security guards with Paul en route to Jerusalem (8:16-24).

OUTLINE

Example of God's Grace in Macedonian Churches, 8:1-6

The Collection Added to List of Gracious Gifts, 8:7-8

The Gift Behind All Gifts, 8:9

Acceptable Balance and Solidarity, 8:10-15

Representatives Recommended, 8:16-24

EXPLANATORY NOTES
Example of God's Grace in Macedonian Churches 8:1-6

At the heart of Paul's appeal for generosity (*charis*, 8:7b) on the part of the Corinthians stands the generosity of God (8:1). Eternal life for mortal beings can only be a grace-gift, a *charis*-gift from the immortal God (Rom. 6:23). "Other charismata [spiritual gifts] only exist because of the existence of this one charisma to which they are all related" (Käsemann, 1964:64). Hence, Paul opens his appeal by setting forth the example of the Macedonian churches. He does not set up the Macedonian Christians as superior to the Corinthians by reason of location, prosperity, or birth. They have *overflowed in a wealth of generosity* (2 Cor. 8:2b) solely through the *charis*-grace of God bestowed upon them.

This central feature of the grace of God among the Macedonian churches gives the example its real poignancy. By their generous gift of money for *the saints* (8:4), the Macedonians have demonstrated their relationship to God, whose gift of life they enjoy. By comparison, the Corinthians, who delight in *charismata* (spiritual gifts; cf. 8:7; 1 Cor. 12-14; 1:7), have failed thus far to demonstrate the central gift of God by their financial gift to Jerusalem.

Paul cites the *severe ordeal of affliction* and the *extreme poverty* out of which the Macedonians have given their share (and more) of the collection (2 Cor. 8:2). The paradox of *abundant joy* in *extreme poverty* is not unlike the power-in-weakness paradox that crops up at various points in 2 Corinthians. We assume that the Corinthians are comparatively wealthy, as the available evidence seems to prove (Murphy-O'Connor, 1983:53-54; Rostovtzeff: 65, 132-133, 482-483). So the example of the impoverished Macedonians, who have given voluntarily *even beyond their means* (8:3b), and that with eager joy (8:2, 4), carries a powerful punch.

One wonders whether Paul, in citing this example of generosity from the poor Macedonians to the Christians of "wealthy Corinth," implies that a surplus of goods blocks the overflow of the gift of God. Perhaps he hints that it is harder for rich Christians to give out of their wealth than for poor Christians to give out of their poverty, or that poor Christians demonstrate a greater measure of the grace of God (cf. Mark 12:41-44). Paul's paradoxical example does not answer such questions from the Corinthians (or from any other reader).

Several terms of reference in the example passage (2 Cor. 8:1-5) call for comment. First, the Macedonians are said to have given *voluntarily* (8:3). This word appears only in this chapter: at 8:3, "with the implication of choice" (Louw: 1:297) the Macedonians had in giving; and again at 8:17, implying the same for Titus in returning to Corinth to collect their offering. Otherwise the word does not appear in the NT. With these two examples of willing hearts before them, the Corinthians are being pushed to ask themselves about the state of their own hearts. On this matter Paul must steer clear of any sign of heavy-handedness, such as applying apostolic authority, for which he may have been criticized at Corinth. The most he can do is to apply his powers of persuasion (cf. 8:8).

Second, the collection for Jerusalem is said to be a *ministry* (8:4). Paul has used the word repeatedly in defense of his work among the Gentiles (2 Cor. 1-7). Now the same word is applied to the collection of money from the Corinthians for *the saints*. At heart, the word connotes service, "often of a humble or menial nature" (Louw, 1:460). In this context it can imply that the Gentile church is rendering a service to the Jewish church in the sacred center of historic salvation. But Paul does not develop the idea here, as he does, for example, in Romans 9–11 (cf. 15:25-29). On the other hand, this *ministry* of gathering money to send to others simply demonstrates the grace of God in Jesus Christ, as 2 Corinthians 8:9 is intended to prove. A *ministry* that fails to bring life and well-being to others is unworthy of Christian confession.

Third, the ministry is for *the saints* (8:4b). Who are these people so designated? Used in this context, as also in the context of Romans 15:25, *the saints* implies something more than "Christians" in the general sense (so Hering: 58). The Greek word *saints* (a plural adjective used as a noun) can refer to people in a community of faith in Christ; Paul does employ the term in this way (e.g., 2 Cor. 1:1). But when he designates a group as *the saints* within a situation-specific argument, he seems to attach a certain cultic notion to the corporate membership of the group (Procksch: 108), not unlike the cult of the people of Israel. Such a communion of *the saints* implies a cultic separateness from the profane in their sacrifice of praise of God. Yet "the focus is not upon a particular state of holiness, but upon a special relationship with God" (Louw, 1:125).

So here in the context of 2 Corinthians 8:4, *the saints* are assumed to belong to a special class for whom the collection is intended. Without further definition of the recipients of the collection in chapters 8 and 9, the Corinthians know who *the saints* are. Earlier Paul has informed them of their identity (cf. 1 Cor. 16:3). *The saints* in this context are to be identified with those of Romans 15:26: they live "at Jerusalem" and they are "the poor" (cf. Gal. 2:10).

Living in Jerusalem, *the saints* probably speak Aramaic and have kept close ties to the temple and to the teaching of the elders of the people. But at the same time they are also believers in the messiahship of the resurrected Jesus. As such, they are allied to Paul (at least from Paul's perspective). But Paul also refers to them elsewhere as "the poor" (Rom. 15:26; Gal. 2:10). As such, they appear to be impoverished, either by circumstances in Judea brought on by the preaching of the Jesus as Messiah, or by famine of some sort (Hughes: 283-284). More likely, though, "the poor" is an "honorific religious title" (Bornkamm: 40-41) given to those who surrendered their personal property and creature comforts for the sake of the community of faith. Collected for *the saints* at Jerusalem, the gift to them becomes a kind of votive offering to God (van Straaten: 78-104), and a sign of solidarity with the faithful remnant of Israel.

Fourth, the Macedonians receive praise as a model in giving themselves *first to the Lord, and, by the will of God, to us.* That the Macedonians should have given themselves to Paul seems strange. The terminology "to give oneself" connotes sacrifice or a form of reverent devotion, as is clear from the first instance: *they gave themselves to the Lord.* Nor should the first phrase be separated from the second, as the NRSV has tended to do in its translation. The *giving* was not in two stages, first to the Lord and then second to Paul (Hughes: 290). The two phrases *to the Lord* and *to us* stand together under the single verb *they gave.* This shows that when the Macedonians gave themselves to the Lord, they simultaneously gave themselves to Paul. The significance of *first (to the Lord)* is not sequence but priority. First and foremost, they gave themselves to the Lord and to us, and that *by the will of God.* Having thus given themselves to the Lord and to his minister, the gift of money for the saints flowed joyfully from their hearts and hands.

Immediately at 2 Corinthians 8:6 and in a rather peculiar sentence structure (Moule, 1982:160-161), Paul moves the example over to the reality of the moment: the urgency for Titus to complete what he has started at Corinth *last year* (8:6, 10). Upon seeing the devotion of the Macedonians, Paul was led "to appoint" Titus (Betz: 54, 71) *so he should also complete this generous undertaking among you.* The idea of appointing Titus is not too strong in this context, even though Paul uses the word *parakalesai,* which frequently means "encourage" or *urge* (8:6). Titus is Paul's partner in the gospel (perhaps junior partner?), not subject to a vote from the churches for carrying out an assignment, as were the two brothers who accompanied him to Corinth (8:18-19, 22-23). So Titus is to represent Paul in an "official" capacity. In this sense, therefore, he is mandated to carry out the task, not merely encouraged.

The Collection Added to List of Gracious Gifts 8:7-8

At 8:7 the form of Paul's appeal shifts from the Macedonian example to an appreciation of gifts the Corinthians hold in high esteem. Paul's aim is to make the gift of the collection equal to the other gifts, and to move the Corinthians to make up their deficiency in giving. Having urged them thus, Paul quickly safeguards his argument from the charge of lording it over the Corinthians. He makes a concession in 8:8 to the Corinthians' freedom of conscience on the matter (a concession rather than self-correction of 8:7).

Verse 7 contains a list of six endowments strung together by the connective *and*, grouped in terms of two triads:

Group 1	Group 2
faith (pistis)	*utmost eagerness (spoudē)*
speech (logos)	*love (agapē)*
knowledge (gnōsis)	*generous undertaking (charis)*

The three in group 1 are endowments well-known to the Corinthians, in which they *excel.* Nor does Paul criticize them here for having these gifts in abundance, although he does chide them in other correspondence for their immature faith (1 Cor. 2:5; 13:13; 15:14, 17; 16:13; 2 Cor. 4:13; 5:7; 10:15; 13:5). *Faith* is doubtless related to the channeling of divine power for the performance of miraculous acts, while *speech* is the powerful word that accompanies faith. *Knowledge* likewise relates to divine power in that the person of faith knows (experiences) the mystery of the power of God and can deploy the powers of spiritual insight. In all of these, the Corinthians *excel.*

The other three in group 2, however, Paul qualifies in an ascending order, the last one receiving something of an imperative force. Each of them admits an administrative or relational character, and all of them together are relevant to the issue at hand, the completion of the collection. *Utmost eagerness* has come up already in connection with the corrective measure toward the wrongdoer (2 Cor. 7:11). The word carries the idea of efficiency in carrying out a worthy task, and of the "rightness" of such speedy dispatch (G. Harder: 559-568). The connection of this endowment with Paul's aim in chapter 8 is clear.

Similarly, *love (agapē)* ties in tightly with the act of giving of one's self, including possessions, for the sake of the other. The construction of the phrase in which the word occurs is puzzling. The NRSV, following the oldest and quite reliable manuscript, reads, *and in our love for you.* Some copyists reversed the syntax: *in your love for us.* The latter simplifies the wording and is therefore less likely to be original to Paul. Literally, the Greek behind the NRSV says, *in the love from us among* (or: *in*) *you.* The phrase implies that the Corinthians possess the quality of love that they witnessed in Paul when he ministered at Corinth. He gave himself to them unreservedly. Now he credits them with the same love.

The third endowment in group 2, which exists in concert with the other two in the same group, is designated simply *charis, generous undertaking.* In the context of chapter 8, *charis* means the generous act of giving material means to assist *the saints.* If the other two, zealous efficiency and self-giving love, are operative in the hearts of the community, then there will be charity as well. Indeed, the purpose for zeal and love is charity (*charis*; Georgi, 1965:60), as Paul's qualifying phrase strongly suggests (more so than the NRSV dash indicates): *so we want you to excel also in this generous undertaking*. This kind of statement beginning with *so* has a certain imperatival (command) force in this context (Furnish, 1984:403). But essentially this connective *so* in a sentence like this indicates purpose or result. In short, by putting these three endowments together in this way, Paul is leading the Corinthians to conclude that if they wish to lay claim to the first two gifts, as they doubtless do since they believe they *excel in everything* (8:7a; cf. 1 Cor. 1:7), they must claim the third. Yet they cannot claim the third, the *charis*, the *generous undertaking*, until they actually take up the collection for the saints.

Paul has more or less cornered the Corinthians into completing the collection. Immediately he is led to offer a concession or disclaimer in 2 Corinthians 8:8: *I do not say this as a command.* The intent, he says to the Corinthians, is to test or prove *the genuineness of your love against the earnestness of others*, the Macedonian Christians. Paul is not averse to applying a competitive factor as a means of persuading his Corinthian audience, and what better model for them than the Macedonians. "Paul must have known of the rivalry, both ethnic and political, between the Macedonians and the Corinthians" (Betz, 1985:48).

The Gift Behind All Gifts 8:9

Finally, the example of the Macedonians gives way to the experience of *the generous act* (*charis*, grace) *of our Lord Jesus Christ*. The phrase is in the form of a common Christian benediction with which the Corinthians are completely familiar (1 Cor. 16:23; cf. 2 Cor. 13:13; Gal. 6:18), hence the introductory formula, *for you know.* . . . Here in 8:9, as nowhere else in the appeal of 2 Corinthians 8, Paul's key word *charis* reaches its apex of significance. The Macedonians have demonstrated remarkable generosity (*charis, grace, privilege,* 8:4), and the Corinthians are called to match them or outdo them in generosity (8:7). Yet in the end the generosity of *our Lord Jesus Christ* outdoes all of them and encompasses all of them in itself.

Paul's way of describing *the grace of our Lord Jesus Christ* in 8:9 fits the form of the appeal for the collection from Christians in "wealthy Corinth" (Murphy-O'Connor, 1983:53). Yet the core thought is the same as that of the early hymn to Christ in Philippians 2:6-8. In that hymn Christ divests himself of his eternal form, assumes the form of a slave, and dies the death of a criminal, "even death on a cross." As in the hymn, so here, the Christ who empties himself is the eternal, cosmic Christ of God, not strictly the earthly Jesus (A. Hanson, 1982:62-64). The divine figure becomes the emptied, earthly figure of Jesus, who gave himself up in death on a cross, a figure of affliction, poverty, humiliation. This is the supreme act of generosity that makes the Corinthians truly rich: *though he was rich, yet for your sakes he became poor, so that by his poverty you might become rich.* Given the reality of this Christ in their experience, how can the Corinthians fail to reflect the same generosity in their collection for *the saints?* The implication is inescapable. Either the Corinthians collect a generous offering for the saints or their claim to the gifts from *the grace of our Lord Jesus Christ* is called into question.

Acceptable Balance and Solidarity 8:10-15

It is part of the genius of Paul's theologizing that he welds reflective insight to practical, ethical agenda, as in the bond between the self-emptying Christ of 8:9 and the collection of money for the saints of 8:10-15. Still, Paul insists he is only *giving advice.* At this point the advice concerns the nature and function of the collection, begun already *last year.* He prefaces the actual advice with the note in verse 10 "that the Corinthians had begun to act and to will rather than vice versa as one would expect" (Fallon: 72). Assuming that their will to act is still alive, Paul counsels them *to do* what their enthusiasm of "will" requires, but only in proportion to what they have, *according to your means* (8:11b). Eagerness in wanting something done (8:11b) is an important principle but acceptable only as it is matched by the corresponding act.

As the argument develops in 8:12, it becomes evident that Paul is not satisfied with the collection as it stands. He considers the work of *last year* under the administration of Titus only a start, not a finish, as the Corinthians might have thought. Paul seems to know the extent of their *means* and cites a commonplace "from business and law" (Betz, 1985:64-65), found also in Jewish and Christian religious tradition: *according to what one has.* This is a way of increasing the amount of the collection so that it is in more accord with the resources in the Corinthian community.

In this regard, the appeal of 8:12 contains three interlocking elements: (1) right motivation stands as the condition of gift-giving (*if the eagerness is there*); (2) motivation, on one side, determines the acceptability of the gift; and (3) material means, on the other side, determines the acceptability of the gift. A person or community may give in excess of the amount proper to their means, but such a gift is not necessary by common standards of gift-giving. *The gift is acceptable according to what one has—not according to what one does not have* (8:12b).

The gift of money to the saints is no less a sacrificial offering to God than any of the traditional Jewish sacrifices, and as such requires the rule of acceptability (Betz, 1985:66). Poor people offer small gifts; their gifts are acceptable. But when rich people offer small gifts, they are not acceptable (cf. Luke 12:47-48; Grundmann: 58-59). However forceful Paul's argument for properly motivated proportional giving may be in this section (8:10-15), prescriptive legislation of amounts or percentages is noticeably absent.

Acceptability and unacceptability of sacrificial gifts in 8:10-12 extends to interdependent community life in 8:13-15. The principle advocated is *a fair balance* or equity, a principle well-known in the Greco-Roman world of oratory. "Justice is equity, giving to each thing what it is entitled to in proportion to its worth" (Cicero: 3.2.3). In 8:14 Paul is aware of a material inequity between the two communities. The Corinthians have an *abundance* at the moment, while *the saints* are in need.

If Paul left his appeal for equity at this point, his audience (then and now) would surely understand his point. But how would his audience understand his corollary point in 8:14b: *so that their abundance may be for your need?* Do the Jerusalem Jewish believers have a spiritual *abundance* to offer the spiritually impoverished Corinthian Gentile believers? Perhaps the theological priority of "to the Jew first and also to the Greek" applies here (Rom. 1:16). The Jewish people inherited an *abundance* of God's salvation centered in Jerusalem, city of the crucifixion and resurrection of the Messiah. That abundance of salvation flowed out to the Gentiles through no less a Jewish-Christian apostle than Paul himself.

Paul could be looking ahead to the time of a mass conversion of Jewish people to Christ along the lines of his vision of the end in Romans 9-11. Apart from the final ingathering of Israel, the Gentiles will not be saved. Hence the "Jerusalem" abundance of the future will enrich the Gentiles (R. Martin, 1986:269-270). Even if Paul is considering this future eschatological program while writing the appeal for the Corinthian collection, it is doubtful that the Corinthians think as he does when they read his words. Furthermore, to impose Paul's later reflection (in Romans) concerning the future of Israel onto this earlier appeal is dubious. Paul assumes that the Corinthians have some idea of the redemptive significance of Jerusalem believers and thus points to *their abundance . . . for your need.* Because of their indebtedness to those believers in Jerusalem, the Gentiles are encouraged to give of their means to equalize the living resources of the two communities, *that there may be a fair balance* (8:14b).

The appeal is then capped with a quotation from the record of that history of salvation (8:15; Exod. 16:18). The saving event echoed in the quotation is the giving of heavenly manna to the desert-dwelling Israelites. Each tribe had to gather enough for its number for the day, without accumulating a surplus. Some gathered little because their number was small; some gathered much because their number was large. But at the end of the day, there was not *too much* or *too little.* Paul's interpretation of the Exodus text by the principle of equality conforms in large measure to Philo's way of understanding the same text. (*Who Is the Heir?* 191).

Representatives Recommended 8:16-24

Here the second major part of the appeal deals with the recommendation of the delegation destined for Jerusalem via Corinth, the kind of authority they possess, the parties they represent, and their function in collecting the gift.

Interestingly, Paul opens the recommendation with a note of *thanks* (*charis*) to God, with the same word he uses for the gracious act of giving a collection to the saints. The gratitude is for the *eagerness* that God has given to Titus on behalf of the Corinthians. The Corinthians know Titus from an earlier encounter (2:12; 7:5-7; Barrett, 1982a:126) and apparently have appreciated his presence among them. Paul wants them to know now that Titus is aligned with him; the zeal of Titus is also Paul's zeal (8:16). Titus is Paul's *partner and co-worker in [their] service* (8:23). At the same time that Paul emphasizes the alliance between himself and Titus, he is careful to underscore to the Corinthians that Titus is *going to you of his own accord* (8:17b). There is only a cooperative missionary endeavor, no apostolic coercion.

The second member of the representative delegation enters on the heels of Titus at 8:18, unnamed except for his general designation as a member of the faith community: *the brother*. Attempts to identify this individual, *famous among all the churches for his proclaiming the good news*, have failed. There is no evidence in the text to tie the person with any name in the history of the early church. Attaching a name to the person is not illuminating, and Paul has chosen not to name him. It does not fit to suggest, as Bruce does, that Paul does not need to name the brother in 8:18 because he is well-known to the Corinthians and will be present at the reading of the letter. Titus is well-known in Corinth, yet Paul names him prominently and repeatedly in chapter 8. Naming the bearer of a letter, or the person responsible for an assignment related to a letter, dignifies the person and encourages respect for his mission in the community.

Why the anonymous *brothers* (8:18, 22)? Should they not also be dignified with their respective names? One answer is that Paul *did* name them in the original letter, but the first name was erased in later manuscripts "because the evangelist, whoever he was, forfeited his credit later on" (Hering: 62; Fallon: 74). This hypothesis is unwarranted: the manuscript evidence does not support it, and the intent of the argument is served better without naming the persons.

Unlike Titus, duly named, *the brother* represents the churches who appointed him by a show of hands, analogous to a modern conference electing a member to a board. The mission of *the brother*, it seems, is to safeguard the substantial gift from the churches. His principal assignment, as representative of the churches, is to accompany Paul during the delivery of *this gracious undertaking for the glory of the Lord himself and to show our goodwill* (8:19; TBC, below). In the meantime, though, Paul dispatches *the brother* with Titus to Corinth to complete the collection there before heading out for Jerusalem. The anonymity of the churches' representative is understandable in the context of Paul's mission. The unnamed representative stands for the Gentiles whom Paul is gathering into Jerusalem as an offering to God in fulfillment of prophecy (Isa. 2:2; 11:10; 66:18; Ps. 18:49; cf. Rom. 15:8-16; Munck: 282-308). This ingathering of the unnamed brother and of the Gentiles will vindicate Paul as God's true ambassador (2 Cor. 5:20) *[Two Appeals for One Collection, p. 280]*.

What applies to *the brother* of 8:18-19 applies also to *our brother* of 8:22, the latter apparently nominated by Paul himself, but still a representative of the churches. Both *brothers* are *messengers of the churches* (8:23). Their task as such is to ensure that the collection arrives at its destination, to represent the Gentile churches of Paul's mission, and to observe Paul's presentation of the money as intended. They are both trustworthy and yet anonymous representatives, not the presenters (8:18, 22). The wording of 8:19 is striking in this regard: the churches appointed the brother *to travel with us while we are administering this generous undertaking.* The distinction is clear between the brothers' function as traveling companions and Paul's function (along with Titus) as administrator of the offering *for the glory of the Lord* (8:19).

Echoing a rule from proverbial wisdom in 8:21 (Prov. 3:4, LXX), Paul sees the benefit to himself in having the churches' representatives with him. Their presence assures him *that no one should blame [him] about this generous gift* (2 Cor. 8:20), and that his intentions, already acceptable *in the Lord's sight,* are also seen to be right *in the sight of others* (8:21b).

At first glance, the elliptical statement of 8:23 looks like a summary of the recommendation of 8:16-22, a view expressed variously in most commentaries (e.g., Furnish, 1984:437; Hering: 63; Kruse: 161). But the structure of verse 23 is like "a formula of authorization" in contemporary "legal and administrative texts" (Betz, 1985:79). Just as there are two kinds of recommendation in 8:16-22, one for Titus and another for *the brothers,* so there are two kinds of authorization in 8:23, each one clearly set off by the introductory particle *as for: as for Titus . . . , as for our brothers.*

The higher rank of Titus in the authorization is signaled by the preposition *hyper* appearing directly before his name (untranslated in NRSV), but not used at all with *our brothers.* This Greek preposition "is etymologically connected with *over* and *upper.*" In the syntax of 8:23, its meaning with the genitive *Titou* gives the sense "on behalf of," "with a view to," "concerning." Even here "the English *over* is still not far off from these senses" (Moule, 1953:63-64). Beyond this signal, Titus is authorized as **my** *partner* and **my** *co-worker,* as compared to the other two delegates, who represent the churches. Titus is the official bearer of the letter, authorized by the apostle to carry out the letter's instructions. The two anonymous *brothers* are *messengers of the churches,* with no such authorization.

The NRSV *messengers* translates *apostoloi,* a highly charged term in Paul's self-defense to the Corinthians (e.g., 1 Cor. 9:1-7; 2 Cor. 11:5, 13). He claims to have been directly commissioned by the risen Lord. Thus Paul carries equal authority with those whom the earthly Jesus commissioned as his *apostoloi* (apostles). But when Paul is writing 2 Corinthians 8, *apostolos* "denotes the commissioned representative of a congregation" (Rengstorf: 422). As such, the two brothers under the title *apostoloi* in 8:23b carry official administrative credentials as appointees of the churches, not as apostles of the risen Christ in the sense that Paul is. Nevertheless, they with Titus are expected to reflect the *glory of Christ*, to think, speak, and act on this mission in accord with the mind of Christ.

Verse 24 concludes the whole appeal with an exhortation for the Corinthians to prove their love and Paul's boast about them before the churches (lit.: *in the face of the churches*). As the Corinthians present themselves to the representatives of the churches, they present themselves also to the churches.

THE TEXT IN BIBLICAL CONTEXT

The subject of the collection from the Gentile churches for the Jerusalem saints appears in four of the principal letters of Paul (Gal. 2:10; 1 Cor. 16:1-4; 2 Cor. 8-9; Rom. 15:25-28). It is not seen elsewhere in the NT except for an oblique reference to Paul's "alms" and "sacrifices" (offering) in Acts 24:17 (on accompanying representatives, cf. Acts 20:4; 21:29; 1 Cor. 16:3-4). If Paul views the collection as a sacrifice to God, as suggested above, then the collection reflects the type of motive and power of the sacrificial system in Israelite tradition. A sacrifice was intended to represent the worshiper's life in all of its dimensions. According to Romans 12:1-2, Paul understands "sacrifice" to mean the presentation of the whole person as "a living sacrifice, holy and acceptable to God, which is your spiritual worship." In this respect, therefore, the collection represents "a sacrifice" (offering) of the persons and congregations from whom it comes (cf. Rom. 15:16, "the offering of the Gentiles").

In making his appeal for the collection, Paul alludes to two texts in support of the two aspects of his appeal. The first text comes from Exodus 16:18, concerning the gathering of "manna" (16:35) for daily nourishment. The manna was "bread from heaven" (16:4), granted solely by the grace of God, analogous (for Paul) to the grace of God in the descent of *our Lord Jesus Christ* from the riches of heaven to the poverty of earth to enrich the poor (2 Cor. 8:9). Grace occurs at a material and spiritual level simultaneously. Paul quotes Exodus 16:18 in particular to prove the principle of equality among people of different heritage in the community of faith in Christ. The tribes of ancient Israel were different one from the other and yet had enough food for the day. Likewise, the Gentile communities outside Jerusalem and the Jewish communities inside Jerusalem should share equally in the resources given by the grace of God.

The rule of equality between human communities occupied a place in Philo's interpretation of Scripture. With respect to the same text of Exodus 16:18, he allegorized the manna to mean wisdom, "the heavenly food of the soul." From the text he proved by the principle of equality that wisdom "is distributed to all who use it in equal portions by the divine Word, careful above all things to maintain equality" (Philo, *Who Is the Heir?* 191).

By using a text from the wisdom tradition of Israel at 2 Corinthians 8:21, Paul supports the "wisdom" of having representatives from the churches accompany him with the collection. However transparent his motive, however forthright his accountability for the collection before God, the administration of the offering must appear right to human eyes as well. His proof text comes from Proverbs 3:4: "You will find favor and good repute in the sight of the Lord *and of people*."

Beyond his use of Proverbs 3:4 in this regard, Paul's thought may interconnect with the tenor of other maxims in Proverbs 3, which deal with the handling of wealth. A few samples illustrate the similarity between the appeal of 2 Corinthians 8 and the instruction of Proverbs 3: "Honor the Lord with your substance, and with the first fruits of all your produce" (Prov. 3:9). "Happy are those who find wisdom, and those who get understanding, for her income is better than silver, and her revenue better than gold" (3:13). "Do not withhold good from those to whom it is due, when it is in your power to do it. Do not say to your neighbor, 'Go, and come again, tomorrow I will give it'—when you have it with you" (3:27-28).

THE TEXT IN THE LIFE OF THE CHURCH

The social problem of rich and poor in the church of "the emptied Christ" intensified in the centuries after Paul. Evidence of the problem is nowhere more apparent than in the second-century writings of *The Shepherd of Hermas*. The "Parables" in particular are meant to give instruction to the rich on their proper relation to their wealth and to the poor of their community. In the first parable, a man of one city comes to dwell in another city and begins to build estates and fine edifices. The lord of the city says to the man, "I do not wish you to dwell in my city; come out from this city, for you do not use my laws. . . . Either use my laws, or depart out of my country." The laws in question relate to the proper Christian view of wealth and property, so the Shepherd instructs his flock:

Take heed therefore, O you who serve the Lord. . . . Let each man therefore, according as he is able, purchase not lands, but souls that are afflicted, visit the widows and orphans, and neglect them not; and expend your
wealth and your preparations on such lands and houses as you have received from the Lord; for to this end did your Master make you rich that
you should fulfill these services for Him. (81-83)

Even more striking is the Shepherd's image of the elm and the
vine in the second parable. This similitude reflects the kind of symbi-
otic relationship Paul envisaged between the rich community at Corinth and the poor group at Jerusalem (whether the Shepherd knew
2 Cor. or not). The vine needs the elm tree to support its branches
and fruit, or its fruit does not come, or if it does, it rots on the ground.
The vine needs the elm, but the elm also needs the vine, for without
the vine the elm does not bear fruit. The Shepherd then applies the
parable to the rich and the poor of the community. He closes by pro-
nouncing a benediction on the rich who have a mind for the poor.

The rich man has much wealth, but in the things related to the Lord he is
poor, being distracted by his wealth. . . . When, therefore, the rich man
has regard unto the poor, he ministers unto him the things that are need-
ful. . . . Therefore the rich man ministers all things to the poor, nothing
doubting, but the poor man, being supplied by the rich, makes interces-
sion for him with God, giving thanks for him that gave unto him. . . . Both
therefore perform their proper work. . . . Blessed are the rich who understand that their wealth is from the Lord. For they who are thus minded
will be able to do some good. (85-86)

The Shepherd of Hermas offers an implicit lesson to the church in
every age on how to translate NT instruction about wealth and poverty, such as that of Paul in 2 Corinthians 8, into a new cultural and social situation. "The author works with the biblical traditions about
wealth and poverty and produces a new interpretation adapted to the
exigencies of his own social situation. Thus he stands in continuity
with the New Testament and carries its legacy into his own age"
(Osiek: 4).

Of the various parts of 2 Corinthians 8 that have played a role in
the life and thought of the church, none reached the pinnacle of acceptance like that of verse 9: *For you know the generous act of our
Lord Jesus Christ, that though he was rich, yet for your sakes he became poor, so that by his poverty you might become rich.* Luther
sought to capture the sentiment of verse 9 in his hymn:

Er ist auf Erden kommen arm,
dass er unser sich erbarm,
uns in dem Himmel mache reich
und seinen lieben Engeln gleich.

He came to earth as poor
that pity he should pour,
to make us rich in terms of heaven,
as love to angels given.

Based on Luther's hymn, reflecting the theme of 2 Corinthians 8:9, Bach composed his *Christmas Oratorio* to celebrate the glorious mystery of the incarnation of the Christ.

Neither was the spiritual blessing of verse 9 lost to the Anabaptists of the Reformation period, many of whom knew firsthand the meaning of poverty, pain, and death. They saw the supreme example of their reproach in the Christ who was rich yet for their sakes became poor. In seeing thus, they found comfort, quoting frequently this verse from 2 Corinthians 8:9 (*MM*: 387, 524, 647, 820, 849, 1004). For support of the doctrine of the incarnation of Christ, groups of believers in the seventeenth century incorporated this text into their articles of faith, hence giving verse 9 the high regard that Luther and Menno had given it before them (*MM*: 1107; cf. Menno: 209, 822).

Paul contextualized the thought of verse 9 into the fabric of the argument of chapter 8. But church authorities to the present time have tended to isolate the verse to hammer out doctrine on the anvil of orthodoxy. For Paul, the sacrificial gift of Christ expressed in verse 9 is inextricable from the act of giving money to the poor saints of Jerusalem. Paul situates his theology concretely in life and culture.

How is the church to translate this text authentically into its ministry? Traditionally the church has used 2 Corinthians 8 to teach stewardship, by which is meant the giving of money to meet the budget of the church. The stewardship of money in this text, however, rests on the bedrock theology of human response to the Creator-God in whose economy human beings live. God's economy embraces money within the whole of life that God redeems, as John Reumann demonstrates in his recent book. Christian stewardship of money in the name of Christ is part of working for "the common good on ecology, peace, and justice issues" (116-117, 123).

Paul calls the gift of money toward the collection for the poor *the partnership of service* (8:4, VGS). In the theological context of grace, Paul did not shrink from "asking for money within the church." The whole enterprise was for him "a matter of fellowship and equality, not enrichment of one group at the expense of the other" (Bassler: 112).

The entire gamut of Paul's appeal in chapter 8 cannot be translated indiscriminately. Yet his persuasive speech contains several attenuating principles that do translate, principles grounded in a theology of grace in the "economy of God" (Reumann: 11-24). The gift in the collection is said to be *voluntary, proportional* to what one has, and *equitable* between groups.

Voluntary. Paul made a concerted effort to persuade the Corinthians to complete (or increase) their portion of the collection. At the same time, he strove to maintain the principle of voluntary giving of one's resources. Otherwise the gift would not spring from grace but from necessity or coercion.

In this regard, congregations and denominations that collect money by legislation should reflect prayerfully on the implications of such a means of raising money within the church. Some churches through a board of stewards (or equivalent body) require an amount of money from each member indiscriminately as "membership dues." But that is in blatant disregard of the principle of voluntary giving explicit in 2 Corinthians 8. Leaders may give pragmatic arguments about meeting budget, supporting good programs, and paying salaries. But such arguments only betray the church's inability to reflect theologically on the profound significance of the principle of voluntarism based on God's grace.

Proportional. Paul expounds unequivocally the principle of proportional giving toward the collection. To the Corinthians he says, complete the gift *according to your means* (8:11). Proportional giving makes the gift acceptable. A member gives relative to what one has, *not according to what one does not have* (8:12). Some churches flagrantly violate this principle. Members are notified of the amount per member that should be given to meet the budget. The stipulated amount in such churches is the same for all members regardless of their income or resources.

In most North American urban churches of 200 members or more, the difference of income and resources between members can be enormous. On one end of the scale, a household earns $200,000 per year; on the other, the same-size household earns $15,000 per year. To impose the same "membership dues" on both constitutes a serious breach of the gospel principle of proportional giving.

Nor is the OT legislation of 10 percent—applicable within the inheritance of the land of Israel (cf. Matt. 23:23)—a solution to the problem in Paul's situation or ours. In our time, the $200,000 household that gives $20,000 may receive acclaim for generosity, but the remaining $180,000 for living expenses is grossly out of proportion to the gift. The $15,000 household that gives $1,500 has scarcely enough left for the bare necessities of life. Such giving is out of proportion to what they have.

Ironically, the state taxation system reflects more adequately Paul's principle of proportional giving than some churches known to this writer. Citizens are taxed according to their income: households on low incomes are taxed minimally, while those on high incomes are taxed at a higher percentage of the total. Less fairly, a flat conference or congregational levy on individuals conflicts with Paul's principle of proportional giving.

As long as church members continue to keep their personal financial state a guarded secret in the community of faith, church authorities should not pass judgment on some members for not giving enough based on guesswork. Let each member give voluntarily *according to what one has—not according to what one does not have* (8:12).

Equitable. Finally, Paul summons the principle of equity in his appeal for a larger gift from the Corinthians. He says, *I do not mean that there should be relief for others and pressure on you, but it is a question of [equity] between your present abundance and their need . . . that there may be [equity]* (8:13). An equitable community does not require an equal distribution of material resources between members or between congregations. Instead, there needs to be an interdependence between them, as exemplified in the Shepherd's parable of the vine and the elm. Rich and poor can share mutually in the grace of God, the rich by giving generously to the poor and the poor by receiving the gift gratefully. As Käsemann puts it, "No one goes away empty, but no one has too much" (1964:76). Both are blessed of God.

A Second Appeal for the Collection

2 Corinthians 9:1-15

PREVIEW

A sharp break in the form and flow of the appeal occurs between 8:24 and 9:1, yet the aim of the appeal is the same in both chapters. Even with the interruption in thought, a number of commentators interpret 9:1-5 in conjunction with 8:16-24. The subject matter is similar (e.g., Furnish, 1984:438; Hughes: 321-322; R. Martin, 1986: 281-282). However, the language of 9:1 definitely marks a new beginning, which must be accounted for in any interpretation of the two chapters on the collection.

After his rather awkward transition in 9:1—*now it is not necessary for me to write you about the ministry to the saints*—Paul returns to the subject of the collection as though a new approach is indeed necessary. He mentions again the eagerness of the Macedonians (cf. 8:1-5). This time, however, he points to the good example of the believers in Achaia (9:2, of which Corinth is the major city) that *stirred up most of them*, the Macedonian churches. As well, Paul resumes the matter of sending *the brothers* ahead to Corinth, explaining that their commission should not be viewed as a form of pressure or extortion, but as a way of validating Paul's boasting about the Achaian churches to the Macedonians. In these opening verses (9:1-5), Paul urges the readers more delicately than he did in chapter 8, that the collection should be a gracious gift of blessing, and therefore bountiful and liberal.

Paul devotes the remainder of the chapter (9:6-15) to making some final points about the collection, similar to those he made in a different way in chapter 8: motives of the givers, the thanksgivings that result from liberal giving, and the enabling grace of God. What appears as new material in 9:6-15 is more an addendum to the appeal of chapter 8, using a somewhat modulated tone. The aim and substance of the appeal itself is the same in chapter 9 as in chapter 8.

While some interpreters view each of chapters 8 and 9 as distinct letters written on different occasions and in reverse sequence (9 before 8), the position adopted here is that the two chapters were composed on the same occasion, in the canonical sequence, and dispatched together to Corinth. *[Two Appeals for One Collection in One Letter, p. 280]*

OUTLINE

Achaia Stimulated the Macedonians, 9:1-2

Another Reason for Sending the Delegates, 9:3-5

Sowing and Reaping: Picture of a Generous Giver, 9:6-10

Many Thanksgivings to a Super-Generous God, 9:11-15

EXPLANATORY NOTES

Achaia Stimulated the Macedonians 9:1-2

As in most English versions, the NRSV glosses over the awkwardness of the transitional Greek phrase of 9:1. Yet by smoothing the phrase for English readers, the translators only aggravate the apparent redundancy of chapter 9.

To make some sense of the function of the further appeal of chapter 9, following that of chapter 8, the opening transitional phrase (*peri men gar*) requires rather more detailed explanation than usual. The NRSV at 9:1 reads: *Now it is not necessary for me to write you about the ministry to the saints.* The two highlighted words, *now . . . about*, are meant to express the transitional notion in *peri men gar*.

The first of these three Greek particles, *peri*, Paul often uses to signify the beginning of a new subject (cf. 1 Cor. 16:1; 8:1; 7:1), but in such cases *peri* is accompanied by an explanatory *de*. Thus in (1 Cor.) 16:1, for example, the translation in the NRSV reads, "Now concerning (*peri de*) the collection." But here in 2 Corinthians 9:1, *peri* (*concerning*) is joined to two different words, *men gar*. The first one, *men*, "serves to prepare the mind for a contrast of greater or lesser sharpness" (Denniston: 359). However, when this particle, *men*, appears alongside *gar*, as it does here, then instead of simple contrast, the reader can expect a modified explanation to balance a preceding statement. A common English expression, "that is to say" or "in other words," serves a similar function (Denniston: 67; cf. Moule, 1953:162).

Consequently, this phrase (*peri men gar*) opening chapter 9 is not introductory, tagging a new topic (or a separate letter: Windisch: 269; Hering: 65; Bultmann, 1985:258; Betz, 1985:90; Fallon: 77). Instead, it signifies a fresh approach to the preceding subject, not merely an extension of the last idea in 8:24 (cf. Dahl, 1977:39; Bruce: 225; Furnish, 1984:425; Barrett, 1973:232).

Paul admits that he is about to broach the subject of the collection from another angle (Denny: 280) and concedes that the additional appeal (chap. 9 in addition to 8) is *superfluous* (*perisson*). The same Greek word, *perisson*, in chapter 8 describes the *abundance* of resources in Corinth (8:14) and the *abundance* of joy in Macedonia (8:2). Here at 9:1 Paul employs the term to acknowledge the tedium of dwelling excessively on the same subject. Though he proceeds with the argument of chapter 9, the result is not an empty repetition but a modulated appeal. Chapter 9 handles the sensitive issues more delicately than did the argument of chapter 8.

Now in 9:2, Paul acknowledges the eagerness of his Achaian readers in making a worthy beginning *last year* (cf. 8:10), making their eagerness *the subject of [his] boasting . . . to the people of Macedonia*. Achaia (the churches of the region, including Corinth) has now become the example to the people of Macedonia! Earlier the Macedonians were hailed as the extraordinary model, a test case for the Achaian readers (8:2-8). Neither Achaia nor its major city Corinth was cited as a worthy model in the earlier appeal of chapter 8. In the new appeal of chapter 9, however, Achaia is set up as a positive example to the Macedonians.

Of the Achaians, Paul now says, *Your zeal has stirred up most of them*. Though some groups in Macedonia are reluctant to participate, most are ready. For Paul to leave the rather hard-hitting appeal of 8:2-8 without this further qualification would jeopardize his desired effect: to stimulate the Corinthians to complete the collection. The readers of chapter 8 could easily feel criticized or even shamed by the glowing example of the Macedonians. Here in the additional appeal, they are duly praised.

Another Reason for Sending the Delegates   9:3-5

In this second appeal, again *the brothers* are not named, nor is Titus mentioned, though he could be included in *the brothers*. Significantly, his special relationship to Paul plays no part in the argument of chapter 9. His prominence in chapter 8 as apostolic representative, on the other hand, together with duly appointed delegates from the churches (of Macedonia?), effectively charged the collection rhetoric of chapter 8 with authority. Hence, the critics at Corinth could construe this as Paul's heavy-handed way of exacting money. The language of 9:3-5 deflects that possibility.

Sending the brothers in advance, says Paul in this second appeal, simply ensures that his boast about the Corinthians will not be empty (9:3). He and by implication the Corinthians will not be put to shame (9:4b) in the presence of some Macedonians who may come along with Paul (9:4a). The collection itself in the end must be a free gift. If it is not a *gift*, it is not an acceptable offering to God (9:5b-c).

In this section explaining the dispatch of *the brothers*, Paul invokes a new word, *eulogia* (often translated "blessing"), in addition to words from the previous appeal. This describes the necessary character of the collection. As in the previous appeal, here again he refers to the collection as a *ministry* (9:1, 12, 13), and sees it once more as a reflection of the *abundant grace* of God (9:8, VGS). But now Paul invests his argument with this new word for the collection, *eulogia*. The NRSV translates the various forms of *eulogia* as *bountiful gift* (9:5b), *voluntary gift* (9:5c), *bountifully* (9:6b). Etymologically, the term means "pleasing word," as in a eulogy for a deserving individual.

In the NT and in other contemporary literature, *eulogia* has to do with praising God or speaking well of God in hope of receiving a blessing. But the noun can signify the gracious benefit received from God (Rom. 15:29; Louw, 1:750). The sense Paul gives the word in 2 Corinthians 9 is peculiar to this context: the gift from the Corinthians should go to *the saints* as a *eulogia*, a *gift of blessing,* as opposed to a sum of money wrung from greedy hearts (9:5c). The contrast, as the NRSV has translated the terms, involves voluntary giving rather than *extortion* (9:5c). The phrasing speaks of a gift from a good heart, hence a *gift of blessing,* as opposed to a small amount that signals greed. "A gift of blessing is given in response to blessings received, while greed represents one's failure to respond in kind, owing to one's failure to receive anything as a gift" (Betz, 1985:97).

Another new word, *hypostasis*, applies to the collection in this section, 9:3-5. The NRSV translates it *undertaking* (9:4b). The word appears five times in the NT, twice here (2 Cor. 9:4; 11:17) and three times in Hebrews (1:3; 3:14; 11:1). In Hebrews, even with a different sense in each case, the implication in each of the three contexts has to do with "reality, substance, proof." These ideas may not be far from Paul's use in 2 Corinthians 9:4b. His concern is that his boasting not be found *empty* (9:3), but rather that it be backed by the reality (*hypostasis*) of the gift of blessing (*eulogia*) from Achaia. Moreover, this important word, *hypostasis*, does not merely cite the project at hand (Köster: 585); it acts to balance the notion of an empty boast and an embarrassed Paul, *to say nothing of [the Corinthians]* (9:4b). This is why Paul is sending the embassy: to protect himself and his converts at Corinth from losing face because of his unsubstantiated boast (9:3) if there is a meager collection of money from Corinth.

Sowing and Reaping: Picture of a Generous Giver 9:6-10

The remainder of the chapter (2 Cor. 9:6-15) develops the idea of a *gift of blessing*, a *eulogia*, a gift that reflects the *indescribable gift* of God (9:15). In the first part, 9:6-10, Paul makes his point by the use of a common agrarian metaphor in the form of a proverb: *The point is this: the one who sows sparingly will also reap sparingly, and the one who sows bountifully (eulogiais) will also reap bountifully (eulogiais;* 9:6).

Ancient farmers took a risk in sowing grain. They believed that the more seed sown, the greater the harvest of grain. But if the rains failed to come, the farmers lost the grain they sowed. Those who risked little would at least have some grain left if the harvest failed (Betz, 1985:98-100). Paul's use of the metaphor to develop his new word for the gift (*eulogia*), places responsibility for the bountiful harvest in the benevolent God (9:7-8), whom the Corinthians know to be abundantly gracious.

God, abounding in grace as he does to the Corinthians, *loves a cheerful giver* (9:7b). *Cheerful* translates *hilaron*, from which comes the English "hilarious." Paul's version of the proverb differs from its source in Proverbs 22:8a (LXX) by one word. In Proverbs, God "blesses" (*eulogei*); in 2 Corinthians 9:7, God *loves* (*agapa*). Strangely, the key word (*eulogia* in verb form) that Paul seeks to develop for the collection in this appeal of chapter 9 sits ready to quote in the proverb he uses, yet he replaces the word "blesses," with *loves*. Paul's version of Proverbs may have the word *loves* instead of "blesses" (Hughes: 331), though that is unlikely, given the available evidence. Nor is it any more plausible to say that Paul has a lapse of memory, thinking the proverb contains the word *loves* instead of "blesses" (Plummer: 259).

Paul knows that of all the texts in his Greek Bible containing the word *cheerful*, this one in Proverbs 22:8a also had his key word, *eulogei*, "blesses." By converting the traditional "blessing" (*eulogia*) of God out of its Hebraic setting into the Christian understanding of the love of God in Jesus Christ, Paul effectively applies the proverb to the situation of the collection. God *loves* humankind unconditionally in Christ and responds in love to those who, like him, give cheerfully rather than *reluctantly or under compulsion* (9:7). Giving is above all a matter of attitude: On what basis does a Christian *decide* to give (9:7a)?

Taking Paul's lead metaphor about sowing and reaping (9:6) at face value, one may infer a selfish motive in giving: the more one gives, the more one gets back for oneself. But Paul expounds his metaphor in quite another direction. God will grant a bountiful blessing to cheerful givers *so that by always having enough of everything, you may share abundantly in every good work* (9:8). Thus, any hint of a self-centered motive is excluded. As proof that the sharing motive is right for God's people, Paul in 9:9 cites verbatim a line from the Greek version of a wisdom Psalm (111:9, LXX; cf. 112:9, NRSV). In the Psalm, the actor is one who fears the Lord (111:1); in Paul's application, the actor is God: *He scatters abroad, he gives to the poor; his righteousness endures forever.*

Lest there be any lingering doubt about the meaning of the agricultural metaphor of sowing and reaping, Paul explains further in 2 Corinthians 9:10 (cf. Isa. 55:10). Since it is in God's nature to supply seed for sowing and bread for food, he will multiply the metaphorical seed of the gift of money for *the saints.* God will increase the metaphorical harvest of *justice* (*righteousness* or *benevolence*) by distributing the surplus of the grace of God. The *righteousness* in this text bears some resemblance to the Jewish practice of almsgiving (Lietzmann: 138).

Many Thanksgivings to a Super-Generous God 9:11-15

In assessing the overall effect of a generous collection from Corinth, Paul identifies four interrelated facets. Then he closes the entire argument with an exuberant paean of praise to God (9:15). First, note the four facets of the effect.

1. A generous gift out of Corinthian wealth will provide for *the needs of the saints* (9:11a, 12a). Paul is a practical Christian thinker. Whatever else the collection may symbolize, its earthly use matters to him. Saints of God should not be poor when other saints are rich. As these two chapters (2 Cor. 8-9) demonstrate, this is a theological imperative for Paul. "As its history unfolded , the collection became for Paul a model of his theology. . . . Pauline theology . . . is directed towards living history" (Georgi, 1965:78-79).

2. A generous gift from Corinth to Jerusalem will result in *many thanksgivings to God* (9:11b, 12b). As Paul relates the collection to thanksgivings, plural, he envisions a worship ceremony at Jerusalem

in celebration of the grace of God. Many people, upon receiving the gift, will offer praises to God like those "related to ancient votive offerings" (Betz, 1985:118). For their part, the Corinthians should rejoice that God mediates his grace through them. In this thanksgiving section, Paul adds yet another new word to the ministry of the collection, *leitourgias* (from which comes *liturgy*), translated *the rendering* in NRSV (9:12).

The word *leitourgia* was current in the sociopolitical setting of the Roman world in which Paul and the Corinthians lived. It indicates a *public service* rendered by citizens under law at their own expense (Betz, 1985:117). Paul borrows the word, transforming its secular function and using it to describe a public service of worship in which both *the saints* of Jerusalem and the Corinthian believers participate jointly and freely. The Corinthians do this by their generous gift of blessing, and *the saints* of Jerusalem by their *many thanksgivings* (Moule, 1961:80).

3. The generous gift will act as proof of the Corinthians' *obedience to the confession* they make (9:13). The first part of verse 13 is difficult to understand. The NRSV translation reads: *Through the testing of this ministry you glorify God by your obedience to the confession of the gospel.* Literally, the ministry of the collection glorifies God *by the obedience of your confession. Of your confession* is genitive and could be the subject or object of obedience. If object (as in the NRSV), then the Corinthians are obedient *to* whatever is represented in the term *confession* (used only here in Paul's letters). If subject, then the obedience is an expression *of the confession.* The latter seems more likely in this context.

Normally where the word *confession* appears in the NT, it refers to a statement affirming faith in Jesus Christ. But here at 9:13, *confession* denotes the particular expression of faith in Christ represented by the *gift of blessing* (9:5-6, notes). The *obedience* or *submission* consists in the act of giving generously, an act that signifies the grace of God in *the gospel of Christ.*

The *confession* is scarcely a legal contract by which Paul's Corinthian converts submit to Jerusalem (so Betz, 1985:123). Paul's consistent sentiment is that neither he nor his Gentile converts need to submit to Jerusalem (cf. Gal. 1-2). Sufficient for Paul is the **mutual benefit** of the two communities to each other, by which their union is validated. Moreover, the Corinthians' *obedience of their confession* relates particularly to their promise a year earlier to take up a collection for *the saints.* Now, a year later, the *gift of blessing* expresses

obedience to their earlier confession, which in effect is a confession
of the gospel of Christ.

4. The generous gift creates a *communal spirit of mutual benefit*
(2 Cor. 9:13b-14). Paul encourages unity within and between the
churches. Of principal concern to him, expressed most pointedly in
Romans 9–11, is the unity of his Gentile mission churches with their
Jewish counterparts. Bringing the collection to Jerusalem will signal
the *participation* (*sharing, koinōnias,* 2 Cor. 9:13b) of the Gentile
communities with the believing remnant in Jerusalem. The Jerusalem group in turn will intercede on behalf of the Corinthians in view
of the *superabundant* (*surpassing,* 9:14) *grace* (or *gift*) *of God* to
them, and through them to *the saints* (9:12).

Paul is gripped by the enormous possibility enshrined in his language of 9:13-14, the union of Jewish and Gentile humanity never
before attained. He exclaims his depth of gratitude to God: *Thanks
(charis) be to God for his indescribable gift!* On this triumphant note
of praise, Paul concludes his appeal for the *gift of blessing* from the
Corinthians for *the saints.*

This exclamation of thanksgiving also concludes the Letter of
Reconciliation of 2 Corinthians (1–9). Originally the letter would
have ended with the usual greetings and benediction. The ending
was either accidentally torn off the scroll and lost, or was deliberately
deleted by the compiler in joining the Letter of Defense (2 Cor.
10–13) to the Letter of Reconciliation (2 Cor. 1–9).

THE TEXT IN BIBLICAL CONTEXT

The biblical context of the collection appears in the TBC after the
notes on 2 Corinthians 8. Arising from the second appeal of chapter
9 are three additional elements: (1) the gift of blessing, the *eulogia*
(9:5-6), (2) the agricultural metaphor of sowing and reaping (9:6-10),
and (3) the concluding exclamation of thanksgiving (9:15). All three
come from within the horizon of the larger biblical world.

First, the *gift of blessing* (*eulogia*). The word usually connotes a
blessing in the sense of a benevolent speech-act. Paul uses the word
in this sense at several points. For example, in 1 Corinthians 10:16 he
refers to the cup of the Lord's Supper as "the cup of the blessing
(*eulogia*)," which involves the act of drinking the memorial wine accompanied with the eucharistic word (11:25). The blessing in this
sense declares the church's right relationship to God in the speech-
act of participation in the Lord's Supper. Similarly, in Galatians 3:14

the blessing from Abraham is mediated to the Gentiles through the speech-act of Christ proclaimed by Paul. In this instance the Gentiles receive "the blessing" of a right relationship with God (cf. also Rom. 15:29; Eph. 1:3; Heb. 6:7; James 3:10).

As used in 2 Corinthians 9:5 for the collection of money from one community for another, the word echoes its antecedents in the Greek translation of the OT. For example, in Joshua 15:19 Caleb's new wife asked him for a gift (*eulogia*) to consolidate their relationship. Other references reveal a similar implication in the word: the act of giving something to another bestows a blessing and confirms a relationship (e.g., Gen. 33:11; 2 Kings 5:15).

Second, the agricultural metaphor of sowing and reaping in 2 Corinthians 9:6-10 was already present in Greco-Roman and Jewish writings of the time. The ancients were adept at integrating agricultural metaphors into their view of life and world expressed in literature. Hesiod's *Works and Days* is the earliest evidence from the Greek side. A similar use of agricultural imagery in Jewish hands spans the entire literature of the OT (Betz, 1985:85 and notes). Thus Paul drew on a common fund of proverbial agricultural imagery to create his own proverb for the opening point about the *gift of blessing*.

For example, Proverbs 11:26 (LXX) reads: "The Gentiles pronounce a curse on those who withhold grain but a blessing (*eulogia*) on the head of the one who distributes it." Or again in Proverbs 22:8, "The one who sows corruption will reap disaster" (cf. Job 4:8; 31:8; Ps. 126:5; Eccl. 11:4; Jer. 12:13; Hos. 8:7; Mic. 6:15). The notion of divine recompense being meted out on human endeavor, negative or positive, occupied the writings of sages, priests, and prophets in Israelite and Jewish tradition (e.g., Sirach 7:3; Test. of Levi 13:6; Philo, *Unchangeableness of God* 166). It conveniently found its way into the NT, as in Paul's formulation here at 9:6 (of 2 Cor.; cf. Matt. 6:26; Luke 19:21; John 4:36-37; Georgi, 1965:67-68; Käsemann, 1969: 73).

Third, the concluding thanksgiving bears some resemblance to the hymn-like praise of the self-emptying Christ of 2 Corinthians 8:9. Yet the final exclamation of 9:15 exults in the **gift** of God and is thereby directly tied to the many thanksgivings accruing from the gift of the collection. Paul can only exult in the gift; he cannot describe it. Paul's word for *gift* (*dōrea*) in verse 15 occurs only here in 2 Corinthians 9, but is commonly used in the NT for God's gift of the Spirit of Christ to the Gentiles. Marvelous and mysterious, the gift is *in-*

describable, the gift of the Son of God to human hearts, bestowing love unconditionally on humankind, as John 3:16 attests. Such a gift defies description, even as God does. Of this indescribable gift of love, Paul declares elsewhere: "I live by faith in the Son of God, who loved me and gave himself for me" (Gal. 2:20).

It is possible that in 2 Corinthians 9:15 "Paul actually cited the first line of an early Christian prayer of thanksgiving" (Betz, 1985: 127). If so, that citation places Paul's concluding thanksgiving and the letter as a whole in the context of early Christian worship. Quoting the first line of a well-known prayer urges the congregation to finish the prayer from memory, thus affirming Paul's argument and appeal in the letter.

THE TEXT IN THE LIFE OF THE CHURCH

Several points arise from the discussion of the collection in 2 Corinthians 8-9 (in addition to TLC after notes on 2 Cor. 8, above). One concerns the **unity of the faith** symbolized in "the gift of blessing" from the Gentile Christians in Corinth to the Jewish Christians in Jerusalem. The religious and cultural differences between the two groups were great, but the differences shrank in the presence of the grace of Christ symbolized in the "offering of the Gentiles." Similarly, the church worldwide is diverse, but united in the Spirit of Christ and the bond of peace.

Paul, in 2 Corinthians exercises **careful accountability** in the handling of the financial "gift of blessing." He gladly endorses the representatives who will ensure the safe deposit of the collection in the treasury at Jerusalem. Churches today can take a lesson from Paul.

Finally, Paul underscores the **bedrock theological motive** for the *gift of blessing* to Jerusalem: the *indescribable gift* of God (2 Cor. 9:15). This word *indescribable* captured the attention of later patristic writers and apologists. It has remained important to Christian thinkers ever since, as seen in creeds and catechisms of the church. God is confessed as inscrutable and indescribable, his gifts and acts of grace beyond compare. What are the implications of such an understanding of the gift-giving God?

The church through the ages "imagines" God, and does so sincerely, else there could be no personal faith. Problems arise, as history shows, when the mental "image" of faith in the indescribable God becomes fixed. Sometimes the image is fixed in wood and stone, but no less so in dogma and system. Of all the snares awaiting the church in any age, the one most subtle is the snare of fixing an image of God. When God is fixed, structured, and God's gift of grace systematized, the worshiper becomes idolatrous.

An exclusively feminist God is an image-become-idol just as surely as an exclusively patriarchal God is also an image-become-idol. An exclusively fundamentalist God is an image-become-idol just as surely as an ultraliberal God. An exclusively denominationalist God is an image-become-idol just as surely as a nondenominational God. So it is with all such particularistic images of God. Folly enters the church when the unfolding mystery of God and his plan of salvation are theologically sculpted into granite figures for human adoration.

Thanks be to God for his indescribable gift of compassionate redemption in Jesus Christ, that enters human minds and cultures in exhilarating new ways in every generation. This is the fundamental motive for believers in giving their material means to provide equity and security.

Letter of Defense

Response to Betrayal in Ministry

2 Corinthians 10:1—13:13

Variation 4: Weak Minister, Strong God

OVERVIEW

There is no recognizable connection between the last verse of 2 Corinthians 9 and the first verse of chapter 10. In addition, the tone and texture of the language of chapters 10-13 are vastly different from anything encountered in chapters 1-9. Only a marked change in relationship between Paul and the Corinthian church can account for the radically new form of writing in these last four chapters. A pause in dictating scarcely spans the rhetorical gulf that exists between these two principal parts of 2 Corinthians (cf. Denny: 289-290; Hughes: 334). The more responsible reading of the last four chapters (10-13) is to regard them as a separate letter written in response to bitter opposition from Corinth.

Paul's Letter of Defense (chaps. 10-13) was probably written and dispatched after chapters 1-9, since Paul in 12:14-18 refers to the visit of Titus and *the brother* to Corinth to collect money for Jerusalem (cf. 8:22-24). Furthermore, Paul still anticipates a third visit in 12:14 and 13:1 (cf. 2:1; 9:4) [*The Integrity of 2 Corinthians, p. 266*].

The situation that prompted the writing of the Letter of Defense can only be reconstructed tentatively by analyzing Paul's selected intimations in his biting polemic against his enemies at Corinth. After sending the Letter of Reconciliation, presumably with Titus and the *brothers* (8:16-24), Paul appears to have learned more precisely what his rivals at Corinth are actually saying against him. He understands how their rivalry is having a negative effect on the congregation(s). Titus may have sent word back to Paul immediately when he discovered the growing enmity among the Corinthians, ag-gravated by eloquent apostles from the outside. Alerted to their high claims for themselves and their efforts to disparage his authority in Corinth, Paul writes his extraordinary response found in the Letter of Defense (2 Cor. 10–13).

The response is extraordinary insofar as it portrays an image of Paul unlike anything else in his writings. Where he willingly defends his *agency* in the gospel ministry, as in chapters 1–9, in the Letter of Defense he defends *himself as agent-apostle*, much against his better judgment. But as he says to the Corinthians, *You forced me to it* (12:11). He plays the boasting game his enemies play, but in a farci-cal and inverted way. Their boast is not his, so he will not compare himself to them (10:12). Their claim to apostolic greatness proves them false. Yet Paul reluctantly must boast of himself to show the en-emies for what they are (11:21b). In so doing, he "enters the world of the agent in order to drive the Corinthians out of it" (Crafton: 104).

Hence, Paul's persuasive defense in these four chapters is trans-parent. Here as nowhere else he proves himself a match for his oppo-nents in wielding conventional rhetorical instruments, but in a way in-tended ultimately to subvert the role he plays as human agent in the gospel (Crafton: 110). The power of the gospel is not in human ability or achievement but in God alone. For the power of God to become effective, the person of Paul must be found *weak,* as indeed he is weak, in the eyes of his detractors (10:10; 11:5; 11:21; 12:7).

To prove his point and *destroy arguments* (10:4) that his oppo-nents level against him, he plays "Paul the fool." He makes fun of himself and expects his readers to laugh with him. But in so doing, they will catch the "truth" behind his irony and side with Paul against his enemies. Throughout his "fool's speech" (11:1—12:13), as also in the rest of the Letter of Defense, Paul's form of writing exhibits the basic elements of the classic orator: human character (*ethos*), emo-tions (*pathos*), and reason (*logos*). The literary contours and tones of the language of the Letter of Defense exhibit all three traits, using the overt literary devices of *sarcasm, irony,* and *parody* (Marshall: 381-391; Betz, 1972:17-19, 34-35; Crafton: 109-136).

Sarcasm pierces the feelings of the audience as they sense their culpability. For example, Paul addresses the question of his refusal to take money from the Corinthians for his apostolic services, thus prov-ing his weakness as an apostle; he says, *How have you been worse off than the other churches, except that I myself did not burden you? Forgive me this wrong!* (12:13). The exclamatory answer is sarcastic.

Irony invites the reader to consider the flip side of a perceived "truth." When Paul engages two sides of an issue, such as weakness and strength, presence and absence, wisdom and foolishness, he is speaking ironically. *Parody* imitates the opposing character for the purpose of ridicule. Paul the fool parades the literary stage dressed like his enemies so as to ridicule them and thus render their authority inoperative at Corinth.

Why does Paul pull out all of these rhetorical stops in 2 Corinthians 10-13? Writing of this sort does not spring from tranquil reflection on a secluded island. Instead, Paul is engaged in a struggle to save his apostolic place as the "parent" of the Corinthian congregations (1 Cor. 4:15). He is fighting against a bitter invective his enemies have executed at Corinth. "Paul's responses in 2 Corinthians must be viewed in the context of the enmity relationship. Paul has been the victim of a successful and damaging invective" (Marshall: 364). His sharp language in these four chapters calls for a reading in that light.

OUTLINE

God's Minister Under Fire: Boasting Ridiculed, 10:1-18

Forced to Boast as a Fool, 11:1—12:13

Warning, Conclusion, Projected Third Visit, 12:14—13:10

Closure, 13:11-13

God's Minister Under Fire: Boasting Ridiculed

2 Corinthians 10:1-18

PREVIEW

The opening words of chapter 10 point immediately to the subject and literary form of the letter. The subject is Paul himself, and the form is a defensive attack. (The usual salutation and thanksgiving are missing, perhaps as part of the compiling procedure. The present 10:1 marks the beginning of the body of the letter). If Paul's personal appeal is *humble,* it is because the Christ of the gospel was humble

(10:1). The enemy attack against Paul's *weak* presence (10:10) therefore is an attack against the Lord, not merely against Paul. Paul admits he is weak by human standards. Weak as he is, divine power fills him, so that he can wage a battle against *every proud obstacle raised up against the knowledge of God* (10:5). Military metaphors are strong in the introductory six verses.

Paul in 10:7-11 challenges the opponents on their own ground, a faulty ground for Paul, but one that he must tread *ever so subtly*. Yes, he will *boast a little too much* (10:8), yet not so much as to compromise his standard, dictated by the gospel (10:15-16). He can cite the invective his enemies have spoken against him at Corinth in his absence: *They say, "His letters are weighty and strong, but his bodily presence is weak, and his speech contemptible"* (10:10). Beside such a pathetic figure of an apostle, the self-commending apostles at Corinth display eloquence, good health, pleasing appearance—everything that Paul is not. By their standard, they have judged Paul inferior to themselves, which he refuses to accept on their terms (12:11).

In the latter part of chapter 10, Paul explodes the folly of comparison (10:12). Comparison leads to boasting in human qualities, and boasting of that sort disqualifies the boaster as an apostle of *the good news of Christ* (10:14). For that reason Paul must handle his own defense in these four chapters with the utmost care lest he finds himself trapped in the same fallacy as his enemies. His guiding watchword comes from Jeremiah 9:23-24: *Let the one who boasts, boast in the Lord* (2 Cor. 10:17; cf. 1 Cor. 1:31).

OUTLINE

Posing the Subject: The Person of the Apostle, 10:1-11

The Folly of Comparative Boasting, 10:12-18

EXPLANATORY NOTES
Posing the Subject: The Person of the Apostle 10:1-11

The forthright opening of the Letter of Defense leaves no doubt of the subject of the appeal: *I myself, Paul, appeal to you* (10:1a). The emphatic pronoun *myself* (*autos*) does not mean that Paul is writing this letter with his own hand; his usual practice is to dictate to a secretary and then add a personal word and signature (cf. 1 Cor. 16:21;

Gal. 6:11; 2 Thess. 3:17). Instead, *I myself* signals that the upcoming appeal concerns Paul's own role as a bone fide apostle.

The terms of the ensuing appeal are stated promptly and poignantly: *the meekness and gentleness of Christ* (2 Cor. 10:1b). Paul is a participant in this Christ and can therefore only present himself according to the character of Christ that governs his life. Paul's reference is probably not to the *meekness and gentleness* of the earthly Jesus but to the character of the eternal Christ of God, who humbled himself in his incarnation, whom *God* raised up (Phil. 2:6-8). *Meekness* and *gentleness* are more or less synonymous terms, and Paul connects them with yet another term for being weak: *humble*. Thus he depicts how he comes across to his rivals at Corinth. This word *humble* (*tapeinos*) "is a servile term" (Marshall: 323-324). In 10:1 Paul casts *humble* in an ironic mold. Its connotation of "weakness" condemns Paul at Corinth (in the eyes of critics). But it connects him with Christ, the same Christ whom the Corinthians claim to follow (cf. Phil. 2:8).

The precise criticism against which Paul seems to direct the irony of 2 Corinthians 10:1 (and indeed the whole letter) is that Paul's personal presence is *humble* or demeaning. Only when he is absent is he bold—in his letters (10:10). But in the world of oratory, in which Paul's rival apostles apparently live, a commanding presence is supposed to give authority to apostolic preaching (Funk: 249-268). From the critics' perspective, when Paul writes in absentia, "he claims more authority than he is able to demonstrate when he is present" (Furnish, 1984:478).

According to the opponents' rule, therefore, Paul was *acting according to human standards* (*kata sarka*, according to the flesh, 10:2) when he exercised authority at Corinth. He flatters himself that he is an apostle, but his *weak* (mean, 10:10) presence proves him to be a charlatan. The burden of the Letter of Defense, for which these early verses set the stage, seeks to turn the thinking of his enemies on its head, yet not by a self-serving defense governed by their rules. Furthermore, his critics' appraisal of his weak presence may be correct; Paul does not attempt to disavow that point. He may have a physical malady of some sort, a *thorn in the flesh* as he says (12:7). Paul has worked as a smelly leather-worker or tentmaker to support himself (Acts 18:3; cf. 2 Cor. 2:16). He probably does not dress the part of a commanding orator. And his manner of public speaking probably leaves something to be desired, compared to that of some of the brilliant orators from Athens and elsewhere. (But there is no evidence that Paul "was apt, when speaking excitedly, to tie himself in grammatical knots"; Barrett: 261).

As the trained orators of Paul's day understand their function, these weaknesses simply disqualify the person for the role of an authoritative ambassador. What Paul does with these "weak" traits, paradoxically, is to turn them to his advantage as a Christ-person, and turn them against his detractors, who are *false* in daring to boast the same apostolic status for themselves (11:12-15; cf. 1 Cor. 1:18—2:5).

By the use of military metaphors in 2 Corinthians 10:3-6—a common practice in Greco-Roman rhetoric—Paul illustrates wherein his real strength lies. *We do not wage war according to human standards,* he says. His instruments of battle *are not merely human,* but are empowered by God (10:4). Their purpose is to demolish fortifications, by which Paul means high philosophical arguments, the kind weighted against him at the moment. His aim in doing so, however, is to open the way to the knowledge of God and to make *every thought* conform to the mind of Christ (10:5).

The military imagery continues in 10:6. Paul stands *ready* (*hetoimō*), like a soldier in the face of a revolt (notes in Furnish, 1984:459). He is ready to *punish* (*ekdikēsai*) every kind of disobedience. If the verb *punish* seems strong (used elsewhere by Paul only at Rom. 12:19), it surely must be so because of the situation that evokes the thought in Paul's mind. Paul does not spell out the kind of punishment he has in mind, nor how he might be able to mete it out. What does come through in 2 Corinthians 10:6, though, is the distinction between the Corinthians and the opponents. At the moment the Corinthians are disobediently listening to Paul's adversaries. When the Corinthians show signs of obedience to Christ, not merely to Paul, then Paul will punish the others who have led them astray.

Verse 6 "suggests that the outsiders represent an alien authority with which Paul is in some relation," but Paul's statement in 10:6 is not "a clear pointer to Jerusalem" (Barrett, 1982b:66-67). How Paul can possibly punish representatives from Jerusalem is baffling! On the other hand, he could punish someone like Apollos, a Diaspora Jewish Christian involved somehow in watering what Paul has planted in Corinth (1 Cor. 3:5-9; 16:12). Persons like Apollos have few (if any) vital links with Jerusalem. Paul can find ways of disciplining such persons.

The absence of the opponents' names from the Letter of Defense does not mean that Paul does not know who they are. On the contrary, the technique of not naming was already recognized as a way of diminishing an opponent's status. "It is a striking feature of Paul's . . . letters that, though he mentions numerous friends and associates by name, he never once names an enemy" (Marshall: 341-342). Instead of naming his enemies, whose names the readers know in any case, Paul paints a caricature of them to expose their inadequacies in comparison to his own qualities. Whoever the opponents are, Paul is prepared to administer some kind of discipline on them when he is assured of the Corinthians' obedience to Christ (2 Cor. 10:6).

Look at what is before your eyes, the NRSV translates 10:7. But the verb *look* (*blepete*) can be indicative as in the NIV, NASB, and NEB, rather than imperative as in the NRSV. If indicative, then the sentence is sarcastic, implying that the Corinthians cannot see behind appearances: "You look at what is in front of your face." Or the sentence can be a question: "Do you look at things after the outward appearance?" (Bultmann, 1985:198). In the present context, the imperative as a warning seems preferable. Paul urges his converts to face "what is patently obvious" (Hering: 71; likewise Windisch: 300; Barrett, 1973:256). This immediately raises the question, What is patently obvious in this text?

The answer must be sought in what follows. At issue is Paul's status as an apostle of Christ. Verse 7 begins to focus the answer, to be continued throughout the following sections. Literally, Paul says, *If anyone is persuaded in himself to be of Christ, let him consider this again with himself, just as he [is] of Christ so [are] we also* (10:7b). The remark is not directed as much to the Corinthians as to an unnamed critic who sets himself up as a valid representative of Christ in Corinth over against Paul. His marks of validation come through later in Paul's parody. At this introductory point, however, Paul is simply stating that he is an authoritative representative of the Christ. Otherwise, the Corinthians themselves would not belong to Christ. Paul can boast *a little too much* of his authority because his mission among the Corinthians has been constructive, not destructive (10:8; cf. notes on 13:10 and following TBC). On that count, he is not ashamed to boast to the extent that he does.

The remainder of this section, 10:9-11, raises specifically the hot issue at Corinth of Paul's epistolary boldness in absentia over against his contemptible appearance of weakness when present. The letters in question are those sent previously to Corinth, which the critics have had a chance to read, and on which they have commented. Aware of this situation, Paul assures his congregation(s), *I do not*

want to seem as though I am trying to frighten you with my letters
(10:9).

The opponents have given Paul a backhanded compliment for his
letter writing, but only to deprecate him on the more important point
relative to his apostolic authority. Paul quotes his detractor as saying,
His letters are weighty and strong [compliment], *but his bodily presence is weak, and his speech contemptible* [deprecation] (10:10).
This becomes the crux around which Paul constructs his defense in
this letter preserved in 2 Corinthians 10–13. How can Paul account
for his weak personal presence as an apostle of Jesus Christ? Clearly
he is not prepared to deny the charge of weakness, but rather to demonstrate its relevance to the Christian paradox. "His weakness is, in
fact, the only thing he can rightly boast of!" (Leivestad: 162).

Apparently the particular weakness the critics have perceived in
Paul is his lack of skill in public speaking. His critics may have construed his lack of dynamic, persuasive speech as an indication of his
lack of the Spirit and of the gift of authoritative apostolic ministry
(Käsemann, 1956:38-43). This view seems to be at the heart of the
attack, judging from 10:10. Other characteristics may have been
cited to supplement the attack, such as weak physique, or weak in
ability to support himself from his preaching. In any case, Paul warns
such a critic in 10:11 that his written word when absent will be
matched by a corresponding deed when present, referring perhaps to
the *punish*ment of 10:6. In view, no doubt, is Paul's *third visit*, coming
soon after this letter (12:14; 13:1). His enemies at Corinth will find
out then that "there is only one Paul; and when plain speech is called
for he will give it, whether on paper or face to face" (Barrett,
1973:262).

The Folly of Comparative Boasting   10:12-18

This section is said to be "one of the most difficult of all passages in
these [four] chapters" (Barrett, 1982b:65). This is especially so if one
tries to tie Paul's use of the phrase *keep within the field* to the apostolic agreement made in Jerusalem (Barrett, 1982b:65; Gal. 2; Acts
15). Paul's text in this section, however, makes no mention whatever
of the Jerusalem agreement that approved Paul's Gentile mission
(Gal. 2:7-10; Barrett, 1982b:65; Louw, 1:707). One word stands out
in 2 Corinthians 10:13, *kanōn*, translated *field* in the NRSV. Only in
this passage (10:13, 15-16: *sphere of action*) and in Galatians 6:16
does Paul use the word. The term usually denotes measurement, as

in a "standard" or "rule" or "principle." This meaning is clearly evident in Galatians 6. The word does not mean something strictly geographic or demographic in 2 Corinthians 10:13, notwithstanding the last phrase *to reach out even as far as you.* "The measure given to Paul is not a sphere marked out in space in which he alone is to work. It is the orientation laid upon him and the blessing which God has caused to rest upon his ministry" (Beyer: 599).

Any connection that *kanōn* might have with geography or demography disappears when the *measure (metron)* and *standard (kanōn)* of 10:13 are viewed in the context of the comparison poignantly depicted in 10:12. There Paul criticizes the measurement his rivals at Corinth use to validate themselves in ministry. Unlike Paul, the rivals *measure themselves by one another, and compare themselves with one another.* Herein lies their folly (10:12b). Paul, on the other hand, measures his ministry by the standard that God has assigned him in *the good news of Christ* (10:14b). He is not about to cave in to the comparison game set up by his enemies.

Paul's boast in 10:15-16 consists not in comparing himself to others, but in checking how diligently he carries *the good news of Christ* to the Corinthians and other Gentiles like them. His commission consists in nothing less, nor will Paul allow himself to be judged by any other standard. Paul belongs to Christ; believes in Christ implicitly; and he treats his apostolic commission with singular devotion. He is, in short, a person of faith in God, and he will not boast beyond that limit. "Faith's only true boast is in Christ" (Furnish, 1984:482).

As often in his arguments, Paul clinches his point by citing a text of Scripture, in this case Jeremiah 9:23-24: *Let the one who boasts, boast in the Lord.* One is tempted to ask how boasting in the Lord differs from boasting in one's self, if in the end the boast is about what one is or what one achieves. How does a Christian relate one's story of moral character or positive accomplishment without self-praise (boasting)? Is it sufficient to tack on a high-sounding phrase such as "to the glory of God"? Paul's apparent answer in the context of this section focuses on the issue of comparison versus noncomparison. Evaluation of life and ministry in comparison to the stature of others is illegitimate for a Christian minister, argues Paul, because the standard is human and the appraisal self-administered. *For it is not those who commend themselves that are approved, but those whom the Lord commends* (2 Cor. 10:18).

THE TEXT IN BIBLICAL CONTEXT

Chapter 10 sets the stage for Paul's most forceful self-defense in all of 2 Corinthians. The early chapters of this epistle implied Paul's knowledge of a growing unease (or disease) at Corinth with respect to his ministry among them. He seemed aware of the presence of outsiders and their posturing at Corinth: some have called for forthrightness and consistency in Paul (1:15-24), for proper apostolic qualifications (2:14-17), for written credentials (3:1-3). In subsequent arguments, Paul validated his ministry within the economy of God (3:4—7:16) and appealed to the Corinthians to join him by giving a generous offering to *the saints* (8:1—9:15). But as the curtain opens on chapters 10 to 13, Paul is more than aware of criticism against him. He knows the invective the alien forces are leveling against him (10:10), and he stands ready to demolish their arguments and to reestablish himself as an authentic apostle at Corinth.

Consistent with his convictions elsewhere in his letters, Paul launches his offensive against his enemies in terms of Christ, who humbled himself, who took on the form of a weak servant, who died the death of a criminal (Phil. 2:6-8; cf. 1 Cor. 1:18-25; Rom. 6:1-4). He thus engages the paradox of the gospel of Christ (2 Cor. 10:1), which safeguards his argument from the pitfalls of the opponents' practice of self-praise and boastful comparison. Their standard is human, and their strength is in themselves. Their works are *according to the flesh* (10:3-4; Gal. 5:16-21).

Paul operates according to another rule, which Jesus called "the kingdom of God" (Mark 1:14-15; Matt. 13:1-53). While Jesus used parable to explain the rule of God, over against conventional wisdom, Paul employs other literary means to make his case, including parody (2 Cor. 11:1—12:10). The underlying principle is the same in the vision of both Jesus and Paul: God's way of acting within the human family contravenes human standards of approval. Prophetic figures like Jesus and Paul are patently misunderstood by the conventional leaders of the day, because prophets and conventionalists operate by different rules. Prophets boast in God; conventionalists boast in themselves.

To press this point, Paul echoes a text of the afflicted prophet, Jeremiah: *Let the one who boasts, boast in the Lord* (10:17; Jer. 9:23, LXX). Paul abbreviates the text to serve his purpose, but he certainly knows its full statement and draws on its resources for his own ministry among the Corinthians. Countered by Jewish-Christian wisdom teachers at Corinth, Paul answers their jibes in the light of

Jeremiah's witness: "Let not the wise boast in their wisdom, and let not the strong boast in their strength, and let not the rich boast in their wealth. But rather let the boasters boast in this, that they understand and know that I am the Lord who acts in mercy and judgment and justice on the earth, because in these my will exists, says the Lord" (Jer. 9:22-23, LXX).

The echo of this text in Paul's mind indicts his rival apostles at Corinth. They boast in their sophisticated prowess as first-rate orator-apostles, overshadowing the pitiful figure of Paul. With the text of Jeremiah at his command, Paul debunks the self-praise that his rivals have paraded in Corinth in their effort to disenfranchise him there. The text of Jeremiah is familiar to the Corinthians. Paul summoned the same text in his earlier correspondence with them (1 Cor. 1:31), in his plea for the saving paradox of the cross (1 Cor. 1:18—2:5; cf. A. Hanson, 1987:11-23).

THE TEXT IN THE LIFE OF CHURCH

Verse 12, pinpointing what chapter 10 is about, is worth quoting here in full. *We do not dare to classify or compare ourselves with some of those who commend themselves. But when they measure themselves by one another, and compare themselves with one another, they do not show good sense.* An early commentator on this text, John Chrysostom, took Paul to mean that he will not compare himself with the false apostles who have entered Corinth. But Paul will compare himself with people like himself. Chrysostom writes, "What [Paul] says is this: 'We do not compare ourselves with them, but with one another,' . . . so we compare ourselves with ourselves, not with those who have nothing: for such arrogance cometh of folly' " (250). Perhaps one could infer with Chrysostom that in this text Paul allows comparison within a group truly devoted to the will of God. Yet Paul seems to say the practice of comparison is at its core unsound in a Christian context. A person of Christ lives up to the moral and spiritual standard of Christ, and ministers according to the specific measure of gifts and ability that God has assigned to that individual in the community of faith (1 Cor. 12:7-11).

Toward the end of the fourth century in North Africa, Augustine read Paul's text of 2 Corinthians 10:12 as good medicine for a strong people. What makes a people strong, Augustine argued, what makes the church truly great, is utter dependence on God. God's strong people give thanks continually, for in doing so, they acknowledge their dependence on divine strength. "Comparing themselves with themselves, as the Apostle says, they do not grasp the meaning of 'I will praise thee in a strong people' " (218).

Many years later, John Calvin, Reformer of Geneva, maintained that Paul does in fact compare himself with the false apostles and demonstrated his superiority to them. If the rivals had compared themselves to Paul, says Calvin, they would soon have been forced to give up their foolish idea of their own superiority and "exchanged boasting for shame" (2:135). As the notes above indicate, this view scarcely fits the parameters of the text in context. From a human point of view, Paul is weak by comparison, and he does not seek to prove otherwise. His *boast* is entirely different from that of his opponents: he boasts in weaknesses that they condemn, and so Paul boasts only in the Lord.

"For an application for this passage," Calvin looks "no farther than the monks, for as they are almost all of them the most ignorant asses, and at the same time are looked upon as learned persons on account of their long robe and hood, if one has merely a slight smattering of elegant literature, he spreads out his features like a peacock" (2:332). Influenced by his own set of circumstances in the ferment of Reformation, Calvin's sarcasm outdoes Paul's. The Reformer, like the apostle, has felt the whip of contempt on his person, no doubt, and he writes from the sting. Both men responded according to their Christian insight and experience and circumstances.

Ministers have no reason to compare themselves with one another, any more than denominations have. Comparison leads to a competitive spirit, and a competitive spirit leads to self-praise, which nullifies the praise of God. One minister may have striking ability to preach, and another special grace to visit terminally ill patients in the hospital. Both are blessed, but both are inherently "weak" in relation to Christ, in that they give themselves away for the sake of the other. Anyone who truly cares for the well-being of the other, not asking recognition in return, takes on the weak posture that so characterized Paul's life in ministry.

Denominations through their leaders have been known to play the comparison game at times. Which one of the denominational groups is more evangelical than the other? Which is more liberal? Which is more biblical? Which is more successful in attracting new members? As we stand in one camp and throw out comparisons, a detracting value is thrust on the other. Comparisons can be insidious and crippling, regardless of the "success" of the church.

Congregations as well need to guard against the comparison game in evaluating the effectiveness of their pastors. The standard of a pastor's preaching is not that of some popular TV evangelist; the standard is the grace of our Lord Jesus Christ. Nor should the current minister be compared to an earlier one; the standard is the grace of our Lord Jesus Christ. The better we all understand that standard of measurement, the more effective will be the witness of the church.

Living in the life-giving light of God's grace, followers of Christ dare not classify or compare themselves with some who commend themselves. To do so is not wise.

Forced to Boast as a Fool

2 Corinthians 11:1—12:13

PREVIEW

Paul is not averse to using satirical irony at various points in his correspondence, especially so in correspondence with the Corinthians. "The rhetoric of irony in 1 Corinthians 4:9-13," for example, is unmistakable (Plank: 33-69). Paul's language of affliction in that passage effectively validates his mission as the mission of Jesus Christ (Plank: 71-90). Yet the ironic tone and texture of Paul's language in 1 Corinthians 4 pales in comparison to that of 2 Corinthians 11:1— 12:13. In this latter passage, "Paul's words drip with irony" (Talbert: 121).

One is bound to approach this passage with caution, careful not to infer too much objective information about the opponents or the Corinthians from Paul's highly charged defensive argument. The "Paul" that speaks in this passage is angry and anxious, in danger of losing his convert-friends to a rival group of Christian missionaries who use whatever means possible to discredit him. In this impressive and yet complicated passage, the reader meets a committed apostle of Christ in a fool's garb. The reader is invited at every point in the drama to figure out the true face of Paul behind the facade of the fool, to feel a little laughter now and then, to shed an empathetic tear, to ask the actor finally to come home.

Reluctant as Paul is to boast, he has to do it (12:11), not to save face but to save the community's Christian life from falling prey to *another Jesus, . . . a different spirit, . . . a different gospel* (11:4), propagated by *false apostles . . . disguising themselves as apostles of Christ* (11:13). Paul's opponents would hardly see themselves in this light, much less describe themselves with such labels. This is Paul's response to their invective aimed at him. If he allows it to stand unchallenged, it will ultimately destroy the Corinthian community Paul founded on the crucified-risen Christ.

Throughout this long section, extending from 11:1 to 12:13, Paul not once yields his status as an authentic apostle of Christ, not once surrenders to the orientation of his opponents. They say he is weak. Paul shouts his weakness back at them through this letter to the Corinthians in a rich mixture of literary color: Yes, I am weak, and weak I shall remain to save others, *for whenever I am weak, then I am strong* (12:10; Plank: 71-90). He uses symbolic imagery, repetition of key words and phrases, parody, irony, and above all paradox in the guise of a fool.

Paul opens the speech with an image of himself as a father protecting his betrothed virgin-daughter community until her eschatological marriage. He fights against the cunning seduction of satanic deceivers appearing as *super-apostles* (11:1-5). Out of love, he has declined taking money from the Corinthians, unlike the so-called *ministers of righteousness* (11:7-15). Then from 11:16 to 12:10, Paul engages in the foolish speech proper: he boasts, not of his prowess as an apostle, but of his weakness. He sums up his folly in the words of 12:11-13.

OUTLINE

The Situation Requiring Foolish Boasting, 11:1-15
11:1-6	Protecting the Betrothed
11:7-11	Money Lovingly Declined
11:12-15	Disguised as Ministers

Speaking as a Fool, 11:16—12:10
11:16-21a	Foolish Confidence
11:21b-33	A Fool's Pedigree
12:1-10	A Fool's Paradise

Conclusion to the Fool's Speech, 12:11-13

EXPLANATORY NOTES

The Situation Requiring Foolish Boasting 11:1-15

The introduction to the Fool's Speech is extraordinarily long, fifteen verses (11:1-15). Yet it is not a "digression" (Talbert: 119) but an extended rationale for making such a "foolish" speech that follows.

11:1-6 Protecting the Betrothed

The wish of verse 1 signals the impending "foolishness" on which Paul is about to embark. *I wish you would bear with me in a little foolishness. Do bear with me!* The wish in this context is a way of begging the readers' indulgence, while admitting "the sorry necessity of self-praise" (Talbert: 110). If the readers miss the significance of the wish-word, they can hardly escape the repeated *bear with me*, first in the indicative (11:1a) and second in the imperative (11:1b). The word invites the readers to be patient "in the sense of enduring possible difficulty" (Louw, 1:308), in this case the difficulty of "watching" Paul donning a fool's cap to make his sharp point. The difficulty also leads Paul into a lengthy rationale for his *foolishness*, beginning with the symbolic image of a father protecting his betrothed daughter until her marriage (11:2).

For his image, Paul draws on a common Jewish practice of his time (see references in Windisch: 320; Furnish, 1984:499). The father jealously guarded his betrothed virgin daughter in the time between betrothal and marriage, lest she become defiled by another man and the father thereby become culpable and disgraced. Paul's jealousy (or zeal) as the apostolic father of the Corinthians is *of God* (NRSV: *divine*), in that he takes responsibility for presenting the community *as a chaste virgin to Christ* (11:2b), unaffected by a message alien to the one Paul delivered to them in the first place. (Paul's metaphors will not stand being pressed beyond the single point he wishes to make.)

The analogy of betrothal, marriage, and the possibility of seduction triggers the Genesis story of the primordial seduction of the first betrothed virgin, Eve, from what is pure and good. Aided by Jewish speculation on the story, (e.g., 1 Enoch 69:6; 2 Enoch 31:16; cf. 1 Tim. 2:13-14), Paul portrays the serpent of Genesis as a beguiling form of Satan, who led Eve astray and corrupted her innocence, which ultimately led into death (Wisdom 2:24; cf. 2 Cor. 11:14; A. Hanson, 1986:64-77). Like Eve, the Corinthian community is at risk of having their thoughts turned from a *sincere and pure devotion to Christ* (11:3b) by emissaries of Satan. Verses 4 to 6 extend the implications of Paul's symbolic image into the current situation at Corinth.

Paul probably does not have a specific individual in mind when he says, *For if someone comes and proclaims another Jesus* (11:4; cf. Barrett, 1973:275). The *someone* (singular) takes off from *the serpent* in the previous verse and is intended to have the same connotations in the context of the subsequent sentences. The message of the deceptive *someone* contains three elements, each one intertwined with the other as nowhere else in Paul's letters: *another Jesus, a different spirit, a different gospel* (11:4). Paul is not at pains to define these three terms of difference, nor is such definition required to make the Fool's Speech effective.

Except for the word order, *a different gospel* is identical to the phrase in Galatians 1:6. However, it is inappropriate to assume that the *different gospel* in 2 Corinthians 11:4 is identical to that of Galatians. The problems inherent in the language of 2 Corinthians 10-13 bear no resemblance to those reflected in Galatians. There is no hint in these chapters of the opponents requiring the Corinthians to practice circumcision, food regulations, or Sabbath keeping. Nor is there any clear indication of opposition stemming from Jerusalem, as there is in Galatians. Thus it is not at all "natural to think that the same meaning will apply in 2 Corinthians" (Barrett, 1973:276; cf. 1982b:60-86). If definition of the three terms is required at all, it must come from the context in which they occur.

Another Jesus could well refer to an elevation of the person of the earthly Jesus, and a corresponding devaluation of the crucified Jesus. Such an elevation of the earthly figure would contradict the very core of Paul's preaching, in which the crucified one is the stumbling block that saves (cf. 1 Cor. 1:18, 23). Paul's protracted weakness in the Fool's Speech corresponds to his preaching of the cross, the ultimate sign of weakness and foolishness. For Paul, however, it is enough to use the phrase without delineation, and so it should be for his interpreters also (Furnish, 1984:500-501, with various views of *another Jesus*).

A different spirit likewise stands undeveloped, although inherently linked to *another Jesus* and *a different gospel*. The Spirit the Corinthians are said to have received through Paul's preaching was the Spirit of the crucified-resurrected Jesus Christ, the same Spirit that guarantees future salvation (2 Cor. 1:22) and present transformation (3:17-18). In the context of the Letter of Defense, the *different spirit* manifests itself in boasting according to human standards rather than the standard of Christ (10:2-6; cf. Georgi, 1985:272-273).

A *different gospel* simply compounds Paul's point of difference, with a focus on the essential character of the good news. Paul expects the congregation to be able to spot the difference when they hear the word preached, but there is nothing to suggest that Paul means "a gospel of works" (Windisch: 328). Whatever the *different gospel* may be, the problem for Paul is that the opponents' manner of speech is persuasive, perhaps beyond Paul's (cf. 11:5). And the Corinthians *submit to it readily enough* (11:4b). Knowing their propensity, Paul prepares his readers for the gusto of his Fool's Speech, the like of which they probably have not heard from him before.

As part of the preparation, Paul affirms his apostolic status without equivocation but with sarcastic irony: *I think that I am not in the least inferior to these super-apostles* (11:5). Paul's use of *super* here should not be taken as a serious reference to the apostles of Jerusalem commissioned by the earthly Jesus, such as Cephas, James, and John in Galatians 2:6-10 (so Barrett, 1973:278; similarly Thrall, 1980:42-57; cf. Käsemann, 1964:81-89). In context, *super-apostles* is sarcastic, as is Paul's remark that he is not *inferior* to them. He repeats the remark at the close of the Fool's Speech in a way that confirms the identity of the *super-apostles* as the ones against whom Paul creates a parody in the Fool's Speech: *I am not at all inferior to these super-apostles, even though I am nothing* (12:11).

Verse 5 constitutes a tongue-in-cheek declaration of indisputable apostolic status. Paul concedes in 11:6a that his detractors might be able to surpass him in persuasive oratory—*I may be untrained in speech*—but they cannot exceed him in *knowledge*. Knowledge, not speech and dramatic acting, establish apostolic status. Furthermore, judging from various statements and innuendo in 1 Corinthians, the people of Corinth (some of them at least) value knowledge above all (cf. 1 Cor. 8:1; 13:2, 8-9). Now Paul declares himself equipped with knowledge, such as he made evident at Corinth *in every way and in all things* (2 Cor. 11:6). The implication of verse 6 is that if the Corinthians will not bear with him in his fool's language, they should bear with him because of his knowledge.

His explication of the betrothal image now complete, Paul broaches the subject of his refusal of financial support from the Corinthians.

11:7-11 Money Lovingly Declined

From this paragraph and its counterpart in 1 Corinthians 9:3-18, we find that Paul has declined financial support from the congregations in Achaia. Why he does so is not clear. In both texts Paul claims he refused gifts to make the gospel *free of charge* (1 Cor. 9:18; 2 Cor. 11:7). The earlier text says he has decided "not to make full use of [his] rights in the gospel" (1 Cor. 9:18). Now here he says he wants *to refrain from burdening [them] in any way* (2 Cor. 11:9).

The criticism behind the plea in 2 Corinthians 11:7-11 is that Paul's refusal of money proves his lack of apostolic authority as well as his lack of friendship. For their part, the opponents take money for their ministry, as is their right, and denigrate Paul at the same time for not doing so (cf. 1 Cor. 9:12). Consider how the poor and "weak" (1 Cor. 9:22) members of the congregation would feel in such a situation. When they listen in on the reading of Paul's speech of weakness, they will likely say among themselves: "This Paul is *our* friend! He loves *us*!"

Second Corinthians 11:7 asks a rhetorical question in exaggerated form, forcing a negative response: *Did I commit a sin by humbling myself so that you might be exalted, because I proclaimed God's good news to you free of charge?* "Paul's irony is here at its most bitter" (Barrett, 1973:281). One hears in the question an echo of the language of 10:1 (*I appeal to you by the meekness and gentleness of Christ—I who am humble when face to face*). The effect of the question is telling. For members of the community to denigrate Paul for humbly declining money is to denigrate Christ, who humbled himself utterly in death (cf. Phil. 2:8), whose *meekness and gentleness* Paul has demonstrated among the Corinthians by delivering "God's gospel, that most precious thing, *for nothing!*" (Plummer: 303).

Second Corinthians 11:8-9 offer Paul's reason for his refusal of money from Corinth; they also raise a question difficult to resolve. He has *refrained* (11:9b) from accepting money, even though he *was in need.* He gives two reasons: first, his *needs were supplied by the friends who came from Macedonia* (11:9a); and second, he did not want to *burden* anyone at Corinth (11:9b). The repetition of *refrain* in the future tense, *I will continue to refrain*, implies a principle that Paul has adopted concerning Corinth. He is now prepared to defend this principle forcefully against his detractors. The exact sense of the principle is difficult to determine. Presumably, if Paul accepts financial support from wealthy members of the congregation, he would feel restricted in his freedom to give his patrons directives, moral and otherwise. They would have become his friends at the expense of the weaker members (Chow: 167-187; cf. Käsemann, 1956:52/37-66/71; Betz, 1972:100-117, 132-137; Furnish, 1984:506-507).

The related question still remains: Why did Paul accept support money from the Macedonians? Would the same principle not apply equally to them? Apparently not. The vivid language at 11:8 has shock value: *I robbed other churches*—presumably those of Macedonia (11:9a). Used only here in the NT, the term *robbed* (*esulēsa*) was commonly used to describe the action of soldiers in plundering captured peoples (Louw, 1:584; Hughes: 385; R. Martin, 1986:346). Paul's metaphorical use of the word in verse 8 stresses his other principle that "those who proclaim the gospel should get their living by the gospel" (1 Cor. 9:14). More than that, the Macedonians are reported to have been extremely poor (8:2), like Paul himself, and could not therefore take up the role of "the powerful patron" in relation to Paul in the same way that the rich Corinthians could (Chow: 123-141, 166).

At 11:10 Paul labels his refusal of support from Corinth as *this boast of mine*, the very reverse of what his opponents are probably boasting. Their self-proclaimed "superiority" has doubtless brought them substantial support from the wealthy of Corinth and gained them high rank among the leaders of the community. From their high position, they are able to criticize Paul, whose *humble* character and performance make him unworthy of Corinthian patronage and therefore devoid of any boast. This scenario about the opponents' perspective on Paul is credible from the language of verse 10. On the other hand, the Corinthians themselves may have interpreted his refusal of support as rejecting their friendship, as in the patron-client relationship. One could infer as much from the question-exclamation form of verse 11. He maintains his *boast* of offering the gospel gratis at Corinth and insists that his boast *will not be silenced in the regions of Achaia*. Then he asks, *And why? Because I do not love you?* He answers boldly by invoking the divine name: *God knows I do!* (11:11).

On another front, the messengers Paul has dispatched, including Titus, have reached Corinth, ready to complete the collection for the saints. Their efforts in raising the money may have aroused suspicions that Paul had chosen a devious means of grabbing money for himself, thus circumventing the parameters of the patron-client relationship. The passage (12:14-18) following the Fool's Speech tends to confirm this view: *(You say) since I was crafty, I took you in by de-*

ceit. Did I take advantage of you through any of those whom I sent to you? (12:16-17). More on that text later.

11:12-15 Disguised as Ministers

Still working toward the Fool's Speech proper in this passage, Paul paints a bold portrait of his rivals as he prepares for the upcoming parody. Several scholars separate the persons targeted in these verses from the *super-apostles* of 11:5 and 12:11 (such as Bruce: 239; Barrett, 1982b:87-103). The argument is that the opponents of 11:12-15 operate under the authority of the Jerusalem apostles, probably with letters of recommendation (3:1), but that they misrepresent the Jerusalem group and Paul's relationship to the group. As noted above under verse 5, such a distinction between the *super-apostles* and those described in 11:13-15 lacks any solid evidence from the Letter of Defense or from any other part of 2 Corinthians. When Paul refers to the *super-apostles* in the introduction and conclusion of his Fool's Speech, he aims merely at deriding their own lofty title of self-praise. The designations in 11:13-15, on the other hand, are Paul's own, in direct response to their invective against him.

Verse 12a reinforces Paul's policy adopted for Corinth, not taking money for his missionary services: *What I do I will also continue to do.* Only now his reason for standing his ground on his policy has altered. He has in his sights now the intruding opponents, not his Corinthian converts (11:12b). If he were to accept money from the Corinthians, he argues, the opponents could then claim equal status with him and his apostolic colleagues, since the opponents also receive payment for their services. Thus his insistence on offering the gospel free at Corinth separates him utterly from his opponents, and from any real comparison with them. His position does *deny* the opponents *an opportunity to be recognized as [apostolic] equals in what they boast about.* Paul's denial is strong; he *cuts off* and *removes* their grounds for boasting. The word *ekkoptō* means literally "to cut in such a way as to cause separation" (Louw, 1:225). Plainly, Paul wants to distance himself as far as possible from the interlopers at Corinth. His refusal of support is one way of doing so.

Another way is to cast the opponents in the worst possible light by construing a list of unflattering labels, as in 11:13: *Such boasters are false apostles, deceitful workers, disguising themselves as apostles of Christ.* Casting subtle irony aside for the moment, "Paul calls a spade a spade" and labels his opponents as he finds them (Denny: 331).

The first label, *false apostles*, turns their self-styled title *super-apostles* (11:5) on its head. Far from being the apostolic heroes they fancy themselves to be, these boasters are mere imitation apostles, inflated with a sense of their own importance. The second term of derision, *deceitful workers*, simply compounds the first. Their actions do not spring from a pure heart. The third label caps the list. They are self-disguised apostles of Christ. They have changed their appearance to look like apostles of Christ. The omen of this final designation is that Paul is about to expose the real character of these self-styled apostles of Christ, in the next two verses and in the Fool's Speech that follows.

The idea of *disguise* points immediately to the master of disguise in Paul's thought world: Satan. "According to some Jewish traditions, Satan *disguised* himself *as an angel of light* to seduce Eve" (Furnish, 1984:510; Life of Adam and Eve 9:1, 3; 12:1; Apoc. Mos. 17:1). By portraying his enemies as ministers of Satan, Paul puts the ultimate insult on his opponents. As Paul sees it, their play-acting as apostles of Christ betrays their real allegiance, not to Christ at all, but to his archenemy, who *disguises himself as an angel of light* and fools them (2 Cor. 11:14). Yet veiled behind the undiluted polemic of 11:15 is a faint image of Christian ministers from some quarter, having come to Corinth with a message of *justice* or *righteousness*. However skillfully they may have expressed their message, however convincing their words in the name of Christ, Paul brands their preaching as the work of Satan's ministers masquerading *as ministers of righteousness*.

The full scope of their message is difficult to reconstruct with any certainty from Paul's rhetoric. One has to assume, however, from the consistent theme of *weakness* throughout the Fool's Speech that one of the main features of their message contains some kind of power theology, whether eloquence, spiritual ecstasy, visions, miracles, or the like.

To complete his derisive portrait of his opponents, Paul pronounces eschatological judgment on them, a kind of "sentence of holy law" (Käsemann, 1969:66-81). *Their end will match their deeds* (11:15b).

Speaking as a Fool 11:16—12:10

With the rationale for this Fool's Speech now in place (11:1-15), Paul embarks, however reluctantly, on the speech proper at 11:16. Throughout the whole argument, he matches the situation at Corinth by invoking conventions from the literary world of the time—comparison, self-praise, and irony. (Missionary counterparts are using the same conventions to undermine his authority as a missionary in a congregation founded by him.) Although not convinced of the value of *comparison* and *self-praise* for a Christian apostle (10:12-18), Paul is able to use these devices in the context of *irony*.

Irony is "the use of words or phrases to mean the opposite of what they normally mean" (Forbes: 10). Hence, when Paul praises himself in this speech, the subject matter is the opposite of what it ought to be, weakness instead of power, trials instead of triumphs, etc. His desire is to regain his rightful place in the Corinthian congregation, but not by yielding to the same conventional ground as his opponents. The ironic fool's discourse provides Paul with a way out of this dilemma. At the same time, the weak character of *a fool* corresponds admirably with Paul's gospel, the social-human weakness of the cross, through which God saves the world (1 Cor. 1:18-31).

11:16-21a   Foolish Confidence

I repeat (11:16) recalls the thought of 11:1 about speaking *a little foolishness*, but the rest of verse 16 advances to the subject of a little *boasting*. The boasting, little or large, has to happen in the context of a Fool's Speech, otherwise Paul contradicts the center of his Christian thought: *Let the one who boasts, boast in the Lord* (10:17). Yet he does not want the Corinthians or the opponents to take him for an actual fool, "with no depth or sense of proportion and therefore not to be taken seriously" (Watson: 123). He is merely playing the part of a fool for two reasons: (1) to convince his readers of his genuineness as their apostle, and (2) to create a parody of his opponents so as to expose their falsehood.

The next two sentences in 11:17-18 set up a sharp contrast by means of two antithetical phrases: *with the Lord's authority* and *according to human standards*. The counterbalance between the two phrases is more apparent in the Greek. Paul implies that even his *little . . . boastful confidence* is not *kata kurion* (*according to the Lord*) but is *kata sarka* (*according to the flesh*). He prefers not to be among *the many* who indulge in self-praise *according to the flesh*. Yet he is irresistibly driven to boast by the sheer force of circumstances at Corinth, but only in the guise of a fool. He uses subject matter that will appear foolish to the arrogant rivals, the real fools in the end.

Verse 19 answers, *You gladly put up with fools.* The fools are Paul's adversaries, who have dared to set themselves up in Corinth against him. If the Corinthians put up with those real fools, surely they can take a little foolish pretense from Paul. So his argument suggests, while he extends a tongue-in-cheek compliment to the Corinthians themselves: *being wise yourselves!*

The wisdom-folly theme pervades the entire section, as it does other arguments in the Corinthian correspondence, particularly 1 Corinthians 1-4. Hence, some validity should be granted to the view that the Corinthians (some at least) have tended toward a form of wisdom Christology rooted in the teaching of the Alexandrian-born Jewish Christian, Apollos. From the combined evidence in 1 Corinthians 2-4 and Acts 18-19, Apollos may have taught and practiced baptism as initiation into the spiritual wisdom of Christ, not into the death of Christ as Paul has taught. "Paul stresses cross and Apollos stresses wisdom" (Richardson: 107).

Wisdom theology can quickly become power theology, as 2 Corinthians 11:20 illustrates, and power theology nullifies the gospel by its oppressive stance. The string of five verbs in verse 20 suggests that Paul is well acquainted with the style of leadership the intruders exercise at Corinth. The Corinthians allow someone *to enslave* them, *to prey* on them, *to control* them, *to oppress* them, and *to slap* them on the face. The whole list is headed up by the compound verb *to enslave,* which occurs also in Galatians 2:4 in connection with the Mosaic Law. Here in 2 Corinthians, however, the law is not in view. Instead, the Corinthians have put themselves in bondage to apostles of wisdom-power. The result is abuse of the socially weak members. Paul will eventually demonstrate in his fool's discourse that any inflated violation of human dignity denies the gospel of the grace of God (cf. 12:7-10; Theissen, 1982:121-140).

With a taste of bitter sarcasm, Paul concludes his ironic appeal for a sympathetic hearing from the Corinthians at 11:21, following his caricature of the opponents in verse 20. *To my shame, I must say, we were too weak for that!* In other words, "What a pity we are not like that—you seem to prefer bullies" (R. Martin, 1986:366).

11:21b-33 A Fool's Pedigree

Finally Paul launches his boast proper in this section, beginning with a comparison in the form of question and answer (11:21b-23a). This is followed by a litany of afflictions in missionary service

(11:23b-29) and capped by an ironically humorous story of his escape down a wall at Damascus (11:30-33). All parts of the boast, however, fall under the flag of the emphatic double parentheses: *I am speaking as a fool* (11:21a); *I am talking like a madman* (11:23a).

If the comparative questions in verses 22 and 23a spring from Paul's knowledge of the opponents, as is safe to assume, then his rival missionaries at Corinth claim to be *full-blooded Jewish-Christian ministers,* and Paul matches or surpasses every claim. There is nothing in the questions that points to a Palestinian Jewish origin for the opponents (cf. Fallon: 99); thus Paul is confident in comparing himself to them.

Are they Hebrews? So am I (11:22). This designation, *Hebrews,* could refer to the language they speak or their skill at reading the Hebrew Bible rather than the Greek translation. More probably the claim has to do with ancestry, true genealogical kinship with the ancient people who left the bondage of Egypt. Paul elsewhere refers to himself as "a Hebrew born of Hebrews" (Phil. 3:5), by which he doubtless means unadulterated descent rather than knowledge of the Hebrew language. The same is probably true for this comparative question in 11:22. "The matter of one's 'good breeding' was a standard topic of Hellenistic rhetoric . . . , whether taken up in order to praise another or in order to commend oneself" (Furnish, 1984:534).

Are they Israelites? So am I (11:22). Related to the first claim to be Hebrews, this one connects the claimants with the religious and cultural heritage of the Hebrew people who became a nation according to the earlier promise of God to Jacob. The order of the questions points to a deepening of the ancestral connection with salvation history, from the Hebrews of the exodus back to Jacob-Israel of national promise.

Are they descendants of Abraham? So am I (11:22). This designation takes the claimants back further to the primal patriarch of promise. His faith-blessing became the paradigm for all the elect of God forever after. For the opponents to be able to make this threefold boast is for them apparently a sign of genuineness if not superiority. On the strength of these three boasts of religious pedigree, they seem to have staked their claim to be first-class Christian missionaries. Yet on all counts Paul can match their boast, *speaking as a fool* (11:21b). To speak boastfully of connection with the dispensation past is foolishness to Paul, because "in the new aeon the only matter of importance was being 'in Christ' " (Fallon: 100).

Are they ministers of Christ? I am talking like a madman—I am a

better one (11:23). Paul does grant his rivals this bold claim, for the
sake of argument at least. But his parenthesis is telling. How can a
true minister of the true Christ, who humbled himself unto death on a
cross, boast of status in the conventional way? For Paul to engage in
any form of boasting about his ministry in the name of this Christ is
madness. His ploy, however, is to perform a parody on his opponents. Yes, he will boast, but of things that any self-respecting person
of the Mediterranean world in their right mind would not dare to
boast about—of hardships and insults, of disgrace and weakness.
Paul's list of hardships is not the kind that a true philosopher presents
to prove his endurance and thus the truth of his ideas. Paul's self-
depiction here, apparently quite unlike that of his opponents, is totally uncomplimentary. There is nothing that "resembles Paul's sustained self-derision in Greek or Roman authors" (Marshall: 360).

Ironically, Paul's opponents are likely to agree wholeheartedly
with his self-derision. It corresponds with their critique of him as an
apostle. But now in the context of the Fool's Speech, their agreement
condemns them as false apostles, because they reject the minister
who bears in his body the offensive marks of the crucified Christ of
God (cf. 4:7-10).

Paul's catalog of hardships and indignities that follows (11:23b-
29) does not exhibit a neat literary structure. Nor are all the various
incidents and situations he cites easy to reconstruct historically. For
that matter, the purpose of listing in such a speech is not for biographical information but for convincing effect. Real events and circumstances in Paul's memory do lie behind the items on the list. But
he selects and lists the items judiciously to make the point at issue,
that he is a true minister of the true Christ.

Everything on the list relates to Paul's personal involvement in
Christian mission, with the incident at Damascus bringing the list to a
climax. The thought in the list moves from general to specific in two
phases.

In the first phase, Paul gives an exaggerated overview in 11:23b
of *far greater labors, far more imprisonments, with countless flog-
gings, and often near death.* Then he illustrates with specific cases
(11:24-25). He recalls five times having *received from the Jews the
forty lashes minus one.* The synagogue had authority to inflict punishment on Jewish recalcitrants based on Deuteronomy 25:3, which
restricted the lashes to forty and no more. To avoid breaking that injunction by a miscount, Jewish leaders established a rule to inflict one
less than forty lashes. For Paul to receive this punishment, he had to

present himself at the synagogue and lay claim to being Jewish, since the synagogue authorities had no power to discipline their non-Jewish neighbors.

When Paul was three times *beaten with rods,* it was at the hands of Roman authorities. Acts records one such beating at Philippi (16:22-23). The one stoning may have happened at the hands of Jewish people, although stoning was a capital punishment in Judaism. Acts 14, however, does record one stoning of Paul at Lystra, in which he was left for dead (14:19). None of the three shipwrecks have any documentation beyond this list. (The shipwreck of Acts 27 comes after 2 Corinthians). Being adrift *for a night and a day* at sea, literally *in the deep,* recalls the ancient Near Eastern mythology of the waters of chaos *(tehom/tiamat).* The ancient Israelites feared being enveloped by the deep and its denizens unless the Creator-God rescued them (Gen. 1:2, 6; Ps. 69:15; 77:16; Hab. 3:10).

In the second phase, Paul reverts to listing general perils, deprivations, and anxieties. He uses repetition of key words (e.g., *danger*) to reinforce the impression of hardship and weakness, and ending with two pivotal questions that focus the boast of weakness (2 Cor. 11:26-29). The perils in general come from rivers, bandits, his own people, Gentile people, the city, the desert, the sea, and *false brothers and sisters* (11:26). The last item is the current situation and appears strategically at the end of the perils.

Then follows a series of physiological deprivations in general: sleeplessness (also at 6:5), hunger, thirst, cold, nakedness. Nakedness in the Jewish context also meant shame. The list of general hardships in phase two ends on a psychological note closely tied to the situation of the moment. He says, *I am under daily pressure because of my anxiety for all the churches* (11:28). This is a veiled reference to the current situation at Corinth. Fledgling Gentile churches such as that of Corinth have become easy prey for charlatans and sophists of various kinds, who win support by replacing the offense of the cross with a power theology in the guise of the Christian gospel.

Paul's two questions at the end of the general list speak poignantly to this last point. *Who is weak, and I am not weak? Who is made to stumble, and I am not indignant?* (11:29). God, in the cross of Jesus, is on the side of the weak, as Paul must be if he is God's minister. Hence, Paul gives his concluding specific example of escaping the powers in Damascus by being lowered down the city wall in a basket. The event shows his weakness (11:30-33).

Some scholars judge the vignette about escape from Damascus to be out of place at the end of a list of hardships and assume that an editor inserted it here in 2 Corinthians (Windisch: 363-364; Betz, 1972:73). They assume the narrative simply does not fit the context and form of what precedes and follows. On the contrary, this short narrative brings the subject of the list to a dramatic climax. Its motif of **descent** provides a bridge to the empty boast about **ascent** that follows.

Paul has called God to witness by an oath-formula in 11:31 as he tells of his escape from the governor of King Aretas at Damascus. He was *let down in a basket through a window in the wall, and escaped from his hands* (11:33; cf. Acts 9:23-24). King Aretas IV ruled the Nabataean kingdom from the city of Petra in the Negeb from 9 B.C. to A.D. 39/40. His kingdom ran from the southern Negeb through Transjordan as far north as Damascus. Paul's escape may be dated in the mid-thirties, during his time in Arabia. "Arabia" was a general designation for the Nabataean kingdom (see Gal. 1:17).

What Paul was doing there to incur the anger of the governor of King Aretas is not immediately apparent in the relevant texts. A reasonable guess is that Paul was preaching the gospel of Christ to Gentiles, in accordance with his call (Gal. 1:16; 2:1:1-2). Perhaps he was still requiring circumcision in this early stage of his Gentile mission (cf. Gal. 5:11). Whatever his activity there, it met with strong disapproval from the Nabataean authority in Damascus (cf. Acts 9:22-23; Faw: 113-114).

Paul's competitors at Corinth could construe his escape as cowardly. But in the context of the Fool's Speech, the humiliating escape down the Damascus city wall in a basket fits his "Christian boast" of weakness. It is the opposite of a Roman soldier's boast on scaling a city wall to take the city. The first soldier up the wall would win the emperor's celebrated *corona muralis* (wall crown) for his bravery (Judge: 45). In Paul's case, the incident of his descent in a basket (perhaps a fish basket; R. Martin, 1986:385) constitutes God's deliverance and Paul's weakness. It thus caps the ironic catalog of hardships and humiliations that make him a genuine minister of Christ.

12:1-10 A Fool's Paradise

Moving beyond his catalog of humiliations that illustrate his weakness, Paul ventures to boast on the same level as his competitors. At least that is how it appears. His boast of ecstasy, however, is probably a parody of his opponents' boasting of the same kind of experience

(Betz, 1972:89-90). To expose their folly, Paul finds it *necessary to boast*. He can match the boast of his rival apostles when he is forced to do so. But then, pointing up the folly in such boasting, he reverts to the ironic* boast of *weaknesses* that mark the life of a true apostle (12:5). Hence, the whole section (12:1-10) exhibits a literary balance between two boasts, the latter of which by its nature is not a boast at all: First, an ecstatic revelation in another world with immortal words that cannot be uttered (12:1-5). Second, a painful experience in this world with a sustaining oracle that can be uttered (12:6-10).

In the first, the fool's boast, *it is necessary to boast* (12:1), but not because Paul believes in the convention of self-praise to make a case for his apostleship. Instead, the Corinthians have pushed him to compare himself with his competitors or admit that he lacks their authority. What happens in the process is that Paul presents "a case for a radically different conception of apostolic authority through his irony" (Forbes: 20).

Necessary as such comparative boasting is in the situation, *nothing is to be gained by it* (12:1). Paul will not build his case for apostleship on this boast, nor will his claim to *visions and revelations* enhance the community's life in any way. Paul's language shows his reluctance to engage in boasting of this kind. This is nowhere more striking than in his use of the third person (*a person*) to describe his own unusual rapture and revelation of fourteen years earlier, about A.D. 42-43 (12:2-4, 7).

This revelation must have been unique for Paul. He apparently kept it much to himself and now has selected it from among his other *visions and revelations of the Lord* (12:1). The experience was his own (12:7), not that of some other person, though on the surface the text may seem to imply otherwise. Why Paul has chosen the third-person form of speech to present his own experience of being *caught up to the third heaven* is unclear. One suspects that he prefers not to make his personal boast too blatant, and thus he distances himself from it. Besides, he scarcely remembers what state he was in when he had the experience. *Whether in the body or out of the body*, he does not know. So he presents this ecstatic person as someone other than himself, other than the earthbound apostle God called him to be.

On the other hand, Paul could be aware of the Socratic tradition that advises against boasting in one's own name, but if necessary in the name of another. "Paul's use of the third person is his way of observing this sort of convention" (Lincoln: 208-209). He knows *a person in Christ* (12:2), *such a person* (12:3), *such a one* (12:5).

Paul's account of the experience makes two key points: (1) His person was raptured to the third heaven, called *Paradise* (12: 2, 4). (2) He *heard things that are not to be told, that no mortal is permitted to repeat* (12:4). The first point corresponds with some Jewish cosmology of Paul's time (2 Enoch 8), which described seven heavens (or even ten, 2 En. 3–22; Charlesworth, 1:115-116, 246-249). The ancients thought of the heavens as levels or realms of existence. The third heaven was supposed to be beyond the astral heaven of physical vision and therefore the realm of the Paradise of God and angels, where the future of the world also resides (cf. Luke 23:43; Rev. 2:7; like the garden or park of Eden: Gen. 2:8, LXX).

Yet the accent of Paul's account falls not on his vision of a mysterious plan of the ages—much less a vision of God or angels—but on the words he *heard*, unutterable words *that no mortal is permitted to repeat*. In this respect, therefore, the ecstatic experience of Paradise is not edifying to the church, and is therefore not a credential for ministry. This is so no matter how much the rival missionaries may recite what they purportedly have heard in their flights of ecstasy.

There is no way of knowing what Paul heard or saw in Paradise, but speculation persists in any case. Some say that the second part of the boast about Paul's thorn in the flesh and the oracle of grace (12:6-10) should be tied to the first part about the rapture to Paradise (12:1-5). The suggestion is that Paul became proud in Paradise and prayed three times while he was there to have the thorn in his flesh removed. An angel or demon rebuked him, after which Paul received the oracle of sufficient grace from the Lord (Price: 37). But this notion lacks support in the text. What Paul heard in the third heaven, he cannot repeat on earth. Why then does he repeat the oracle he received in Paradise?

More likely the oracle belongs to a separate nonecstatic episode (12:6-10) by which Paul counters the boast-value of the rapture to Paradise (12:1-5). Verse 5 makes the transition from the foolish boast about revelations in Paradise to the ironic *"boast"* of the true apostle: *On behalf of such a one* [raptured to Paradise] *I will boast, but on my own behalf* [as apostle of Christ] *I will not boast, except of my weaknesses* [which is not really a boast at all].

There is a second side of the balance, a painful experience in this world with a sustaining oracle of grace that can be uttered (12:6-10). For this second part, Paul shows something of his true Christian self behind his fool's cloak. He can boast if he wishes without being a fool, for he would at least be *speaking the truth* (12:6). He implies that the boast of his opponents about their revelations is false; that makes them real fools. But even given the truth about the *exceptional character* of his otherworldly revelations, Paul still refrains from boasting about them (12:6-7). The test of his ministry in the name of Christ lies in what people can see and hear for themselves. Does his ministry measure up to the standard of the crucified Christ? This is the crucial question the Corinthians must answer concerning Paul. It is one that Paul answers distinctively for himself in the verses that follow (12:7b-10).

To keep me from being too elated, a thorn was given me in the flesh, a messenger of Satan to torment me, to keep me from being too elated (12:7b). Remarkably, Paul takes some humiliating factor in his person, perhaps the same despicable feature his opponents hold against him (10:10), and casts it in the brilliant light of God's grace. The search for the specific identity of Paul's metaphoric *thorn in the flesh* is a blind alley that adds nothing to the meaning of the text. The metaphor itself carries the meaning: a thorn in the flesh is painful, tormenting, uncomfortable. Yet conjectures are myriad, most in the physical sphere: malaria, earache, blindness, epilepsy, persecutions, etc. Some have proposed a psychological malady such as depression, or Paul's grief over the unbelief of his own Jewish people, or his problem with opponents. Still others suggest a spiritual-moral meaning, as in a tormenting temptation to yield to sexual desire, hence the appellation *messenger of Satan* (Hughes: 442-448).

Indulging in conjectures about Paul's *thorn in the flesh* can detract from the significance of the text in its setting. Yet Paul has suffered from a tormenting condition in his physical being (*flesh*). He personifies it as *a messenger of Satan*, but claims it is authorized by God and is intended to keep him *from being too elated*. Paul ascribes the pain itself to Satan, but its usefulness in Christian ministry he ascribes to God. In this respect, Paul's thorn resembles the redemptive cross of Jesus Christ.

Like the triple prayer of Christ in Gethsemene, when he faced the cross in his flesh (Matt. 26:39-44), Paul prayed three times to the Lord to remove the thorn from his flesh. The thorn remained, but with it came the two-line oracle of divine grace that etched its benediction indelibly on Paul's mind and irreversibly shaped his ministry. *My grace is sufficient for you, for power is made perfect in weakness* (12:9). This is the shining centerpiece of the Fool's Speech. The light of the oracle illuminates the story of Paul's descent of the wall in a basket, and explains his refusal to boast in anything mortal except his weakness.

With a few succinct strokes of his quill to bring his Fool's Speech to its climax, Paul has created a classic nugget of Christian literature that has drawn preacher, poet, peasant, and philosopher to it like a magnet. In an astounding paradox, Paul depicts his personal appropriation of the divine oracle; as any paradox, it invites reflection and response rather than logical explanation: *So, I will boast all the more gladly of my weaknesses, so that the power of Christ may dwell in me. Therefore I am content with weaknesses, insults, hardships, persecutions, and calamities for the sake of Christ; for whenever I am weak, then I am strong* (12:9-10).

Conclusion to the Fool's Speech   12:11-13

Paul concludes his Fool's Speech as he opened it (11:1-15), with justification for his foolish boasting. The closing word echoes to the same ironic tone that has marked the speech throughout, the only new material being *the signs of a true apostle* (12:12).

I have been a fool! A *fool* first for boasting as a minister of Christ; a fool also in the sense of jester, to mock the self-praise of his rival apostles. In this closing defense of his foolish boast, he lays responsibility on the back of the Corinthians themselves. **You** *forced me to it;* the *you* is emphatic (12:11a). He was compelled, not because the Corinthians persuaded him overtly to boast of his apostleship, but because they were silent about Paul in the presence of boastful apostles who reduced Paul to *nothing* (12:11b). *Indeed you should have been the ones commending me*, says Paul. After all, he is their spiritual father (11:2; 1 Cor. 4:15), the one who brought them to faith in Christ and founded the community in their city. They themselves are his letter of recommendation, *to be known and read by all* (2 Cor. 3:2). Yet they have failed to commend their founding apostle to the self-styled *super-apostles* (12:11; 11:5).

Paul declares himself *not at all inferior to these super-apostles*, and then adds, *even though I am nothing* (12:11b). The last phrase juxtaposed to the first probably echoes the opponents' critique of Paul as *nothing* alongside them. If they do refer to him as *nothing* of an apostle, he agrees ironically, as he did before when he cited their bitter comment about his weakness (10:10). Yes, it is true I am nothing, he argues implicitly, but that makes me a true apostle of Christ as compared to those who claim to be superior. Thus he can assert that he is not at all inferior to these super-apostles, not that he is claiming to be their equal (cf. Watson: 137). On the contrary, he is not in their league at all, since they are *false apostles*. The *super-apostles* and the *false-apostles* are the same group of rival interlopers at Corinth against whom Paul is forced to defend himself as a fool [*Super-Apostles, p. 279*].

At 12:12, Paul incorporates a new item, *the signs of a true apostle*, which the Corinthians probably feel they had a right to expect. Early Christian tradition soon adopted *signs* of a true apostle of Christ, with which Paul is familiar. The *signs* were said to confirm the presence and power of God in the life and work of the apostle. The threefold category of miracles as *signs and wonders and mighty works* is attested in several early Christian documents (Acts 2:22; 2 Thess. 2:9; Heb. 2:4). Together they usually refer especially to healings and expelling demons. Paul points to illustrations of such miraculous acts that have happened at Corinth, even though neither Acts 18 nor any other part of the Corinthian correspondence mentions them. Even in this brief note about the *signs*, Paul is careful not to take any credit for them himself. They *were performed among you*, not "I performed the signs." Through the passive voice, he attributes the miracles to God.

Paul then moves quickly from the traditional signs of an apostle to his last item of closure, one that surfaced earlier (11:7-11): his refusal of financial support from Corinth. Their complaint apparently is that Paul slighted them by accepting support from other churches while refusing help from Corinth. His stated motive remains consistent with what he said at the beginning of the Fool's Speech (11:7, 9): he did not want to burden the Corinthians. Paul considers his action and stated motive a mark of compassion, not a reason for condemnation. His terse ironic line at the end depicts his frustration with their complaint: *Forgive me this wrong!* (12:13).

THE TEXT IN BIBLICAL CONTEXT

The theme pervasive throughout the Fool's Speech is the foolishness and weakness of the gospel that Paul embodies and preaches. In the end, this turns out to be a paradox, *for whenever I am weak, then I am strong* (12:10). Paul presents the theme of weakness ironically as self-praise, inherently a contradiction in terms. Hence, he plays the fool to make his boast, while performing a denigrating parody of the unacceptable self-praise of his opponents. The strength-in-weakness paradox can be traced through the biblical landscape: prominently in the Corinthian correspondence, in other Pauline letters, in later NT writings, and in the story of Israel's covenant relationship with God.

The weighty and sometimes tortured arguments Paul advances on wisdom and foolishness in both extant Corinthian letters implies the high premium the Corinthians have placed on wisdom. They apparently believe that the person initiated into wisdom connects with God, the Author of all wisdom, and is thus delivered from the tyranny of mortality in the world of time and flesh. With the blessing of divine wisdom in a person's life comes a demonstration of divine power in the conventional sense of power, they think.

Paul's argument in 1 Corinthians 1:18—2:16 challenges this view of divine wisdom and power. The grotesque image of a crucified Messiah, which the Corinthians apparently have minimized, cuts through the conventional ideas of power and wisdom. From a human perspective, the cross is a sign of weakness and foolishness "to those who are perishing" (1:18). The Messiah crucified is "a stumbling block to [Jewish minds] and foolishness to Gentiles" (1:23), but he emerges paradoxically as God's wisdom and power. "For God's foolishness is wiser than human wisdom, and God's weakness is stronger than human strength" (1:25). Moreover, Paul's "foolish" discourse in 2 Corinthians 11:1—12:13 about his status as a minister of Christ, in comparison to that of his opponents, reflects his theology of the cross expressed in 1 Corinthians 1 and 2.

Elsewhere in the Pauline letters, the strength-in-weakness theme surfaces. Paul's exhortation to nonretaliation in Romans 12, for example, expresses the theme in another way. The Christian response to the power of a persecuting opponent is not one of equal or superior power, but one of apparent weakness. Believers are called not to retaliate but to bless persecutors and do good, trusting God for deliverance (12:14-21).

The later Pauline letters also exhibit traces of the strength-in-weakness motif. In Colossians 3, for example, God's chosen ones are to manifest compassion, kindness, humility, meekness, and patience in their lives (3:12-15). These are not the attributes of a powerful warrior, but of a "weak" follower of the crucified Messiah.

The Gospels reveal a similar form of the theme. Luke highlights the lowly birth of the Messiah in an animal shelter. The recipients of the heavenly announcement are lowly shepherds in a field, not a powerful ruler in an urban center (Luke 2). In all three synoptic Gospels, the Messiah enters the waters of Jordan along with the lowly penitents of the land. The disciples misunderstand this kind of Messiah. Peter expected a powerful figure, able to deliver the nation by conventional wisdom, but he and his colleagues have to learn that God's deliverer "must undergo great suffering, and be rejected by the elders, the chief priests, and the scribes, and be killed" (Mark 8:31). Out of this posture of human weakness, God's otherworldly resurrection power emerges. The cross (human weakness/foolishness) and resurrection (divine wisdom/power) constitute the theological foundation on which Paul builds his strength-in-weakness paradox in 2 Corinthians 11-12.

This pattern of thought extends well beyond the bounds of the early Christian literature of the NT. The theme punctuates the story of Israel's covenant relationship with God. Paul views the theme as a self-evident principle to the eyes of faith in these words from 1 Corinthians: "God chose what is foolish in the world to shame the wise; God chose what is weak in the world to shame the strong; God chose what is low and despised in the world, things that are not, to reduce to nothing things that are, so that no one might boast in the presence of God" (1:27-29).

Numerous examples from the story of Israel illustrate the principle. The Hebrew slaves were the weak of their world, yet God chose them (Exod. 1:8-10; 5:10-21; Deut. 7:7-9). Rahab the prostitute of Jericho, a weak one of her city, became God's agent of salvation for Israel and ancestor of the Matthean Messiah (Josh. 2:1-7; 6:25; Matt. 1:5; Heb. 11:31). David was the youngest of his family and least likely for kingship, yet God chose him through Samuel to be monarch of Israel and forerunner of the Messiah, "for the Lord does not see as mortals see" (1 Sam. 16:6-13). None of these could boast of their human qualification for the divine mission. Their weak social status required that they boast only in the Lord (Jer. 9:23-24; 1 Cor. 1:31; 2 Cor. 10:17).

THE TEXT IN THE LIFE OF THE CHURCH

The long section from 11:1 to 12:13 is all of one piece. A preacher may wish to sever one small part from the whole and give that part independent status for a sermon. But such a procedure violates that part's place and function in the structure of the Fool's Speech. Even such a striking text as the oracle of sufficient grace at 12:9 does not stand alone; it crowns the stinging polemic of the whole speech. All the literary parts have integrity within the warp and woof of the speech as a whole.

Some questions arise for the life of the church concerning Paul's language as a whole in this section. Are the biting sarcasm, irony, and parody to be considered standard fare in teaching and preaching? How does a Christian minister handle Paul's denigrating of other ministers who criticize him? Is there a valid self-defense in Christian service?

One way of handling the text of the Fool's Speech (11:1—12:13) is to identify themes that pepper the argument or come to the surface at key points. Then one can use a thematic structure in conjunction with striking texts. Some church leaders have not had much success in mastering this skill. In their writings, especially their sermons and treatises, they seem to have found it easier to pluck a small text out of its literary structure and weave it into a new form of address in keeping with current theology. This practice may show little regard for the place of the selected text in the original argument and thought of the first writer and readers. At least three theme-issues in the Fool's Speech can provide a frame for the several striking texts in this section: boasting of weakness, nonretaliation, and sufficient grace for suffering.

Boasting of Weakness. One can boast of weakness only as a fool. By definition, self-praise requires qualities that meet the conventional standard of high value. Weakness, whether in social standing or in personal characteristics, excludes self-praise. Paul says he will boast of the things that show his weakness. *On my own behalf I will not boast, except of my weaknesses* (2 Cor. 12:5, 9). In this boast, he is speaking ironically. He means the opposite of what he says. If his words are taken out of the context of the Fool's Speech and treated as serious reflective prose, the result is absurd. Imagine one Christian comparing their degree of weakness with the weakness of another, to boast of their superior Christian experience: "My weakness is weaker than your weakness!"

Yet Paul's words have received such treatment. Pilgram Marpeck, for example, taught that "in our weakness, of which we ought to boast, as Paul did," Christians become free from sin and enjoy the love of God and eternal life. The weakness in Marpeck's understanding is the tendency to transgress God's will (Marpeck: 330-331). Of that weakness one should "boast," according to Marpeck. On the other hand, Paul is not addressing the problem of transgression or moral lapses in the Fool's Speech. The weakness in the setting of 11:1— 12:13 relates to the hardship and suffering incurred in ministry in the name of Christ crucified. It relates to Paul's own physical and personal handicap, as in his *thorn in the flesh* (12:7) and his *contemptible speech* (10:10).

Paul's ironic boasting of weakness simply turns the tables on his opponents. What they condemn in him, he uses to validate his ministry as an apostle of the suffering Messiah of God. Weakness is a human posture that accompanies faith in Christ crucified, a posture that necessarily excludes conventional self-praise, one that issues in the gift of divine strength. For this reason, Paul is *content with weaknesses . . . for the sake of Christ; for whenever I am weak, then I am strong* (12:10).

Nonretaliation. One of the problems a peace-church interpreter of this Fool's Speech faces is Paul's defensive attack on his opponents. How can this apostle of the nonretaliating Christ level such a scathing attack against his critics at Corinth? Does Paul not teach nonretaliation in keeping with the coming peace of God?

Gordon Zerbe has argued that Paul's teaching on nonretaliation, emphatically enjoined in Romans 12:14, 17-21, is fundamentally coherent throughout the letters (Zerbe: 180). While Zerbe cites one text from the Fool's Speech (2 Cor. 11:20) to illustrate Paul's exhortation to slaves to endure abuse, he leaves the problem of Paul's invective against his opponents unresolved. Yet Zerbe's thesis that Paul consistently exhorted his congregations not to render evil for evil is well supported from numerous texts besides Romans 12. What then is the explanation of Paul's abusive verbal response to his opponents' mistreatment of him among the Corinthians?

Several points help alleviate the tension between Paul's repeated admonitions to nonretaliation and his own apparent retaliation to his opponents' accusations against him.

First, he addresses his defense to the Corinthians, not to the opponents themselves. The intended effect of denigrating the rival missionaries to the Corinthians is to steer the Corinthians clear of the interlopers' teaching, which Paul considers to be false. Moreover, Paul is not paying back the interlopers directly with the evil they have done to him. Instead, he is trying to save the community he founded from the destructive effects of the opponents' misguided teaching about Christ.

Second, what comes across as a strong polemical self-defense is actually a defense of the gospel of the suffering Messiah of God and of the agency (Paul) through which that gospel must flow to the world. If Paul allows the opponents' "gospel" to stand undisputed, then there is nothing new in the world. Their standard of power and righteousness accords with the conventions in the world already. Paul's sarcastic deriding of the opponents is his way of counteracting an erroneous message propagated as the true gospel of God. If their gospel is true, then his must be false. But Paul is thoroughly convinced that his gospel of the cross is true to the story of the word and act of Jesus Christ. Thus his defense of his own "weakness" in ministry is in effect a defense of the character of the good news of God's action in Jesus, and therefore not simply rendering evil for evil.

Third, Paul can say in good conscience that his life and ministry is a genuine imitation of the Christ of God, as he does say in so many words (2 Cor. 10:1; 1 Cor. 11:1). Thus his sharp defense is not so much of his own person but of the person of the Christ who loved him and gave himself up for him (Gal. 2:20). If Paul accepted the power theology of his opponents in Corinth, he would betray the Christ who changed his life and thought.

How then does a Christian respond to opposition? Is the form of Paul's rhetoric in the Fool's Speech a model for all time and for all circumstances of criticism? The attack against Paul in 2 Corinthians 10-13 undermined the distinctive foundation of the Christian mission. Paul's strong polemical response to the opponents reveals his profound commitment to the particular character of the Christian missionary message. There is a marked difference between defending one's own personal identity and defending the "truth of the gospel" (Gal. 2:14).

In a different situation of rivalry, as in Philippians 1:15-18, Paul patiently ignores the abuse and rejoices that the gospel of Christ is preached, even while he languishes in prison. Moreover, each case of critical opposition calls for assessment based on the fundamental nature of the gospel of Christ crucified. In principle, the response of the gospel is one of love, not retaliation.

Sufficient Grace for Suffering. For many people, the grace of God means the abundance of material possessions, good health, a happy family, and the like. For Paul, the grace of God carries him through the hardship of Christian mission in the world. Paul's lists of hardships in 2 Corinthians (4:7-12; 11:23-29; 12:10) illustrate his endurance of suffering and his weakness as a human being. He counts both as necessary for the missionary service to which God has called him. Instead of a miracle to remove his thorn in the flesh, for which he quite naturally has prayed, he is given an oracle of *sufficient grace* (12:9).

The loving, enabling grace of God in Christian experience constitutes the greatest quality of life possible in the present universe of human suffering and mortality. In Christian experience, without a miracle of healing, for example, a person can cling to the oracle of sufficient grace and draw on the deep resources of divine strength in human weakness. As Paul received the oracle and passed it on, so now every burden-bearer can hear the sustaining word of God: *My grace is sufficient for you, for [my] power is made perfect in weakness* (12:9).

Warning, Conclusion, Projected Third Visit
2 Corinthians 12:14—13:10

Preview

Paul has rounded out his Fool's Speech in 12:11-13 and now launches a substantial conclusion to his entire defense of his status as God's minister. The conclusion of this Letter of Defense has two parts. First, Paul treats his relationship to the community by using the analogy of the parent-child relationship: the loving parent supports the child, not the child the parent. The apostle will continue to serve his community unconditionally without accepting financial support from them (12:14-21). Second, he points to the relationship of the community to the living reality and power of the once-crucified Christ, and to the responsibility of both apostle and community for maintaining a right relationship with God in Christ (13:1-10).

Both stages of the conclusion are couched in the promise of a third visit that will bring with it Paul's apostolic judgment and correction. He fears the worst in the community, and thus inserts a list of vices that he suspects will characterize the Corinthians who have themselves come under the spell of Paul's opponents. Paul also fears for his own reception at Corinth. Yet he will not spare his converts the necessary correction, even if his discipline will mean his humiliation.

The projection of the third visit, in which the warning is couched, has a judicial ring to it. Paul cites the legal text of Deuteronomy 19:15 about two or three witnesses as foundation for his investigation of the community's life. Even this weighty conclusion, in the form of a projected judicial third visit, Paul laces with the ironic thread he wove into the earlier parts of this Letter of Defense (2 Cor. 10-13). The analysis that follows is again suggestive of the movement of thought that runs through this concluding text.

OUTLINE

EXPLANATORY NOTES

Parent-Apostle Related to His Family at Corinth   12:14-21

This whole section (12:14-21)—if not the entire conclusion—revolves around the metaphor of parental support of dependent children. The metaphor, as Paul spins it out in the context of the critique against him, establishes above all his refusal of financial support from the Corinthians, his children in the faith.

12:14-18 Loving More, Not Taking Advantage

Paul has duly noted his impending third visit (12:14a) and proceeds immediately to two of the serious charges leveled against him: his overt refusal of support, and his covert siphoning of funds from the collection for the Jerusalem saints. He gives a short answer: I was merely loving you more, and not taking advantage of you, as you charge. But before entering a discussion of the details of his answer, the third visit calls for comment.

The phrasing in 12:14a of the NRSV retains the ambiguity of the Greek word order. Both the NRSV and the Greek text allow the inference, *For the third time I am preparing to come to you.* The sense is that Paul earlier prepared himself twice to make the visit and now is preparing for the third time. Taken in isolation, this reading of the word order in 12:14a is possible. But with the clear reference to a third visit in 13:1-2, such an inference is impossible. Instead, when writing, Paul has already visited the Corinthians twice, once at the founding of the community and again on the occasion of his painful experience there (2:1-4; cf. 7:12). Now he is projecting a third visit to deal with those who have brought charges against him, and to build up the community again in their faith. One implication of this interpretation is that chapters 10–13 cannot constitute the so-called tearful letter mentioned in 2:4 and 7:8 (Batey: 139-146).

With the metaphor of the caring parent (12:14c), Paul persists in his practice of refusing donations, maintaining that, like a good parent, he does not want their possessions. He wants *them* (*you*, 12:14b). He desires only to *spend* himself, *and be* utterly *spent* of energy for the lives (*psuchōn*) of the community, his spiritual children. Here is a statement of complete self-sacrifice, like the sacrifice of the crucified Christ. Elsewhere Paul can say that Christ "loved me and gave himself for me" (Gal. 2:20).

Along the same line of expending himself in love for the Corinthians, Paul asks poignantly, *If I love you more, am I to be loved less?* (12:15). The question expects the answer no. The puzzle comes with the comparative. More than what or who? Can he mean that he loves the Corinthians more than the opponents do? If the idea "is almost grotesque" (Plummer: 363), it is none the less possible. Alternately, Paul could be alluding to the monetary gifts he accepted from the Macedonian churches while he declined support from the Corinthians. His comparative then would imply that he loved the Corinthians more than he loved the Macedonians. This alternative appears to be just as grotesque as the first. A better choice is to take the *more* as a generic term for *abundantly*. If Paul loved the Corinthians abundantly, why is their return minuscule?

So be it, he says: *I did not burden you* (12:16). That is Paul's view of his refusal of support. But it is not the view of the Corinthians as prompted by the opponents, no doubt. Paul knows his view is not theirs and reckons with that contingency in the second part of 12:16. *Nevertheless (you say) since I was crafty, I took you in by deceit.* The veiled reference in this verse and in the two following is to the collection for Jerusalem. Did Paul take personal expenses out of the offering to fund his travels? The Corinthians seem to have thought so or were led to believe so by the *false apostles* (Hughes: 464).

Paul answers the charge in four rhetorical questions, the first two expecting a negative answer and the latter two expecting a positive answer. *Did I take advantage of you through any of those whom I sent to you? . . . Titus did not take advantage of you, did he?* (12:17-18). The answer to both is no. The Corinthians are not about to cast aspersion on Titus, their respected collaborator. Paul likewise respects Titus as partner and friend in the ministry. Moreover, the first two questions are weighted in Paul's favor. The other two extend the effect of the first two. *Did we not conduct ourselves with the same spirit? Did we not take the same steps?* (12:18). The expected answer is yes. The plural *we* could be editorial, meaning the singular *I*, Paul. More likely the *we* aligns Paul deliberately with the favored Titus and the unnamed brother.

Paul's reference to sending Titus and *the brother* (12:18a) echoes the earlier dispatch of Titus with two trusted brothers in 8:16-24 to collect money for Jerusalem. Not everyone agrees with this connection between 12:18 and 8:16-24 (R. Martin, 1986:447-448). Accordingly, 12:18 is said to point to a visit prior to the writing of 8:16-24, and to the presence of Titus with Paul while he writes chapters 10–13. In support of this interpretation, 12:18 mentions only one brother, whereas 8:16-22 refers to two. In this view, Paul must have sent a *brother* with Titus on the earlier visit alluded to in 8:6, even though Paul makes no such mention in 8:6.

Despite the mention of only one brother in 12:18, Paul alludes to the event in the past (aorist) tenses of the verbs. This seems to point to the emissary (with Titus) in 8:16-24. In that passage, Paul commended each of the two brothers separately. One represented the churches, and the other likely represented Paul himself. Which one of these two from chapter 8 is identified here in 12:18 is not certain. The *famous* brother (8:18) representing the churches seems more likely, though the *eager* brother (8:22) is a possibility (Furnish, 1984:566) since that brother was Paul's associate along with Titus. "The two questions of 12:18c-d have more point if both Titus and the other man of whom the Corinthians have been reminded were Paul's own associates" (566).

However Paul intended to identify *the brother* with Titus and himself in 12:18, the best assumption is that the embassy of 8:16-24 has already visited Corinth prior to the writing of chapters 10–13, and have returned to Paul with information about the critique against him. Hence, at 12:18 Paul can appeal to the vigilant efforts of the emissaries, Titus in particular, as evidence for his case that he defrauded no one in Corinth. Paul walks in the same footsteps as the ones he sent, the ones for whom the Corinthians have high regard.

12:19-21 Saving the Community, Not Self-Defense

Paul then turns more directly to the matter of his self-defense. The NRSV (following many earlier versions) renders the opening sentence of the section as a question: *Have you been thinking all along that we have been defending ourselves before you?* (12:19). Paul's Greek sentence, however, can just as readily be read as a statement capping the sequence of rhetorical questions preceding: *You sup-pose all along that we are defending ourselves before you* (Furnish, 1984:556). Certainly the tenor and texture of Paul's argument in chapters 10-13 comes across as a defense of his person and status. But he dare not leave that impression unqualified. His detractors have already accused him of catering to his own self-interest, and the apology of this letter (2 Cor. 10-13) could easily serve to enhance their charge. For this reason Paul casts his apology (1) as a forthright statement of fact *in Christ before God* (12:19b), and (2) as a way of building up the beloved Corinthian community (12:19c).

The *fear* Paul records in 12:20 is a suspicion. He seems not to have solid evidence that the Corinthians have degenerated to the lev-el of the vices he lists. But, given their alignment with the *false apostles* (11:13), Paul suspects that they have lapsed morally and communally. Should that be so, he says, *When I come, I may find you not as I wish.* In which case, *you may find me not as you wish*—ex-ercising authority to discipline the community as he has done before (2:1-4; 1 Cor. 5).

The vices listed in 12:20 are not peculiar to this text or to this community (cf. Phil. 1:17; 2:3; Rom. 2:8; Gal. 5:20; 1 Pet. 4:3; Sirach 40:5). Paul has drawn the terms from traditional Hellenistic lists of vices. Yet his structuring of the eight social sins may be deliberate, to fit the disruptive situation in the community at Corinth. The structure seems to contain four pairs (Plummer: 369): strife and jealousy, an-ger and factions, slander and gossip, conceit and disorder. Together these pairs of social vices constitute destruction of community life, an intolerable state of affairs for Paul. The Christ-life of the community is his assurance that his divine call to world mission is authentic. Hence the need to come a third time to Corinth to build up again a commu-nity fraught with moral disturbance.

The second list of sexual sins in (2 Cor.) 12:21 is reminiscent of the lists in 1 Corinthians and elsewhere in Paul's letters. Nowhere else in 2 Corinthians (except for the questionable text of 6:14—7:1) does Paul concern himself with sexual immorality in the Corinthian church. At this point in the Letter of Defense, however, he *fears* a re-currence of the sexual laxity of an earlier time, and so lists three gross sexual sins: *impurity, sexual immorality,* and *licentiousness* (12:21b). The presence of such sins in the Christ-community is unthinkable to Paul's Jewish-Christian mind. The presence of immorality in the com-munity would, he says, cause him to fear *that when I come again, my God may humble me before you, and that I may have to mourn over many who previously sinned and have not repented* (12:21a).

The emphatic word *again* is somewhat ambiguous in Paul's Greek text. It could imply *God may humble me again*, as he did when I confronted the same problem in the community in the earlier painful visit (R. Martin, 1986:465). Or it may point simply to the third visit to Corinth, as in the NRSV, *when I come again*. The two words, *come again* stand together in the Greek text, making the latter meaning preferable. Furthermore, Paul did not consider his earlier experience at Corinth to be God's humbling of him. But if this third visit finds the community lapsed into sexual immorality despite Paul's corrective measures in his earlier mission, the situation would prove Paul's mission ineffective, and would represent God's humbling of him.

"The legitimacy of [Paul's] apostleship is demonstrated by the Christian faith and life of the congregations he has founded and over which he exercises pastoral care" (Furnish, 1984:567). For their part, the Corinthians should know well enough that Paul is thoroughly convinced of his divine call to mission, and he will consequently discipline the congregation, mourning as he does so. The alternative, they should know, will not be God's humiliation of Paul by rendering his ministry at Corinth inoperative. This is the force of the sentence of 12:21 that projects Paul's third visit to Corinth. The Corinthians are forewarned: they should prepare themselves for a severe Paul, not a humiliated Paul.

Corinthians Related to the Living Christ Crucified 13:1-10

That Paul aims to discipline the community, rather than be humiliated by God, becomes clear in the opening four verses of chapter 13. In the next four verses (13:5-10), Paul urges the community to correct itself and avoid the pain of his chastisement.

13:1-4 Apostolic Responsibility to Correct Members

Once more Paul announces his third visit (13:1). Was he very conscious of the chronology of his visits to Corinth? Was it unusual to pay three visits to a church he founded? Why the repeated mention of the third visit? The answer to these questions may lie in Paul's use of the legal text of Deuteronomy 19:15 which he echoes in 13:2: *Any charge must be sustained by the evidence of two or three witnesses* (cf. Matt. 18:16). Paul is quite at home interpreting his Scripture in the freedom of the Spirit. "Paul's hermeneutical skill exhibits a creative freedom that allows the gospel tradition to become living speech within the exigencies of the daily life of his churches" (Beker: 33).

In the first two verses of chapter 13, Paul refers to his *second* and *third* visit to Corinth, and implies by his use of the legal text of Deuteronomy 19:15 that the second and third visits constitute the *two* and *three* witnesses required for trying a case. "The ordinals *third* and *second* in these two verses cannot fail to be connected with the cardinals *two* and *three* in the quotation" from the LXX (Barrett, 1973:333). The text does not make clear exactly how the second and third visits function as witnesses in Paul's defense, or in Paul's case against the Corinthians. Perhaps the third visit speaks to the ongoing existence of the community Paul founded, and thus bears ample testimony to his right to be called an apostle of Jesus Christ (cf. 2 Cor. 3:1-2). Again, the third visit may carry a note of finality in keeping with the implicit meaning of the third witness in the Deuteronomy formula: one witness is not sufficient, two witnesses are adequate, but three witnesses establish the testimony completely.

As rightful apostle, Paul warns that he *will not be lenient* when he comes this third time (13:2). The third visit will bear sufficient testimony on two fronts: (1) it will exonerate Paul as apostle of Jesus Christ, and (2) it will indict the offenders at Corinth at the same time. Paul will mete out discipline (the form is not mentioned) on those who have sinned. His action, he says, will be the proof the Corinthians desire *that Christ is speaking in me* (13:3). Paul's language of warning in the name of Christ here has a ring of power in it, calling up again the paradox of strength-in-weakness. Earlier he claimed to be weak, as Christ crucified was weak. He even boasted ironically of his weakness (12:6-10). Now he stresses the power side of the paradox. Christ *is not weak in dealing with you, but is powerful in* (or *among*) *you* (cf. Phil. 2:6-11).

What appears as weakness in the crucified Christ, and in Paul his follower, is the power of God that challenges sin in its myriad forms. Paul is not here distinguishing two forms of Christ, one crucified in weakness and the other resurrected in power. Rather, the living Christ moves within the community as the crucified one, manifesting God's power to judge human sin. Paul will likewise move among the people of Corinth on his third visit, crucified with Christ but exercising the power of God to pass judgment on wrongdoers. Hence his concluding statement about his responsibility for the community. *For we are weak in him, but in dealing with you [in the third visit] we will live with him by the power of God* (13:4b).

13:5-10 Members' Responsibility for Self-Correction

Paul's alternative to his disciplinary action on the community in the forthcoming visit is the community's self-examination and restoration to the good life (13:5-7). In such a happy circumstance, Paul will rejoice (13:9) even if their strength makes him appear weak to their eyes. He would prefer not to exercise authoritative discipline on them and prove his apostolic power. Hence his reason for writing in this vein: that the Corinthians will mend their ways and make his discipline unnecessary (13:10). In this final section (13:5-10) of his whole apology, Paul puts a cap on all of his earlier arguments of this Letter of Defense (2 Cor. 10-13). Several elements of these six verses call for more detailed explanation.

Examine yourselves (13:5a), Paul commands, with the heavy emphasis falling on *yourselves*. Rather than testing others, including Paul, test yourselves. Perhaps this admonition marks the goal to which Paul's irony was leading all along in his apology of the Letter of Defense. (Betz makes the point that Socrates did the same to his students; 1972:135). *Examine* and *test* (NRSV) might better read *test* and *prove*. Test yourselves and prove whether you are in the faith, whether you are living according to your faith in Christ. The emphasis is not on the principle of faith that leads to salvation, but on the behavior of life that flows from the experience of being in Christ (5:17). Hence, Paul's ensuing question is ironically tinged: *Do you not realize that Jesus Christ is in [among] you?—unless, indeed, you fail to meet the test* (13:5b; *you* is plural). The Corinthians, of course, will not want to fail the test of their faith in Christ and appear unapproved. If they pass the test, by implication they must also say that Paul passes their test as well, for without his mission they would not be in Christ. Verse 6 points to this conclusion: *I hope you will find out that we have not failed.* Paul could be perceived from 13:6 as defending himself again. To avoid that perception, he focuses his reason for the test more sharply on the well-being of his readers.

But we pray to God that you may not do anything wrong—not that we may appear to have met the test, but that you may do what is right, though we may seem to have failed (13:7). While the sentence of verse 7 is somewhat convoluted, the controlling thought of Paul is clear. He prays (present tense) that the Corinthians will not commit evil (*poiēsai . . . kakon*), for in doing so they would only hurt themselves by proving themselves counterfeit. He prays that they will do good (*poiēte . . . kalon*) for their own sake, not merely to have Paul come out looking good. Paul's hope is that the Corinthians will mend their ways before he arrives, so that he will not have to use his authority to discipline them. Paul's enemies will continue to accuse him of being weak. So be it. What matters most to Paul is that the gospel takes firm hold in the community for good.

However, it is misleading to say that Paul is "not concerned for his own reputation . . . so long as his converts in Corinth are doing what is good" (Barrett, 1973:339); to say so contradicts the intent of Paul's statement in 13:7. If the Corinthians really turn from their wrongheadedness, how could they at the same time reject the apostle? His life epitomizes the good of the gospel of Christ, which the Corinthians are urged to adopt. The disapproval Paul expects is not from the reformed Corinthians, but from the interlopers who seek to discredit him. The two groups should not be confused in sorting out Paul's argument. The Corinthians and the false apostles are held in tension throughout the argument.

For we cannot do anything against the truth, but only for the truth (13:8). Paul is bound by the truth, not by how he fares personally in the opponents' case against him. And the truth he has in mind, no doubt, is "the truth of the gospel" (Gal. 2:14) or *the truth of Christ* (2 Cor. 11:10). Truth determined by philosophical or judicial logic is not at issue here. What is at issue is the truth inherent in the nature of the gospel of Christ crucified. Moreover, the *truth* in 13:8 is pitted against the *different gospel* (11:4) propagated by the *false apostles* (11:13; Bultmann, 1964:244).

Earlier Paul spoke of boasting in his weakness (12:9). Now at 13:9 he rejoices when he is weak. His weakness and rejoicing spring from the strength of his converts at Corinth. When they are strong in the faith, he has no need to demonstrate his authority in chastising them. He will appear weak, but rejoicing. He prays for their restoration to wholeness (13:9b). The NRSV reads, *that you may become* **perfect**. The word rendered *perfect* could be misleading. It suggests "the attainment of religious and moral perfection" (R. Martin, 1986:484), but the word denotes primarily the setting of joints so as to restore the body to its proper function (Liddell and Scott, 1:910). Paul's use of the word is probably metaphoric. He is praying for the knitting together of the members into true community in the name of Christ, where mutual love builds wholesome relationships among the people of Christ, and especially with Paul.

Verse 10 is Paul's last word of conclusion to the letter that began at 10:1 in our 2 Corinthians. *So I write these things while I am away from you, so that when I come, I may not have to be severe in using the authority that the Lord has given me for building up and not tearing down* (13:10). The Letter of Defense (2 Cor. 10–13) is laden with warning and admonition from an apostle on the verge of being seriously estranged from his beloved congregation. He has appealed to them at the beginning of the letter in meekness and gentleness (10:1). At the same time, he exercises his authority that the Lord has given him for building up and not for tearing down (10:8). What appears throughout the letter as self-defense is Paul's attempt to steer his converts clear of deceptive forces that have entered the community (11:1-6).

As Paul writes these four chapters, he has the third visit in view. By writing in advance, he hopes to restore faith in the community, and to restore the community's trust in himself before he arrives. The present-absent theme comes through again in the last verse (13:10), as in the opening of the letter (10:1-2). This letter represents Paul's admonition in absence. If the letter accomplishes its goal, Paul will not have to be severe when he is present at Corinth. Whether present or absent, he assures his readers again, his authority to execute discipline is *for building up and not for tearing down.* On that note Paul's argument comes to a close. It remains for him only to close the letter with a farewell, greeting, and benediction (2 Cor. 13:11-13).

THE TEXT IN BIBLICAL CONTEXT

Paul draws on the model of the Mediterranean family to describe the relationship between himself and the Corinthians (Malina:158-160). He sees his missionary role as a loving parent providing for children freely. The image of the church of Christ as a family figures prominently in Paul. For example, he closes 2 Corinthians by calling the believers *brothers and sisters* (13:11), a common designation in his letters. Familial kinship terminology is common in the rest of the NT, too.

The Gospel of Mark makes much of "domestic domains" in setting forth the new relationship between Jesus and his disciples (Poetker: 14-23). In Mark, Jesus disrupts the family kinship bond in favor of his new family of disciples who "do the will of God," the Father of Jesus and his new family (Mark 3:20-21, 31-34). Mark may have drawn on an early Christian tradition, evident in Paul, of viewing the new groups of believers that met in private homes as families of God, bonded by the grace and love of Christ.

The domestic domain plays a meaningful role in the development of the NT theology. In Israelite tradition, nationalistic thinking included the symbols of holy land and holy temple. These were transformed in the new community of Christ to accommodate the vision of the world mission of the early church. People of Christ from both Jewish and Gentile heritage are born into the family of God by a new kind of birth (John 3:1-10). They live in loving relationship with the members of the church group, as brothers and sisters live in the bond of kinship.

The picture in 1 John is highly instructive along this line. "Whoever says, 'I am in the light,' while hating a brother or sister, is still in the darkness. Whoever loves a brother or sister lives in the light, and in such a person there is no cause for stumbling" (1 John 2:9-10). In the Mediterranean village community, it was shameful to be out of relationship with the kinfolk. The NT draws freely from this domestic model in constructing a vision for the new groups of Christians living under the love of Father-God (1 John 3:1; 2:13).

Paul finds reason to pass judgment on the strained relationship within the new Corinthian family—their relationship with each other and their relationship with him. To do so he enlists the help of a prescriptive rule of Deuteronomy 19:15 about two and three witnesses to establish a case. In the biblical way of thinking, judging the thinking and behavior of others is not a matter of personal whim. The Torah required proper procedure for making a judgment and applying correction. In Israel, elders were appointed to sit in the gate of the city, to decide between parties in a dispute (e.g., Deut. 17:2-13; 22:15; 25:7). These judges were obliged to invoke the rule of law in deciding the rightness of a charge. Part of "right" procedure in establishing cases in Israelite society was to hear from two or three eyewitnesses. Matthew 18:15-20 commends the rule for settling disputes between members of the community of Christ.

Yet Paul does not settle his case by the presence of the *two or three witnesses* alone (2 Cor. 13:1). He rests his judgment of the Corinthians on the truth (13:8). The truth in Pauline context is not simply statements that correspond to physical reality, as in truth-telling. Instead, Paul relies on what he calls elsewhere "the truth of the gospel" (Gal. 2:14). For Paul, the new reality that has broken into his Jewish life is that of God's crucified Messiah on behalf of the world. The theology of the cross has become for Paul the center and source of all moral and spiritual judgment and correction. His case rests ultimately on that truth; it follows the course that the truth of the cross directs in his dealing with the Corinthians. What the crucified Messiah represents finally is God's unfailing, redeeming, gracious love. The same love rescued the Hebrews from Egypt, the exiles of Judah from Babylon, Jesus from the grave, and believers from the plight of sin and death.

In keeping with his conviction about the truth of the gospel, Paul uses his apostolic authority *for building up and not for tearing down.* At the beginning and end of his appeal in the Letter of Defense, Paul makes the same point, using the same words (2 Cor. 10:8; 13:10). God is Creator-God and Redeemer-God. The story of the people of Israel is the story of God building the people up, not tearing them down. Paul's phrase echoes Jeremiah's oracle of the Lord:

> I will set my eyes upon [the exiles from Judah] for good, and I will bring them back to this land. I will build them up, and not tear them down; I will plant them, and not pluck them up; I will give them a heart to know that I am the Lord; and they shall be my people and I will be their God, for they shall return to me with their whole heart. (24:6-7; cf. 1:10)

The story of Jesus crucified and raised is the continuing story of God acting to re-create the world, not to tear it down. And Paul works in concert with the continuing story of God's renewing of creation, starting with those who are *in Christ* (2 Cor. 5:17). The giving of gifts to the community is for building up, not tearing down (1 Cor. 12-14; cf. Matt. 16:13-19). Pastoral authority within the community of grace is creative, healing, life-giving authority.

THE TEXT IN THE LIFE OF THE CHURCH
The Church as Family

As noted above, order and harmony were the expected norms of the Mediterranean family. Breakup in the family brought dishonor and shame on the family name, and hence on the parents and children who lived under that name. The metaphor of the kin-family thus became singularly significant for the witness of the early church. In more recent history, a number of Christian groups discovered the prominence of family imagery in the NT and incorporated a component of the image into their group (or denominational) name. Examples are "Mennonite *Brethren,*" "*Brethren* in Christ," and "Plymouth *Brethren.*"

The term *brethren,* from the Elizabethan English of the King James Bible, was initially gender-inclusive, as Paul's term *adelphoi* (lit.: *brothers*) was. Both men and women of the new congregations of

Paul's mission were considered brothers and sisters (*adelphoi*) in the new family of God. Language, like culture generally, is dynamic, always open to new associations and new terms of reference. The Elizabethan term *brethren* is now anachronistic on two counts. First, the word *brethren* is no longer in common use in spoken English and sounds antiquated today. Second, *brethren* is not universally gender-inclusive in English-speaking cultures. Hence, *brethren* no longer serves to identify the church as God's kindred people, bonded together harmoniously by the sacrificial love of Christ.

Denominational names are not sacred. God's family is. A breakup in God's family brings shame and dishonor on the name of Christ. Disunity and disorder between brothers and sisters in the family of God denies the center of grace and love that brought the members together in the first place. "Jesus marks this center," says Ulrich Luz. "Paul lays out *how* Jesus marks the center, an approach that applies as well to other New Testament proposals. It is as the crucified and risen One that Jesus determines the life reality of Paul's congregations" (247). So also now, the gift of Jesus crucified and raised creates a new family of God. Broken kinship families of the present culture need a new family, God's new family of Christians, in which to find healing and love. If the new Christian family, the church, has no sense of shame in quarreling and breaking up, what good service can it render to broken lives in need of a new family relationship?

Building Up, Not Tearing Down

Both principal parts of the canonical 2 Corinthians exhibit variations on the theme of Christian ministry. Two coordinated phrases at the end of the conclusion to the second part (13:10) pinpoint the essence of ministry in the name of Christ: (a) *authority that the Lord has given me*, and (b) *for building up and not for tearing down*. Authority in ministry, whatever its expression in a church setting, is a gift from the Lord. The exercise of authority (or power) in the Christian church, following Jesus and Paul, is for constructive purposes, *for building up and not for tearing down*.

In this respect the church distinguishes itself from popular culture, where the strong win out over the weak, the opposing party is overcome by the use of force, criticism is squelched by eliminating the critic, etc. As Walter Wink has it, the ancient Babylonian myth of human domination lives on in modern cultures and politics (13-31). The myth is re-fashioned variously through the ages, but repeatedly exerts violence for self-preservation and self-esteem.

The myth is present not only in the political domain but in the domestic as well. Domination, whether in a nation or a home, is said to be necessary for redemptive purposes, violence for the sake of the good. Wink writes:

> The myth of redemptive violence inundates us on every side. We are awash in it yet seldom perceive it. This myth speaks for God; it does not listen for God to speak. . . . It does not seek God in order to change. It claims God in order to prevent change. . . . Its metaphor is not the journey but a fortress. Its symbol is not the cross but a rod of iron. Its offer is not forgiveness but victory. Its good news is not the unconditional love of enemies but their final liquidation. . . . It is blasphemous. It is idolatrous. And it is immensely popular. (17)

The gospel of Jesus Christ reverses the torrent of human domination and violence. It was this gospel that transformed Paul from persecutor to pastor. Out of his new pastor's heart in the experience of Christ crucified, Paul builds up the other and does not tear down. He himself may be humiliated, beaten, imprisoned, but he will not retaliate by using a "strongman" posture. His goal in exercising his authority with the Corinthians is not to dominate them and gain his own self-preservation and self-esteem, but to restore their soul through his own self-sacrifice.

Closure

2 Corinthians 13:11-13

PREVIEW

Paul's closure to the Letter of Defense corresponds to the form of letter closing in the Mediterranean world: a farewell and greeting, followed by a prayer or wish for the well-being of the recipient. Within this standard form, however, Paul incorporates ideas that match his appeal throughout the Letter of Defense (2 Cor. 10–13). His *farewell* of 13:11 recalls the earlier assessment of the sorry state of community life at Corinth at the hands of Paul's opponents: *Put things in order, listen to my appeal, agree with one another, live in peace.* In the greeting of 13:12, Paul aims at binding the members at Corinth together in love by the *holy kiss;* he also links the Corinthian community as a whole to *all the saints* of like mind in other communities, probably Ephesus in particular if Paul is writing from there.

The prayer of benediction in 13:13 is the most elaborate of all the benedictions in Paul's letters. The three names or titles invoked—Lord Jesus Christ, God, Holy Spirit—are common in Paul but not usually found together as they are here. With such a comprehensive benediction resting on them, the Corinthians should feel abundantly blessed.

OUTLINE

Farewell and Greeting, 13:11-12

The Benediction, 13:13

EXPLANATORY NOTES

Farewell and Greeting   13:11-12

There is some debate whether the farewell, greeting, and benediction of 13:11-13 belong at the end of the Letter of Defense (2 Cor. 10-13) or at the close of the Letter of Reconciliation (2 Cor. 1–9). Or did the later compiler of 2 Corinthians supply this benediction to close the canonical 2 Corinthians? If 2 Corinthians is a composite of at least two letters *[Integrity, p. 266]*, then the questions are valid.

Two factors suggest that the closing of 2 Corinthians is in its proper place at the end of the argument of the Letter of Defense. First, an editor in combining two letters would probably leave intact the opening of the letter placed first, and likewise the closing of the letter placed last (Furnish, 1984:585). The assumption here is that the letters in the hands of the compiler were complete, not fragmentary. Second, the admonition of 13:11 uses the Greek word for *restore* (verb: *put things in order*), also found at 13:9 as a cognate (noun: *perfect*). Since no substantial argument exists for placing the three-part closure elsewhere, and its form fits here, its place at the conclusion of the Letter of Defense (2 Cor. 10–13) remains secure.

The word *finally* in 13:11a introduces the letter ending, not the conclusion of an argument. *Brothers and sisters* occurs nowhere else in chapters 10–13, although once in these chapters Paul calls the Corinthians *beloved* (12:19). Elsewhere in the Pauline letters, the familial designation *brothers and sisters* is a common description of the Christian community (TBC and TLC, above). *Farewell* translates the verb most often rendered *rejoice*, as in 13:9, where Paul rejoices when he is weak and the Corinthians are strong. The word was a common greeting in the Greek world, much like the English "good-bye" (Barrett, 1973:342). In Paul's hand, though, the word addresses the character of Christian life. In the present verse, it stands at the top of a string of four concise admonitions strategically located within the closing greeting.

The first admonition recalls a key word from 13:9 (*katartisin*) denoting restoration, wholeness, etc. Here it is an imperative verb (*katartizesthe*), translated in the NRSV *put things in order*. The second, *listen to my appeal*, looks back to the argument and advice of the letter (10:1-6; 12:19—13:10). The last two admonitions carry the same idea. They encourage harmony and community: *agree with one another, live in peace*. The admonitions do not stand alone. They find support in the promise that the God of love and peace, both key ingredients for Christian community life, will be with them. God's love and peace is not the reward for obedience to Paul's demands (Windisch: 426), but the enabling of God for restoration to wholeness.

The greeting of 13:12 is somewhat alien to a modern congregation. In the culture of the time, *a holy kiss* was distinguished from other kinds of kissing, such as an erotic kiss. In the ancient Mediterranean world, "a kiss could take many forms: it could be placed on the foot, the knee, the hand, the breast, the cheek, the forehead, the mouth [the erotic kiss specifically]" (Furnish, 1984:583). The kiss was used as part of the initiation rite in some of the mystery cults of the time.

As it appears in Paul's final greeting here, the *holy kiss* was probably a sign of association in the same religious community. It may also have been part of the fellowship liturgy of the Lord's Supper. In modern Anglo-American culture, the practice has all but vanished, yet the meaning of the holy kiss remains or should remain. Members of the community of Christ can greet each other in mutual love and respect, according to the accepted norms of the culture and time. In some present-day cultures, when parties meet, the greeting may be in the form of a hug, in others a handshake (cf. Phillips). When parties are absent from one another, a letter can carry a unifying greeting, as here at 13:12b: *All the saints greet you.*

The Benediction 13:13

Of the closing benedictions to Paul's letters, none compares to that of 2 Corinthians 13:13. *The grace of the Lord Jesus Christ, the love of God, and the communion of the Holy Spirit be with all of you.* The theological sweep in the three short lines is breathtaking. Frequently Paul ends his letters with the shorter benediction: *The grace of the Lord Jesus be with you* (1 Cor. 16:23; Gal. 6:18; Phil. 4:23; 1 Thess. 5:28; Philem. 25). This shorter version was probably more common, which might explain why it appears first in the series of three connected blessings (R. Martin, 1986:504).

The three divine designations (Christ, God, and Holy Spirit) in the benediction sometimes function interchangeably in Paul's letters, as in Romans 8:1-11. But here at the close of 2 Corinthians, Paul invokes the three functional titles of deity in relation to the life of the community at Corinth. He sets the titles within three neatly formulated lines:

> *the grace of the Lord Jesus Christ,*
> *the love of God,*
> *the communion of the Holy Spirit.*

While his tri-unity of divine invocation anticipates the later doctrine of the Trinity, Paul's order (Christ, God, Holy Spirit) is clearly not that of the later creed (Father, Son, Holy Spirit). Paul's order corresponds to his understanding of how the grace of the gospel should take hold in the congregation at Corinth. The grace of **Christ** opens human hearts to the love of **God**; the love of God revealed in Christ creates community through the dynamic activity of the **Spirit**. All three designations of deity are subjective, not objective; they generate the threefold blessing of *grace, love,* and *communion* among the believers at Corinth. And Paul's prayer for blessing encompasses *all* members of the community, including any factions.

The yearning of the benediction has currency for churches in the modern (or postmodern) world. *The grace of the Lord Jesus Christ, the love of God, and the communion of the Holy Spirit be with all of you* (13:13).

Outline of 2 Corinthians

LETTER OF DEFENSE: RESPONSE TO
BETRAYAL IN MINISTRY   10:1—13:13

Variation 4: Weak Minister, Strong God   10:1—13:13

God's Minister Under Fire: Boasting Ridiculed   10:1-18
    Posing the Subject: The Person of the Apostle   10:1-11
    The Folly of Comparative Boasting   10:12-18
Forced to Boast as a Fool   11:1—12:13
    The Situation Requiring Foolish Boasting   11:1-15
        Protecting the Betrothed   11:1-6
        Money Lovingly Declined   11:7-11
        Disguised as Ministers   11:12-15
    Speaking as a Fool   11:16—12:10
        Foolish Confidence   11:16-21a
        A Fool's Pedigree   11:21b-33
        A Fool's Paradise   12:1-10
    Conclusion to the Fool's Speech   12:11-13
Warning, Conclusion, Projected Third Visit   12:14—13:10
    Parent-Apostle Related to His Family at Corinth   12:14-21
        Loving More, Not Taking Advantage   12:14-18
        Saving the Community, Not Self-Defense   12:19-21
    Corinthians Related to the Living Christ
        Crucified   13:1-10
        Apostolic Responsibility to Correct Members   13:1-4
        Members' Responsibility for Self-correction   13:5-10
Closure   13:11-13
    Farewell and Greeting   13:11-12
    The Benediction   13:13

Essays

CONTENTS

THE CANONICAL SHAPE OF 2 CORINTHIANS Second Corinthians
as it now stands in the NT was first used to address concerns of the post-
apostolic church in the Roman world of the second century. Brevard Childs
in his 1984 publication, *The New Testament as Canon: An Introduction*,
calls for an interpretation of the final form of the books in the NT. In approaching 2 Corinthians, Childs is particularly interested in the theological
reason for bringing the disparate fragments in 2 Corinthians together in one
book, with the sharp judgment passage (chapters 10–13) coming at the end.
He does not underestimate the importance of studying the primary contexts
of each of the incorporated fragments. But he insists on a careful study of the
role of the composite document as normative for the church:

> The canonical role of the final form of [2 Corinthians] has its own integri-
> ty which functions in a way distinct and often different from the original
> letters. . . . By the turn of the second century, Paul's occasional letters
> had increasingly been assigned a continuing authoritative status, and
> were being assembled into an expanding corpus. Within this context, in-
> dependent letters and fragments were joined into a new composition

largely from the conviction that their authority transcended the original situation to which they were first delivered. (290, 295-296)

Unlike 1 Corinthians, cited in 1 Clement as though already well-known, 2 Corinthians does not appear in the writings of church leaders until late in the second century. Noted heretic, Marcion, put 2 Corinthians on his list of books intended to guide the life and thought of his churches. Thereafter the two letters of First and Second Corinthians in their present form became normative for the post-apostolic church. None of the church leaders of the second and third centuries made any attempt to identify parts of 2 Corinthians, as scholars do today. The early leaders were able to see in the received form of 2 Corinthians a sustaining word for their life of faith in the world. Church authorities recognized Paul as a principal apostolic authority, whose ministry they had inherited. They identified Paul's opponents as their opponents; Paul's ministry of reconciliation was theirs as well; his stern warnings (6:14—7:1 and 10:1—13:10) undergirded their warnings to congregations.

Bishops and local ministers of the late second century, believing as they did in a coming judgment on apostates, would have found Paul's harsh judgment on *false apostles* (11:13) meaningful in their time. After Paul's time, the church faced false teachers as Paul did. They no doubt heard chapters 10-13 speaking poignantly to their own situation. Similarly, the editorial effect of placing the sharp "warning fragment" of 6:14—7:1 in the midst of a letter dealing with reconciling ministry alerts readers not to "over-reconcile" to the point of unworthy compromise. The little fragment of sharp warning also prepares readers in advance for the closing arguments of (2 Cor.) 10-13, in which Paul gives censure to false teachers and discipline to the congregation.

THE COLLECTION Viewed as a collection for Jerusalem (1 Cor. 16:3; Rom. 15:26), the gift of funds from Paul's Gentile mission churches is reminiscent of the temple tax. Jewish representatives collected that tax from Jewish communities of the Diaspora. They were willing to pay (if they had the money) to keep their ties with the Holy City and to guarantee their share in the redemptive agency of the temple.

Viewed as an offering for "the poor" (Gal. 2:10; Rom. 15:26), the collection reflects the Jewish piety of almsgiving. This is how Acts understands Paul's reason for his visit to Jerusalem: "I came to bring alms to my nation and to offer sacrifices" (24:17). Why Acts does not explore further the significance of the collection from the Gentiles to Jerusalem remains a mystery.

Paul rests his appeal for the collection for Jerusalem on some sturdy theological and ethical planks: the gift of grace in the Lord Jesus Christ, who was rich but became poor to enrich humankind (2 Cor. 8:8-9; 9:14-15); and the just requirement of a fair balance between groups of believers (8:10-14; 9:5-9). An even weightier agenda doubtlessly lies behind these explicit reasons for the collection of money for the Jerusalem saints.

The collected money was not for generally poor people anywhere in the Mediterranean basin, of whom there were many. It was specifically for poor Jewish believers in Jerusalem, and it was coming from Gentile believers in the Greek-Roman provinces of Achaia, Macedonia (cf. 2 Cor. 8:1-4; 9:1-4;

Rom. 15:25-26), and probably Asia Minor (Acts 20:1-4). By means of the collected money, Paul was able to tie his Gentile world mission to Israel's symbolic center of historic salvation, and he viewed the event as God's way of fulfilling the prophecy in Isaiah (66:18; cf. 2:2) and Haggai (2:6-9). The Lord would shake the nations and gather the Gentiles to meet in Zion to witness his glory and rejoice in his deliverance.

Moreover, the collected money was not merely pragmatic relief for the impoverished of Jerusalem. It was as well an offering representing the Gentiles who believed the word of the gospel of Jesus Christ, God's agent of salvation whom Paul preached. Nowhere is the sacral sense of the collected money more pronounced than in the closing section of Romans, written after Paul and his co-workers completed the mission in the north and just before he departed for Jerusalem. Paul declares his ministry to the Gentiles to be a priestly service of the gospel of God. He sees the collection from the Gentile churches an acceptable offering "sanctified by the Holy Spirit," and a "ministry to Jerusalem" (Rom. 15:15-16, 25-26, 31; Munck: 282-308).

Noteworthy also is "the uncommonly large number of traveling companions that accompany [Paul]" (Munck: 303; Acts 20:1-4). As representatives of the various Gentile churches, they vouchsafe the collection of money from the Gentiles. But their significant number coupled with Paul's risk of life in going to Jerusalem says something more, as Johannes Munck found some forty years ago. The explanation lies in Paul's view of "the connexion between the mission to the Gentiles and the mission to the Jews" (303; Rom. 11; Acts 26:6-7; 28:20) in fulfillment of the prophecy that "the wealth of the nations shall come to you [Jerusalem]" (Isa. 60:5-6; cf. Mic. 4:1-2).

No wonder Paul's appeals in 2 Corinthians 8-9 are forceful. The collection from the Gentiles was more than an optional nicety tacked on to the gospel. It was a theological necessity, rooted in Israel's God, and symbolized in Jerusalem and in its believing Jewish remnant: "to the Jew first and also to the Greek" (Rom. 1:16).

A DIFFERENT GOSPEL   Second Corinthians 11:4 speaks of *a different gospel* which proclaims *another Jesus* and *a different spirit*. The Greek phrase translated *a different gospel* appears in Galatians 1:6, and we may be tempted to assume that the sense must be the same in both texts. With that assumption in place, another usually follows, that the meaning of the phrase in the context of Galatians must be the same as in the context of 2 Corinthians 10–13. C. K. Barrett exemplifies this method. It is "natural to think that the same meaning [operative in Galatians] will apply in 2 Corinthians" (1973:276; cf. 1982b:60-86). Barrett does not make clear why it should be "natural" to think this way.

The situation depicted in the language and context of 2 Corinthians 10–13 bears no resemblance to those identified in the language and context of Galatians. Opponents do exist behind the rhetoric of both letters, but their particular stance implied in each of the two arguments is quite different. In 2 Corinthians 10–13, there is not the slightest hint of the opponents requiring the Corinthian believers to observe circumcision, dietary rules, or the Sabbath. Nothing in 2 Corinthians 10–13 suggests that the different gospel is "a gospel of works," as Windisch proposes (328). Likewise, there is no clear sign that the opposition stemmed from Jerusalem (cf. Gal. 2:11-14).

Granted that an opponent *makes slaves* of the Corinthians in some way (11:20), the form of the enslavement should not be tied uncritically to that of Galatians 2:4. Particular aspects of observing the law, such as circumcision, are not at issue anywhere in the letter of 2 Corinthians 10-13. Each letter calls for a reading focused on the language structure of the particular argument directed to a particular community where the other letters of Paul are not available. Within the structure of 2 Corinthians 10-13, moreover, *a different gospel* is probably one that boasts of unusual spiritual experiences with a corresponding loss of emphasis on the crucified Jesus-Messiah (see, e.g., 10:15-18; 11:16—12:5).

THE INTEGRITY OF 2 CORINTHIANS   One long-standing puzzle about 2 Corinthians concerns how the various parts of the letter hold together. Are the different parts integrated as though written at one sitting by one writer in the same frame of mind from start to finish? No one seriously questions who wrote the different parts of 2 Corinthians. The historical Paul did, in the midst of his north-Mediterranean mission at about A.D. 54-55. The way the parts of 2 Corinthians fit together, however, is quite a different matter. This is the puzzle of integrity.

Reading through 2 Corinthians in one sitting, an attentive reader will experience abrupt breaks in the form of writing and flow of thought at several points in the text. This phenomenon has led to a wide range of scholarly opinion about the origin of the parts and their place in the present letter.

At one end of the spectrum, a few scholars feel compelled to treat the letter in its present form as a unity. Paul wrote all of 2 Corinthians on one scroll at one period for the same situation, abrupt changes of mood and language notwithstanding. At the opposite end, more than a few scholars see in 2 Corinthians a composite of no less than five fragments of letters, some large and some small, written at different times about different situations at Corinth. The combining of the fragments happened after Paul's mission and death at approximately the same time as the collection of Paul's letters from the different churches around the Mediterranean. A second-generation Christian (or group) devoted to Paul and his work must have gathered together all available writings of the great apostle. Some of the material from Corinth would have been fragmentary, either from wear and tear or from the deliberate cutting of one piece of papyrus from the scroll. The collected fragments of different letters, if they came from one area, Corinth, were then transferred to one scroll to make a composite letter.

The practice of combining written (or oral) materials from an important community leader started long before the second-generation church. Many documents of the Hebrew Bible are composite works, the prophets being a prime example. The large scroll of Isaiah, for example, contains speeches from different years and different situations of the prophetic ministry. The combining of the different prophetic oracles and narratives then served the larger (and later) community of Israel. A similar process happened for Paul's combined letters or parts of letters in 2 Corinthians. A generation after Paul's death, this composite document identified with Paul's ministry at Corinth was put into the service of the church at large.

Whatever the position concerning the number of letter fragments in 2 Corinthians, some account should be given for the unexpected interruptions of thought and literary texture at several points in 2 Corinthians. The disjuncture from one section of text to the next is sharper at some points than at others, as the following analysis indicates.

From 2:13 to 2:14. At 2:12-13 Paul begins a personal account of his traveling from Troas to Macedonia to find Titus. Suddenly the thought changes into a triumphant thanksgiving that leads Paul into another train of thought lasting until 7:4. At that point the travelogue about Macedonia resumes and concludes in 7:5-16. This juxtaposition of texts has led some readers to the opinion that the conciliatory text of 1:1—2:13 and 7:5-16 once stood together in the same letter, and that 2:14—7:4 (minus 6:14—7:1) belonged to another letter in the form of a defense for Paul's mission and ministry.

From 6:13 to 6:14; and 7:1 to 7:2. At 6:11 and 13 Paul cites his openness and compassion toward the Corinthians and asks that their hearts also be open to him: *open wide your hearts also* (6:13). Abruptly at 6:14 the text becomes a stern, sermon-like warning for believers to avoid an unequal yoke with unbelievers. A striking number of the words in this small passage (6:14—7:1) appear only here in the NT and are not characteristically Pauline. Much of the thought compares well to that of the Dead Sea Scrolls from Qumran. At 7:2 the conciliatory language returns as suddenly as it left: *Make room in your hearts for us.* A number of interpreters view 6:14—7:1 as a Pauline fragment of a lost letter, inserted between 6:13 and 7:2 by a later editor. Others believe the passage was written by someone other than Paul and inserted at this point by the later compiler of Paul's correspondence.

From chapter 8 to chapter 9. Both chapters 8 and 9 deal with the collection of money for the saints at Jerusalem. The appeal of chapter 8 reaches an apt conclusion at the end of the chapter. Chapter 9 begins another appeal for the collection as though chapter 8 did not exist prior to it. This observation has led some scholars to interpret the two chapters about the collection as two separate letters. Some suggest that chapter 9 is an earlier appeal than the letter of chapter 8.

From chapters 1-9 to chapters 10-13. Of the noticeable interruptions in language and thought throughout chapters 1-9, none compares to the radical change of tone at the beginning of chapter 10. In chapters 1-9 the tone generally is conciliatory, even though Paul appears to be aware of visiting preachers at Corinth who commend themselves unduly in distinction from him (3:1-3). In marked contrast, the language of chapters 10-13 is sarcastically biting. In these four chapters, Paul attacks the rival missionaries who have made themselves welcome at Corinth. He goes on to chastise the Corinthians for allowing these preachers to present themselves at Corinth in opposition to him. Hence, most scholars read chapters 10-13 as a letter written at a different time and situation from the time and circumstance of chapters 1-9. Some place the last four chapters chronologically before chapters 1-9, and identify chapters 10-13 as part of the so-called "severe letter" or "letter of tears" referred to in 2:4 and 7:8. Many other interpreters consider chapters 10-13 to be a letter in response to a later development of opposition to Paul in Corinth.

The position adopted. Rather than enter a detailed discussion of the various composition theories of 2 Corinthians, a short explanation of the position adopted in this commentary must suffice.

With the exception of the alien character of the warning inserted between 6:13 and 7:2, and assuming that Paul digresses from one line of thought to pursue another related idea, the unity of chapters 1-9 can be affirmed. The same cannot be said for all thirteen chapters. The thirteen chapters comprising 2 Corinthians have two distinct literary parts: chapters 1-9 and chapters 10-13. These two literary types brought together onto the one scroll of 2 Corinthians represent two letters of Paul, or parts of letters, written out of two different sets of circumstances. The sequence is the same. The letter of chapters 1-9 predates the letter of chapters 10-13. The latter does not qualify for the earlier "letter of tears" alluded to in 2:1-4.

Even though there is no evidence in the available manuscripts for two original letters, the literary evidence points strongly in the direction of two originals. Paul ends the collection appeal of chapter 9 thankful to God *for his indescribable gift* (9:15). Then immediately in chapter 10, he lashes out at opponents in Corinth, and at the Corinthian believers themselves. He uses sustained invective, the like of which is completely missing from chapters 1-9. Someone may say that Paul composed the two parts at two intervals, or that he had "a sleepless night" between the end of chapter 9 and the beginning of 10 (Lietzmann). But that is hardly enough to account for Paul's placing the two very different ways of writing to his congregation on the same scroll to be read at Corinth at one sitting.

It is difficult to imagine Paul mailing one scroll with one part gentle and conciliatory and the other censuring and defensive; one part saying, *I often boast about you; I have great pride in you; I am filled with consolation; I am overjoyed* (7:4), and the other saying, *I fear that when I come, I may not find you as I wish. . . . Examine yourselves to see whether you are living in the faith* (12:20; 13:5). In the letter of chapters 1-9, Paul has no reason "to boast" about himself in ministry. In chapters 10-13 the Corinthians have forced him "to boast" at length. The word *boast* is prominent in chapters 10-13, and the first person singular (*I*) is frequent. These terms signal a new situation of opposition and estrangement that has prompted the kind of writing found in these last four chapters of 2 Corinthians.

The relational sequence of chapters 1-9 to 10-13 needs further comment. Chapters 10-13 are severe and sarcastic, but not tearful or sorrowful any more than 1 Corinthians is. Neither the letter of 1 Corinthians nor the letter of the last four chapters of 2 Corinthians qualifies for the letter Paul describes in 2:3-4 and again in 7:8. The letter Paul cites in these texts refers to his second visit, when someone opposed him shamefully. Paul denounced the man for his outburst against him. The congregation apparently stood apart apathetically. Paul left the congregation dishonored, lacking moral support from his converts, and sorrowful at such a heavy loss of honor. Out of sorrow, he wrote a letter chiding the congregation for their strategic withdrawal from him when he needed their support, and calling on them to discipline the individual involved. The congregation felt hurt by Paul's letter, but they followed his directive in any case, according to the report that Titus brought back to Paul (7:5-13). Upon learning of their obedience, Paul wrote the conciliatory letter now preserved in 2 Corinthians 1–9, urging the church to show compassion to the man who had wronged him (2:8-9). While the conciliatory letter survived in 2 Corinthians 1–9, the "tearful letter" did not survive.

The substance and rhetoric of 2 Corinthians 10–13 make it an unlikely candidate for the tearful letter on several counts. Those four chapters make no mention of the offender or of the offense, and they give no advice to the congregation on how to deal with the man. Instead, these chapters represent quite another situation in which intruding missionaries have led members of the congregation to question Paul's credentials for apostolic ministry. With such a charge against him, Paul writes the Letter of Defense (chaps. 10–13) and plans a third visit to deal with the charge face to face (12:14; 13:1).

One can only assume that Paul and the Corinthian believers ultimately resolved their differences. If he later wrote Romans from Corinth, as most believe he did, then indeed Paul and the Corinthians were united. He would have lived in Corinth for some time, and he probably accepted food and lodging from the Corinthians, particularly the Corinthian women responsible for such provision (Wire: 39-97). The epistle to the Romans from Corinth carries virtually no hint of the earlier conflict with the Corinthians. By the end of Romans, Paul can report that the collection from Achaia, the area of Corinth, is already complete (Rom. 15:25-26). Furthermore, the Letter of Defense survived, is preserved in chapters 10–13 (of 2 Cor.), and thus is testimony in itself that the letter and third visit accomplished their aim: the conflict was resolved, relations restored, and the letter preserved as a memento.

The thorny question on the place of the warning of 6:14—7:1 in chapters 1–9 is more difficult to decide. As for the literary unity of 2 Corinthians 1–9, this small warning passage does not fit well into the context of chapters 6-7. Its presence in that context "looks like an erratic boulder" (Plummer: xxiv).

From the number of "foreign words," coupled with rather un-Pauline ideas and forms, one could reasonably assume that this fragment had currency at Corinth and came into the hands of the collector of Paul's letters and letter fragments. The collector then incorporated the warning into the scroll of 2 Corinthians between 6:13 and 7:2. The language and ideas of the fragment have much in common with some texts in the Qumran scrolls. But warnings of this sort were common in the synagogues of Greek-speaking Jewish people in Mediterranean culture, not strictly in the Qumran community. The fragment has some of the marks of a synagogue sermon; it may well have made its way into the Corinthian Christian context, where it was picked up and incorporated into the larger scroll of the biblical 2 Corinthians.

The fragment contains a significant number of un-Pauline elements and fits marginally in the rhetorical context of 2 Corinthians 6-7; yet its insertion in that unlikely place gives it canonical status in the tradition of the Corinthian correspondence of Paul, whether Paul wrote it or not. This justifies its interpretation and application in the commentary.

JEWISH-CHRISTIAN RELATIONS   The argument of 2 Corinthians 3 contains the raw material for the later notion (fourth century onward) that God has replaced "inferior" Judaism with "superior" Christianity. Yet Paul's thought is not that of ascendant Christianity over Judaism. At face value, the language of chapter 3 seems to cater to the church's mind-set, developed especially after Constantine's favor toward Christianity, that Christianity superseded Judaism. Consider the surface character of Paul's remarks about the ministry of Moses espoused in Judaism as compared to the new ministry of Christ adopted by Paul: *What once had glory has lost its glory because of the greater glory; for if what was set aside came through glory, much more has the permanent come in glory!* (3:10-11). From this language Alfred Plummer, at the beginning of this century, judged Paul to mean that "Christianity is so superior to Judaism that it has extinguished it" (92).

Paul, however, was not arguing from the perspective of the world religion of Christianity against the religion of Judaism. Paul was Jewish, writing from within the borders of his own religious heritage against a view—rejection of Jesus as Messiah—held by some of his own people. Paul disagreed with that view and accepted the Jewish Messiah, Jesus crucified and raised. Paul never ceased to be Jewish, as his later letter to the Romans attests (11:1-6). Moreover, his statement about the all-sufficiency of Jesus-Messiah in the new time frame of Gentile mission is tinged with polemic against his own Jewish detractors, who say that Moses and Messiah stand together. Paul argues, rather, that Messiah has taken over from Moses in ways appropriate to the new age of the Spirit and world mission.

Consequently, the language of 2 Corinthians 3 cannot be used in support of the superiority of Christianity over Judaism, much less in maintaining an anti-Semitic attitude on the part of non-Jewish Christians. Paul's rhetoric in this text and elsewhere in his letters proves that he was in dialogue with his own Jewish and Jewish Christian contemporaries, with whom he sometimes disagreed out of conviction. He thought his nonbelieving kinsfolk should see the light of Christ as he did, and he was ready to put his life on the line for them. This shows the depth of his new conviction about Messiah, and the breadth of his love for his own Jewish people. Jewish-Christian dialogue now underway does not require bland agreement between the two groups, but a wholesome respect one for the other in the name of the sovereign God of all humankind.

LETTERS OF RECOMMENDATION   Only at 2 Corinthians 3:1, of all the letters of Paul, is there reference to *letters of recommendation*. The texture and tone of Paul's argument at the beginning of chapter 3 points to rival missionaries at Corinth who carry these letters. Their presence on Paul's trail is especially evident in the telltale phrase in 3:1, *as some do.*

These missionary persons with letters in hand came from an established congregation. Yet there is no indication that they originated in Palestine, as Plummer suggests (78); nor that the letters were written by leaders in the mother church in Jerusalem, as Käsemann intimates (1956:25). These missionaries probably originated in a Greek-speaking Jewish-Christian community somewhere in the North Mediterranean area, possibly at Ephesus or Antioch, with some ties to a Diaspora synagogue.

What of the letters they carried? The commending letter was a functional form of the day in the Mediterranean world of the Roman empire, much like a letter of reference today. Persons could move through the Roman world and find access into social settings by means of the letter of recommendation. Christians also used the letter of recommendation to vouch for their good standing. Paul's letter to Philemon on behalf of the runaway slave-become-Christian, Onesimus, exhibits this form. Onesimus probably carried the letter with him to Philemon's house church.

In the hands of the missionaries who came to Corinth, these commending letters functioned as credentials for ministry among the believing community that Paul founded. Paul's second question implies that the visiting preachers requested similar letters of recommendation from the Corinthians in return for their ministry among them: *Surely we do not need, as some do, letters of recommendation . . . from you, do we?* Since these rival apostles carried letters of recommendation, a question must have dawned on the Corinthians: Why did Paul not show us letters of recommendation when he first came to us? Who authorized his mission in our city? Is he a true apostle? No doubt the rival missionaries helped to raise this query. They may have played up Paul's beleaguered reputation with the synagogue, that five times he had received the thirty-nine stripes for his radical teaching (2 Cor. 11:24; Sanders, 1986:85-90). If the interloping missionaries happened to belong to a group authorized by Apollos (cf. 1 Cor. 3:4-9), they may not have known Paul personally at all, and thus felt at liberty to speak against his apostleship.

NEW COVENANT   On two occasions in Paul's surviving letters, the term *new covenant* occurs. Both occurrences are in the Corinthian correspondence, and one of them (1 Cor. 11:25) in a quotation of the eucharistic words of Jesus, found also in the Synoptic Gospels (Luke 22:20). Jeremiah had already foretold a "new covenant" (31:31) before the term appeared in the words of Jesus or in the argument of Paul in 2 Corinthians 3:6.

The idea of covenant has its roots in the relationship between Israel's God (Yahweh) and Israel's life as a people in the Land of Promise. The Greek term, *diathēkē,* means to cut in two, and it implies two sides to the relationship: God takes the initiative to save the people and give them life in the land; in response, the people observe the rule of God for their lives in the land and world as expressed in the Law (*Torah*).

The idea of a *new* covenant implies a previous covenant. The question of the *new* covenant is whether it renders inoperative the one that led up to it. Or does the new one subsume the former covenant within itself and thus render the old inoperative? The latter seems to be the case in Paul's argument and thought in 2 Corinthians 3. Paul does, after all, quote the Law as though it still exists as proof for what he is saying about it. But the old covenant no longer has saving significance in itself since the coming of the Messiah. The new constituent component in the new covenant is Christ, who encompasses all that the Law intends. The Law points to Christ, is fulfilled in Christ, and in that sense is *new.* The old form has been rendered inoperative. The newness of the covenant in Christ's death and resurrection corresponds to the new age manifesting itself in Paul's activity in world mission (Hickling, 1980:208f.). The new covenant is therefore "cut" between God and a new people made up of *both Jewish and Gentile people,* not one to the exclusion of the other. The new covenant further corresponds to Paul's idea of *new creation,* which includes anyone in Christ, whose life is governed by the life-giving Spirit (2 Cor. 3:4-6; 5:17)

OPPONENTS IMPLICIT IN 2 CORINTHIANS That Paul experienced bitter opposition from some rival missionaries is inescapable, especially from the rhetoric of 2 Corinthians 10-13. Yet the identity of the adversaries is veiled, and so is their criticism of Paul. The only primary source for identifying the rivals depicted in 2 Corinthians is this extant letter (particularly chaps. 10-13). The opposition may already begun when Paul was writing 1 Corinthians (cf. 1 Cor. 1:12-17; 3:3-15), but it came to a head by the time Paul wrote the Letter of Defense (2 Cor. 10-13). Even in the Letter of Defense, the opponents are veiled behind (or within) the various forms of argument, but strangely also revealed therein at the same time. The job of locating the real identity and character of Paul's opponents in 2 Corinthians remains unfinished. But certain advances have been made.

Historical reconstructions of various allusions Paul makes in his arguments are usually not necessary for grasping the sense of a given text. In the case of the implied opponents at Corinth, however, the matter is somewhat different. The rival ministry of these figures lies intertwined in the rhetoric of chapters 10-13. An informed, imaginative reconstruction of the identity and character of the persons denounced in the argument is therefore possible.

The following is a brief review of scholarly opinion regarding Paul's opponents at Corinth, including (last) the position assumed throughout the commentary.

Judaizers. To some modern readers, the opponents behind 2 Corinthians appear as "Judaizers" from Jerusalem. Unlike Paul, they insist that Gentile converts to Christ (the Jewish Messiah) observe the regulations of the Jewish law. These people came to Corinth under the auspices of the conservative branch of the Jerusalem Church, to ensure that Corinthian believers in the Jewish Messiah adhere to the law of Israel's God. These opponents, according to this view, are cut from the same cloth as those characterized in Galatians. They appeal to Moses (2 Cor. 3:1-18) and preach *another Jesus than the one we proclaimed . . . and a different gospel from the one you accepted* (2 Cor. 11:4; cf. Gal. 1:6-9; 2:11-14). These same critics are also implied in Paul's rhetorical questions in 2 Corinthians 11 and are found to be Hebrews, Israelites and descendants of Abraham (11:22; cf. Gal. 3:6-14). This school of interpretation takes such clues to mean that Paul's opponents at Corinth warrant the designation "Judaizers."

However, the way these clues are construed is misleading. The problems of law observance in Galatians (such as circumcision and the food code) are not mentioned in 2 Corinthians. Nor is the opponents' place of origin identified. As Meeks points out, "Where they came from, we do not know, for there is nothing in the text to connect them with Jerusalem" (132). Hints in 2 Corinthians portray them rather as charismatic missionaries (or self-styled "apostles") who seek to outdo Paul in missionary leadership (apostleship), in spiritual insight and ministry (12:1, 11-12), and in Christian social manners (12:14-18). The traits of these opponents in 2 Corinthians are different from those of Galatians.

Gnostics.   More than anyone else, Walter Schmithals detected "Christian" Gnostics at Corinth. According to him, these were the opponents Paul faced. Paul's extravagant rhetoric in 2 Corinthians 10-13 stems from Paul's misunderstanding of his Gnostic opponents. Gnosticism in Corinth, by Schmithals' description, was a religious movement that viewed human beings as essentially divine. Salvation comes to those with inner, spiritual knowledge (gnōsis) of their substantial self, of the nature of the world, and of God's redemption of the soul (25-32).

Schmithals' conclusions stretch the evidence beyond proper limits. If Paul in his letters to the Corinthians appears to misunderstand the Gnostics that Schmithals constructs, it is because they did not exist as such in Paul's time. The force with which Paul addresses the situation in 2 Corinthians, especially in chapters 10-13, demonstrates that he recognized quite well what his opponents were up to in Corinth; he rejected their stance unequivocally.

Jewish "Divine-Men" Missionaries.   Dieter Georgi's elaborate research into *The Opponents of Paul in Second Corinthians* deserves more detailed evaluation than this space allows. His analysis of the situation depicted in 2 Corinthians reveals a group of outside missionaries competing with Paul for the allegiance of the Corinthians. They touted their credentials as superior to Paul's, their ties to salvation-tradition as stronger, their spiritual experience as higher, and their rhetoric as more persuasive and pleasing. Georgi thus identifies Paul's opponents as Jewish missionaries of Palestinian origin who think they have reached the status of "divine men," like Moses and Jesus.

Georgi's designation of the opponents of Paul in 2 Corinthians relies heavily on material from the Corinthian correspondence. Yet it takes liberties with Paul's rhetoric without due warrant. If the opponents claimed to be *Hebrews* (2 Cor. 11:22), for example, does that really mean they were also of Palestinian Jewish origin and spoke Aramaic? Paul himself claimed to be "a Hebrew born of Hebrews" (Phil. 3:5), but he was a citizen of the Roman city of Tarsus and a Roman citizen, and he spoke Greek (Acts 21:37—22:29; 16:37-39). Is Paul's reduction of the glory of Moses in chapter 3, and his own claim to spiritual ecstasy in chapters 11-12, sufficient ground to classify the opponents as belonging to a "divine-man" school of thought? The evidence scarcely carries the weight of the conclusion.

Pneumatics.   A more modest proposal came from Ernst Käsemann. He signaled the importance of key words in 2 Corinthians 10-13 for identifying the opponents. He acknowledged the Jewish-Christian background of the rivals but emphasized their claim to pneumatic experience, their spiritual giftedness, including their ability thus to perform miracles. In comparing their credentials and experience of the Spirit (pneuma) with Paul's, they portrayed Paul as *weak* (10:10). The strength of Käsemann's conclusion about Paul's rival missionaries in 2 Corinthians is that he limited his search to 2 Corinthians 10-13. The problem with working primarily with Paul's language, however, is that Paul argues polemically, in a way that will cast his opponents in the worst possible light.

The result of Käsemann's analysis is rather general. To say in the end that the opponents were "pneumatics" and "Jewish-Christian" is scarcely telling for the interpretation of the text of 2 Corinthians.

Strategic Alliance of Judaizers and Spirit-People. Jerome Murphy-O'Connor put his finger on a very important point in his recent book on *The Theology of the Second Letter to the Corinthians*. His clue to part of the identity of the opponents comes from the figure of Apollos in 1 Corinthians. Apollos like Philo, his Alexandrian Jewish counterpart, taught initiation into a higher spiritual wisdom. A group in the church at Corinth had aligned themselves with this Apollos. They adopted his teaching on the Spirit to an extreme, from Paul's perspective. Paul put this group of "spirit-people" in their place with his own instruction on spiritual wisdom and knowledge in 1 Corinthians 1–3. The group must have felt hurt when the letter was read. When an outside group of Jewish-Christian missionaries came to Corinth to bring the community in line with the Jewish law, these "spirit-people" in the community saw an opportunity to get back at Paul. They formed a coalition with these Judaizers to devalue Paul's status and mission in the community. "Such 'Corinthianization' of the Judaizers is the best explanation of the combination of apparently incompatible traits that appear in 2 Corinthians" (15).

Welcome as Murphy-O'Connor's insight on Apollos at Corinth is, his attempt at combining two groups, (1) insider "spirit-people" in league with Apollos and (2) outsider "Judaizers," is really not required by the evidence of 2 Corinthians to the extent that he thinks.

Another explanation of the opponents, adopted in the commentary, makes the most sense of the available evidence:

Hellenistic-Jewish Christian Missionaries from the Same Diaspora Synagogue Setting as Paul. Scholars in search of Paul's opponents in 2 Corinthians have felt reasonably secure in placing the opposing group at Corinth outside the circle of Paul's Christian mission. The opponents must have another origin, another language and culture, and a deficient Christian confession. The inquiry has operated on the premise that "opponents" must be sharply distinguished from the religious and social thought and life of Paul. Hence, scholars have tended to highlight their *difference* from Paul to account for Paul's dramatic rhetoric of denunciation.

A case can be made the other way. Paul is upset, as his polemical argument shows, because he has expected Christian missionaries from his own religious and social world, speaking his own Greek language, wandering charismatically in mission as he does, to respect his person and the primacy of his apostolic place in the church he founded at Corinth. These other "apostles" followed Paul to Corinth, arriving after he had left, and they should have supported him and his missionary work. Instead, they criticized him. Out of this sense of betrayal, Paul writes with such passion in 2 Corinthians 10–13. The subjects of his scathing rhetoric, the "opponents," seem far removed from Paul's Christian thinking and mission, *disguising themselves as apostles of Christ* (11:13). But the distancing factor is itself a key part of the rhetoric of denunciation.

According to Paul in (2 Cor.) 11:12, the interlopers at Corinth take *every opportunity to be recognized as our equals*. As far as their Jewish background and spiritual gifts are concerned, they are Paul's equals (11:22). They also claim to be ministers of Christ as Paul is (11:23). Yet on several points, they are not his equal. They arrive in Corinth after Paul founded the community. On that score, they are secondary. They carry letters of recommendation. Paul did not carry such letters because he was breaking new ground. They take sustenance from the Corinthians for their labors in the gospel. Paul did not do so [Refusing Money from Corinth, p. 277].

However, from Paul's perspective, one critical point renders them unequal to him as an apostle: they boast competitively in the name of Jesus Christ. Paul does not, indeed cannot. Their vain boasting and competitive behavior brands Paul's critics as false apostles (2 Cor. 11:13), not merely secondary apostles, and certainly not their claimed status of super-apostles (11:5). The purported Christian message they preach is another Jesus, . . . a different spirit, . . . a different gospel (11:4). In short, these persons, despite their claim to have come from the same Jewish-Christian circle as Paul, have lost their grasp on the distinctive character of the gospel: the paradox of the power of God in the weakness of the cross of Jesus Christ and manifested in the apostle (12:9; cf. 1 Cor. 1:18-25).

At another level, these "apostles" to Corinth from within Paul's missionary circle in the North Mediterranean society may have been able to maintain a better relationship to the Jewish synagogue than Paul was able to maintain (2 Cor. 11:24); they may have related to the one at Ephesus (cf. Acts 19:8-10). For one thing, Paul's Roman citizenship, associated with the Hellenistic city of Tarsus, may not have worked in his favor among the Jewish synagogue elite, who regarded Roman domination as a violation of the rule of the Lord their God. To complicate matters even more, Paul emphasizes a saving Messiah killed in Roman fashion, by crucifixion. These elements considered, Paul's preaching is bound to create no small animosity. Suppose that Paul's competitors, on the other hand, are not associated with Roman imperialism by citizenship and play down the significance of the cross-theology that Paul plays up; then their stance may be helping them retain their tie to the synagogue, with little repercussion.

The Jewish synagogue in the cities of the Greek-speaking world ensured its members a link with the saving tradition of Israel. Greek-speaking Jews, like Apollos from Alexandria and Paul from Tarsus, could listen to Moses being read (2 Cor. 3:15) in the Greek language, and know in their hearts that their Jewish inheritance in salvation was secure. Judging from the description of Apollos in 1 Corinthians 3 and in Acts 18–19, he and others like him have made converts to Christ from Diaspora synagogues. In turn, the more outstanding of these converts to Christ have become recognized missionary preachers among the Gentiles, especially in Gentile congregations already established by someone else, Paul in particular (Acts 19:13-19).

Their credentials, like those of Apollos, are first rate. Coming from Jewish parents and aligned with the synagogue, they are Hebrews, . . . Israelites, . . . descendants of Abraham (2 Cor. 11:22). Aligned with the new Christ-movement, they are ministers of Christ and filled with the Spirit; they have visions of the Lord, performed miracles (11:23; 12:1, 12), and accept support for their labor in the gospel. They come from the same Jewish background as Paul himself and stand essentially in the same circle of Hellenistic-Jewish Christian thought.

Judging from Paul's dramatic rhetoric of denunciation in 2 Corinthians 10-13, he perceives the criticism from his rival apostles to be aimed at denying his status and function as apostle of Jesus Christ at Corinth. His scathing denunciation of his critics is understandable if they come from within his own circle of Christian missionary friends and colleagues from the Diaspora synagogue setting, people like Apollos. Paul and his gospel were being discredited in the Corinthian congregation he founded, by Christian missionaries of his own kind of Jewish-Christian thought and life. His pain at having his apostleship and his gospel thus discredited best accounts for the display of emotion in the rhetoric of denunciation in chapters 10-13.

By analogy, a Christian minister in a denomination today feels deeply hurt when another leader of the same denomination calls one's own ministry and motives and message into question. The response to such betrayal is understandably defensive.

Of the number of possible factors that could account for the sharp criticism of Paul at Corinth, the sociological ones doubtless play a significant part. In his essay on the "Sociology of Early Christian Missionaries," Gerd Theissen (1982:27-67) deals with the legitimation of "primitive Christian itinerant preachers," of which both Paul and his opponents are members. Theissen identifies two types of missionary preachers in the early stages of the Christian movement: (1) itinerant charismatics and (2) community organizers. Paul and his co-workers represent community organizers, who break new ground and establish independent communities of believers. "The most important difference between [the two types] is that each adopts a distinctive attitude to the question of subsistence" (28).

Paul recognizes his right to subsistence from preaching the gospel. He has a word from Moses and a word from the Lord Jesus to authorize his privilege of expecting a living from his preaching (1 Cor. 9:8-14). But he renounces the privilege, choosing rather to support himself independently in his ministry at Corinth (1 Cor. 9:15). Paul's competitors view their right to food and lodging as a mark of apostleship in relation to Jesus, himself a wandering charismatic teacher. Their criticism against Paul is that by renouncing his privilege of subsistence, he has renounced true apostleship in the name of Christ. By seeking his own living, rather than accepting livelihood from the Corinthians, Paul is *acting according to human standards* (2 Cor. 10:2). On this count, among others, Paul's rivals hold his apostleship suspect. Paul is obliged to establish the legitimacy of his apostolic ministry, but not by the standards of his competitors. He cites his *weakness* as identification with Christ (2 Cor. 12:6-10), and his renunciation of support as abundant love for the Corinthians (2 Cor. 12:14-18).

Theissen's reconstruction of the crisis between Paul and his rival missionaries at Corinth is instructive:

Itinerant charismatics arriving in Corinth made a claim on support from the community. The members reacted at first by pointing to Paul: our apostle Paul never raised any such claims. In response, the itinerant charismatics could point to the words of Jesus as a justification for their position. As regards Paul, that left but two choices. Either they must convert him to their style of life or deny him his claim to apostolicity. . . . They contested Paul's apostolicity—not out of personal malice, but in self-defense. (1982:53)

Antoinette Clark Wire adds yet another possible dimension to the mixed crisis that developed at Corinth. The social status of some members has improved after Paul's mission in the city, especially the status of the Corinthian women prophets. These would consider themselves Paul's friends, whose hospitality he has refused while maintaining his right to it. "When Paul refuses their hospitality—whether offered or not—and refuses to join them in mutual gain, they are offended, rejecting a friendship based on mutual loss. . . . The result is enmity" (195). The rival apostles to Corinth, discovering this situation among the Corinthians, are then able to use Paul's refusal of hospitality against him to their own social advantage.

All of this sifted evidence for the identity of Paul's opponents in 2 Corinthians points persuasively to Hellenistic-Jewish Christian missionaries from a setting in a diaspora synagogue. The leader of the group may very well be Apollos.

REFUSING MONEY FROM CORINTH Why does Paul take financial aid from the poorer churches of Macedonia but not from the wealthier Corinth? Corinth could better afford to give Paul money for his service in the gospel. Perhaps Paul refuses money from the richer Corinthians to avoid the conflict of interest in the patron-client relationship prevalent in that culture. How could he exercise his apostolic prerogatives, as he did in 1 Corinthians 5, if certain members were his patrons, giving him material support? John K. Chow has written an illuminating "study of social networks in Corinth" under the title *Patronage and Power.* He concludes that "Paul's conflict with some of the Corinthians resulted partly from Paul's refusal to accept money from the church, which, in effect, constituted a violation of the convention of friendship or patronage and which would therefore be seen by some at least to bring dishonor to the rich patrons in the church" (188-189).

Paul considers receiving financial support from the congregation an apostolic privilege, but not an obligation (1 Cor. 9:12-14). He can refuse money if the situation demands it, as the situation at Corinth apparently does. He wants to "make the gospel free of charge" (1 Cor. 9:18; 2 Cor. 11:7). The accusation against him is threefold: he is not a friend of (some of) the Corinthians (2 Cor. 12:15), he lacks apostolic authority (12:12-13), and he is dipping into the collection (12:16-18; cf. 1 Thess. 2:3-8). His answer to all three comes from apostolic privilege. He has the right as an apostle to take money from the Corinthians or to refuse it. He chooses consistently to refuse money from Corinth for reasons that are not altogether clear (2 Cor. 11:7-11). He does not want to burden them (11:9); he exalts them by living humbly himself (11:7). But these reasons do not fully explain why he takes money from the poorer churches of Macedonia but not from Corinth.

The city of Corinth is known to be rich, and doubtless some of the members are well off (1 Cor. 1:26) and can afford to provide Paul's needs as an apostle. If Paul were to align himself with the rich of the congregation, he would violate one of the central tenets of his own confession and preaching:

that God chooses the weak of the world to accomplish his redemptive purpose (1 Cor. 1:27-31; 9:22; 2 Cor. 11:9; 12:9). On a practical and ethical level, he would not be in a position to exercise discipline for the rich members of whom he was client. What if the incestuous man (1 Cor. 5) were Paul's principal patron? How could Paul remove him from the congregation as he does? Paul advises and disciplines his converts out of love for the congregation. His refusal of money from patrons at Corinth, or from the church as patron, frees him to love them more (2 Cor. 12:15; cf. 1 Cor. 9:18).

SATAN   Paul mentions the figure of Satan at three points in 2 Corinthians. At 2:11 he counsels the congregation to forgive the wrongdoer in order to avoid the tricks of Satan. At 11:14 he characterizes his opponents as ministers of Satan disguised as ministers of righteousness. At 12:7 he views his *thorn in the flesh* as *a messenger of Satan* to keep him from being too elated. Satan is also connected with the name of *Beliar*, in the inserted text of 6:14—7:1 (cf. Jub. 1:20; Test. Dan 1:7; 3:6; Fitzmyer, 1971:205-217, on Dead Sea Scrolls).

Paul inherited his view of Satan from his Jewish tradition. The Greek term *(Satana)* is a carry-over from the Hebrew *(ha)-satan*. The Greek version (LXX) rarely uses this term. When it does, the meaning denotes an *adversary* on the earthly plain, as in 1 Kings 11:14, where Hadad of Edom is Solomon's *adversary (satanas;* cf. Sirach 21:27). The sense is that the adversary is like an accusing prosecutor in a court *(TDNT,* 2:73). Where the archenemy of God is in view, the LXX renders *(ha)-satan* with the Greek *ho diabolos.* This Greek term, like its Hebrew counterpart, *(ha)-satan,* denotes an evil figure opposed to the will of God, and standing again like a prosecutor in God's court *(TDNT,* 7:151-163). Depending on the context, such a figure could be called in English: Accuser, Adversary, or Devil. This is the same figure that provoked David to number Israel (1 Chron. 21:1); Job suffers under his power (Job 1:6—2:7); the same *Satan* resists the high priest in the reestablishing of the remnant in Israel (Zech. 3:1; cf. Ps. 109:6). In each of these instances in the OT, the *Satan* figure is not a demon of the underworld totally separated from the court of the Lord. On the contrary, Satan is seen in the same judicial assembly with the Lord, discussing the destiny of the people of God in the world. Satan's chief aim in these texts is to oppose the Lord of Israel *(TDNT,* 2:73-75).

This sinister yet lordly figure appears under other titles in the OT. One of the less-notable references to the rival of God appears in the priestly text of Leviticus 16 under the name Azazel (traditionally translated "scapegoat"). Here Aaron the priest presents a goat to the Lord and another to Azazel. He puts the sins of the people on the goat dedicated to Azazel. That goat is led out of the camp into the desert and handed over to Azazel for destruction, to rid God's holy community of its iniquities. In later Judaism, this figure of Azazel became identified with the arch opponent of God, otherwise known as Satan (Grabbe: 152f.).

Another name for the figure opposed to God occurs at Isaiah 14. In that prophecy the figure comes through as a high angelic being under the name "Lucifer" (KJV), meaning "Day Star, son of the Dawn." Embodied in the evil king of Babylon, his ambition in Isaiah 14 is to raise his throne "above the stars of God" and to make himself like the Most High (14:12-14). '

The same negative character from the other world and invading this world bears the name *Belial* or *Beliar*. In almost all the texts in which his name appears in the OT, Belial begets children like himself. These lawless persons think and act like their progenitor "Belial" (KJV: Deut. 13:13; Judg. 19:22; 20:13; 1 Sam. 30:22; 2 Sam. 16:7; cf. John 8:42-44; Col. 3:6, KJV; 1 John 3:8-10).

How do Paul's images of Satan in 2 Corinthians match these from his Scripture? Taking the name Belial/Beliar first, the rhetorical questions of 2 Corinthians 6:14-16 assume that those who participate in Beliar bear his image, just as the participants in Christ bear the image of Christ. A person cannot participate in both at the same time (cf. 1 Cor. 10:21). This image is consistent with the prevailing notion from the OT that Beliar has his offspring, who do his will by nature.

Second, the beguiling character of Satan in the OT comes through in every reference in 2 Corinthians. Forgiveness prevents the kind of outwitting tricks Satan played on David (2:11). Satan's ministers opposing Paul are in disguise to deceive the Corinthians: they are in league with Lucifer, the Day Star, *an angel of light* (11:14-15) who opposed God and fell from heaven (Isa. 12:14).

Finally, Satan torments Paul with the thorn in the flesh to keep him from being too elated (2 Cor. 12:7). This characterization of Satan carries a mild echo of the story of Job, who suffered at Satan's hand but was ultimately acquitted and restored.

The Azazel figure of the scapegoat tradition does not appear anywhere in 2 Corinthians, though it probably does lie behind 1 Corinthians 5:5. In that context, Paul consigns the incestuous man to Satan for the destruction of the flesh so that the spirit may be saved in the day of the Lord. Here the echo resembles the figure of the destructive desert demon, Azazel, under the name Satan (see Caird, 1994:107-111).

Paul believes that Satan's ultimate defeat was sealed by Jesus' death and resurrection, to be completed in the Day of the Lord (Col. 2:14-15; Rom. 16:20; cf. Luke 10:18; John 12:31-32; Rev. 12:7-12; 20:2, 10).

THE SUPER-APOSTLES Who are the *super-apostles* of 2 Corinthians 11:5? Are they the same persons identified in 11:12-15 as *false apostles* and ministers of Satan *disguising themselves as apostles of Christ?* Barrett maintains that the *super-apostles* correspond to the primary Jerusalem apostles mentioned in Galatians 2:9 as "pillars." Barrett thus distinguishes between the *false apostles . . . disguising themselves as apostles of Christ* (2 Cor. 11:13) and the *super-apostles* with whom Paul is said to claim equality. The distinction, however, is fabricated essentially on the assumption that Paul seriously claims equality with the *super-apostles* in 12:11 and distances himself from the false apostles of 11:13 (1973:320, 277-279, 286, 28-32).

However, *super-apostles* is a highly sarcastic term, one that Paul would not likely use for such Jerusalem figures as Peter, James, and John. Paul's claim not to be inferior to the *super-apostles* is an ironic tongue-in-cheek boast, in keeping with the rest of his Fool's Speech, not a serious claim apart from the fool's boast in which the term is located. The irony is made obvious by the additional remark, *even though I am nothing* (12:11). Moreover, the *super-apostles* and the *false apostles* are the same group of rival interlopers at Corinth against whom Paul was forced to defend himself as a fool. They claim to have greater oratorical skill (10:10; 11:6), higher spiritual experiences (12:1-5), better connection with the Jewish heritage of faith (11:21-22), and apostolic status as ministers of Christ (11:23). By their own estimate, they are above Paul. Paul's verdict is that their claim renders them *false* by the standard of Christ crucified in weakness (10:1-6; 13:4).

TWO APPEALS FOR ONE COLLECTION IN ONE LETTER The strained literary relationship between chapters 8 and 9 of 2 Corinthians has long been a subject of debate. Echoes of the appeal of chapter 8 reverberate in chapter 9 in the form of a *recitative*. Yet these echoes are not, as some suggest, mere repetitions to drive home the point of the appeal more forcefully (Plummer: 252; Hughes: 322). There are repetitive elements in chapter 9: the collection as a ministry, the Macedonian contribution, the anonymous delegates, generosity encouraged, resulting thanksgiving, the great grace of God. Yet these all are clothed in additional rhetorical dress. The tone and texture of speech in chapter 9 is modulated, and the sensitive subject of the collection of money is handled more delicately in chapter 9 than in chapter 8.

This observation has led numerous scholars, notably Betz, to separate chapter 9 from chapter 8 completely. Betz argues from a literary analysis of the two chapters that each chapter constitutes a substantial fragment of an independent letter: "Paul wrote two letters at about the same time, that is, when the envoys were about to leave for Corinth" (1985:94). Betz accounts for the difference between the two appeals by comparing the destination of each letter: the letter of chapter 8 goes to the city of Corinth; the letter of chapter 9 goes to the churches of Achaia, excluding Corinth (cf. 1:1b).

Other interpreters think Paul wrote and dispatched the letter of chapter 9 a short time prior to the writing of chapter 8. The opening of chapter 9—*it is not necessary for me to write to you about the ministry to the saints*—is said to signal Paul's first attempt to reactivate the collection after the brief reminders in 1 Corinthians 16:1-4. When Paul realized that the letter of chapter 9 had not achieved its goal, he wrote a somewhat sharper appeal, the letter of chapter 8, to spur the church on to complete the offering.

However, chapter 9 assumes prior knowledge on the part of the Corinthians, available to them nowhere else than in chapter 8. The wording of 9:3, for example, assumes the more elaborate introduction of the brothers in 8:16-24. The note about the people of Macedonia in 9:2-4 assumes the readers' prior knowledge of the state of the collection in Macedonia, which they have heard in 8:1-5.

The peculiar transition in 9:1 notwithstanding, there is a more promising approach to chapter 9. First, treat that appeal for the collection in the sequence in which it occurs. Second, regard chapter 9 as composed on the same occasion, but not necessarily at the same moment. Third, interpret the appeal of chapter 9 as an addendum to the rhetoric of chapter 8. The latter needs more discussion.

In the appeal of chapter 8, two features dominate the agenda of the rhetoric: the extraordinary example of sacrificial giving in the Macedonian churches, which tests the mind and will of the Corinthians (8:1-15); and the authorization and recommendation of an embassy to ensure that the collection is completed (8:16-24). Around these two major elements, Paul weaves his plea for a generous gift for *the saints*. Both elements appear again in chapter 9, but Paul construes their persuasive role differently. He significantly qualifies the example of the Macedonians: the Achaians, not mentioned as an example in chapter 8, were the first to start the collection; their example was effective in stimulating the majority of Macedonians.

As for the delegation of *brothers*, their description in 9:3-5 diminishes their implied authoritative role. Paul is sending them simply to ensure that the churches of the area are not put to shame (cf. 8:19, 22-23). Titus, whose authority in collaboration with Paul is highlighted in 8:23, is not even mentioned beyond *the brothers* of 9:3-5. Throughout the rest of chapter 9 (9:6-15), Paul makes a last call for a generous collection, but as Martin states, he does so with "unusual delicacy" (R. Martin, 1986:283). In short, the so-called "redundancy" of chapter 9 is best described as added qualification to the preceding appeal of chapter 8. Why Paul found it wise to parallel the appeal of chapter 8 with a more delicate wooing of the Corinthians in chapter 9 can only be conjectured (or imagined!).

F. W. Farrar remarks: "it looks as if [Paul] had been interrupted, or had left off dictating at the end of the last verse [of chapter 8]. Such breaks must often and necessarily have occurred in the dictation of the Epistles, and doubtless help to account for some of their phenomena" (218; cf. Bruce: 225). Paul may have ended a session of dictation at 8:24, retired for the night or for lunch. Upon his return, he could have read what he had written in chapter 8 (or had his scribe read it back to him) to feel its effect, as the Corinthians would feel it later. He likely recognized the sharpness of his argument directed toward the Corinthians, contrasted with his praise for the Macedonian example. So Paul decided to append a second appeal aimed at creating a more amicable feeling in the hearts of his readers toward himself and his collection of money for the Jerusalem saints. Paul's (2 Cor. 8) text on papyrus was too costly to throw away and was still useful when joined to a more delicate addition.

THE "UNEQUAL YOKE" PASSAGE   The place of the passage about the "unequal yoke" (6:14—7:1) in 2 Corinthians has occasioned no small debate among biblical interpreters. The questions surrounding the text are manifold, but two stand out. First, what is the origin of this distinctive text as it stands in 2 Corinthians? And second, how does one explain its place and purpose within the context of 2 Corinthians 6?

On its origin, judging from its position in a letter under Paul's name, and without any manuscript evidence to the contrary, one could answer simply that Paul wrote this directive to the Corinthians. Analysis of the internal features and substance of the text itself, however, points in another direction.

Un-Pauline words are frequent in this short text (not taking into account the quotations from Scripture). There are no less than eight Greek words that do not appear elsewhere in the undisputed letters of Paul. In the NRSV they appear as *mismatched* (6:14a), *partnership* (6:14b), *agreement* (6:15), *Beliar* (6:15), *share* (6:15), *agreement* (6:16), *cleanse* (7:1), *defilement* (7:1).

Terms function differently here than elsewhere in Paul's letters: *Fellowship* (6:14), *believer* (6:15), *promises* (7:1), *making . . . perfect* (7:1).

The citations from Scripture (6:16-18) are unique to this text within Paul's letters.

The formulas introducing and concluding Scripture citations (6:16c, 18c) are unlike any that Paul uses regularly (e.g., Rom. 10-11; Gal. 3).

The thrust of the passage is quite uncharacteristic of Paul's ideas in any of his arguments. This observation is perhaps the most telling and warrants some discussion. For Paul, who made it a mark of his ministry "to become all things to all people" (1 Cor. 9:22), now to prohibit association with *unbelievers* is strange indeed. Earlier he informed the Corinthian church that he did not intend them "to go out of the world" (1 Cor. 5:10) like an ascetic community. He told members to marry "only in the Lord" (7:39) but encouraged them to maintain previously covenanted marriages with unbelievers (7:12-16).

Ideas related to the central thrust of 2 Corinthians 6:14—7:1 are no less peculiar within Paul's thought. Paul is not known to teach that the fulfillment of God's promises depends on the members' observance of the commandments of God (6:17-18). In the rhetorical question of 2 Corinthians 6:14b, righteousness implies obeying the law; for Paul, righteousness is a term of salvation in relation to Christ apart from "righteousness under the law," which he "counted as loss because of Christ" (Phil. 3:6-7). The name "Christ" at (2 Cor.) 6:15 stands strangely undeveloped in a strong appeal to remain undefiled in moral and religious communal life. Avoidance of defilement, according to 7:1, applies to both *flesh* (*body*) and *spirit*. In contrast, Paul elsewhere consistently opposes flesh and spirit where they occur together (e.g., Gal. 5:16-21). Furthermore, on the perfecting of moral purity in Christian life, Paul regularly attributes this to the power of God in the Spirit of Christ, not so much to human initiative, as 2 Corinthians 7:1 strongly implies.

The weight of internal evidence is compelling against this text having originated with the apostle Paul himself. Nor is it likely that Paul found the passage in another source and incorporated it into 2 Corinthians 6. If he would not think to write in this vein, why would he choose to incorporate what he would not think to write? The question of the origin of this little text in 2 Corinthians is still open.

Joseph Fitzmyer concluded that this passage is "a Christian reworking of an Essene paragraph which has been introduced into the Pauline letter" (1971:217). His examination of the Qumran scrolls alongside this text suggested to him five points of contact with the Jewish covenantors of Qumran: (1) The triple dualism of uprightness and iniquity, light and darkness, Christ (or Messiah) and Beliar. (2) The opposition to idols. (3) The temple of God. (4) Separation from all impurity. (5) A rhythmic stringing together of OT texts (208-216). There is significant similarity of attitude and terms of reference between the texts of Jewish Qumran and this passage in 2 Corinthians 6. Yet this observation does not exclude other possibilities. Dualism (in various forms) was widespread in Diaspora Judaism, as shown in Philo's writings, and so was opposition to idols, reverence for the temple of God, and moral purity.

Hans Dieter Betz claims to have found in this passage the theology of Paul's "opponents" as represented in Paul's letter to the Galatians. These "opponents" were Jewish Christians with ties to the Jerusalem church. They belonged to the same Jewish-Christian camp that sought to impose purity regulations of the law on Gentile Christians at Antioch, against Paul's judgment about "the truth of the gospel" that required no such imposition (Gal. 2:11-21; Betz, 1973:88-108). Because he located the passage in a setting of "opponents" of Paul, Betz was unable to explain how this text found its way into a letter written by Paul.

William Webb has cited evidence of new-covenant and second-exodus traditions in this fragment (especially in the chain of OT quotations) and in the literary context in which it appears in 2 Corinthians. According to Webb, Paul (assumed to be the author of the fragment) prompts the Corinthians' return to him and to God "with the cry for a new exodus . . . and with promises related to their homecoming. . . . Paul effectively parallels the Corinthians' need to return to him as their apostle with their need to return to God" (177-178). Traditional covenantal categories do exist within the unit itself. But the Pauline-Christian "newness," so evident in the surrounding material, is scarcely present in the thought of 6:14—7:1.

Sweeping thoughts of new creation and world reconciliation charge the language of 2 Corinthians 5:1—6:13, with Christ as the supreme re-Creator of the world, Paul as God's earthly agent, and the Corinthians as the benefactors. Furnished with these conciliatory ingredients, which show little trace of Jewish covenantal categories (cf. Sanders, 1977:548), Paul opens his heart without covenantal (or other) restriction to the Corinthians in hope of their reciprocation. Hence, Webb is correct in his assessment that the unit itself contains signs of covenant and exodus traditions. But he is less so in citing an element of **new** covenant in 6:14—7:1 after the pattern Paul sets forth in chapter 3, and still less in his appraisal of the thematic coherence of the fragment within the Pauline landscape of chapters 5-7.

J. D. M. Derrett put his finger on a moot point, scarcely touched by most commentators on 2 Corinthians 6. The passage, says Derrett, is "a midrash [commentary] on Deut. 22:10, which forbids the placing of unlike animals, specifically the clean ox and the unclean ass, under the same yoke" (250). With this regulation as a model, the Jewish sage, Ben Sirach, taught that human beings associate with their equals (as in Sirach 13: rich and poor should not associate). The Mosaic Law above all marked the Jewish people off from their Gentile neighbors. For a faithful observer of the law to associate closely with a lawless Gentile was deemed an unequal yoke that should be avoided, in keeping with the typological interpretation of Deuteronomy 22:10. The text of 2 Corinthians 6:14—7:1 reflects this attitude.

The second question is equally difficult: what is the place and purpose of this passage in 2 Corinthians? If it exhibits a pattern of thought that places it outside Paul's horizon, how then did it find its way into the extant 2 Corinthians in the context of chapter 6? This question has the ring of Luther's query concerning the inclusion of James in the same canon alongside Paul's letters. Does the epistle of James really come from the same community that Paul founded? Paul holds "that a person is justified by faith apart from works prescribed by the law" (Rom. 3:28); the epistle of James holds "that a person is justified by works and not by faith alone" (2:24). The epistle of James appears to have come from a Jewish branch of the Christian church that feared the moral implications of Paul's lawfree gospel among the Gentile-Christian communities that continued to flourish after Paul's death. That epistle, like 2 Corinthians 6:14—7:1, teaches "religion that is pure and undefiled" and instructs the members to remain "unstained by the world" (1:27).

Jewish-Christian communities continued to exist after Paul had accomplished his mission to the Gentiles. These communities (probably maintaining some ties to the synagogue) continued to believe as Christians that God's law contained in their Scriptures (OT) was still valid for all practical purposes. Such Jewish communities, even though a minority group by the end of the first century, carried considerable influence and belonged assuredly to the body of Christians throughout the Mediterranean world. The epistle of James reads like a homily coming from one such branch, as does this passage in 2 Corinthians 6:14—7:1.

The passage probably found its way into 2 Corinthians 6 long after Paul had completed his Gentile world mission and departed from this life. Paul's writings were collected many years after they were written. Some of them were fragmentary by the time of collection. In combining parts of letters onto one scroll, the collector-compiler had this fragment from another quarter and thought it wise to incorporate it where it is now, to bring a balance to Paul's overly open attitude.

USE OF SCRIPTURE   Of the many puzzling elements of Paul's letters, few outrank the way he interprets Scripture in his arguments. Perhaps the last phrase is key: he interprets Scripture in his *arguments*. 2 Corinthians 3 is no exception, even though several scholars have pointed to that chapter as a prime example of Pauline exegesis: discovering meaning inherent in a text. Paul's reference to the glow and the veil on Moses' face are said to be in line with the Palestinian-Jewish way of commenting on a text (*midrash pesher*), in which the present significance of a text is found in its details, words, sequence, numbers, etc. In the argument of 2 Corinthians, however, where the text of Exodus 34 is clearly in view, Paul alludes to particular elements to speak a word on target into the particular situation of the moment at Corinth. His method is more that of allusion and echo than it is reflective commentary, much less historical critical exegesis.

The recent work of Richard Hays on Paul's use of Scripture offers valuable clues to solving "the puzzle of Pauline hermeneutics" (1989:1-33). Paul *alludes* to the LXX where he cites a text specifically within an argument (e.g., Rom. 11), and *echoes* texts at other points without direct reference. He brings his Scripture to bear on a situation in a congregation by linking one element from one text with another element from another, making an intertextual chain around which his argument is cemented. The intertextual linkage acts as authoritative reinforcement within the given discourse. As Hays puts it, Paul's scriptural allusions and echoes "generate new meanings by linking the earlier text (Scripture) to the later (Paul's discourse) in such a way as to produce unexpected correspondences, correspondences that suggest more than they assert" (Hays: 24).

What an echoed text of Scripture *meant* originally and what the same text *means* in the echo are not identical but analogous. Even in the more sustained echo of Exodus 34 in 2 Corinthians 3, the meaning for Paul is mediated by his experience of Christ, his call to Gentile mission, and the rival mission of his own Jewish-Christian contemporaries among his converts at Corinth. On the fading glory of Moses' face and the veil that covered the glow, his interpretation merges auspiciously with the thrust of his appeal in the argument: people who turn to the Lord, Jesus Christ, permanently reflect the greater glory to which the law (Moses) points as its end-fulfillment.

Paul's method of interpretation may not find a ready home among modern (or postmodern) readers steeped in the scientific method of Euro-American culture. Yet there is a hermeneutical lesson to be learned from Paul. The word of Scripture should be a word on target, an energizing word that speaks authentically to the issues of the moment. Such useful speech from Scripture will leave some textual elements behind, because they do not merge with the current life setting. The Jewish-Christian Paul set aside circumcision, a traditional sign of the covenant, in keeping with his Gentile mission. In many modern church settings, where women and men are now equally gifted and educated, it should mean lifting the traditional gender restriction for ministry. The role of Scripture is generative, not restrictive, as Paul's reading of Exodus 34 illustrates.

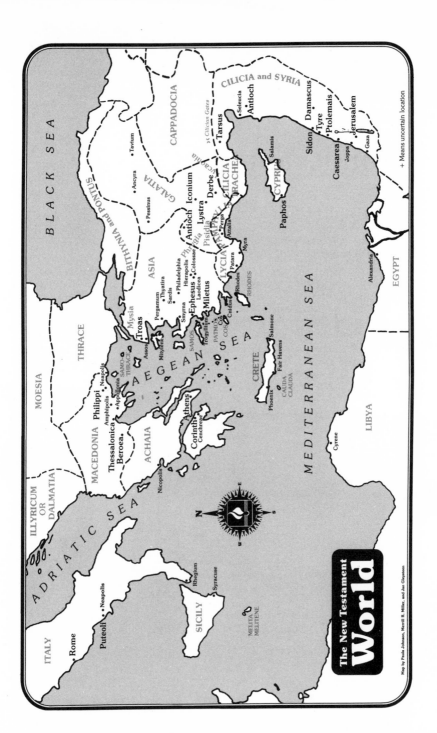

The New Testament **World**

Map by Paula Johnson, Merrill R. Miller, and Jan Gleysteen

Bibliography

Works by Ancient Authors
Aristotle
    1954   *Rhetoric*. Trans. W. R. Roberts. New York: Modern Library.
Augustine of Hippo
    1948   *Basic Writings of St. Augustine*. Ed. Whitney J. Oates. 2 vols.
            New York: Random House.
Charles, R. H., ed.
    1913   *The Apocrypha and Pseudepigrapha of the Old Testament in*
            English. 2 vols. Oxford: Clarenden.
Charlesworth, James H., ed.
    1983-85 *The Old Testament Pseudepigrapha*. 2 vols. Garden City,
            N.Y.:
            Doubleday.
Chrysostom, John
    1848   *The Homilies of St. John Chrysostom: The Second Epistle of St.*
            Paul the Apostle to the Corinthians. Trans. Members of the En-
            glish Church. Oxford: John Henry Parker.
Cicero
    1954   *Rhetorica ad Herennium*. Loeb Classical Library. Trans. Harry
            Caplan. Cambridge: Harvard Univ. Press.
Clement of Rome
    1937   *The First Epistle of Clement to the Corinthians*. Ed. W. K. L.
            Clarke. London: SPCK.
Hermas
    1870   *The Shepherd of Hermas*. Trans. Charles H. Hoole (used with
            slight alterations). London: Rivingtons.
Josephus
    1987   *The Works of Josephus Complete and Unabridged*. Trans. Wil-
            liam Whiston. Peabody: Hendrickson Publishers.
Philo
    1929   *Philo*. Trans. F. H. Colson and G. H. Whitaker. 10 vols. 2 suppl.
            vols. Loeb Classical Library. Cambridge: Harvard Univ. Press.
Quintilian, M. F.
    1920   *The Institutio Oratoria of Quintilian*. Loeb Classical Library.
            Vol. 1. Trans. H. E. Butler. New York: G. P. Putnam's Son.
Vermes, G.
    1987   *The Dead Sea Scrolls in English*. 3d ed. Harmondsworth: Pen-
            guin Books.

Wise, Michael, Abegg Martin Jr., and Edward Cooke
1996   *The Dead Sea Scrolls: A New Translation*. San Francisco: Harper San Francisco.

Other Sources
ABD   Ed. D. N. Freedman et al.
1992   *The Anchor Bible Dictionary*. 6 vols. New York: Doubleday.
Baird, William
1980   *Knox Preaching Guides: 1 Corinthians, 2 Corinthians*. Atlanta: John Knox.
Barrett, C. K.
1970   "Ho adikēsas (2. Cor 7, 12)." In *Verbortum Veritas*, 149-157. Wuppertal: Theologischer Verlag Rolf Brockhaus.
1973   *The Second Epistle to the Corinthians*. Black's New Testament Commentary. Reprint. Peabody, Mass. Hendrickson Publishers.
1982a   "Titus." In *Essays on Paul*, 118-131. London: SPCK.
1982b   "Paul's Opponents in II Corinthians." In *Essays on Paul*, 60-86. London: SPCK.
Bassler, Jouette M.
1991   *God and Mammon: Asking for Money in the New Testament*. Nashville: Abingdon.
Bates, W. H. "The Integrity of 2 Corinthians." *New Testament Studies* 12 (1965): 56-69.
Batey, Richard
1965   "Paul's Interaction with the Corinthians." *Journal of Biblical Literature* 84:139-146.
Beale, G. K.
1989   "The OT Background of Reconciliation in 2 Cor. 5-7 and Its Bearing on the Literary Problem of 2 Cor. 6:14—7:1." *New Testament Studies* 35:550-581.
Becker, Jürgen
1993   *Paul, Apostle to the Gentiles*. Trans. O. C. Dean Jr. Louisville: Westminster John Knox.
Beker, J. C.
1980   *Paul the Apostle: The Triumph of God in Life and Thought*. Philadelphia: Fortress.
Belleville, L. L.
1989   "A Letter of Apologetic Self-Condemnation: 2 Corinthians 1:8—7:16." *Novum Testamentum* 31:142-163.
Best, Ernest
1987   *2 Corinthians*. Interpretation. Louisville: John Knox.
Betz, Hans Dieter
1972   *Der Apostel Paulus und die sokratische Tradition: Eine exegetische Untersuchung zu seiner "Apologie" 2 Korinther 10-13*. Tübingen: J. C. B. Mohr (Paul Siebeck).
1973   "2 Corinthians 6:14—7:1: An Anti-Pauline Fragment?" *Journal of Biblical Literature* 92:88-108.
1985   *2 Corinthians 8 and 9*. Hermeneia. Philadelphia: Fortress.

Beyer, H. W.
    1980   "*Kanōn*." In *TDNT*, 3:596-602. See *TDNT*
Billerbeck, Paul
    1926   *Kommentar zum Neuen Testament*. Bd. 3. München: C. H.
            Beck.
Black, David Alan
    1984   *Paul, Apostle of Weakness: Astheneia and Its Cognates in the
            Pauline Literature*. New York: Peter Lang.
Bornkamm, Günther
    1971   *Paul*. Trans. D. M. G. Stalker, New York. Harper & Row.
Bosch, David
    1979   *A Spirituality of the Road*. Scottdale: Herald Press.
Braght   See *MM*
Bruce, F. F.
    1971   *1 and 2 Corinthians*. New Century Bible. Greenwood, S. C.: At-
            tic Press.
Buck, Charles R. Jr.
    1950   "The Collection for the Saints." *Harvard Theological Review*
            45:1-29.
Bultmann, Rudolf
    1964   "*Alētheia*." In *TDNT*, 1:238-247. See *TDNT*
    1969   "The Significance of the Historical Jesus for the Theology of
            Paul." In *Faith and Understanding*, 220-246. Trans. L. P. Smith.
            London: SCM.
    1985   *The Second Letter to the Corinthians*. Trans. Roy A. Harrisville.
            Minneapolis: Augsburg.
Caird, C. B., with L. D. Hurst
    1994   *New Testament Theology*. Oxford: Clarendon.
Calvin, John
    1948   *The Epistles of Paul the Apostle to the Corinthians*. *Calvin's
            Commentaries*, vols. 1-2. Trans. John Pringle. Grand Rapids:
            Eerdmans.
Chamblin, J. Knox
    1957   *Paul: A Study in Social and Religious History*. Trans. William E.
            Wilson. New York: Harper & Row. First published 1912.
    1993   *Paul and the Self: Apostolic Teaching for Personal Wholeness*.
            Grand Rapids: Baker Books.
Childs, Brevard S.
    1977   "A Fragment in Its Context: 2 Corinthians 6:14—7:1." In
            Studies in Paul, 40-69. Minneapolis: Augsburg.
    1984   *The New Testament as Canon: An Introduction*. Philadelphia:
            Fortress.
Chow, John K.
    1992   *Patronage and Power: A Study of Social Networks in Corinth*.
            Sheffield: JSOT.
Collange, J. F.
    1972   *Énigmes de la deuxième épître de Paul aux Corinthiens: Étude
            exégétique de 2 Corinthiens 2:14—7:4*. Cambridge: Univ.
            Press.

Cousar, Charles B.
1981   "II Corinthians 5:17-21." *Interpretation* 35:180-183.
Crafton, Jeffrey A.
1991   *The Agency of the Apostle: A Dramatistic Analysis of Paul's Responses to Conflict in 2 Corinthians.* JSNT Supplement Series, 51. Sheffield, U.K.: Sheffield Academic Press.
Dahl, Nils A.
1967   "Paul and the Church at Corinth According to 1 Corinthians 1-4." In *Christian History and Interpretation: Studies Presented to John Knox.* Ed. W. R. Farmer et al. Cambridge: Univ. Press.
Dana, H. E., and Julius R. Mantey
1927   *A Manual Grammar of the Greek New Testament.* New York: Macmillan.
Deissmann, Adolf
1927   *Light from the Ancient East.* Trans. L. R. M. Strachan. London: Hodder & Stoughton; Grand Rapids: Baker Book House. 1965 reprint. 4th German ed., 1922.
Delcor, M.
1968   "The Courts of the Church of Corinth and the Courts of Qumran." In *Paul and Qumran.* Ed. J. Murphy-O'Connor. London: Chapman Publishers.
Denniston, J. D.
1950   *The Greek Particles.* 2d ed. Oxford: Clarendon.
Denny, James
1894   *The Second Epistle to the Corinthians.* The Expositor's Bible. London: Hodder & Stoughton.
Derrett, J. D. M.
1978   "2 Cor. 6, 14ff. a Midrash on Deut. 22, 10." *Biblica* 59:231-250.
Dirk Philips
1992   *The Writings of Dirk Philips, 1504-1568.* Classics of the Radical Reformation, 6. Trans., ed. C. J. Dyck et al. Scottdale, Pa.: Herald Press.
Doty, W. G.
1969   "The Classification of Epistolary Literature." *Catholic Biblical Quarterly* 31:183-199.
Duling, Dennis C., and Norman Perrin
1982   *The New Testament: An Introduction.* 2d ed. San Diego: Harcourt Brace Jovanovich.
Dunn, James G. D.
1970   "2 Corinthians III 17: The Lord Is the Spirit." *Journal of Theological Studies* 21:309-320.
1974   "Paul's Understanding of the Death of Jesus." In *Reconciliation and Hope.* Exeter: Pater Noster.
Elias, Jacob
1995   *1 and 2 Thessalonians.* Believers Church Bible Commentary. Scottdale, Pa.: Herald Press.
Ellis, E. Earle
1975   "Paul and His Opponents: Trends in Research." In *Christianity,*

> *Judaism and Other Greco-Roman Cults: Studies for Morton Smith at Sixty.* Ed. Jacob Neusner. Leiden: E. J. Brill.

Fahy, T.
1964   "St. Paul's Boasting in 'Weakness.' " *Irish Theological Quarterly* 31:214-227.

Fallon, Francis T.
1980   *2 Corinthians.* New Testament Message, 11. Wilmington: Michael Glazier.

Farrar, F. W.
1885   *II Corinthians.* The Pulpit Commentary. London: Kegan Paul, Trench.

Faw, Chalmer E.
1993   *Acts.* Believers Church Bible Commentary. Scottdale, Pa.: Herald Press.

Fee, Gordon
1977   "2 Corinthians VI.14—VII.1 and Food Offered to Idols." *New Testament Studies* 23:140-161.

Finkelstein, Louis
1971   "The Jewish Religion: Beliefs and Practice." In *The Jews: Their Religion and Culture,* 469-531. 4th ed. New York: Schocken Books.

Fitzgerald, John T.
1988   *Cracks in an Earthen Vessel: An Examination of the Catalogues of Hardships in the Corinthian Correspondence.* Atlanta: Scholars Press.
1990   "Paul, the Ancient Epistolary Theorists, and 2 Corinthians 10-13." In *Greeks, Romans, and Christians,* 190-200. Ed. David L. Balch et al. Minneapolis: Fortress.

Fitzmyer, Joseph A.
1961   "Qumran and the Interpolated Paragraph in 2 Corinthians 6:14—7:1." *Catholic Biblical Quarterly* 23: 271-280.
1971   "Qumran and the Interpolated Paragraph in 2 Cor 6:14—7:1." In *Essays on the Semitic Background of the New Testament,* 205-217. London: Geoffrey Chapman.
1981   "Reconciliation in Pauline Theology." In *To Advance the Gospel,* 162-185. New York: Crossroad.

Foerster, Werner
1971   *"Satanas."* In *TDNT,* 7:151-163. *See TDNT.*

Forbes, Christopher
1986   "Comparison, Self-praise and Irony: Paul's Boasting and the Conventions of Hellenistic Rhetoric." *New Testament Studies* 32:1-30.

Frost, Robert
1969   "The Tuft of Flowers" and "Mending Wall." In *The Poetry of Robert Frost.* Ed. Edward Connery Lathem. New York: Holt, Rinehart and Winston.

Funk, Robert W.
1967   "The Apostolic *Parousia:* Form and Significance." In *Christian History and Interpretation: Studies Presented to John Knox,* 249-268. Ed. W. R. Farmer et al. Cambridge: Univ. Press.

1982   "The Apostolic Presence: Paul." In *Parables and Presence: Forms of the New Testament Tradition,* 81-102. Philadelphia: Fortress.

Furnish, Victor Paul
1984   *II Corinthians.* The Anchor Bible. Garden City: Doubleday.
1993   *Jesus According to Paul.* Cambridge: Univ. Press.

Garrett, Susan R.
1990   "The God of This World and the Affliction of Paul: 2 Corinthians 4:1-12." In *Greeks, Romans, and Christians,* 99-117. Ed. David L. Balch et al. Minneapolis: Fortress.

Gaventa, Beverly Roberts
1993   "Apostle and Church in 2 Corinthians: A Response to David M. Hay and Steven J. Kraftchick." In *Pauline Theology,* vol. 2: *1 and 2 Corinthians,* 182-199. Ed. David M. Hay. Minneapolis: Fortress.

Georgi, Dieter
1965   *Die Geschichte der Kollekte des Paulus für Jerusalem.* Hamburg: Herbert Reich. Trans.: *Remembering the Poor: The History of Paul's Collection for Jerusalem.* Nashville: Abingdon, 1992.
1985   *The Opponents of Paul in Second Corinthians.* Philadelphia: Fortress. German, 1964.

Getty, Mary Ann
1983   *First Corinthians and Second Corinthians.* Collegeville Bible Commentary, 7. Collegeville: Liturgical Press.

Gnilka, J.
1968   "2 Corinthians vi. 14—vii. 1 in the Light of the Qumran Texts and the Testaments of the Twelve Patriarchs." In *Paul and Qumran: Studies in New Testament Exegesis,* 48-68. Ed. by J. Murphy-O'Connor. London: G. Chapman.

Goppelt, Leonhard
1982   *Typos: The Typological Interpretation of the Old Testament in The New.* Trans. Donald H. Madvig. Grand Rapids: Eerdmans.

Grabbe, Lester L.
1987   "The Scapegoat Tradition: A Study in Early Jewish Interpretation." *Journal for the Study of Judaism* 18:152-167.

Griffiths, Michael
1985   *The Example of Jesus.* London: Hodder & Stoughton.

Grundmann, Walter
1964   *"Dektos."* In *TDNT,* 2:58-59. See *TDNT*

Gundry, Robert
1976   *Sōma in Biblical Theology with Emphasis on Pauline Anthropology.* Cambridge: Univ. Press.
1993   "Corinthians, Letters to the." In *Dictionary of Paul and His Letters.* Eds. Gerald F. Hawthorne and Ralph P. Martin. Downers Grove: InterVarsity Press.

Hafemann, Scott
1990   *Suffering and Ministry in the Spirit: Paul's Defense of His Ministry in II Corinthians 2:14—3:3.* Grand Rapids: Eerdmans.

Hanson, A. T.
  1968   "Eve's Transgression." In *Studies in the Pastoral Epistles,* 64-77. London: SPCK.
  1982   *The Image of the Invisible God.* London: SCM.
  1987   *The Paradox of the Cross in the Thought of St. Paul.* Gospel Perspectives, 3. Sheffield, U.K.: Sheffield Academic Press.
Hanson, R. P. C.
  1967   *The Second Epistle to the Corinthians: Christ and Controversy.* London: SCM.
Harder, Günther
  1971   "*Spoudazō.* . . ." In *TDNT,* 7:559-568. See *TDNT*
Harder, Leland, ed.
  1985   *The Sources of Swiss Anabaptism: The Grebel Letters and Related Documents.* Scottdale: Herald Press.
Harvey, A. E.
  1996   *Renewal Through Suffering: A Study of 2 Corinthians.* Edinburgh: T & T Clark.
Hay, David M.
  1993   *Pauline Theology.* Vol. 2: *1 and 2 Corinthians.* Minneapolis: Fortress.
Hays, Richard B.
  1989   *Echoes of Scripture in the Letters of Paul.* New Haven: Yale Univ. Press.
Hendry, George S.
  1947   "*Hē gar agapē tou christou sunechei ēmas*—2 Corinthians v. 14." *Expository Times* 59:82.
Hengel, Martin
  1976   *The Son of God: The Origin of Christology and the History of Jewish Religion.* Philadelphia: Fortress.
  1977   *Crucifixion in the Ancient World and the Folly of the Message of the Cross.* Philadelphia: Fortress.
Hering, Jean
  1967   *The Second Epistle of Paul to the Corinthians.* Trans. A. W. Heathcote and P. J. Alcock, London: Epworth. French, 1958.
Hickling, C. J. A.
  1975a   "The Sequence of Thought in II Corinthians, Chapter Three." *New Testament Studies* 2:380-395.
  1975   "On Putting Paul in His Place." In *What About the New Testament?* 76-88. London: SCM.
  1980   "Center and Periphery in the Thought of Paul." In *Studia Biblica,* vol. 3: *Papers on Paul and Other New Testament Authors,* 199-214. Ed. E. A. Livingstone. Sheffield: JSOT.
Hooker, Morna D.
  1971   "Interchange in Christ." *Journal of Theological Studies* 22:349-361.
Hubmaier, Balthasar
  1989   *Balthasar Hubmaier: Theologian of Anabaptism.* Classics of the Radical Reformation, 5. Ed. H. Wayne Pipkin and John H. Yoder. Scottdale, Pa.: Herald Press.

Hughes, Philip E.
    1962   *Paul's Second Epistle to the Corinthians.* New International Commentary on the New Testament. Grand Rapids: Eerdmans.

Hyldahl, Niels
    1973   "Die Frage nach der literarischen Einheit des Zweiten Korintherbriefes." *Zeitschrift für die neutestamentliche Wissenschaft* 64:289-306.

Jervell, Jacob
    1960   *Imago Dei: Gen 1, 26f. im Spätjudentum, in der Gnosis und in den paulinischen Briefen.* Göttingen: Vandenhoeck & Ruprecht.

Jewett, Robert
    1993   "Earthen Vessels and *Ordinary People.*" In *Saint Paul at the Movies: The Apostle's Dialogue with American Culture.* Louisville: John Knox.

Judge, E. A.
    1982   *Rank and Status in the World of the Caesars and St. Paul.* Univ. of Canterbury.

Käsemann, Ernst
    1956   *Die Legitimität des Apostels: Eine Untersuchung zu II Korinther 10-13.* Darmstadt: Wissenschaftliche Buchgesellschaft.
    1964   "Ministry and Community in the New Testament." In *Essays on New Testament Themes,* 63-134. London: SCM.
    1969   "Sentences of Holy Law in the New Testament." In *New Testament Questions of Today,* 66-81. Trans. W. J. Montague. Philadelphia: Fortress.
    1971a   "The Spirit and the Letter." In *Perspectives on Paul,* 138-166. Philadelphia: Fortress.
    1971b   "Some Thoughts on the Theme 'The Doctrine of Reconciliation in the New Testament.' " In *The Future of Our Religious Past,* 49-64. Ed. James M. Robinson. London: SCM.
    1971c   "The Saving Significance of the Death of Jesus in Paul." In *Perspectives on Paul,* 32-59. London: SCM.
    1984   "Cultural Conformity and Innovation in Paul: Some Clues from Contemporary Documents." *Tyndale Bulletin* 35:3-24.

Kennedy, George A.
    1963   *The Art of Persuasion in Greece.* Princeton: Univ. Press.
    1972   *The Art of Rhetoric in the Roman World, 300 B.C.-A.D. 300.* Princeton: Univ. Press.
    1984   *New Testament Interpretation Through Rhetorical Criticism.* Chapel Hill: Univ. of North Carolina Press.

Klaassen, Walter
    1981   *Anabaptism in Outline.* Scottdale: Herald Press.

Koester, Helmut
    1982   *History and Literature of Early Christianity.* Philadelphia: Fortress. German, 1980.

Köster, Helmut
    1972   "Hupostasis." In *TDNT,* 8:572-589. See *TDNT*

Kraftchick, Steven J.
   1993   "Death in Us, Life in You." In *Pauline Theology*, vol. 2: *1 and 2 Corinthians*, 156-181. Ed. David M. Hay. Minneapolis: Fortress.
Kruse, Colin G.
   1987   *The Second Epistle of Paul to the Corinthians: An Introduction and Commentary*. Leicester: Inter-Varsity Press.
Kümmel, Werner Georg
   1975   *Introduction to the New Testament*. Trans. Howard Clark Kee. Nashville: Abingdon.
Lampe, G. W. H.
   1961   *A Patristic Greek Lexicon*. Oxford: Clarendon.
Leivestad, R.
   1966   " 'The Meekness and Gentleness of Christ': II Cor X. 1." *New Testament Studies* 13:156-164.
Liddell, H. G., and R. A. Scott
   1940   *Greek-English Lexicon*. 2 vols. Ed. Henry Stuart Jones. Oxford: Clarendon.
Lietzmann, D. Hans
   1949   *An Die Korinther I-II*. Tübingen: J. C. B. Mohr.
Lincoln, Andrew T.
   1979   "Paul the Visionary: The Setting and Significance of the Rapture to Paradise in II Corinthians XII. 1-10." *New Testament Studies* 25:204-220.
   1981   *Paradise Now and Not Yet: Studies in the Role of the Heavenly Dimension in Paul's Thought with Special Reference to His Eschatology*. Cambridge: Univ. Press.
Lochman, Jan Milic
   1980   *Reconciliation and Liberation: Challenging a One-Dimensional View of Salvation*. Trans. David Lewis. Philadelphia: Fortress.
Loewen, Howard John, ed.
   1985   *One Lord, One Church, One Hope, and One God: Mennonite Confessions of Faith in North America*. Text-Reader Series, 2. Ed. W. M. Swartley. Elkhart, Ind.: Institute of Mennonite Studies.
Louw, J. P., E. A. Nida, et al.
   1989   *Greek-English Lexicon of the New Testament Based on Semantic Domains*. 2d ed. 2 vols. New York: United Bible Societies.
Luedemann, Gerd
   1989   "Anti-Paulinism in the Pauline Churches." In *Opposition to Paul in Jewish Christianity*, 64-111. Trans. M. Eugene Boring. Minneapolis: Fortress.
Luther, Martin
   1959   *Luther's Works: Sermons*. Vol. 51, ed., trans. John W. Doberstein. Philadelphia: Muhlenberg.
   1973   *Luther's Works: Commentaries on 1 Corinthians 7; 1 Corinthians 15; Lectures on 1 Timothy*. Vol. 28, ed. Hilton Oswald. St. Louis: Concordia Publishing House.
   1974   *Luther's Works: Sermons*. Vol. 52, ed. Hans J. Hillerbrand. Philadelphia: Fortress.

1976   *Luther's Works: First Lectures on the Psalms.* Vol. 11. St. Louis: Concordia Publishing House.

Luz, Ulrich
1992   "The Significance of the Biblical Witness for Church Peace Action." Trans. Walter Sawatsky. In *The Meaning of Peace: Biblical Studies,* 234-252. Ed. Perry B. Yoder and Willard M. Swartley. Louisville: Westminster John Knox Press.

Malina, Bruce J., and Jerome H. Neyrey
1996   *Portraits of Paul: An Archaeology of Ancient Personality.* Louisville: Westminster John Knox.

Marpeck, Pilgram
1978   *The Writings of Pilgram Marpeck.* Classics of the Radical Reformation, 2. Ed. William Klassen and Walter Klaassen. Scottdale: Herald Press.

Marshall, Peter
1987   *Enmity in Corinth: Social Conventions in Paul's Relations with the Corinthians.* Tübingen: J. C. B. Mohr.

Martin, Ernest D.
1993   *Colossians, Philemon.* Believers Church Bible Commentary. Scottdale, Pa.: Herald Press.

Martin, Ralph P.
1981   *Reconciliation: A Study of Paul's Theology.* London: Marshall Morgan and Scott.
1986   *2 Corinthians.* Word Biblical Commentary, 40. Waco: Word Books.

Martyn, J. Louis
1967   "Epistemology at the Turn of the Ages: 2 Corinthians 5:16." In *Christian History and Interpretation: Studies Presented to John Knox.* Ed. W. R. Farmer et al. Cambridge: Univ. Press.

Marxsen, Willi
1968   *Introduction to the New Testament: An Approach to Its Problems.* Philadelphia: Fortress. German, 1964.

ME   *The Mennonite Encyclopedia.* Scottdale, Pa.: Herald Press.
1955-59 Vols. 1-4, ed. H. S. Bender et al.
1990   Vol. 5, ed. C. J. Dyck et al.

Meeks, Wayne A.
1983   "Governance." In *The First Urban Christians: The Social World of the Apostle Paul,* 111-139. New Haven: Yale Univ. Press.

Mell, Ulrich
1989   *Neue Schöpfung: Eine traditionsgeschichtliche und exegetische Studie zu einem soteriologischen Grundsatz paulinischer Theologie.* Berlin: Walter de Gruyter.

Menno Simons
1956   *The Complete Writings of Menno Simons.* Ed. J. C. Wenger. Scottdale: Herald Press.

Menzies, Allen
1912   *The Second Epistle of the Apostle Paul to the Corinthians.* London: Macmillan.

Meyer, Ben F.
   1989   *Critical Realism and the New Testament.* Allison Park, Pa.: Pick-wick.
Milton, John
   1962   *Paradise Lost.* In *Representative Poetry.* Vol. 1. 3rd ed. Toron-to: Univ. Press.
Minear, Paul S.
   1979   "Some Pauline Thoughts on Dying: A Study of 2 Corinthians." In *From Faith to Faith: Essays in Honor of Donald G. Miller,* 91-106. Pittsburgh Theological Monographs, 31. Ed. D. Y. Hadi-dian. Allison Park, Pa.: Pickwick.
Mitchell, Margaret M.
   1991   *Paul and the Rhetoric of Reconciliation: An Exegetical Investi-gation of the Language and Composition of 1 Corinthians.* Louisville: Westminster John Knox.
MM   Thieleman J. van Braght.
   1938   *Martyrs Mirror.* Trans. Joseph F. Sohm. Scottdale, Pa.: Herald Press. Dutch, 1660.
Moule, C. F. D.
   1953   *An Idiom Book of New Testament Greek.* Cambridge: Univ. Press.
   1961   *Worship in the New Testament.* London: Lutterworth.
   1965   "St. Paul and Dualism: The Pauline Concept of Resurrection." *New Testament Studies* 12:106-123.
   1982   "Peculiarities in the Language of II Corinthians." In *Essays in New Testament Interpretation,* 158-161. Cambridge: Univ. Press.
Munck, Johannes
   1959   *Paul and the Salvation of Mankind.* Atlanta: John Knox.
Murphy-O'Connor, Jerome
   1983   *St. Paul's Corinth: Texts and Archaeology.* Wilmington: Michael Glazier.
   1985   "Paul and Macedonia: The Connection Between 2 Corinthians 2:13 and 2:14." *Journal for the Study of the New Testament* 25:99-103.
   1987   "Relating 2 Corinthians 6:14—7:1 to Its Context." *New Testa-ment Studies* 33:272-275.
   1991   *The Theology of the Second Letter to the Corinthians.* Cam-bridge: Univ. Press.
Murphy-O'Connor, Jerome, and James H. Charlesworth, eds.
   1990   *Paul and the Dead Sea Scrolls.* New York: Crossroad.
Nickle, Keith F.
   1966   *The Collection.* Naperville: Allenson.
Olson, Stanley N.
   1985   "Pauline Expressions of Confidence in His Addressees." *Catholic Biblical Quarterly* 47:282-295.
Osiek, Carolyn
   1983   *Rich and Poor in The Shepherd of Hermas: An Exegetical-Social Investigation.* Catholic Biblical Quarterly Monographs, 15. Washington, D.C.: Catholic Biblical.

Otis, W. S. C.
 1870 "Exposition of 2 Cor. V. 14." *Bibliotheca Sacra* 27:545-564.
Pagels, Elaine
 1975 *The Gnostic Paul: Gnostic Exegesis of the Pauline Letters.* Philadelphia: Trinity Press.
Pate, C. Marvin
 1991 *Adam Christology as the Exegetical and Theological Substructure of 2 Corinthians 4:7—5:21.* Lanham, M.D.: Univ. Press of America.
Pherigo, Lindsey P.
 1949 "Paul and the Corinthian Church." *Journal of Biblical Literature* 68:341-350.
Philips *See* Dirk Philips
Plank, Karl A.
 1987 *Paul and the Irony of Affliction.* Atlanta: Scholars Press.
Plummer, Alfred
 1915 *A Critical and Exegetical Commentary on the Second Epistle of St. Paul to the Corinthians.* International Critical Commentary. Edinburgh: T. & T. Clark.
Poetker, Katrina
 1995 "Domestic Domains in the Gospel of Mark." *Direction* 24/1:14-23.
Price, Robert M.
 1980 "Punished in Paradise (An Exegetical Theory on II Corinthians 12:1-10)." *Journal for the Study of the New Testament* 7:33-40.
Procksch, Otto
 1964 "*Hagios.*" In *TDNT*, 1:100-115. See *TDNT*
Rebell, Walter
 1992 *Christologie und Existenz bei Paulus: Eine Auslegung von 2. Kor 5, 14-21.* Stuttgart: Calwer Verlag.
Rengstorf, Karl Heinrich
 1964 "*Apostolos.*" In *TDNT*, 1:407-445. See *TDNT*
Renwick, David A.
 1991 *Paul, the Temple, and the Presence of God.* Atlanta: Scholars Press.
Reumann, John
 1992 *Stewardship and the Economy of God.* Grand Rapids: Eerdmans.
Richardson, Peter
 1984 "The Thunderbolt in Q and the Wise Man in Corinth." In *From Jesus to Paul: Studies in Honour of Francis Wright Beare*, 91-111. Ed. Peter Richardson and John Hurd. Waterloo: Wilfrid Laurier Univ. Press.
Roetzel, Calvin
 1991 *The Letters of Paul: Conversations in Context.* 3d. ed. Louisville: John Knox.
Rostovtzeff, M.
 1926 *The Social and Economic History of the Roman Empire.* Oxford: Clarendon.

Sanders, E. P.
    1977   *Paul and Palestinian Judaism.* Philadelphia: Fortress.
    1978   "Paul's Attitude Toward the Jewish People." *Union Seminary Quarterly Review* 33:175-187.
    1983   *Paul, the Law and the Jewish People.* Philadelphia: Fortress.
    1986   "Paul on the Law, His Opponents, and the Jewish People in Philippians 3 and 2 Corinthians 11." In *Anti-Judaism in Early Christianity*, vol. 1: *Paul and the Gospels*, 75-90. Waterloo: Wilfrid Laurier Univ. Press.
Sattler, Michael
    1973   *The Legacy of Michael Sattler.* Trans. John H. Yoder. Scottdale, Pa.: Herald Press.
Schelkle, Karl
    1969   *The Second Epistle to the Corinthians.* Trans. Kevin Smyth. London: Burns and Oates.
Schmithals, Walter
    1971   *Gnosticism in Corinth: An Investigation of the Letters to the Corinthians.* Trans. John E. Steely. Nashville: Abingdon.
Schweizer, Eduard
    1991   *A Theological Introduction to the New Testament.* Trans. O. C. Dean Jr. Nashville: Abingdon.
Seifrid, Mark A.
    1992   *Justification by Faith: The Origin and Development of a Central Pauline Theme.* Leiden: E. J. Brill.
Shillington, V. George
    1991   "Paul's Success in the Conversion of Gentiles." *Direction* 20/2:125-134.
    1985   "The Figure of Jesus in the Typological Thought of Paul." Dissertation. Hamilton: McMaster Univ.
    1986   "People of God in the Courts of the World: A Study of 1 Cor. 6:1-11." *Direction* 2:40-50.
Simons. *See* Menno
Spicq, C.
    1954   "L'étreinte de la charité (II Cor. V, 14)." *Studia Theologica* 8:123-132.
Stählin, Gustav
    1965   "*Isos, isotēs, isotimos.*" In *TDNT*, 3:343-355. See *TDNT*
Stendahl, Krister
    1976   *Paul Among Jews and Gentiles and Other Essays.* Philadelphia: Fortress.
Stephenson, A. M. G.
    1965   "The Defense of the Integrity of 2 Corinthians." In *The Authorship and Integrity of the New Testament*, 82-97. SPCK Theological Collections, 4. London: SPCK.
Strachan, R. H.
    1935   *The Second Epistle of Paul to the Corinthians.* London: Hodder & Stoughton.
Stuhlmacher, Peter
    1967   "Erwägungen zum ontologischen Charakter der *kainē ktisis* bei Paul." *Evangelische Theologie* 27:1-35.

1985   *Gerechtigkeit Gottes bei Paulus.* Göttingen: Vandenhoeck & Ruprecht.
1986   *Reconciliation, Law and Righteousness: Essays in Biblical Theology.* Trans. Everett R. Kalin. Philadelphia: Fortress.
Sumney, Jerry L.
1990   *Identifying Paul's Opponents: The Question of Method in 2 Corinthians.* Sheffield, U.K.: Sheffield Academic Press.
Talbert, Charles H.
1989   *Reading Corinthians: A Literary and Theological Commentary on 1 and 2 Corinthians.* New York: Crossroad.
Taylor, Louis H.
1958   *The New Creation.* New York: Pageant.
Taylor, N. H.
1991   "The Composition and Chronology of 2 Corinthians." *Journal for the Study of the New Testament* 44:67-87.
TDNT   Ed. G. Kittel et al.
1964-76   *Theological Dictionary of the New Testament.* 9 vols. Trans. and ed. G. W. Bromiley. Grand Rapids: Eerdmans.
Theissen, Gerd
1982   "Legitimation and Subsistence: An Essay on the Sociology of Early Christian Missionaries." In *The Social Setting of Pauline Christianity: Essays on Corinth*, 27-67. Ed. and trans. John H. Scheutz. Philadelphia: Fortress.
1987   *Psychological Aspects of Pauline Theology.* Trans. John P. Galvin. Philadelphia: Fortress.
Thrall, Margaret E.
1967   "The Pauline Use of *suneidēsis*." *New Testament Studies* 14:118-125.
1980   "Super-Apostles, Servants of Christ, and Servants of Satan." *Journal for the Study of the New Testament* 6:42-57.
1982a   "A Second Thanksgiving Period in 2 Corinthians." *Journal for the Study of the New Testament* 16:101-124.
1982b   "Salvation Proclaimed, V. 2 Corinthians 5:18-21: Reconciliation with God." *Expository Times* 93/8:227-232.
1994   *A Critical and Exegetical Commentary on The Second Epistle to the Corinthians.* Vol. 1. Edinburgh: T. & T. Clark.
Van Braght   *See MM*
Van Straten, F. T.
1981   "Gifts for the Gods." In *Faith, Hope and Worship: Aspects of Religious Mentality in the Ancient World.* Ed. H. S. Versnel. Leiden: E. J. Brill.
Van Unnik, W. C.
1973   "Reisepläne und Amen-Sagen: Zusammenhang und Gedankenfolge in 2 Korinther 1:15-24." In *Sparsa Collecta: The Collected Essays of W. C. Van Unnik*, 144-159. Novum Testamentum Supplement, 29/1. Leiden: E. J. Brill.
1963   "With Unveiled face." *Novum Testamentum* 6:153ff.
Versnel, H. S.
1970   *Triumphus: An Inquiry into the Origin, Development and Meaning of the Roman Triumph.* Leiden: E. J. Brill.

Von Rad, Gerhard
   1964   "The O. T. View of Satan." In *TDNT*, 2:73-75. *See TDNT*
Watson, Nigel
   1993   *The Second Epistle to the Corinthians*. Epworth Commentaries.
             London: Epworth.
Webb, William J.
   1993   *Returning Home: New Covenant and Second Exodus as the
             Context for 2 Corinthians 6.14—7.1*. Sheffield, UK.: Sheffield
             Academic Press.
Wedderburn, A. J. M.
   1985   "Some Observations on Paul's Use of the Phrases 'In Christ' and
             'With Christ.' " *Journal for the Study of the New Testament*
             25:83-97.
Weiss, Johannes
   1909   *Paul and Jesus*. Trans. H. J. Chaytor. London: Harper & Broth-
             ers.
Williamson, Larmar Jr.
   1968   "Led in Triumph: Paul's use of *Thriambeuō*." *Interpretation*
             22:317-332.
Wills, Lawrence
   1984   "The Form of the Sermon in Hellenistic Judaism and Early
             Christianity [2 Corinthians 6:14-7:1]." *Harvard Theological
             Review* 77:277-299.
Wilson, R. M.
   1972   "How Gnostic Were the Corinthians?" *New Testament Studies*
             19:65-74.
Wink, Walter
   1989   *Engaging the Powers: Discernment and Resistance in a World
             of Domination*. Minneapolis: Fortress.
Windisch, Hans
   1924   *Der zweite Korintherbrief*. Göttingen: Vandenhoeck &
             Ruprecht.
Wire, Antoinette Clark
   1990   *The Corinthian Women Prophets: A Reconstruction Through
             Paul's Rhetoric*. Minneapolis: Fortress.
Young, Frances Margaret, and D. F. Ford
   1987   *Meaning and Truth in 2 Corinthians*. Grand Rapids: Eerdmans.
Zahn, Theodor
   1909   *Introduction to the New Testament*. Edinburgh: T. & T. Clark.
Zerbe, Gordon
   1992   "Paul's Ethic of Non-retaliation." In *The Love of Enemy and
             Nonretaliation in the New Testament*, 177-222. Ed. by W. M.
             Swartley. Louisville: Westminster John Knox.
Ziesler, John
   1972   *The Meaning of Righteousness in Paul*. Cambridge: Univ. Press.

Selected Resources

Best, Ernest. *Second Corinthians.* Interpretation. Louisville: Westminster John Knox, 1987. Intended to help church leaders in their preaching ministry. Illustrative and contemporary in style.

Fallon, Francis, T. *2 Corinthians.* NT Message Series, 11. Wilmington: Michael Glazier, 1980. Concise commentary on large sections of text. A usable tool for preachers.

Fitzgerald, John T. *Cracks in an Earthen Vessel: An Examination of the Catalogues of Hardships in the Corinthian Correspondence.* Atlanta: Scholars Press, 1988. Clearly written. Probes the rhetorical significance of listing hardships as Paul does in 1 and 2 Corinthians. Discusses the place of suffering in the theology of Paul's Christian mission.

Furnish, Victor Paul. *Jesus According to Paul.* Cambridge: Cambridge University Press, 1993. Assesses the place of Jesus as the Messiah of God in Paul's understanding of his faith, life, and mission.

Harvey, A. E. *Renewal Through Suffering: A Study of 2 Corinthians.* Edinburgh: T & T Clark, 1996. Focuses on two themes in 2 Corinthians, renewal and suffering, and treats the relationship between them.

Hay, David M., Editor. *Pauline Theology, vol. 2: 1 and 2 Corinthians.* Minneapolis: Augsburg Fortress, 1993. NT scholars write on various points of theology arising out of 2 Corinthians: "The Shaping of Theology," "Death in Us, Life in You," and "On Becoming the Righteousness of God."

Hengel, Martin. *The Pre-Christian Paul.* Philadelphia: Trinity Press International, 1991. Traces the origin, education, and career of Paul through his persecution of the church to his conversion. Assists in understanding the context of Paul's thought.

Malina, Bruce J., and Jerome H. Neyrey. *Portraits of Paul: An Archaeology of Ancient Personality.* Louisville: Westminster John Knox Press, 1996. Up-to-date analysis of the makeup of Paul's personality as a Jewish-Christian missionary to the Gentile world. Throws light on some of the puzzling statements in 2 Corinthians.

Murphy-O'Connor, Jerome. *St. Paul's Corinth: Texts and Archaeology.* Collegeville: The Liturgical Press, 1983. Provides evidence from inscriptions and contemporary literature about the character of the city of Corinth and its people. The incisive comment for each item illuminates many of Paul's arguments in the Corinthian correspondence.

Murphy-O'Connor, Jerome. *The Theology of the Second Letter to the Corinthians.* Cambridge: Cambridge University Press, 1991. Highlights Paul's Christian thought behind ministry, the collection, and the Fool's Speech. Explores significance for today.

Talbert, Charles H. *Reading Corinthians: A Literary and Theological Commentary on 1 and 2 Corinthians.* New York: Crossroad, 1989. Explores Paul's use of literary devices to make his case. As the arguments unfold, so do elements of Paul's theology.

Theissen, Gerd. *The Social Setting of Pauline Christianity: Essays on Corinth.* Philadelphia: Fortress Press, 1982. Explains some of the social codes in 2 Corinthians: how to subsist, class structure, the strong and the weak at Corinth.

Index of Ancient Sources

(Other than 2 Corinthians)

The Author

V. George Shillington writes out of a rich cultural and educational background. Born in Northern Ireland of Presbyterian parents, he emigrated to Canada in the late 1950s and met Mennonites for the first time in the late 1960s.

He attended the Kitchener (Ont.) Mennonite Brethren Church and came to appreciate the Anabaptist understanding of the gospel of Jesus Christ. The Kitchener congregation ordained him to the gospel ministry in 1977.

Since 1981 Shillington has served as professor of biblical studies and theology at Concord College (Winnipeg) and has lectured in other institutions, including Harvard University, Trinity College (Dublin), and New College (Edinburgh). He is well-known in congregations for his enthusiastic biblical sermons. He is the author or editor of three other books and numerous articles and book reviews.

He teaches courses on Paul, the parables of Jesus, modern biblical interpretation, Jews and Christians in Greek society, among others, and has led several study tours to Israel, Jordan, Syria, Turkey, and Greece.

Shillington holds a Ph.D. in New Testament literature and history from McMaster University (Hamilton). He studied with E. P. Sanders and Ben F. Meyer. His M.Div. is from Central Baptist Seminary (Toronto). George and his wife, Grace (McClurg), have two grown sons (to whom this commentary is dedicated) and are members of the Portage Avenue Mennonite Brethren Church in Winnipeg.